# NEW CULTURE, NEW RIGHT

First edition published in 2004 by 1stBooks.

Second edition published in 2013 by Arktos Media Ltd.

Copyright © 2013 by Michael O'Meara and Arktos Media Ltd.

All rights reserved. No part of this book may be reproduced or utilised in any form or by any means (whether electronic or mechanical), including photocopying, recording or by any information storage and retrieval system, without permission in writing from the publisher.

Published in the United Kingdom.

This book is printed on acid-free paper.

ISBN 978-1-907166-89-1

BIC classification:
Social & political philosophy (HPS)
Nationalism (JPFN)

Editor: Matthew Peters
Cover Design & Layout: Daniel Friberg

ARKTOS MEDIA LTD
www.arktos.com

Michael O'Meara

# NEW CULTURE, NEW RIGHT

Anti-Liberalism in Postmodern Europe

ARKTOS
London
2013

*In memory of my brother
Martin (1949–1972)*

# Table of Contents

Preface to the Second Edition . . . . . . . . . . . . . . . . . . . . . . . . . . 7

Introduction: The True Right . . . . . . . . . . . . . . . . . . . . . . . . . . 9

I. From the Old Right to the New . . . . . . . . . . . . . . . . . . . . . 26
    The Passing of the Old Right . . . . . . . . . . . . . . . . . . . . . . 27
    The GRECE's Founding . . . . . . . . . . . . . . . . . . . . . . . . . 30
    1968 . . . . . . . . . . . . . . . . . . . . . . . . . . . . . . . . . . . . . 31
    Postmodern Antinomies . . . . . . . . . . . . . . . . . . . . . . . . . 36
    Across Three Decades . . . . . . . . . . . . . . . . . . . . . . . . . . 42
    The Conservative Revolution . . . . . . . . . . . . . . . . . . . . . 46

II. Metapolitics . . . . . . . . . . . . . . . . . . . . . . . . . . . . . . . . . . 61
    The War of Position . . . . . . . . . . . . . . . . . . . . . . . . . . . 62
    World-Openness and Will to Power . . . . . . . . . . . . . . . . . 65
    The Identitarian Challenge to Liberal Modernity . . . . . . . . 72

III. Liberalism's Reign of Quantity . . . . . . . . . . . . . . . . . . . . 77
    The Quantitative Character of Political Rationalism . . . . . . 77
    Contemporary Measures . . . . . . . . . . . . . . . . . . . . . . . . 97
    Virtual Totalities . . . . . . . . . . . . . . . . . . . . . . . . . . . . . 107

IV. Twilight of the Gods . . . . . . . . . . . . . . . . . . . . . . . . . . 125
    Christianity . . . . . . . . . . . . . . . . . . . . . . . . . . . . . . . . 125
    Paganism . . . . . . . . . . . . . . . . . . . . . . . . . . . . . . . . . 128
    Myth . . . . . . . . . . . . . . . . . . . . . . . . . . . . . . . . . . . . 133
    Tradition . . . . . . . . . . . . . . . . . . . . . . . . . . . . . . . . . 136

V. Archeofuturism . . . . . . . . . . . . . . . . . . . . . . . . . . . . . . 146
    The Christian/Modernist Concept of Time . . . . . . . . . . . . 146
    The Longest Memory . . . . . . . . . . . . . . . . . . . . . . . . . 148
    The Wellspring of Being . . . . . . . . . . . . . . . . . . . . . . . 151
    The Future of the Past . . . . . . . . . . . . . . . . . . . . . . . . 164

VI. Anti-Europe . . . . . . . . . . . . . . . . . . . . . . . . . . . . . . . . 176
    Europe and America . . . . . . . . . . . . . . . . . . . . . . . . . . 176
    The Homeland of Modernity . . . . . . . . . . . . . . . . . . . . 184
    Planet of the Clowns . . . . . . . . . . . . . . . . . . . . . . . . . 190
    Toward Zion . . . . . . . . . . . . . . . . . . . . . . . . . . . . . . . 196

VII. The West Against Europe . . . . . . . . . . . . . . . . . . . . . . . . . . . 210
    The Cold War Condominium . . . . . . . . . . . . . . . . . . . . . . . . . 210
    Third World Alliance . . . . . . . . . . . . . . . . . . . . . . . . . . . . . . 217
    The System That Destroys Nations . . . . . . . . . . . . . . . . . . . . . 218

VIII. Imperium . . . . . . . . . . . . . . . . . . . . . . . . . . . . . . . . . . . . 226
    The Decline of the Nation-State . . . . . . . . . . . . . . . . . . . . . . 227
    The Imperial Idea . . . . . . . . . . . . . . . . . . . . . . . . . . . . . . . . 231
    The Geopolitics of Eurosiberia . . . . . . . . . . . . . . . . . . . . . . . 235
    Organic Democracy . . . . . . . . . . . . . . . . . . . . . . . . . . . . . . 244

Conclusion . . . . . . . . . . . . . . . . . . . . . . . . . . . . . . . . . . . . . . 258
    Liberalism's War on Identity . . . . . . . . . . . . . . . . . . . . . . . . . 258
    The New Right Project . . . . . . . . . . . . . . . . . . . . . . . . . . . . 260
    Critique of the GRECE . . . . . . . . . . . . . . . . . . . . . . . . . . . . 263
    Achievement . . . . . . . . . . . . . . . . . . . . . . . . . . . . . . . . . . . 270

Index . . . . . . . . . . . . . . . . . . . . . . . . . . . . . . . . . . . . . . . . . . 279

# Preface to the Second Edition

In early 2003, when the final draft of this book was completed, the various tendencies associated with the European New Right—and, more specifically, with the Groupement de Recherche et d'Études pour la Civilisation Européenne (GRECE)—were already growing in different directions. Today, these differences have become such that the same book, in endeavoring to chart the principal contours of New Right thought, could not be written. This second edition is thus not an update of the now fragmented New Right (or, better said, the now multiform identitarian resistance)—for that would require a different format, with a different aim. This edition re-presents the same "global critique of liberalism"—and of the system now threatening the existence of European peoples everywhere—that grew out of the earlier New Right. I have thus refrained from revising my interpretations of 2003, adding new references, or changing the text to allow for recent developments, which would have entailed changing the spirit of the whole work. This edition is "new" in having been edited and reformatted; and in having certain errors and awkward expressions corrected, an index added, and an obsolete appendix of New Right organizations and publications removed. In a word, it is a more polished version of the first edition.

—San Francisco, January 2013

"For institutions to exist there must exist the kind of will, instinct, imperative which is anti-liberal to the point of malice: the will to tradition, to authority, to centuries-long responsibility, to *solidarity* between succeeding generations backwards and forwards *in infinitum* . . . The entire West has lost those instincts out of which institutions grow, out of which the *future* grows: perhaps nothing goes so much against the grain of the 'modern spirit' as this."
—Friedrich Nietzsche

"Europe has one aim: to actualize its Destiny. This means, to reconquer its sovereignty, to reassert its mission, to establish its imperium, to give to the world an era of order and European peace."
—Francis Parker Yockey

"Here's to all Cork men,
Likewise New York men,
Who stand for Ireland the world around."
—T. D. Sullivan

Introduction

# The True Right

Notions of "conservatism" and "liberalism," which have come to us from English public life, the ideological categories of "Right" and "Left," taken from French politics, or more blanket terms like "reaction" and "progress," derived from nineteenth-century Continental usage, have always meant something quite different in the United States than they have in Europe. In an American work on the European Right, it may be in order, then, to begin with a definition of these terms, though the difficulty in doing so is quite formidable. To start, the historical context out of which they evolved is entirely remote to the American experience, which has never known a culture-bearing aristocracy, an enrooted peasantry, or an insurgent bourgeoisie. In addition to these incommensurable histories, Right and Left originated as parliamentary polarities, whose one-dimensional spatial references rarely did justice to the ideological complexities they represented.[1] Finally, the Right poses a special problem in that its different tendencies define themselves largely in opposition to the Left, which often gives them a negative or reactive character.[2]

Due to this latter peculiarity, any attempt at approaching these elusive and not very stable designations must start with the Left. What, then, is the Left? While it too eludes easy definition, having assumed multiple guises, in more cases than not it stands for those rationalist ideological tendencies favoring the political impulses of a "modernity" opposed to "the divine order of creation." Inspired by the spirit of Protestant individualism, Newtonian science, and a latent Gnosticism, it believes in "the infinite progress of knowledge and the infinite advance toward social and moral betterment."[3] The past for it is identified, as such, with the world's imperfections, particularly its entrenched privileges, and the modern with reason's capacity to ameliorate outmoded practices. On this basis, it holds that every age adds to the achievements of its predecessors, as it gradually progresses toward a condition of ever greater rationality. Just as modernity "heroizes the present" (Michel Foucault) and makes "an increasingly intense cult of the new" (Gianni Vattimo), the Left champions the progress, possibility, and emancipation modernity promises, as history (in the Hegelian sense) evolves toward a condition of "absolute rationality."[4]

It consequently places the claims of recent and future experience over and above the alleged irrationalities of traditional ones, whose continuity it endeavors to break.[5] This causes it to reject hierarchy, authority, and tradition, which it treats as obstacles to change, and to favor the "liberation" and "perfection" of the individual, whose "rational being" is placed at the heart of the modernist enterprise. It similarly privileges pluralism and fashion, along with debate, dialogue, and revision. And though it too comes to possess traditions and to serve as a *status quo*, these are modernist ones, based on innovations of an ostensibly ameliorative sort.[6] The Left, in a word, identifies with the "myth of progress," which undergirds its vision of man's possibility, its individualistic faith in reason, its penchant for models, plans, and reforms, and its opposition to the heritage of past generations.

In reaction to the Left's idealism, the Right opposes its realism. The Right as such emerges in defense of ancestral legacies and of the larger spiritual order sustaining these legacies. Unlike the Left, the traditional heritage for it is not "a dismal catalogue of absurdities and crimes against humanity," but the backdrop to the way the present is to be apprehended and the future worked out. It likewise believes this heritage offers a glimpse of the transcendent—of that which stands outside of time—and of the larger possibilities latent in the human condition. Indeed, when true to itself, it is less concerned with "conserving" customary forms than with realizing their potential in the present.[7] Its identification with "the mellowing civilizing influence of tradition, of written and unwritten laws, and ... of the lasting values which have been crystallized in the course of history" is, then, with the substance of these things and not necessarily with their transitory forms.[8] For the Right resists not innovation *per se*, but "reforms" endeavoring to change "the order of creation." Nor, must it be insisted, does it defend the past simply for its own sake. As Arthur Moeller van den Bruck writes, it has no ambition "to see the world as a museum."[9] Its principal concern is for "what is" and "what will be," both of which are inseparable from "what was." A "True Right" (of which there have been few historical examples) prefers, thus, to reason in terms of the specific geographic, cultural, racial, religious, and historical realities situating and defining it. This means its immediate references are generally long established ones, not ideas about how the world might be if reason were to make a clean sweep of the past. It similarly accepts that man is a flawed creature, adopts a skeptical view of progress and a tragic sense of life; favors enrootment, continuity, and natural hierarchies; and distrusts crusading spirits ignoring "what is" for the sake of a rationalistic "what ought to be."

Because "Right" and "Left," like "conservative" and "progressive," are terms inextricably entwined in modernity's historical weave, they are perhaps better understood in terms of the role they have played in its introduction and development.[10] For though it was only at the end of the eighteenth century that these terms acquired ideological definition, as "subjective dispositions," they appeared with the earliest stirrings of modernity. This was especially evident in the late medieval struggle over the state. Against a myriad of provincial particularisms and in alliance with the urban merchant class (which tradition assigned to the lowest estate), the "progressive" forces associated with the French monarchy sought to introduce a centralized political system whose rational, bureaucratic mold aimed at concentrating all sovereignty in the king's hands.[11] Key to this anti-traditional concentration of power was a "defeudalization" of aristocratic prerogative and ecclesiastical authority. The conservative forces of custom, language, and regional identity, combined with upper-class and Church resistance, would make this, however, a slow, uncertain process. Nevertheless, it was in opposition to monarchical-bourgeois innovations threatening the feudal foundations of state and society that the Right first emerged as a political force opposed to modernist, anti-feudal subversions. (From this perspective, one might argue that the political history of Europe since the Middle Ages is the story of the Right's progressive decline.)[12]

Along with the centralizing monarchical state, the traditional ramparts of late medieval Europe were assailed by modernist forces inherent in the rapidly developing market economy, whose moneyed wealth challenged the landed interests identified with the existing forms of hierarchy and authority. The founding of the Portuguese East India Empire and the Spanish conquest of the New World at the end of the fifteenth century dramatically accelerated this process, especially in unleashing economic forces powerful enough to sweep away all "the motley feudal ties that bound" men to their traditional relations. Yet, it was only with the Protestant Reformation (harbinger of both the modern world and the "Jewish revolutionary spirit") that the embryonic Left assumed an openly insurrectional stance.[13] Beginning in the German-speaking lands (but assuming their most influential expression in Western Europe, especially England and Holland), anti-papal reformers launched a frontal assault on the traditional, hierarchical, and liturgical bases of ecclesiastical authority. Driven by the radical Hebraic promptings of early Christianity and the considerable financial resources of anti-Spanish Jews, these dissidents attracted the support of a diverse alliance of princes, burghers, and peasants, many of whom were motivated not solely by hostility to Roman corruption, but by their predatory designs on Church real estate.

Protestantism's most representative champions, especially in Western Europe, came, though, from "the rising bourgeoisie," whose economic initiative and sense of self-reliance made it especially resistant to papal practices. Able to read the recently translated and printed Bible without the aid of a priest and inclined to make moral decisions outside the collective framework of the faithful, the burgher favored a spirituality attuned to the analytical workings of the early modern conscience—an attunement whose most immediate consequence would be a growing individualism of thought, theory, and practice. It was thus the solitary experiences of prayer, conscience, and faith, not the religiously ordered community associated with medieval Catholicism and its rites, through which the Protestant hoped to mediate his relationship with God.[14] From this religious individualism challenging traditional ecclesiastical authority, most future manifestations of the Left would take their cue. With some justice, Louis de Bonald called the Reformation "the mother of all political revolutions."[15]

The Reformers' greatest success came, ironically, not in re-ordering Christian spiritual life, but in setting off a process that would undermine the authority of Christianity in any of its forms, for in challenging the established Church they inadvertently let loose the forces of skepticism and secularism, relativism and tolerance—as "objective revelation" was supplanted by practical ethico-religious subjectivities.[16] Thus, even though their more Puritanical elements sought a greater doctrinal exactness than Rome and an intrusion of God's realm into Caesar's (as in the merchant oligarchy of Calvin's Geneva), their clash with Catholicism made the public expression of religion (as in the "Church civilization" of the Middle Ages) increasingly difficult, especially after the murderous havoc of the great seventeenth-century religious wars. The sole possible remedy to such fratricidal strife would be the privatization of faith, the gradual secularization of civil society, and an acceptance of pluralist, even atheistic, beliefs. The ensuing toleration could not, however, but lead to greater spiritual indifference, as the essential and eternal truths of the Christian tradition were not only differently interpreted, but eventually ignored for the sake of civil harmony and an increasingly sensate culture.

Impelled by this secularizing process—which was simultaneously a process of societal dissolution—modernity "took off," as other institutions, such as the family, the trades, and the various corporate bodies, began shedding their traditional communal trappings for the sake of individual and market interests. The first and most grievous casualty of this dissolution of medieval Christian civilization was, of course, the religious world view of the Middle Ages. The old Aristotelian-Catholic understanding of the natural world and the skeptical nuanced one of Renaissance humanism were both forced to give way to a rationalist one in which a clock-like nature was to be measured, analyzed, and rendered into the language of mathematics.[17] On this basis, the New Science of the seventeenth century would endeavor to replace scriptural and ancient authorities with an "objectivity" derived from principles of empirical observation and logic. Henceforth, all that could not be conveyed in the detached utterances of a disembodied reason, measured quantitatively, and expressed in mathematical formulas that reduced natural phenomena to statistical probabilities ceased to count as an authority. This, of course, impoverished the European imagination, but science's appeal was nevertheless contagious, for it seemed to "emancipate" Europeans from superstition and ignorance. With it, it was as if a veil had lifted, revealing the actual mechanical workings of the world. Fontenelle recounts that the angels formerly inhabiting the heavens were suddenly seen as actors "flying" about a stage with the aid of invisible wires.[18] Science, in effect, allowed Europeans to go backstage and see for themselves how the wires were pulled—to see, in a word, how the natural forces operated irrespective of providential ordinance.

    The decisive step in modernity's advent, and hence the Left project, would come in the eighteenth century, when Europeans began applying the abstract, mathematical, and individualistic principles of scientific rationality to political and social institutions. If liberation from traditional strictures had brought about a greater mastery of the material world, then reason, it seemed, might do the same for man's social world. By eliminating the irrationalities inherent in a pre-modern order based on tradition and religion, it was hoped that a scientific one might take its place to the benefit of all. This would give modernity a decidedly optimistic slant, for it was assumed that reason had the capacity to remake reality in ways that the existing heritage did not. The philosophical movement known as the Enlightenment, ideologically legitimizing these modernizing forces, would thus aspire to rid society of what John Dryden called the "rust and ignorance of the past." Positing that the lived world was governed by *a priori*, homogeneous, and quantitative properties whose law-like principles were accessible to the modalities of modern science, this "second Protestant Reformation" (Christopher Dawson) sought to disenchant the cosmos, organize the universal brotherhood of man, and prepare the way for the inevitable progress that was to issue from reason's reign.[19] As it did, every form of tradition was challenged, every idea of familial or communal obligation rejected, all historic authorities undermined.

However unreasonable, the Enlightenment's crusading rationalism overwhelmed its traditionalist critics. But this was due less to its alleged "cogency" than to certain changes in the nature of European society, specifically the growing economic significance of the urban merchant class, which conceived of man in matter-of-fact terms and accepted as truth or certainty only the tangible evidence of the visible world.[20] Given "reason's" embrace by this powerful social actor, especially after the Whig Revolution of 1688 enfranchised it and the forces of usury, the claims of property began to supersede those of blood and heritage. In the process, the contract would come to supplant status as the juridical foundation of society, moorless capital to join landed tenure as a source of political power, and the state to serve as a rational (or bureaucratic) monitor of the free market. Moreover, since God and all transcendent references, along with tradition and custom, were expected to cede to the more credible persuasions of reason, previous moral references were forced to give way to the one value that the bourgeoisie raised above all others: money. Enlightenment liberalism would thus sanction not merely the rationalization (or de-traditionalization) of European society, but the ascent of the capitalist class, whose moneyed powers henceforth took priority over every political, moral, and religious obstacle opposing it.

Clerical, aristocratic, and popular supporters of the *ancien régime*—those whom Isaiah Berlin grouped under the term "Counter-Enlightenment"—had, as one might suspect, a less sanguine view of the professed "age of lights."[21] With the French Revolution's bloody institutionalization of reason's reign in 1789, the worse of their fears were confirmed. The Counter-Enlightenment's ensuing struggle to defend traditional institutions from the Revolution's "abuse of reason" would impose a certain coherence on these traditionalist forces, in the process, spurring the first ideological articulation of what would become the politically conscious Right—though, paradoxically, this articulation could not but announce its fated demise, for the very need to formulate what had always been assumed indicated that it no longer dominated the established order. Nevertheless, it was opposition to the Enlightenment's disenchantment of the world and its disregard for custom, station, and propriety that led these late eighteenth- and early nineteenth-century counter-revolutionaries to take up the cause of "organic" (that is, historically evolved rather than rationally planned) society. As they did, they elevated tradition above reason, enrootment above mobility, community above individualism, the particular above the universal, growth above progress. At the same time, they rejected reason's dismissal of the poetic, mythic, and religious influences shaping the European mind and, though not at all opposed to science, tended to emphasize its epistemological limitations and its insufficiency in supporting the normative foundations of communal life. It would be wrong, however, to think these counter-revolutionaries opposed change *per se*. As Edmund Burke put it, "change is the means of our preservation." The Counter-Enlightenment's resistance to modernist reforms was thus less a rejection of innovation than of the belief that abstract reason—especially a reason animated by the plebeian impulses of bourgeois materialism—had the power to regenerate man's nature and create a new order *ex abruptio*. In the course of the nineteenth century, the Right's reaction "to the French Revolution, liberalism, and the rise of the bourgeoisie" would assume various shapes, but in whatever guise it continued, when true to itself, to oppose the Left's anti-traditionalist subversions.[22] Negatively, this would make it a form of anti-liberalism; positively, a proponent of certain perennial values associated with the transcendent in the European heritage.

Given modernity's ongoing assault on traditional European institutions, particularly those accompanying the jarring onset of early nineteenth-century industrialization, there also emerged—but on the far Left side of the recently formed Right-Left spectrum—a socialist reaction to the way men were "materialized and commodified" in modern society. In contrast to the True Right, these socialists identified with Enlightenment values—and hence with the powers of reason and progress, the principles of individualism, egalitarianism, and universalism, and the primacy of the economic. They differed with the liberal Left mainly in emphasizing a more equable and compassionate distribution of labor's fruits (thus their anti-capitalism) and, in the form of planning, a rational alternative to the disorders and injustices that came with unregulated markets.[23] In this and in their struggles for popular sovereignty and solidarity, socialists took their stand against the alienating forces of liberal modernity—which is arguably what is greatest in their history. On the other hand, the destruction of traditional culture, the desacralization of the world, the imposition of the market's reign of quantity, and the denigration of virile, aristocratic values, all of which stimulated the oppositional forces of the Right, had but little effect on the socialist version of the Enlightenment's rationalist social project.[24]

Quite typically, Karl Marx (whose anti-capitalist critique has never been more pertinent) was entirely ambivalent in his treatment of the bourgeois values animating modern society, for he envisaged his classless society in ways that were bourgeois, even as he sought to dispense with the bourgeoisie. As Oswald Spengler argues, "Marxism is the capitalism of the working class."[25] Given this ambivalence, Marxian socialists tended to follow liberals in believing that higher living standards imply a higher standard of life, that greater rationalization brings greater freedom, that economics is the heart of social life, and that the ethical and customary forms of European culture count for less than material achievement. Their collectivist project in a word represented more a variant of, than an alternative to, the capitalist one they opposed, just as their economic doctrines and larger world view were a "debauched hangover" of bourgeois economics and philosophy. Their agitations and legislative reforms may therefore have opposed the more oppressive facets of industrial capitalism, but, in the last instance, they too adhered to its underlying tenets.[26]

Not coincidentally, the anti-liberal Left's commitment to modernity has often taken aberrant or oppressive form. Serge Latouche describes the "real existing socialism" of the former Soviet Union as having entailed little more than "the gulag + the nomenclature + Chernobyl."[27] Since the collapse of Russian Communism, most socialists have even abandoned their former anti-capitalism, defining themselves as simply more efficient and equable managers of capitalism's market economy. In many quarters, they have, in truth, become almost indistinguishable from social liberals—which follows the fact that socialism, even Marxian socialism (which Eduard Bernstein called "organized liberalism"), has always been a derivation of the Enlightenment project and hence a complicit participant in liberalism's war on tradition.[28]

It was in America, though, that Enlightenment liberalism found its greatest champions and modernity its fullest realization. Born in a wilderness, without the heritage of authority and hierarchy that was Europe's, the American people began its history with a clean slate, the *tabula rasa*, extolled by liberal reformers, experiencing but slight resistance to an order based on the constitutional, economic, and social embodiments of reason. Modernity, in truth, had little to overcome in this land "liberated from the dead hand of the European past." Even its Protestant Christianity, central to New World institutions, bore little relation to the historical expressions of European Christianity, being largely a radical or Puritanical expression of the bourgeois ethos. Above all, America lacked an aristocracy, with an ancient tradition and a high culture to defend. It lacked, as a consequence, an alternative to modernity's materially impressive but existentially shallow achievements and lacked thus the patrimony that was at the heart of European conservatism.

This "first great experiment in social engineering" (Thomas Molnar) also fostered a political tradition that was pre-eminently progressive in spirit.[29] Indeed, no country has remained as committed to the Enlightenment's liberal project as the US, bound as it is to the rationalist/materialist principles upon which it was founded. Whatever anti-liberalism the country has known has typically been confined to the political periphery and been more populist or nativist than conservative in character. Even the constitutional legacy American "traditionalists" presently defend in face of New Class innovations is essentially an Enlightenment, hence liberal, legacy.

The terms "Left" and "Right" have come thus to denote quite different things in the US than they have in Europe. Specifically, the American Right (in its Old Right, Buckleyite, traditionalist, neoconservative, and paleoconservative forms) represents an offshoot, however conservative, of bourgeois liberalism, allied with the constitutionalism, economism, egalitarianism, and individualism against which the True Right historically defined itself.[30] Relatedly, the theoretical father of liberal capitalism, Adam Smith, is usually taken as the Right's chief philosopher, big business its principal constituency, and middle-class boosterism its cultural ideal.[31] It can even be argued that American politics has known only a false Right. As the English academic John Gray notes, US conservatism is "merely a variant of the Enlightenment project of universal emancipation and universal civilization"—that is, a variant of classical liberalism and, thus, of the Left project.[32]

In France, by contrast, where the Enlightenment culminated in the psychic epidemic of 1789 and liberal principles were taken to a murderous extreme, it is impossible to say that the political tradition is or has ever been primarily liberal. Until a generation ago (when Socialists and globalists began their reign), the French remained conservative and anti-bourgeois in ways entirely foreign to American life.[33] The national consciousness was simply not influenced to the same degree by the Enlightenment. The French and, more generally, the European system of Right-Left politics tended, as a result, to overlap the struggle between tradition and modernity, conservatism and progressivism, that was absent in the US. For nearly a century and a half, this situation enabled the conservative forces of the *ancien régime* to stage a certain rearguard resistance to liberal modernity. It also gave European political life a far greater diversity of ideological affiliation and a weaker national consensus than was the case in the US.

In recent decades, however, this too has changed. Like their American counterparts, European parties today increasingly differ only in nuance, with the Right serving more and more as the Left's redundant appendage. The advocates of progress and modernization have, in fact, gained control of all their executive committees—among Germany and Italy's former Christian Democrats, Britain's Tories, France's former Gaullists, *et cetera*. Though this "Americanization" of the European Right can be traced back to the late nineteenth century, when industrialization shifted power from agriculture to commerce, eliminating conservatism's historical social base and forcing its defenders into the arms of the moderate bourgeoisie, the decisive realignment came only after 1945.[34]

In the wake of Germany's crushing defeat, which was simultaneously a defeat for traditional Europe, Continental politics underwent a profound re-ordering.[35] In the Eastern half of the Continent, the Soviets imposed a totalitarian modernity which reduced all politics to their party dictatorship. In the West, the Old Right was implicated in fascism's excesses, stigmatized, and nearly everywhere driven from the political arena. The existing hierarchies were likewise extirpated and their representatives excluded from the political arena. Wherever the Right managed to survive in the postwar West, it was obliged to adapt to Washington's "liberal consensus," accept its ground rules, and deny that it was, indeed, a Right—for otherwise it risked being accused of "fascism" (defined by the Left as virtually any non-effacing Rightist doctrine or movement).[36] The most common expression of this postwar Right (*Demutskonservatismus* that it was) would take the form of "economic liberalism" (associated in the US with "conservatism") or else Christian Democracy.[37] Characteristically, both tendencies identified with free markets, individual rights, and Americanization—which made them closer in spirit to the historical Left than the Right.

The notion of an economic or democratic Right, as Julius Evola contends, is indeed a contradiction in terms, for it was opposition to market society and the mass politics born of the "Dual Revolution" that gave the Right its defining essence.[38] For Evola's True Rightist, all evil comes from the bourgeoisie and its liberalism. Not surprisingly, traditional Right-wing parties almost everywhere passed from the scene after the American occupation of Europe.[39] Of the surviving remnants, most ended up embracing the Left's economism, especially after the Reagan-Thatcher forces carried out their neo-liberal market reforms in the early 1980s. This false Right would, in fact, act merely to moderate the Left's angelic reformism, ensuring that the nation's economic and financial health was such as to sustain the Left's social experiments. What is presently called the European Right is actually an unabashed proponent of liberal modernity, and, implicitly, of the Left project, having become little more than a vestige of earlier manifestations of the Left. For this reason, today's so-called Right might be characterized as a "center," constituting the Left's Right.

Yet, in winning the battle of modernity, the Left too has been compromised. As an established order, with a greater stake in conformity than opposition, it increasingly defines itself in centrist terms.[40] Even doctrinally, its socialist wing has abandoned its anti-capitalism and, in some cases, its commitment to social policy, moving closer to the market forces associated with the false Right. Recent socialist governments, for example, have been responsible for greater job insecurity, a higher concentration of wealth at the top, a breakdown of traditional forms of social solidarity, and the privileging of Third World immigrants to the detriment of the European working class. Given this sort of political environment, traditional Right-Left antagonisms have diminished to the extent that nuances alone distinguish them, as each competes to outdo the other as the most ardent champion of the market, the most self-righteous guardian of democracy and human rights, and the most stalwart foe of racism and xenophobia.

Fortunately, this is not quite the whole story. Any American newspaper reader will have heard the names of Le Pen's National Front, Haider's Freedom Party, or the "List" of Pim Fortuyn (who had to be murdered to prevent his ascension to the Dutch premiership); less well known are the plethora of identitarian, national-revolutionary, populist, and far Right formations opposing the false Right. These anti-liberal tendencies situated on the fringe of European politics, but more and more posed to enter the "mainstream," are usually characterized as closet forms of fascism, Right-wing expressions of anti-globalism, or insignificant exceptions to a generally healthy parliamentary system. Ignoring for the moment the ideological slant of these characterizations, let us simply note that Continental politics is again beginning to deviate from the American model. Europe in general, but particularly France, Italy, Belgium, and Germany (not to mention Russia, parts of Eastern Europe, Spain, and Greece), are today experiencing a revival of anti-liberal politics that portends major changes in the European political system. Though traditionalist and conservative in many ways, the forces associated with this "New Right" bear little resemblance to either the conservative liberalism of the false Right, the lingering traditionalism of the Old Right—or even the ideal type represented by Evola's True Right.

This book is about the most intellectually formidable of these New Right forces.

## Notes to Introduction

1. Donald E. Stokes, "Spatial Models of Party Competition," *The American Political Science Review* 57:2 (June 1963).
2. The reactive character of the Right was especially pronounced in the period of the French Restoration (1815–30), when the Left served as the *parti du Mouvement* and the Right as the *parti de la Résistance*—that is, as the party resisting the Left's reforms. See Jacques du Perron, *Petit bréviaire de la Droite* (Paris: Consep, 2002), 68. Somewhat less clearly, this tendency was also at work in late eighteenth-century England, where the politics of Whig and Tory followed a somewhat similar logic of movement and resistance.
3. Jürgen Habermas, "Modernity and Postmodernity," *New German Critique* 22 (Winter 1981); Eric Voegelin, *The New Science of Politics: An Introduction* (Chicago: University of Chicago Press, 1952).
4. Michel Foucault, "What is Enlightenment?," in *The Foucault Reader*, ed. Paul Rabinow (New York: Pantheon, 1984). Cf. Georges Sorel, *The Illusions of Progress*, trans. John and Charlotte Stanley (Berkeley: University of California Press, 1969).
5. Pierre Manent, *The City of Man*, trans. Marc A. LePain (Princeton, NJ: Princeton University Press, 1998), 17.
6. In his great dictionary, Émile Littré defined the "Left" as the "*parti de l'opposition dans les chambres français*." This was not merely its status under Louis Napoleon, when the dictionary was first published, for subsequent editions under the Third Republic retained the same definition—implying that the Left is in perpetual opposition to all traditional forms of authority, even when it holds power. One Rightist interprets this as sign of the Left's inherent "opposition to the reality of things," to "the order of creation," to "natural laws," to "original sin"—its opposition, in other words, to whatever natural or traditional order man has known. See Yves Daoudal, "La Gauche et le péché originel," in *Droite-Gauche: Un clivage dépassé?*, ed. Bernard Mazin (Paris: Éds. CDH, 1998).
7. Klaus Motschmann, "Vorwort," in *Abschied von Abendland? Die Moderne in der Krise*, ed. Klaus Motschmann (Graz: Stocker, 1997).
8. Kay Heriot, "The Conservative Imagination," *National Democrat* 2 (Spring–Summer 1982).
9. Arthur Moeller van den Bruck, *Germany's Third Empire*, trans. E. O. Lorimer (London: George Allen and Unwin, 1934), 223.
10. The Right, in other words, is not purely situational in character. It has a distinct and defining origin and, as such, channels its evolving identity between references whose ultimate referent is the tradition formed in reaction to the eighteenth-century liberal revolutions. This lends it those perennial qualities that allow one to speak of a True Right. *Pace* Russell Kirk, conservatism does not amount "to the consensus of the leading conservative thinkers and actors over the past two centuries" (which would confuse it with the false Right), but rather to the anti-liberal project born in the wake of 1789. Cf. *The Portable Conservative Reader* (New York: Viking, 1982), xv.

11. Alain de Benoist, "Le Bourgeois," in *Critiques-Théoriques* (Lausanne: L'Âge d'Homme, 2002). In England, which would play the leading role in opening the way to liberal modernity, the state formed on the basis of the Norman Conquest was a fairly uniform and centralized one and its aristocracy, which was compelled after its decimation in the War of the Roses and the Civil War to recruit its members from the gentry and merchant classes, was early on implicated in the modernizing process. The Whig Revolution of 1688 then imbued these developments with their specifically modern political and economic forms, helping to usher in modernity earlier, more effectively, and more organically than on the Continent—which is why they lack the same explicative force of the more self-conscious Continental process.
12. For example, see Olivier Tholozan, *Henri de Boulainvilliers: L'anti-absolutisme aristocratique légitimé par l'histoire* (Aix-en-Provence: Presses Universitaire d'Aix-en-Marseille, 2000).
13. Some historians see the Left as essentially a secularized Christian heresy—a this-worldly salvation religion. For example, Norman Cohn, *The Pursuit of the Millennium: Revolutionary Messianism in Medieval and Reformation Europe*, rev. ed. (New York: Oxford University Press, 1970); Jacques du Perron, *La Gauche vue de Droite* (Puiseaux: Pardès, 1993); Jules Monnerot, *Sociologie du Communisme: Échec d'une tentative religieuse au XXe siècle* (Paris: Hallier, 1979).
14. Ernst Troeltsch, *Protestantism and Progress: A Historical Study of the Relation of Protestantism to the Modern World*, trans. W. Montgomery (Boston: Beacon Press, 1958), 18–23.
15. Quoted in Perron, *Petit bréviaire de la Droite*, 101.
16. Harold J. Laski, *The Rise of European Liberalism* (London: Unwin, 1971), 22–25.
17. Paul Hazard, *The European Mind, 1680–1715*, trans. J. Lewis May (Cleveland: Meridian, 1963), 8–26.
18. Bernard le Bovier de Fontenelle, *Conversations on the Plurality of Worlds*, trans. H. A. Hargreaves (Berkeley: University of California Press, 1990), 12. On the "impoverishing" effects of the New Science, see René Guénon, *East and West*, trans. Martin Lings (Ghent, NY: Sophia Perennis, 1995), 46–81.
19. Christopher Dawson, *The Gods of Revolution* (New York: New York University Press, 1972), 146–47. Also Carl L. Becker, *The Heavenly City of the Eighteenth-Century Philosophers* (New Haven, CT: Yale University Press, 1932).
20. Here, as elsewhere in this work, all suggested correspondences between cultural/intellectual forms and socioeconomic developments should be taken as "elective affinities." As will be evident in subsequent chapters, I follow Heidegger in seeing "truth" as an ontological event and causality a naturalistic one. But while ideas are never the mere reflexes of their socioeconomic context, the context is nevertheless often decisive in stimulating them and influencing their reception. Ideas may therefore have their own logic of development and their own ends, which transcend purely social interests, but only when they are embraced by "objective forces," social classes, or individual passions do they become historically important. Cf. Karl Mannheim, "Conservative Thought," in *From Karl Mannheim*, 2nd ed., ed. Kurt H. Wolff (New Brunswick, NJ: Transaction Publishers, 1992).

21. Isaiah Berlin, "The Counter-Enlightenment," in *The Proper Study of Mankind: An Anthology of Essays*, ed. Henry Hardy and Roger Hausheer (London: Chatto and Windus, 1997).
22. Samuel P. Huntington, "Conservatism as an Ideology," *The American Political Science Review* 51:2 (June 1957). This "aristocratic" concept of the Right is neither that of Huntington nor of those who are at the center of this study, but, in this century, of Julius Evola. *Pace* Huntington, this concept is not bound to the "interests of a continuing social group," but to a tradition whose forms, however aristocratic, transcended class affiliations. See Evola, "La Droite et la Tradition," in *Explorations: Hommes et problèmes*, trans. Philippe Baillet (Puiseaux: Pardès, 1989). Because I take the Evolean conception to be the single philosophically coherent representation of the Right, I use the term "True Right" in his sense. The chief ideologues of this Right, whose principles were anticipated in the works of Antoine de Rivarol and Gabriel Sénac de Meilhan during the French Revolution, are Joseph de Maistre, Louis de Bonald, Donoso Cortés, and, in our age, Evola. For the closest thing to a contemporary programmatic formulation of this Right, see Julius Evola, *Orientations*, trans. Philippe Baillet (Puiseaux: Pardès, 1988). On Evola, who has had a formative impact on the New Right discussed in the body of this text, see Christophe Boutin, *Politique et Tradition: Julius Evola dans le siècle (1898–1974)* (Paris: Éds. Kimé, 1992); Adriano Romualdi, *Julius Evola, l'homme et l'œuvre*, trans. Gérard Boulanger (Puiseaux: Pardès, 1985); Guido Stucco, "The Legacy of a European Traditionalist: Julius Evola in Perspective," *The Occidental Quarterly: A Journal of Western Thought and Opinion* 2:3 (Fall 2002).
23. Alain de Benoist, *Les idées à l'endroit* (Paris: Hallier, 1979), 84–89. These differences also derived from the differing emphasis that liberals put on distribution (markets) and Marxists on production (labor).
24. Pierre Vial, "Le camarade charpentier," *Éléments pour la civilisation européenne* (henceforth *Éléments*) 42 (June 1982). It should be noted that part of the socialist Left—the tradition that runs from Proudhon to Sorel to Niekisch to Oberlercher—rejects the Enlightenment heritage and affirms the importance of community and spirit. In opposing the Marxist/cosmopolitan distillation of the socialist idea, this "Left" has always been closer to the far Right than to tendencies on its side of the political spectrum, insofar as it saw socialism as an ethical-social principle opposed to bourgeois individualism and materialism, and not as an economic program based on a rationalist, inorganic ideology committed to pitting one stratum of the social organism against another. See Oswald Spengler, *Preussentum und Sozialismus* (Munich: Beck, 1919); Marc Crapez, *Naissance de la Gauche* (Paris: Éds. Michalon, 1998); Michael Freund, *Georges Sorel: Der revolutionäre Konservatismus* (Frankfurt am Main: Klostermann, 1932); Otto-Ernst Schüddekopf, *Linke Leute von rechts: Die nationalrevolutionäre Minderheiten und der Kommunismus in der Weimarer Republik* (Stuttgart: Kohlhammer, 1960); René Binet, *Socialisme national contre marxisme* (Montreal: Éds. Celtiques, 1978); Alexandre Dougine (Dugin), "La Métaphysique du National-Bolchevisme," at *Archivio Eurasia* (http://utenti.tripod.it/ArchivEurasia); "Zwei Gespräche mit Reinhold Oberlercher," at *Deutsches Kolleg* (http://www.deutsches-kolleg.org).

25. Spengler, *Preussentum und Sozialismus*, § 20. Also Jan Waclav Makhaïski, "La banqueroute du socialisme du XIXe siècle" (1905), in *Le socialisme des intellectuels*, ed. Alexandre Skirda (Paris: Seuil, 1979); Jean Baudrillard, *The Mirror of Production*, trans. Mark Poster (St. Louis, MO: Telos Press, 1975).

26. Historically, the chief obstacle to the market's onslaught was not the political forces of socialism, but the workers themselves, for their trade unions, cooperatives, and mutualities did more to mitigate the modern commodification of labor than all the socialists' Sunday speeches or parliamentary horse trades. Thus, though long associated with the Left, the labor movement remained conservative insofar as it sought to defend its communal, corporate traditions from the liberal modernist principles of 1789. See Frank Tannenbaum, *A Philosophy of Labor* (New York: Knopf, 1951); Michael Torigian, *Every Factory a Fortress: The French Labor Movement in the Age of Ford and Hitler* (Athens: Ohio University Press, 1999).

27. Serge Latouche, *The Westernization of the World: The Significance, Scope and Limits of the Drive towards Global Uniformity*, trans. Rosemary Morris (Cambridge: Polity, 1996), xiv.

28. Alain de Benoist, *Orientations pour des années décisives* (Paris: Le Labyrinthe, 1982), 74; Jean Desperts, "D'un sociale démocratie à l'autre," *Éléments* 42 (June 1982); John Schwarzmantel, *The Age of Ideology: Political Ideologies from the American Revolution to Postmodern Times* (New York: New York University Press, 1998), 106. Cf. Jules Monnerot, *La guerre en question* (Paris: Gallimard, 1951), 151.

29. Cf. Louis Hartz, *The Liberal Tradition in America* (New York: Harcourt, Brace and World, 1955); Alan Brinkley, "The Problem of American Conservatism," *American Historical Review* 99:2 (April 1994); Bernard Crick, "The Strange Quest for an American Conservatism," *The Review of Politics* 17:3 (July 1955).

30. Admittedly, this conservative defense of America's liberal republican foundations, with its emphasis on individual autonomy, local rights, and civic responsibility (which I associate with "conservative liberalism"), is a far different and less subversive "liberalism" than the liberal managerialism practiced by the post-New Deal New Class. Between these defenders of liberal republicanism and the New Right discussed herein, there is, indeed, room for cooperation. But from the latter's perspective, it is the liberal republicanism derived from the Enlightenment political tradition that was responsible for laying the basis of the managerial Leviathan, which they both oppose.

31. Alongside Smith, especially on the traditionalist wing of the postwar American Right, there stands Edmund Burke. However significant a role Burke played in articulating the first ideological expression of conservatism (no figure, indeed, comes close to his stature), he nonetheless belongs to the pre-revolutionary distillation of liberalism, with its roots in the Whig Revolution of 1688 and its affiliation with the newly arising commercial society of eighteenth-century Britain. On the specifically American appropriation of "the Irish adventurer," see Russell Kirk, *The Conservative Mind: From Burke to Eliot*, 7th ed. (Chicago: Regnery, 1986). Because Burke's so-called "conservatism" contained a large admixture of Whiggery, whose replacement of traditional social roles with commercial or utilitarian ones allied it with bourgeois interests, he has

been readily embraced by the American Right and, for the same reason, has a more ambivalent status among Europeans. Similarly, Smith considered Burke a kindred spirit and anarcho-capitalists like Friedrich von Hayek have paid repeated homage to him. See E. G. West, *Adam Smith: The Man and His Works* (Indianapolis: Liberty Fund, 1976), 237; Alain de Benoist, *Horizon 2000: Trois entretiens avec Alain de Benoist* (Paris: GRECE pamphlet, 1996), 5–14.

32. John Gray, *Enlightenment's Wake: Politics and Culture at the Close of the Modern Age* (London: Routledge, 1995), x; also John Gray, *Endgames: Questions in Late Modern Political Thought* (Cambridge: Polity, 1997), 1–11. Charles W. Dunn and J. David Woodard, *American Conservatism from Burke to Bush* (Lanham, MD: Madison Books, 1991), I thought, much confirmed Gray's assessment. See also Jonathan M. Schoenwald, *A Time for Choosing: The Rise of Modern American Conservatism* (Oxford: Oxford University Press, 2001). In this context, it is significant to note that Kirk's *The Conservative Mind*, which has had a formative influence on America's postwar "Right," is almost exclusively devoted to Anglo-American "conservatism" (i.e., conservative liberalism), with hardly a word on the more muscular forms of Continental conservatism.

33. Dominique Venner, "La bourgeoisie, stade suprême du communisme," in *Gauche-Droite: La fin d'un système. Actes du XXVIIIe colloque national du GRECE* (Paris: Le Labyrinthe, 1995).

34. Thomas Molnar, "Metamorphosen der Gegenrevolution," *Criticón* 115 (September–October 1989). Equally credible, it can be argued that since the appearance of the terms "Right" and "Left" in the National Assembly of 1789, the Right has been compelled to operate within the parliamentary and institutional parameters established by the bourgeoisie and thus been implicitly implicated in them—as its conservative, but loyal, opposition. See Frédéric Julien, "Droite, Gauche et Troisième Voie," *Études et recherches* 5 (Fall 1987). The historical evolution of the Right—especially as a representative of what I call the "false Right"—has consequently always been compelled to accept a significant admixture of the liberalism it formally opposes. This was especially the case with the tradition founded by Burke and Peel, which was infused from the start with Whiggery. See Robert Blake, *The Conservative Party from Peel to Churchill* (London: Fontana, 1970), 3–9, 13–16. In recognizing that this Right is a false one, my argument accords with the above notion. By contrast, René Rémond's frequently cited depiction of the French Right as divided into monarchical, liberal, and Bonapartist tendencies, while touching a certain historical reality, characterizes only a fraction of its subject and, then, misleadingly, for it confuses earlier expressions of the Left (Bonapartism and Orleanism) with the Right. His trifold schema also fails to grasp the historical contours of the Right outside France. See *The Right Wing in France: From 1815 to De Gaulle*, 2nd ed., trans. James M. Laux (Philadelphia: University of Pennsylvania Press, 1969). Relatedly, it is disputable if it is even plausible to speak of French "conservatism" as a Right-wing phenomenon. Armin Mohler points out that *conservatisme* refers to the *juste milieu* of the nineteenth-century liberal bourgeoisie and its Orleanist (i.e., liberal) politics. What I refer to as "anti-liberalism" or what a German signifies when speaking of *Konservatismus* is, historically, *la Droite traditionnelle*—whose heirs, however entangled in modern politics, are to be

found today only in the ranks of the so-called far Right. See Armin Mohler, *Von rechts gesehen* (Stuttgart: Seewald, 1974), 120. Cf. Pamela Pilbeam, "Orleanism: A Doctrine of the Right?," in *The Right in France, 1789-1997*, ed. Nicholas Atkin and Frank Tallett (London: Tauris, 1998).

35. Cf. Tage Lindbom, *The Myth of Democracy* (Grand Rapids, MI: Eerdmans, 1996), 68.
36. Benoist, *Orientations pour des années décisives*, 19; Jean-Jacques Mourreau, "La Droite et la politique," in *Aux sources de la Droite: Pour en finir avec les clichés*, ed. Arnaud Guyot-Jeannin (Lausanne: L'Âge d'Homme, 2000); Paul Piccone, "21st Century Politics," *Telos* 117 (Fall 1999).
37. Erik von Kuehnelt-Leddihn, "Conservative or Rightist?," *Chronicles: A Magazine of American Culture* (January 1999). (Hereafter *Chronicles*.)
38. Julius Evola, *Le fascisme vu de Droite*, 2nd ed., trans. Philippe Baillet (Puiseaux: Pardès, 1993), 22. On the "dual revolution" (the bourgeois economic revolution in England and the bourgeois political revolution in France), see Eric Hobsbawm, *The Age of Revolution, 1789-1848* (New York: Random House, 1996).
39. Jean-Christian Petitfils, *La Droite en France de 1789 à nos jours* (Paris: PUF, 1973), 105.
40. Alain de Benoist, "Mais où est donc passée la Gauche?," *Éléments* 99 (November 2000); Alain de Benoist, "L'implosion de la Droite" (1997), in *L'écume et les galets, 1991-1999: Dix ans d'actualité vue d'ailleurs* (Paris: Le Labyrinthe, 2000). Cf. Jean Baudrillard, *La Gauche divine* (Paris: Grasset, 1985), 70, 91-104, 108.

Chapter I

# From the Old Right to the New

In 1978, the French media "discovered" the Groupement de Recherche et d'Études pour la Civilisation Européenne. Led by a brilliant young journalist named Alain de Benoist, the GRECE constituted an association of Right-wing intellectuals dedicated to the renewal of European culture. Those identifying themselves as *Grécistes* believed the foundations of European civilization had slipped and that a cultural shift was requisite to any recovery of its former vigor. Given the media's inherent bias, the initial reports were uncharacteristically neutral. *Grécistes*, in fact, were treated as something of an oddity. Since the war, France's intellectual life had been almost exclusively monopolized by the Left. That Rightists (aside from the "conservatives" of the *droite affairiste*) might contribute to the realm of ideas or take a commanding position in the leading debates seemed entirely newsworthy.

In the course of 1978 and 1979, nearly a thousand articles on this "Parisian fashion" appeared in the French and European press, alongside a handful of books and several university dissertations.[1] Then, after Benoist's *Vu de Droite* was awarded the *Grand Prix* of the Académie Française, and especially after the GRECE gained access to *Le Figaro Magazine*, reaching a national and occasionally a European-wide audience, the media began to take alarm. With Thatcher's recent triumph in Britain and Reagan's imminent victory on the horizon, it seemed to be riding an international wave of anti-liberal revival. Of perhaps greater concern, its erudition and sophistication posed a not easily dismissible challenge to Left principles. For some, like *Le Nouvelle Observateur*, the arbiter of French political correctness, the GRECE constituted a "*Risorgimento* of the extreme Right*"* and hence a force to be crushed.[2] In this spirit, an American academic accused it of being an "open conspiracy" whose goal was "to restore respectability, if not popularity, to positions that have been outside the bounds of permissible [that is, liberal] discussion since the end of the Second World War."[3] Another commentator went so far as to see "SS financing" behind the GRECE.[4] Then, as the Left's indignation mounted and media neutrality melted away, Benoist's group was branded

"New Right" (*Nouvelle Droite*), as if it shared the politics of the Thatcher-Reagan forces, and denounced as a menace to the liberal consensus.[5]

## The Passing of the Old Right

This new school of anti-liberal thought originated not in 1978, but a decade prior to its media discovery. Like the New Left of the sixties, the GRECE represented a break with as well as a continuation of earlier traditions. It needs, therefore, to be situated against this larger historical horizon, whose dominant reference point was the Second European Civil War. Between late 1944, when France was "liberated," and 1946, when the Fourth Republic was founded, the Old Right, particularly its anti-liberal nationalist wing, was decimated by a murderous purge. That this bloodletting resembled those that had earlier occurred in the Soviet Union was not at all fortuitous, for Communists were its principal organizers. The entire Left, however, had a hand in it, motivated as it was by the war's bitter legacy, as well as by earlier anti-Rightist campaigns, particularly those of the Popular Front, which had promoted the notion that "fascism" was the mirror opposite of the Left and that anti-liberalism of any persuasion (especially if anti-Stalinist) represented a variant of the "brown plague."[6] The nationalist regime Marshal Pétain established at Vichy following France's defeat in 1940, modest effort that it was to maintain the institutional legacy of the French state, only enhanced this association, for Vichy's unavoidable collaboration with the occupying forces—a collaboration without the slightest ideological affinity to National Socialism—tainted the Right as a whole.[7]

Once the Allies captured Paris in August 1944, the Left—with the French Communist Party (PCF) at its head and the US Command in the rear—lost no time in taking its revenge on the "collaborators." All Rightists, whether they had actively supported the occupying forces or simply cooperated with Pétain's legally established government for the sake of the defeated nation, were threatened by the ensuing terror. Having opposed the triumphant liberal-Communist coalition, they were automatically labeled "fascists" and targeted for the same punishments as their alleged German and Italian homologues. With this "orgy of summary vengeance," as many as a hundred thousand so-called "fascist collaborators" were murdered by the anti-fascist Resistance (the figure is disputed), over a million interned, several tens of thousands sentenced to hard labor, a quarter million deprived of their civil rights, and an unknown number of others driven into exile.[8] Of these imprisoned, hounded, and murdered French Rightists, more than a few, it turns out, had been veterans of the anti-German resistance.⁹ This, however, mattered little to the Left-wing vigilantes, who were not only in the pay of, but under the command of, the invading American forces.

Besides hunting down collaborators, the American occupation forces hoped to extirpate the roots of "collaborationism." In the same way the victors in the seventeenth-century religious wars forcefully imposed their beliefs on conquered populations, determining who would be Protestant and who would be Catholic, the US and its anti-fascist allies endeavored to re-order the ideological character of the postwar European population. Thus, while the Soviets began to demolish the class structure of and set up one-party dictatorships in the East European lands occupied by the Red Army, France's former ruling class was similarly slated for replacement by the victors. What Thomas Molnar calls a "monoclass" of *déclassé* administrators, recruited from the most opportunist social elements (pre-eminently traitors and renegades loyal to the "Anglo-Saxons") and trained in the newly founded École Nationale d'Administration, was charged with implementing the liberal managerial principles of the American conquerors. As this monoclass (or "New Class") assumed control of the government, the media, and the major corporate structures, it sought to "democratize" the country.¹⁰ In principle, this meant replacing Europe's traditional aristocratic standards with the liberal ones of postwar capitalism. In practice, it meant establishing a new state bureaucracy, economic elite, and intelligentsia dependent on their American analogues, which, in the process, meant fostering a system infused with "abstract individualism, utilitarian beliefs, a superficial humanitarianism, an indifference to history, an avoidance of high culture, a preference for the virtual, and an inclination to corruption, nepotism, and vote buying."¹¹

These de-Europeanizing practices would abate somewhat in the late 1940s, after Charles de Gaulle broke ranks with the new liberal order to form the Right-wing Rassemblement du Peuple Français (RPF). Although his RPF immediately undermined the Left's monopoly and provided anti-liberals an opportunity to regroup, it failed to prevent their anti-Communism and old-style nationalism from being recuperated by America's Cold War Establishment (whose objectives were less anti-Communist than anti-European). The RPF consequently ended up accepting Europe's divided status, inadvertently "playing the game of the extra-European forces" (Yockey). The formation of Pierre Poujade's Union de Défense des Commerçants et Artisans in the mid-1950s, representing a more "muscular" expression of anti-liberal electoralism, continued this collaborationist tendency. The same holds for the anti-liberal mobilization to defend the "white Christian West" from the national liberation movements spreading throughout the colonial world—as if these movements were mainly of Communist and not American inspiration. The subsequent collapse of the Fourth and the founding of the Gaullist Fifth Republic would again rally nationalists and anti-liberals, but their brief and tenuous association with De Gaulle came to a bloody impasse, once his new government "betrayed" *Algérie française*. Of the Right's numerous postwar humiliations, Algeria's loss was certainly the most grievous, for it revealed—or at least seemed to reveal—that the enemy had captured not simply the Metropolis and the State, but the nationalist forces.[12]

For anti-liberals coming of age in this period of liberal ascendancy, these repeated failures could not but provoke a soul-searching self-examination. Not only had they failed to regain the high ground of the pre-war years, they no longer addressed the constituency that had once given Charles Maurras' Action Française and Colonel La Rocque's Croix de Feu their mass following. That constituency, in fact, had ceased to exist, as postwar France made the transition to a liberal-democratic consumer society. In the process, the still large rural population was forced off the land by tractorization and urbanization; American production techniques crowded out traditional artisanal methods; US-style universities, with mass enrollments and semi-literate students, were founded and became, along with the introduction of television, part of a new programmable process of socialization; de-Christianization spread to the majority of the population; and high culture experienced its greatest setback since, perhaps, the fall of the Roman Empire. With the ensuing consumption of such deculturating products as Hollywood films, jazz, and standardized commodities reflecting *le look américain*, French culture, like European culture as a whole, began to retreat. This naturally alarmed the anti-liberals, but their old-style nationalism and anti-Communism made it difficult for them to realize the degree to which their Cold War allegiance to America and, implicitly, its cultural order, had implicated them in this deculturating process.

As family and nation, community and church continued to recede before the country's technologically engineered makeover, Dominique Venner, Jean Mabire, and a handful of other revolutionary Rightists were forced to the conclusion that the "European way of life" was becoming a thing of the past. Triumphalist American liberalism had not only vassalized their government, sundered the coherence of their culture, and prevented Europeans from discovering themselves in the achievements of their ancestors, it succeeded in co-opting the anti-Soviet forces for its own sake.[13]

Unsurprisingly, the precocious Alain de Benoist, after an adolescent stint in the Action Française, joined Venner and Mabire's Europe-Action, the first Right-wing group to embrace issues anticipating the cultural and identitarian concerns that would hereafter define the *European New Right*.[14]

## The GRECE's Founding

In founding the GRECE in early 1968, when the anti-liberal Right was at its historical nadir, Benoist and his compatriots had no intention of creating another groupuscule to revive the *opposition nationale*. There were no want of such organizations and no sign that they had had the slightest impact. Instead, the GRECE's young founders, with only tangential links to the Old Right and shaped largely by the challenges of the postwar order, saw their task in different terms. In their view, an anti-liberal movement against the de-Europeanizing forces of Americanization, consumerism, and the liberal capitalist regimes established by the US after 1945 would never succeed as long as the culture remained steeped in liberal beliefs. As Benoist formulated it: "without Marx, no Lenin."[15] That is, without an offensive of anti-liberal ideas and thus a revolution in the spirit, there could be no movement against *le parti américain*.[16] The GRECE was established, then, not as a political organization concerned with *la politique politicienne*, but as a school of thought to contest the ruling ideology and redeem the soul of European culture and identity. Its decision to found journals, organize study groups, promote research projects, and sponsor conferences for the sake of its anti-liberal *Kulturkampf* lent it, ironically, a certain resemblance to the Frankfurt School of Social Research, even if it lacked the financial and institutional resources of this Jewish Marxist think tank, "founded in 1923 to oppose the philosophy of National Socialism" (Alain Pascal). For like the earlier phenomenon of "Western Marxism," the Continental New Right, to which the GRECE would give life, was a product of political defeat.[17] The waning of political opportunities in the mid-sixties, particularly after the loss of Algeria, meant that anti-liberal intellectuals, like Marxists after the failed Communist revolutions of 1923, had little alternative but to seek a new center of gravity in philosophical and theoretical work.

The GRECE's decision to pursue an intellectual vocation stressing culture and identity rather than politics would mark a paradigm-forming break with previous Rightist practices. Not only did it privilege the cause of Europe's cultural heritage (which had never previously needed defending), it adopted an entirely novel approach to the field of political contestation, defining itself in terms that were pagan rather than Catholic, postmodern rather than anti-modern, European rather than Western. At the same time, its young founders distanced themselves from the discredited legacies of Pétainism, neo-fascism, traditional Catholicism, colonialism, Poujadism, and economic liberalism (not to mention bourgeois conservatism and Americanism), taking up issues that were "new" in evoking the archaic impulses of their European heritage. This reformulation of the Right project quite naturally alienated many conventional Rightists, but it also spoke to an apparently unaddressed need, for it attracted an immediate audience and helped rearm many flagging Right-wing and nationalist forces. Within but a few years of its founding, GRECE publications were reaching an ever-widening French, then European, readership. Benoist's brilliance as a writer and the polyvalent talents of his collaborators soon made the *Nouvelle École*, its theoretical organ, one of Europe's leading Rightist organs. Then, as the journal's prominence grew, scores of world-class intellectuals began to flock to its *comité de patronage*, further enhancing its influence. The growth of its international reputation in the late seventies and early eighties would eventually culminate in the formation of similar tendencies in other European countries, most notably in Italy, Belgium, and Germany. By the time of its media discovery, it had established itself as the single most influential intellectual force on the European Right.

## 1968

The GRECE was no sooner founded—the first number of *Nouvelle École* appeared in March 1968—than a near revolutionary upheaval lent its cultural project a significance that could never have been anticipated. As noted above, the postwar makeover had eliminated many traditional ways of life—in France and throughout Europe. With this, Europeans began liquidating much of their cultural heritage. Then, in 1968, it seemed as if they were about to liquidate the institutional foundations of Continental life, for in this frenzied period, whose closest historical parallel was the "revolutionary springtime" of 1848, there erupted the most spectacular expression of the postwar modernization process: the "May Events."

Retrospectively, the French student rebellion of May 1968 appears to have been less a revolutionary challenge to the liberal order, which it seemed at the time, than a radical spur to its ongoing subversions.[18] Its modernizing thrust was especially effective in facilitating the replacement of the existing elite, still tied in various ways to older notions of national and regional hegemony, with a cosmopolitan bourgeoisie—a

"Yuppie International" (Peter Berger)—made up of administrators, experts, and businessmen thoroughly immersed in the spirit and logic of the American-style techno-economic system they were responsible for managing. This post-Sixty-Eight "circulation of elites" (in which the order created by the "lions" of 1945 succumbed to the subtle modifications of its "foxes") suggested to the Italian Catholic philosopher Augusto Del Noce that the May Events were essentially intra-bourgeois rather than anti-bourgeois in character and effect.[19] That the rebellion was carried out by middle-class youth unfamiliar with the pre-American Europe of their parents also seems relevant.[20]

The rebellion's origins accordingly lay in the late 1950s and early 1960s, when the French government introduced an American-style university system, foreign to the elite models previously dominating European education.[21] As one of the world's foremost educational systems proceeded to dismantle itself, Greek and Latin were purged from the curriculum; the character and orthography of the French language were simplified; moral and civic instruction was suppressed; political-national history was replaced by a "new social history"; memorization was eliminated; and various pedagogical and psychological methods, supplemented with audio-visual aids, were substituted for more rigorous methods of instruction. At the same time, Communist and Leftist educators dominant in the new mass universities endeavored to make the classroom a "handmaiden of democracy." The university's traditional role as the enculturating transmitter of knowledge, as well as heritage and value, thus gave way to a new one, as an American-imported pedagogy fostered the forces of "individual self-expression": code for subjectivism, relativism, and pragmatism.[22] Like their US counterparts, Parisian university students—with minds "incapable of discrimination according to proper judgement" (Evola)—were encouraged to reject the "stale" accumulations of previously transmitted bodies of learning and prejudice for the sake of certain ideological fashions. Together with consumerism, these "educational reforms" would set the stage for the May Events.

Though France at the time was governed by De Gaulle's mildly anti-American government, his nationalism had failed to inspire French youth with a new vocation.[23] (That the CIA and its "cultural" services campaigned to disparage his policies and controlled numerous facets of French opinion were probably also a factor.)[24] French life, though, was already succumbing to American mass culture, which Gaullist modernization inadvertently fostered.[25] As Elvis, blue jeans, and the television screen started crowding out indigenous references, the French began to fall under the spell of America's Culture Industry and its antipathy to traditional forms of taste and value.[26] America's media-inspired civil rights movement and the student protests at Berkeley especially lit up the imagination of French youth. Then, in early 1968, following a dispute over the sexual "segregation" of university dormitories, Parisian students spontaneously re-enacted the psychodrama that had earlier convulsed Berkeley. Events quickly escalated, exceeding anything that had occurred on US campuses. At their height, the state even teetered. The young rebels nevertheless resembled the Americans in their "indiscipline, irrationalism, and inferior sort of anarchism."[27] While spouting the revolutionary teachings of Mao Zedong or extolling the heroism of Che Guevara, they displayed an occasional idealism. But this was mostly the gloss of an individualism whose anti-authoritarian and hedonistic impetus constituted less a revolt against postwar society, as Herbert Marcuse thought, than a youthful assertion of its underlying tenets.[28] "*La Révolution*," one New Rightist would later say of 1968, "*c'est je*"—for it unleashed an insurgence of narcissistic individualism.[29]

The Maoist Marxism of the period accordingly favored counter-cultural and individualistic more than class issues. Not the militant trade unionist opposing capitalist exploitation in the name of worker solidarity, but the pioneer of "emancipatory" lifestyles, personal freedoms, and political correctness now embodied the ideal of its "cultural revolution." The slogan "the personal is political" signaled, then, not merely the entry of feminists, homosexuals, non-whites, and counter-cultural groups into the "revolutionary struggle," but the advent of a "whole new political space" committed to individual "liberation."[30] Instead, then, of assailing the socioeconomic structures of bourgeois society, the May Events actually sought the final liberal triumph over whatever "obscurantist" traditions still lingered in European life, as intellectual, moral, racial, and cultural standards were razed in the name of certain libertarian ideals, such as the admonition to "prohibit all prohibitions."

Like their spiritual godfather, Karl Marx, the Sixty-Eighters took liberal modernist principles for granted. The *simulacre de révolte* they had staged before the TV cameras would thus play itself out as a "liberation" from whatever restraints family, Church, and custom still exerted over the individual. The path to fullest self-realization and hence happiness, they claimed, pointed to precisely this sort of freedom.[31] The ensuing fall of taboos would predictably sanction the most unrestrained of the "progressive" forces. Sex, for example, was hereafter dissociated from its reproductive function, came into the open, and turned into an object of commercialization, politicization, and media exploitation. The Marquis de Sade, impossible to publish before May, gained a similar respectability, as the Sadean state of permanent libidinal insurgence established itself as a fixture of the post-1968 order.[32] Marriage, family, and natality underwent analogous "liberations."[33] Even Christians, whose theology became noticeably more profane and socially mindful, began abandoning or downplaying transcendent references for the sake of self-fulfillment. Feminism, gay pride, ethnomasochism, hedonism, multiculturalism, and anarcho-capitalism—the great "isms" issuing from *la philosophie soixante-huitarde*—would naturally bloom in this hothouse atmosphere, just as Europe's high culture and distinct identity began to wither and fade.[34] In elevating personal desire above all else, the Sixty-Eighters could not, though, but stimulate the "nihilism" latent in the modernist project—the nihilism that comes with the collapse of traditional beliefs and values. Indeed, some Rightists have been inclined to think of them in terms of Nietzsche's "Last Man," oriented as they are to the here and now, concerned only with their own happiness, and indifferent to what went before and what might pass in their wake.[35]

In the decade following the rebellion, the *enfants de Marx et de Coca-Cola* (Jean-Luc Godard) gradually made their way back to the bosom of bourgeois society.[36] As they did, the banners of Third Worldism, anti-Americanism, and Maoism they had waved in the streets began giving way to flags bearing even more insidious insignia. Like their American counterparts, the former rebels remained attached to many of the sixties' causes, particularly the hedonistic ones associated with their individualism. But in outgrowing their revolutionary rhetoric and making their peace with consumer society, they also exchanged the Marcusian ideals of their youth for America's human rights rhetoric and free market ideology—again revealing that not liberalism and capitalism, but those traditionalisms they wrongly associated with them, had been the unconscious target of their earlier rebellion.[37] Their new-found Americanism would accordingly be as doctrinal and inquisitional as their abandoned Marxism. By the 1980s, French anti-Americanism (which had traditionally served as a defense of national identity from US cosmopolitanism) had become largely "synonymous with xenophobes, antiquarians, the cold-hearted, Marxists, fascists, shopkeepers, and authoritarians, [while] pro-Americanism [was associated] with all that is creative, modern, open, universal, and liberated. . . . In 1960 [Jean-Paul] Sartre [had] said an anti-Communist was a dog; thirty years later the dog [was] the anti-American."[38]

In passing from the Marxism of their youth to the "social Reaganism" of their adult years—from what Régis Debray calls the "Manichaeism of the poor" (Communism) to the "Manichaeism of the prosperous" (liberalism)—the former rebels continued to adhere to "the party of the foreigner," only the American now replaced the Russian. Then, as this *gauche caviar* began assuming positions of social and political responsibility, especially after François Mitterrand's Socialist party took power in 1981, it readily signed on to American-programmed globalization, Third World immigration, multiculturalism, and the various other "progressive" forces warring on the remnants of Old Europe.[39] This, of course, was entirely predictable, not least of all to those corporate and multinational interests that would most profit from it. For individualism and universalism have always gone hand in hand, one serving not as the opposite, but as the verso of the other.[40]

The rejection of traditional European values at the individual level, posed in anti-capitalist terms during the sixties, now converged with the universalizing, anti-European ones of *le parti américain*. For a time, this would make France one of America's most docile allies, as it disclaimed the Gaullist policies that had momentarily re-established the nation as a force in the world. Then, as the country's gates were thrown open to all who would trade in and sell off its welfare, human rights moved to the center of the Left's value system, liberal individualism became all the vogue, and entrepreneurial "culture" crowded out more traditional references.[41] At the same time, these new-found champions of America's planetary civilization showed not the slightest reluctance in demonizing the lingering vestiges of their European identity and the distinct facets of their patrimony—although their term was not "distinct," but "racist," "exclusionary," or "irrelevant."[42] This situation, moreover, was not confined to France, but affected the entire Continent, just as the May Events took their toll in virtually every European country. In Germany, for instance, anyone disputing the cosmopolitan modernism of the Sixty-Eighters, even those upholding the social democratic ideals of the old SPD, was henceforth suspected of "fascism."[43] In Britain, Belgium, and elsewhere, similar inquisitional and anti-European forces have come to dominate the public sphere.

What provoked this sea change that converted the Mao-jacketed rebels into business-suited collaborators of American-style globalism? The answer is complex. One can point to the increasing dysfunctionality, and hence unattractiveness, of the Communist model; the blood-stained record of many Third World regimes; the decline of the nation-state and its great integrating structures (army, class, school, union, party); the multinational and then global evolution of capitalist relations; the spread of sensibilities nurtured by television, electronic stimulations, and computerization; the unrelenting Americanization of European life; the universalization of Guy Debord's spectacle; the transition from Fordist mass production, based on fixed labor markets and Keynesian fiscal policies, to flexible post-Fordist systems geared to just-in-time production, restructured patterns of work, and new technologies. Each of these trends undoubtedly affected the *zeitgeist*. But for *Grécistes* the decisive factor was the cultural one. As the European monoclass increasingly mirrored the New Class forces in control of US institutions and as traditional values retreated before those of American mass culture, it was only natural, they believed, that political and social developments took a similar track.[44] This especially seemed the case since the capitalism the Sixty-Eighters had attacked in the name of hyper-modernism had itself become hyper-modern, linked to the growing globalization of the market and the denationalization of European economies.[45] Their embrace of the new economic forms was no less affected by a development of perhaps even greater cultural consequence: postmodernism.

## Postmodern Antinomies

Whether conceived as a break with modernity or as a late modernist innovation, the "postmodern condition" marks the advent of a new epoch in Western history. The first, most influential philosopher to interpret this condition, Jean-François Lyotard, describes it in terms of the collapse of the *grand récit*, the Great Narrative, animating modernity.[46] He claims a narrative of this sort establishes the philosophical disposition that allows knowledge and meaning to be transmitted in terms of a single overarching outlook. In the case of modernity's Great Narrative, whose collapse ushers in postmodernity, a secularized version of the Christian salvation myth served to legitimate the universalizing discourse of Western rationality and progress.

For more than two centuries, this metanarrative had imbued scientific reason with the authority of the divine *logos*, representing the world with objective certainty, scoffing at "irrationality, superstition, and prejudice," as it established a universal system of truth that was to emancipate man from his "self-incurred tutelage." Then, with the advent of the postmodern condition in the closing decades of the twentieth century, reason's "perpetual process of self-critique" (William Connolly) turned against modernity itself, whose totalizing discourse was revealed to rest on similar narrative foundations.[47] Progress, freedom, and objectivity—the alleged products of scientific reason and the forces that were to liberate modern man from his irrational beliefs—were suddenly discovered to be fictions, no more real than the stories primitives tell about their world.[48]

In this sense, postmodernity marks that stage in late modern consciousness when modernity began to recognize the subjective foundations of its own narrative projections.

Including in their ranks such figures as Michel Foucault, Gianni Vattimo, Gilles Deleuze, Jacques Derrida, and Jean Baudrillard, postmodernists see themselves as "denaturalizing (or "dedoxifying") the foundationalist character of modern representations.[49] Against the rational, objective, and universal claims of the modern narrative, as it applies the timeless truths of mathematical reason to man's contingent world, they argue that the narrating subject is never autonomous, never situated at an Archimedean point beyond space and time, never able to perceive the world with detachment and certainty. Rather, representations of all kinds are inevitably entwined in sociolinguistic webs of signification that know no all-embracing truth, only their own truths, which are indistinguishable from their will to power. Different "language games," to use Lyotard's Wittgensteinian terminology, play with different rules. Instead of logically ordering the various manifestation of the objective world with neutral, naturalistic categories, modern reason, like every language game, functions according to rules and with concepts that are self-referential, making sense of the world it views in ways already presupposed. This makes reason primarily "significatory" rather than representational. As a consequence, there can in actuality be no overarching narrative to structure reality's multiple dimensions and hence no single, unsituated objective category to describe or explain them. On this basis, postmodernists conclude that there are no cognitively privileged and canonical forms of knowledge—only different styles, voices, and registers reflecting different perspectives, different premises, and different systems of symbolization. Every representation of reality, they emphasize, is a mediated one, reflecting not reality *per se*, but a subjective and highly contextualized system of significatory representations.

Once it is accepted that different narratives impose different representations on the world and that these representations are irreducible to one another, modernity's Great Narrative is forced to cede to the various micro-narratives (*petits récits*) standing outside it. For if there is no single overarching narrative, and hence no single absolute truth, to explain history and justify the modernist project, then multiple developments, each with their own particularistic justification and local determination, are not only possible, but viable and desirable. Postmodernists thus celebrate the differentiation of authority that follows and the heterogeneous possibilities freed from modernity's homogenizing abstractions, particularly those of a pluralistic politics of difference and identity.[50] The implications of this "anti-foundationalism" are, though, more than epistemological. Since "one cannot transcend language" (Richard Rorty) and appeal to universal truths unaffected by time and place, there can be no "totalizing, essentializing logic," no commonly accepted vision of the good, and hence no great collective agent (such as modernity's classes, parties, nations, or states) to serve as bearers of an emancipatory politics. All forms of human action, even (or especially) the most lofty, inevitably shatter before an elusive, polymorphous reality, represented by a now self-conscious throng of incompatible discursive traditions. This leads postmodernists to a "radical pluralism" that "deconstructs" modernist notions of truth, value, and justice in the interests of a wider field of localized representations and practices.[51]

While opposing modernity's philosophical presumptions, especially its "sovereignty of reason," postmodernists nevertheless do so in ways favoring the individualistic tendencies of liberal politics. In many respects they are, in fact, simply more philosophically sophisticated liberals, although ones whose principal reference is no longer the ethnically homogeneous nation-state, but rather the rainbow world of the global market. As *Grécistes* point out, the postmodern view of reality as a shifting field of discursive relations is less concerned with re-legitimating the micro-narratives of the pre-modern tradition than with privileging their antithesis: the anarchist fragments of a hyper-modern world linked to the nomadic logic of the new international economy. Thus, while criticizing the Great Narrative's denigration of traditional communities, the "micro-groups" and "tribal identities" (Michel Maffesoli) postmodernists celebrate as alternatives to modern individualism and expressions of a new polyvalent sociality are typically ones geared to the libidinal impulses of changing markets and seasonal fashions.[52]

The proliferation of shifting identities and the "heterotopic" world of free-floating signifiers that comes with the metanarrative collapse are similarly prized as a liberation from modernity's totalizing structures, just as modernists earlier touted an atomizing individualism as a liberation from traditionalist restraints. Accordingly, the identity and community of a particular people, elaborated in history and involving a circumscribable subject (such as an *ethnos* or a nation), has for them no more legitimacy than one fabricated by a counter-cultural movement or a marketing agency. Indeed, since the history of such a people unfolds within a destining framework conditioning the range of individualization, postmodernists are wont to treat it as having less legitimacy. For this reason, "B and D" groups, racial minorities, trance freaks, lesbian bikers, squatters, immigrants, and grunge rockers all register in their count, while Basque nationalists, Swiss communards, and Lombard regionalists, whose communities are ancient and intergenerational, are generally suspected of being "closed" or repressive variants of the Great Narrative.[53]

In celebrating the "imagined" racial, sexual, and counter-cultural "identifications" that the metanarrative collapse makes possible, postmodern liberals also refuse to hypostatize the ones with which they are temporarily identified. In William Connolly's political theory, this is called "the cultivation of agnostic respect among interwoven and contending constituencies"—implying that no single one is or could be primary.[54] Such "respect" inclines postmodernists to champion "minorities in politics, sex, and language" and to refuse the "tyranny of wholes" (Ihab Hassan). Paradoxically, this agnosticism ends up culminating in a universalism even more embracing than the modernist one they oppose. For once stable identities are dismissed and everything is rendered fluid, the Other becomes an analogue of the Same, somewhat in way that modern individualism became the counterpart of modernity's totalizing structures. A postmodern world of absolute differences is hence a world in which difference ceases to be significant, as the toleration of multiple tribal codes is generalized into a global principle of arbitrary caprice. Vattimo observes that "what Kant legitimately . . . regarded as a call to the universal human community . . . has in the present . . . become an expedient referral to multiplicity."[55] Baudrillard makes a similar observation, characterizing postmodern tribalism as part of a process by which the existing "macro-structures" are metamorphosed "into innumerable particles [bearing] within them all the stigmata of the [existing] networks and circuits—each one forming its own micro-networks and micro-circuits, each one reviving for itself, in its micro-universe, the now useless totalitarianism of the whole."[56]

Once postmodernity collapses the universal into the particular, the global into the local, the objective into the subjective, then narcissistic identities and idiosyncratic communities (tribes) cannot but assume the stature of modernity's fixed monolithic ones.[57] This makes the postmodern condition both highly uniform and highly atomized, reflecting a world market that situates a rootless individual within a multitude of incommensurable micro-groups, each of which resembles the other in lacking stability, coherence, and social cohesion.[58] "Everything," as a result, "now equals everything" and "nothing equals nothing."[59]

In attacking "the cogito of Western philosophy" (that is, the Archimedean narrator of modernity's *grand récit*), postmodernists, in the libertarian spirit of '68, "transgress" the objectivizing totalities of the modern *épistémè*, hoping to multiply the number of possible narratives available to the individual. In practice, however, they usually end up repeating modernity's founding gestures—in refusing the past, rejecting the significance of the established cultural heritage, and fostering a corrosive individualism at odds with every traditional form of community. More tellingly, they ignore the new "mechanisms of domination and decision" which have assumed unprecedented power in postmodern society, as the fragmentation of the social order and the destabilization of identity enhance the interventionist compass of the state, the media, and the major corporations. Old-line Marxists, nostalgic in their attachment to modernist certainties, find this inattention to the totalizing nature of the postmodern condition as testament to postmodernity's complicity with the new hegemonic system of global capitalism.

Against a postmodernism intent on reducing cultural affiliations (identity) to a "superficial decoration" suitable to globalism's shifting market forms—that is, against a postmodernism that not only stops short of its anti-liberal implications, but celebrates the trivial novelties of a totally consumerized reality—*Grécistes* defend an ontology rooted in Europe's cultural-historical specificity. Being-in-the-world, the fundament of identity, is neither arbitrary nor infinitely malleable. In their view, an individual who constantly reinvents himself, as he circulates among postmodernity's nomadic tribes, is an individual lacking any meaningful ontological grounding. As a "substance," identity is thrown, rooted, cultivated. According to the philosophies of Nietzsche and Heidegger, from which postmodernists derive their most fundamental insights, the specific histories and cultures informing human subjectivity (identity) are dismissible at the cost not only of authenticity, but of one's humanity.[60] Identity in this sense is inseparable from its determinants, even if the old objective certainties no longer hold and all existing formations are recognized as "social constructs" or micro-narratives. The history of the world may lack a totalizing unity and exhibit a multitude of incommensurable narratives, as postmodernists rightly insist, but its innumerable expressions are hardly the same as a chaos in which everything is possible.

As ego, self, or actor, the individual, *Grécistes* hold, is inseparable from his community and heritage, for (as subsequent chapters will make clear) every individual is eventual, historical, particular, and hence dependent on his context for whatever sense of identity he endeavors to realize—or escape. Again, following Nietzsche and Heidegger, *Grécistes* view identity and the possibility of intersubjective relations as interwoven facets of the traditional micro-narratives which liberal modernity sought to supplant.[61] Accepting that there are no universals in the sense posited by liberal modernity and that knowledge is always provisional, they also emphasize that within a specific culture, the existing structures of belief offer what might be called "localized universals" to frame the parameters of its specific discourse.[63] In this sense, the "living past" of European culture constitutes not only the historical basis of Europe's particular discourse, but the sole one constitutive of its particular will to power.

Though *Grécistes* acknowledge that "truth" is an interpretative product of a particular tradition (that is, anti-foundational), they also believe that this does not imply, as postmodernists assume, that "truth" is entirely free-floating, that any "truth" can be embraced by any subject, or that empirical reality can bend to any subjective intent. Against a bourgeois/academic postmodernity committed to the nihilistic "reconstructionism" of modern liberal politics, *Grécistes* argue that "truth" is a function of culture and history, "authorized" by context alone—a context, moreover, that is never arbitrary, but lived, felt, rooted. In a word, the metanarrative collapse does not dispense with the need for meaningful forms of identity, but is significant precisely because it revives—and hence re-legitimates—those particularistic discourses and identities that liberal modernity dismissed and that liberal postmodernity is wont to misconceive. Indeed, once the fiction of an absolute, universal narrative is abandoned, the world becomes again a place of willed action and the European project assumes a legitimacy that liberal modernity sought to repress. Rather than succumbing to the market-inspired communitarianism of the postmodernists, *Grécistes* assert that some truths are superior to others—if only because they express their own particular will to power.

Foucault has argued that a narrative order based on modern rationality (in the form of Jeremy Bentham's panoptical model of power) leads not to emancipation, as the Enlightenment promised, but to one in which new forms of control and domination are able to subjugate the individual.[63] One might similarly argue that the present bourgeois/academic recuperation of postmodernity liberates individuals and peoples from modernity's metanarrative constraints only to delegitimize their resistance to the centrifugal forces of the global market. Against such a postmodernism, as it justifies the extirpation of the European life world, *Grécistes* defend the integrity of ontologically rooted identities, contending that competing micro-narratives need not lead to complicity with globalism's hyper-individualistic, and ultimately anti-European, modes of consumption and control. There are, they insist, still relevant identities and viable micro-narratives, rooted in lived traditions, that speak to the particularities of the present, while eschewing the nihilistic implications of postmodern tribalism. Instead, then, of accepting the metanarrative collapse as justification for the culturally corrosive logic of global capital, they look to breathe new life into the historical sources of European identity, fully aware that there are no universal foundations to such an identity, only a subjective affiliation to a tradition whose living present is the only one they can possibly know.

The breakdown of the modernist paradigm needs not, therefore, culminate in a tribalizing atomization dispensing with organic attachments. As *Grécistes* hold, it can, just as readily serve as an alternative to present developments, insofar as the historically rooted truths of the European heritage offer a potentially more meaningful path to the future than does modernity's empty metaphysical postulates—or postmodernity's atomized and libidinal alternatives.[64] Based on a recuperation of postmodernism's anti-liberal core, GRECE-inspired identitarians claim the only viable narratives for Europeans—and hence the only viable communities and identities—are those posited by the cultural, historical, and racial legacies native to their heritage.[65] Unlike the New Left, then, whose rebellion in 1968 ostensibly targeted the American-centric system founded in 1945, the New Right fights this system not in the name of a postmodernism that extends and radicalizes its underlying tenets, but for the sake of freeing Europeans from its deforming effects.

## Across Three Decades

The intellectual horizons postmodernity brought into view were not immediately evident to *Grécistes*. It was only in 1979 that Lyotard's *La condition postmoderne* appeared and later still that the postmodern critique took hold. *Grécistes*, moreover, never wholeheartedly signed on to it and some in their ranks disavowed it in the name of a pre-modern traditionalism. Postmodernism would influence their anti-liberalism, but postmodernists have tended to occupy a different mental universe. A brief overview of the GRECE's evolution—an evolution to which the entire New Right is today heir—might better explain why this has been the case.

In the more than three and a half decades that now make up its history, the GRECE has worked out its anti-liberal project in a number of different philosophical languages. Many of these have been quite divergent, some opening paths that continue to be pursued, others that have been abandoned or gradually rethought over the years. It is important, then, in characterizing the GRECE's general trajectory, to indicate its abiding concerns. Put simply, its project has always focused on a defense of Europe's identity. Whatever philosophical language its members have spoken over the years, whatever theoretical references they have made or themes they have explored, they have done so as patriots of the "European idea," seeking to safeguard the integrity of Continental life from the anti-identitarian implications of liberal modernity. Such a defense, as will be evident below, has had little to do with ideology *per se* or even with a particular philosophical current, but rather reflects a world view—and a will to power—opposed to liberalism's anti-European impetus.

While shedding the irrelevant trappings of the Old Right and experimenting with a variety of strategies to revive the European idea, the first decade of the GRECE's existence, as one might expect, was somewhat transitional in character. Its initial challenge to liberal culture, for instance, took place in the realm of science and bore many characteristics, such as a positivist faith in scientific reason, that it later rejected. Science, however, was a "natural" starting point for its anti-liberal project. In the eighteenth century, the champions of liberal modernity had mobilized the New Science against their conservative foes and have since represented themselves as the political vanguard of the most advanced scientific ideas. Twentieth-century science, however, has proven to be far less amenable to liberal claims.[66] The basic tenets of evolutionary psychology, behavioral genetics, molecular biology, sociobiology, and ethology, all seem to contradict liberal notions of environmental primacy, natural "goodness," the individualist nature of the social world, the irrelevance of race, and the plasticity and equality of human nature.[67] Given liberalism's vulnerability in this field, it was here that *Grécistes* staged their initial assault on modernist ideas, targeting what the most recent scientific research revealed about the social, hierarchical, genetic, and hence anti-liberal foundations of human life.[68]

Besides mobilizing the latest scientific research against Leftist claims, the early GRECE devoted considerable attention to Europe's Indo-European, classical, and medieval origins—with the aim of affirming not merely Europe's biological, but also the specific historical character of its identity. Through a popularization of Indo-European prehistory, *Grécistes* thus hoped to make Europeans aware of their culture's primordial attributes and the ways these distinguish them from other peoples. With similar intent, they have done the same for the Greco-Romans, who brought to fruition the greatest Indo-European characteristics and established the foundations of European civilization. And though critical of Christianity's non-European origins, *Grécistes* looked on the Catholic Middle Ages as integral to the integration of the Celtic, Germanic, and Slavic peoples of Northern and Eastern Europe into the civilizational fold established by the Greco-Romans.[69] All these historical experiences, they argue, are constituent of European identity and need to be affirmed, if Europeans are to regain confidence in their civilizational project.

History and the life sciences dominated the GRECE's early publishing concerns, but it was philosophy that would play the leading role in orienting it to the larger cultural realm.[70] As mentioned, its first attempt at philosophical definition took positivist form. The young Benoist, who was 25 at the time of the GRECE's founding, had been much influenced by the eminent historian, classicist, and philosopher of science, Louis Rougier, who was best known as the foremost French proponent of "logical positivism."[71] As a school, logical positivism sought to purge philosophy of its lingering "metaphysical" elements and center the discipline on the verifiable claims of science and logic. By the early seventies, however, when *Grécistes* attempted to rouse interest in it, logical positivism had already spent itself as a philosophical force. Once this was realized, Rougier's influence began to decline and that of Giorgio Locchi, a Paris-based Italian journalist and accomplished Germanist, to rise. From this point on, the GRECE would orient mainly to Continental, particularly German, thinkers.[72] This would lead it to Nietzsche and then to Heidegger, two thinkers who have since played commanding roles in its project. But while the GRECE's Nietzscheanism and Heideggerianism remain enduring features of its philosophical identity, they also tend to obscure the more subterranean influences of Julius Evola, Armin Mohler, Thierry Maulnier, Ernst Jünger, Raymond Abellio, Jules Monnerot, Raymond Ruyer, Julien Freund, and others, whose ideas have been assimilated over the years, but never systematically formulated. As a consequence of this philosophical *bricolage*, the GRECE cannot be defined in terms of a single philosophy or fixed body of ideas. Nevertheless, its identitarian world view possesses a definite coherence: for its anchorage in the European heritage influences the ideas it takes up and how they are incorporated into its anti-liberal project. Subsequent chapters should make this clearer.

In the second half of the seventies, the ethological studies of Konrad Lorenz took center stage in the GRECE's cultural politics. Against behaviorists and environmentalists emphasizing the significance of milieu, and hence the promises of liberal reform, Lorenz's work on animal behavior stressed the primacy of the evolutionary heritage.[73] Buttressed by the research of Irenäus Eibl-Eibesfeldt and the writings of Robert Ardrey, his studies helped popularize such anti-liberal concepts as territoriality, hierarchy, aggression, and human nature. While giving currency to Lorenz's ideas in this period, especially to the anti-egalitarian implications of his thought, *Grécistes* were nevertheless already in the process of moving away from the life sciences and toward a more culturally specific anti-liberalism. It was Lorenz's "debate" with the great German philosophical anthropologist, Arnold Gehlen, that prepared the way for this reorientation. In this exchange, Lorenz was compelled to make certain concessions to Gehlen's understanding of culture and Gehlen to attribute a greater role to nature in establishing a platform for human behavior.[74] Yet, it was the latter's "culturalism," the subject of the next chapter, which would most affect the GRECE's evolving project.[75]

In addition to its cultural turn, the late seventies witnessed the introduction of what has since become a hallmark of the European New Right. Despite his Catholic upbringing, the young Benoist considered Christianity a Near Eastern distortion of Europe's indigenous spirit. Under Rougier's influence, his opposition to Christianity was mainly of atheistic inspiration.[76] But once Locchi's Nietzscheanism took hold, it was increasingly informed by the heritage of pre-Christian paganism, which was seen not simply as a positive alternative to Christianity's Abrahamic tradition, but as a culturally more faithful expression of the European spirit. Then, as *Grécistes* began investigating the pagan heritage, a series of larger questions arose, reflecting back on earlier positions and forward to new ones, such as those broached in the early eighties, when they discarded all reference to "biological realism," took their distance from Nietzsche, oriented to Heidegger, and intersected the postmodern debate.

By the time the Soviet empire showed the first signs of collapse, the GRECE had ceased emphasizing such ethological themes as anti-egalitarianism, which seemed to sanction the social Darwinian ramifications of "third age capitalism," and begun making a systematic critique of modern forms of alienation (individualism, economism, technology), as well as focusing on *la cause du peuples* and the defense of identitarian differences (*le droit à la différence*)—themes that had been introduced earlier, but assumed greater urgency in the latter half of the eighties, as Americanism, cosmopolitanism, and global capitalism assumed increasingly menacing forms. To the degree these themes emphasized ethnopluralism and cultural relativism—and thus victimized minorities and principles of self-determination—they owed a good deal to the Left and to the anti-colonial movements still influencing the Third World. In time, this *stratégie de retorsion* would culminate in a Right-wing form of Third Worldism, which called for an alliance between Europe and the Third World to rebuff the Cold War system of *blocs*. Then, as these larger geopolitical considerations were broached, the GRECE's conception of European union was similarly affected, prompting it to advocate a federal democratic imperium to unite Europeans on the basis of biocultural rather than simply economic criteria.

Though Communism's collapse in 1991 validated much of the GRECE's previous trajectory, it also brought new problems. At one level, the growing diffusion of its ideas and the evolving political situation provoked a series of splits within its organization, giving rise to various New Right tendencies that would take their distance from Benoist's specific distillation of the anti-liberal tradition.[77] At the same time, the demise of Russian totalitarianism brought about not a new openness in European affairs, but an immediate narrowing of permissible freedoms, as another "iron curtain"—this time of political correctness and *la pensée unique*—was drawn across the Continent. As Alexandre Zinoviev describes it: "Hardly had Communism collapsed than the West began adopting certain characteristics of its discredited adversary."[78] Freedom of speech and certain historical forms of belief have since been abridged, and in many cases criminalized for the sake of certain high-sounding but dogmatic precepts. Threatened by this "new inquisition," the GRECE and other New Right tendencies challenging the established order must now also struggle against those powerful forces that seek to muzzle them.[79] This curtailment of traditional freedoms in the West has, though, diminished neither the audience nor the relevance of New Right ideas, for at the dawn of the third millennium its defense of the European project continues to represent the most relevant alternative to the regnant liberalism.

## The Conservative Revolution

In the literature devoted to the GRECE—a literature whose plethora is one testament to its significance—the leading question inevitably is: how "new" is the New Right? Some commentators insist that the followers of Alain de Benoist have merely repackaged traditional far Right ideas and that their novelty lies in their form, not their content. Others claim there are radically innovative aspects to this anti-liberal tendency and that it is a mistake to ignore its contributions to contemporary thought. A third current, found within many traditional Rightist formations and even among some *Grécistes*, disputes that the New Right is Right-wing in any historical sense of the term and is best seen as a Third Way tendency, transcending conventional Right-Left polarities.

In seeking to characterize the GRECE and, more generally, the various tendencies that today make up the New Right, it is important not to lose sight of the fact that these formations are, above all, schools of thought and not political parties. Their adherents ought to be seen, then, as the Voltaires and Rousseaus of the new anti-liberalism, not its Robespierres and Saint-Justs. As such, New Rightists struggle for a revolutionary cultural synthesis in the realm of ideas, not the overthrow of the liberal order in the streets or parliaments. Yet even as a school of thought, the New

Right does not represent a specific ideology, only a certain anti-liberal disposition committed to the integrity of European culture and identity. This makes it a polyvalent tendency, difficult to pigeonhole.

The leading French commentator on the New Right has, for example, identified five distinct currents running through the GRECE.[80] One of these is associated with the anti-modern traditionalism of René Guénon and Julius Evola, which has influenced much of the European far Right since the seventies. A second current is communitarian or *völkisch*, emphasizing "European nationalism" and the centrality of a Continental identity. Another is neo-pagan, opposing the Judeo-Christian heritage in the name of primordial European values. A fourth is postmodern, celebrating the cultural pluralism that comes with the breakdown of modernity's totalizing structures and the possibilities it poses for the European project. A final current is scientist, oriented to the life sciences and their genetic, eugenic, and ideological implications. While all these currents are reflected to one degree or another in GRECE publications, the exact relationship between them remains unclear. The vast literary corpus of Alain de Benoist, expressing aspects of each, constitutes the sole axis around which they all seem to revolve.[81] Again, this polyvalence attests to the New Right's philosophical diversity and its potential for divergent expression.[82]

In adopting a cultural, rather than a distinctively political, project, most of the GRECE's founders, as well as most subsequent New Right tendencies, did so because of their alienation from the postwar Right—specifically from its Americanism, colonialism, economic liberalism, Catholicism, and misleading understanding of fascism. The various historical manifestations of the Right have accordingly been subject to numerous critiques. Benoist, for example, designates not the Left *per se* as Europe's enemy, but rather the liberal modernist ideology that seeks the destruction of European culture (even if the Left is most identified with this ideology). On several occasions, he has claimed he can conceive of situations where he might take his stand with the Left and not the Right. He thus stresses that while *on* the Right, he is not necessarily *of* it.[83] Indeed, he is renowned for voting for Reds or Greens whenever they mount a genuine opposition to the liberal order.[84] Not surprisingly, Catholic traditionalists and *Lépenistes* have occasionally accused him of being a *crypto-gauchiste*.[85]

While a strong argument can thus be made that Benoist's GRECE is not Right-wing at all, there is no question that the prevailing political consensus situates it on the Right.[86] But perhaps more important than where it lies on the political spectrum is how it approaches the leading ideas—for above all the New Right is to be judged as a school of thought. Whether, in fact, there are inherently Right-wing or Left-wing ideas is, of course, disputable. (On a host of issues—regionalism, ecology, religion, state centralization, nationalism, colonialism, science, race, the Jews, *et cetera*—both Right and Left have shifted from side to side over the last two centuries.) There does, however, seem to be a Right-wing way of rendering ideas and a Left-wing way of rendering them.[87] In contrast to the Right, the Left is inclined to engage and assimilate the leading ideas, which means that intellectual and cultural developments usually work to its advantage. In a self-conscious break from the traditional Right and its refusal to take the intelligentsia seriously—that is, to acknowledge that an unexamined and intellectually disarmed culture no longer suffices in an age seeking the extirpation of the European heritage—the New Right follows the Left in recuperating from contemporary thought what it can for its identitarian project.

Despite, then, their ambivalent relationship to the historical Right, New Rightists are nevertheless most indebted to its legacy. They have, to be sure, borrowed from the Left, especially from its critique of liberal society, which is evident in all they have taken from the Frankfurt School's "dialectic of reason," Baudrillard and Debord's dissection of *la société du spectacle*, Debray's Gaullist nationalism, Tönnies' vindication of community, Foucault's "micro-physics of power," Dumont's studies of traditional hierarchical societies, *et cetera*. But the deepest roots of their identitarian world view are lodged in the heritage of the Counter-Enlightenment and the True Right. When Edmund Burke, Joseph de Maistre, Louis de Bonald, and others in the period of the French Revolution worked out what would be the conservative or Right-wing critique of liberal modernity, they took their stand with the traditions, identities, and hierarchical principles of organic communities.[88] However much the New Right has updated and rethought these principles, they remain integral to its project. It is no less indebted to the second great resurgence of Right-wing thought: the so-called anti-positivist revolt of the late nineteenth century, which gave birth to various national-populist, national-socialist, and revolutionary nationalist movements—or to what Zeev Sternhell aptly calls "the Revolutionary Right."[89] From Barrès, Sorel, Le Bon, Pareto, Nietzsche, and others rejecting liberalism's mechanistic world view for a vitalist one, the New Right has taken much, particularly from their critique of mass society, parliamentary democracy, and the pathologies of a machine-made civilization.

Charles Maurras' Action Française, which grew out of the revolt's anti-bourgeois opposition to the Third Republic, is often compared to the

GRECE.[90] This comparison is not entirely ill-conceived, but the two tendencies are only remotely akin. Maurras and his followers were erudite, uncompromising anti-liberals who played a major role in French cultural life in the period between the Dreyfus Affair and the Vichy regime. In this, they were superbly readable critics of the republican bourgeoisie and its egalitarian and individualistic beliefs. As such, they militated against the heritage of 1789, upheld the primacy of the political, and defended the organic foundation of French communal life. Here, though, the resemblances tend to end. New Rightists differ from Maurras' followers in being democrats, not monarchists; pagans, not Catholics; Europeanists, not French nationalists. They also share none of Maurras' Germanophobia or "white Jacobinism."[91]

The historical current having the greatest affinity to the New Right—*die konservative Revolution*—is indeed not French at all, but German.[92] This "Third Way" movement, representing perhaps the most fertile intellectual movement of the twentieth century, emerged from the hecatomb of the First European Civil War (1914–18). In unparalleled fashion, it probed the great catastrophes provoked by the Enlightenment's collapse at Verdun, in the market, and within the European soul. Involving such figures as Arthur Moeller van den Bruck, Hans Freyer, Werner Sombart, Ernst Niekisch, Carl Schmitt, Ernst Jünger, Martin Heidegger, and Oswald Spengler, the Conservative Revolution arose in opposition to the bankrupt conservatism (*Altkonservatismus*) of the old parliamentary Right, doing so for the sake of "eliminating a newly emerged disorder and of re-establishing a state of normality" (Evola). Its refusal of liberal modernity would make it conservative, but its realization that conventional efforts to revive the living heritage of the *ancien régime* had failed caused it to look for a revolutionary way out of the crisis. As Dostoevsky formulated it, it was "revolutionary out of conservatism."[93] It thus believed that the traditional order could no longer be restored, only redeemed through an overthrow of the liberal regime. In an era when global capitalism poses an even greater threat to European existence, it should not be surprising, then, that the New Right has been vigilant in keeping its memory—and project—alive.[94]

\* \* \*

The Conservative Revolution to which *Grécistes* and other New Right identitarians commit themselves targeted not just the structures compromising the integrity of European existence, but every view and orientation conducive to modernity's anti-traditionalist subversions. Unlike economic liberals who label themselves "conservatives" or unlike traditionalists bemoaning the moral degradations of their age while refraining from social action, Conservative Revolutionaries assailed both the principles and practices of the liberal order. Given their integrity and the richness of their thought, their anti-liberalism has come to inform virtually every meaningful alternative to liberal modernity in the twentieth century. That New Rightists have revived their heritage in our postmodern world makes them—arguably—the most pertinent political tendency presently affecting Europe's future.

But the New Right's appeal, I want to emphasize, is not simply to Continental Europeans. As will be evident in the following pages, in which its ideas will be surveyed and synthesized, its project bears on the most pressing concerns of New World Europeans, who, in the former white homelands of the United States, Canada, Australia, Argentina, Chile, Afrikanerdom, and New Zealand, are today no less threatened by liberalism's anti-identitarian assault on their racial and cultural heritage.

## Notes to Chapter I

1. Jean Desperts, "La ND tient la forme," *Éléments* 56 (Winter 1985). Some of the more important articles of 1978 and 1979 have been collected in Julien Brunn, ed., *La Nouvelle Droite: Le dossier de "procès"* (Paris: Nouvelles Éditions Oswald, 1979). For an exhaustive bibliography of articles devoted to the work of Alain de Benoist, see "Bibliographie" at *Les Amis d'Alain de Benoist* (http://www.alaindebenoist.com).
2. "Les habits neufs de la droite française," *Le nouvelle observateur* (July 2, 1979).
3. Allen Douglas, "'La Nouvelle Droite': G.R.E.C.E. and the Revival of Radical Rightist Thought in Contemporary France," *The Tocqueville Review* 6:2 (Fall 1984).
4. *Le canard enchaîné* (December 20, 1972).
5. Guillaume Faye, "Le libéralisme, ça ne marche pas," *Éléments* 44 (January 1983). As a term, the "New Right" originally applied to the union-busting, budget-cutting, market-fixated Anglo-American Right of the late 1970s and 1980s, as represented by the monetarist regimes of Thatcher and Reagan and the theories of Friedrich von Hayek and Milton Friedman. Programmatically, this "Right" was a neo-liberal tendency that sought to diminish state intervention in the economy, dismantle the postwar system of Keynesian regulation, roll back the welfare state, and mobilize popular electoral support around certain Protestant fundamentalist themes. The present globalist order is very much a product of its policies. That it was termed "conservative" is merely symptomatic of the current inversion of values, for this Right's slash-and-burn commitment to free markets and economic individualism opposed everything the historical Right represented. See John Gray, *Endgames: Questions in Late Modern Political Thought* (Cambridge: Polity, 1997). By contrast, the *Nouvelle*

*Droite* is anti-liberal and anti-Christian, hostile to the Anglo-American Right of Thatcher and Reagan, and more concerned with culture than economics. Typical of the prevailing inability to distinguish between these tendencies is Ruth Levitas, ed., *The Ideology of the New Right* (Cambridge: Polity, 1986), and Ted Honderich, *Conservatism* (London: Hamish Hamilton, 1990). On the GRECE's view of the "Anglo-Saxon" New Right, see Alain de Benoist, "Hayek: A Critique," *Telos* 110 (Winter 1998); Alain de Benoist, "Le libéralisme contre les identités," in *Aux sources de l'erreur libérale: Pour sortir de l'étatisme et du libéralisme*, ed. Benjamin Guillemand and Arnaud Guyot-Jeannin (Lausanne: L'Âge d'Homme, 1999). The GRECE's association with the Club de l'Horloge, a prestigious "national-liberal" think tank, did, however, lend a certain substance to this label up until 1981, when the relations between these two groups fractured. See Pierre-André Taguieff, "La Nouvelle Droite et ses stratégies," *Nouvelle revue socialiste* (July–August 1984). Given, though, the purely journalistic significance of the term, "New Right" is used herein largely for convenience sake—to refer to those formations whose anti-liberalism stems from GRECE-style identitarianism. Cf. Pierre Krebs, "Die Tätowierungen durch die Medien des Systems: Neue Rechte, Konservatismus oder Neue Kultur?," *Thule Briefe* 3 (September 1997).

6. "Fascism," it might be noted, was largely an invention of Soviet Communism. Italian Fascism, for example, was a specific national phenomenon entirely unlike German National Socialism. The differences between the Spanish Phalange, Romania's Legion of the Archangel, Belgium's Rex, etc., were equally great. Academics nevertheless tend to follow Soviet usage and speak of a global "fascism," even though they have consistently failed to define it theoretically. Roger Griffin's *Fascism* (Oxford: Oxford University Press, 1995), in grouping every anti-liberal "bad guy" under its rubric, is quite typical of what passes for scholarship in this field today. For a critique of this tendency, see François-Georges Dreyfus, "Le mythe de l'"extrême Droite' et les dangers du 'Front républicain,'" in *Droite-Gauche: Un clivage dépassé?*, ed. Bernard Mazin (Paris: Éds. CDH, 1998); Alain de Benoist, *Communisme et nazisme: 25 réflexions sur le totalitarisme au XXe siècle* (Paris: Le Labyrinthe, 1998), 83–87; Armin Mohler, "Le 'style' fasciste," *Nouvelle École* 42 (Summer 1985); Paul Gottfried, "La Gauche et le fascisme," *Nouvelle École* 46 (Fall 1990).

7. Pierre Vial, "Vichy devant l'histoire," *Éléments* 70 (Spring 1991); Dominique Venner, *Histoire de la Collaboration* (Paris: Pygmalion, 2000); François-Georges Dreyfus, *Histoire de Vichy: Vérités et légendes* (Paris: Perrin, 1990).

8. These figures, found in official sources, have all been disputed. For an important collection of documents reflecting the anti-liberal view, see Maurice Bardèche, ed., *L'épuration* (Paris: Éds. Confrérie Castille, 1997). Also Philippe Saint-Germain, *Le livre noir de l'épuration* (Paris: La Librairie Française, 1975); and, academically, Henri Amouroux, "L'épuration dans tous ses états," *Historia* 581 (May 1995).

9. Dominique Venner, in his *Histoire critique de la Résistance* (Paris: Pygmalion, 1995), authoritatively dismantles the fiction that the Left dominated the Resistance, showing instead that it originated with the nationalist Right—especially the far Right—and was as much Right-wing as Left-wing in membership.

Also see Jean-Claude Valla, *L'extrême Droite dans la Résistance* (Paris: Les Cahiers Libres d'Histoire, nos. 2 and 3, 2000). In this context, it is worth citing François Mauriac's lament of 1940: "In our country, it is the destiny of Rightwing ideas, even the most equitable, even the wisest of them, never to triumph except as a result of the misfortune of the country." Quoted in Philippe Burrin, *France Under the Germans: Collaboration and Compromise*, trans. Janet Lloyd (New York: The New Press, 1996), 25.

10. Thomas Molnar, *The Emerging Atlantic Culture* (New Brunswick, NJ: Transaction Publishers, 1994). Molnar's "monoclass" is conceptually akin to the "New Class," a term with a rather complicated genealogy, used to denote the functionaries, politicians, and professionals who "manage" the bureaucratic/technocratic apparatus not only of the state, but of the large corporations and institutions. See James Burnham, *The Managerial Revolution* (New York: John Day, 1941); Alfred D. Chandler, Jr., *The Visible Hand: The Managerial Revolution in American Business* (Cambridge, MA: Belknap Press, 1977); Bruno Rizzi, *The Bureaucratization of the World*, trans. Adam Westoby (New York: The Free Press, 1985); Milovan Djilas, *The New Class: An Analysis of the Communist System* (New York: Praeger, 1957); Daniel Bell, *The Coming of Post-Industrial Society* (New York: Basic Books, 1976); Christopher Lasch, *The Revolt of the Elites and the Betrayal of Democracy* (New York: Norton, 1995); Paul Edward Gottfried, *After Liberalism: Mass Democracy in the Managerial State* (Princeton, NJ: Princeton University Press, 1999); and Samuel Francis, *Revolution from the Middle* (Raleigh, NC: Middle American Press, 1997). Here I use the terms "monoclass" and "New Class" interchangeably. Of related interest, the historian Robert H. Wiebe uses the term "new national class" to describe the historical and sociological character of America's New Class—a term, I think, that is especially suitable for the US situation, though less so for Europe. See *Self-Rule: A Cultural History of American Democracy* (Chicago: University of Chicago Press, 1995), 202–22.

11. Charles Champetier and Alain de Benoist, "The French New Right in the Year 2000," *Telos* 115 (Spring 1999); Hans-Dietrich Sander, "Das erste Kriegsziel der amerikanischen Politik," *Staatsbriefe* (December 1999).

12. Régés Constans, "Français d'Algérie: Une histoire occultée," *La Nouvelle Revue d'Histoire* 1 (July–August 2002). While the socially divisive nature of the Algerian War and the revolutionary activities of the OAS galvanized many first-generation New Rightists, most have since come to accept the wisdom of De Gaulle's decision to abandon *Algérie française*. See Dominique Venner, *Le cœur rebelle* (Paris: Les Belles Lettres, 1994), 183–201.

13. Jean-Christian Petitfils, *L'extrême Droite en France* (Paris: PUF, 1983), 109–13; Dominique Venner, *Histoire et tradition des européens: 30,000 ans d'identité* (Paris: Rocher, 2002), 264. The American way of life that came with consumerism was so threatening not just because of its poisonous effects on European culture, but also because it constituted an insidious form of political domination. As one German anti-liberal characterizes it: "*Der vielzitierte American way of life ... ist eine Droge, an der man sich zu Tode lachen kann, ein Prinzip und einen Stil, aus dem sich ein Herrschaftsanspruch über andere Menschen und Völker ableiten könnte, verkörpert diese unendliche Amüsiermaschine gerade*

*nicht.*" See Thor von Waldstein, "Die 'Idee Deutschland' in postamerikanischen Jahrhundert," *Staatsbriefe* (September–October 2000).
14. On the organizational roots of the GRECE, see Pierre-André Taguieff, *Sur la Nouvelle Droite* (Paris: Descartes et Cie, 1994), 111–47; for a first-person account, see Pierre Vial, *Une terre, un peuple* (Villeurbanne: Terre et Peuple, 2000), 42–50; for an account of the milieu shaping the intellectual concerns of the young Rightists who took up the identitarian cause, see Venner, *Le cœur rebelle*, 143–81; for an excellent collection of articles symptomatic of the ideas animating this milieu, see Jean Mabire, *La torche et le glaive* (Paris: Éds. Déterna, 1999 [1966]).
15. Alain de Benoist, "La Droite introuvable," *Éléments* 20 (n.d. [c. 1977]).
16. Alain de Benoist, *Les idées à l'endroit* (Paris: Hallier, 1979), 62–65.
17. Perry Anderson, *Considerations on Western Marxism* (London: Verso, 1976), 24–48.
18. Benoist, *Les idées à l'endroit*, 287; Robert de Herte, "Anniversaire," *Éléments* 26 (Spring 1978).
19. Augusto Del Noce, "Le Marxisme meurt à l'Est parce qu'il s'est réalisé à l'Ouest," *Krisis* 6 (October 1990); Alain de Benoist, *Orientations pour des années décisives* (Paris: Le Labyrinthe, 1982), 69; Alain de Benoist, "Mai 68, c'est bien fini!," *Éléments* 64 (December 1988).
20. As in America, the permissive Dr. Spock was France's principal child-rearing authority in the postwar period.
21. Cf. Caspar von Schrenck-Notzing, *Charakterwäsche: Die Politik der amerikanischen Umerziehung in Deutschland* (Frankfurt am Main: Ullstein, 1993).
22. Fabrice Valclérieux, "Phantasme de la pédagomanie et réalités de la pédagogie," *Études et recherches* 3 (June 1976). Once it is accepted that "education" is formation in a culture and "instruction" is the conveyance of mere technique, then it is difficult to disagree with Le Bon's argument that: "It requires only a few years to instruct a barbarian [i.e., someone foreign to one's culture] but sometimes centuries to educate him." See Alice Widener, ed., *Gustave Le Bon: The Man and His Works* (Indianapolis: Liberty Press, 1979), 288.
23. Robert Poulet, *J'accuse la bourgeoisie* (Paris: Copernic, 1978), 23.
24. Vincent Jauvert, *L'Amérique contre De Gaulle: Histoire secrète, 1961–1969* (Paris: Seuil, 2000). Robert Steuckers, among others (including De Gaulle's successor Georges Pompidou), believes the rebellion may have been instigated by American secret agents intent on detracting De Gaulle from challenging US hegemony in Europe. See "Interview mit Robert Steuckers: 'Vitales Denken ist inkorrekt,'" *Eurocombate* (http://www.geocities.ws/eurocombate).
25. Richard F. Kuisel, *Seducing the French: The Dilemma of Americanization* (Berkeley: University of California Press, 1993), 149.
26. Jacques Thibau, *La France colonisée* (Paris: Flammarion, 1980), 35. On the Culture Industry, see Max Horkheimer and Theodor W. Adorno, *Dialectic of Enlightenment*, trans. John Cumming (New York: Seabury Press, 1972), 120–67.
27. Jean Mabire, ed., *Julius Evola: Le visionnaire foudroyé* (Paris: Copernic, 1977), 119. Cf. Jacques Duclos, *Anarchistes d'hier et d'aujourd'hui* (Paris: Éds. Sociales, 1968).

28. Henri Gobard, *La guerre culturelle: Logique du désastre* (Paris: Copernic, 1979), 13-17.
29. Pierre Bérard, "Cours camarade, le Nouveau Monde est devant toi!," in *Le Mai 68 de la Nouvelle Droite* (Paris: Le Labyrinthe, 1998), 26.
30. Fredric Jameson, "Periodising the Sixties," in *Postmodernism: A Reader*, ed. Patricia Waugh (London: Edward Arnold, 1992).
31. Alain de Benoist, "La France aurait mieux fait de garder Daniel Cohn-Bendit," in *Le Mai 68 de la Nouvelle Droite* (Paris: Le Labyrinthe, 1998).
32. Gerd Bergfleth, "Sade, notre contemporain," *Éléments* 82 (March-April 1995); Philippe Baillet, *Julius Evola ou La sexualité dans tous ses "états"* (Chalon-sur-Saône: Hérode, 1994), 53-59.
33. Cf. Agathe Fourgnaud, *La confusion des rôles: Les toujours-jeunes et les déjà-vieux* (Paris: J. C. Lattès, 1999).
34. Cf. Michel Houellebecq, *Les particules élémentaires* (Paris: Flammarion, 1998).
35. Nietzsche's "Last Man," to which further reference will be made, is the representative modern man ("the most contemptible man"), who abandons all Faustian strivings for the sake of security, comfort, and self-satisfaction. See Friedrich Nietzsche, *Thus Spoke Zarathustra*, trans. R. J. Hollingdale (London: Penguin, 1969), Prologue, § 5. (Hollingdale, though, translates *der letzte Mensch* as "the Ultimate Man.")
36. Benoist, *Les idées à l'endroit*, 289; Philippe Conrad, "Réflexions sur la 'révolution' de Mai 68," in *Le Mai 68 de la Nouvelle Droite* (Paris: Le Labyrinthe, 1998).
37. Venner, *Le cœur rebelle*, 169.
38. Régis Debray, "Confessions d'un antiaméricain," in *L'Amérique des français*, ed. Christine Fauré and Tom Bishop (Paris: Éds. François Bourin, 1992).
39. Alain de Benoist, "C'est encore loin, l'Amérique" (1991), in *La ligne de mire II: Discours aux citoyens européens, 1988-1995* (Paris: Le Labyrinthe, 1996); Frank Costigliola, *France and the United States: The Cold Alliance Since World War II* (New York: Twayne, 1992), 191-94; Kuisel, *Seducing the French*, 221-24; Denis Lacorne and Jacques Rupnik, "France Bewitched by America," in *The Rise and Fall of Anti-Americanism: A Century of French Perception*, ed. Denis Lacorne, Jacques Rupnik, and Marie-France Toinet, trans. Gerald Turner (New York: St. Martin's Press, 1990).
40. Cf. William R. Garrett, "The Reformation, Individualism, and the Quest for Global Order," in *Religion and Global Order*, ed. Roland Robertson and William R. Garrett (New York: Paragon House, 1991).
41. Alain de Benoist, "Les fausses alternatives" (1983), in *La ligne de mire II*.
42. Keith A. Reader, *Intellectuals and the Left in France Since 1968* (London: Macmillan, 1987), 108-38. As Guillaume Faye notes, Mitterrand's Socialists, however destructive, were "old-fashioned, opportunist, and amateurish," almost conservative in comparison to Lionel Jospin's recent semi-Trotskyist Socialist government (1997-2002), whose ideologically driven agenda has frontally assaulted Europe's cultures and peoples in the name of certain "pseudo-proletarian" principles ("pseudo" because they confused an abstract, petty bourgeois radicalism with tenets no French worker ever contemplated). See "Le trotskisme au pouvoir," *J'ai tout compris!* 12 (August 2001); Jérôme Bourbon, "Une taup trotskiste en Matignon?," *Écrits de Paris* 634 (July-August 2001);

Louis-Marie Enoch and Xavier Cheneseau, *Les taupes rouges: Les trotskistes de Lambert au cœur de la République* (Paris: Manitoba, 2002). Less predictably, recent Right-wing governments, in their unqualified commitment to globalization, seem bent on outdoing the anti-identitarian policies of the Socialists. See Jean-Gilles Malliarakis, *La droite la plus suicidaire du monde* (Paris: Trident, 1998), 122–26; Guillaume Faye, "Que fait le gouvernement Raffarin pour combattre l'immigration?," *J'ai tout compris!* 29 (January 2003).

43. Karlheinz Weissmann, "Ein paar einfache Wahrheiten," *Criticón* 130 (March–April 1992); also Alain de Benoist, "La Nouvelle Droite allemande," *Éléments* 86 (October 1996).
44. Less critically posed, this is also Kuisel's thesis in *Seducing the French*.
45. Cf. Gérard Desportes and Laurent Mauduit, *La Gauche imaginaire et le nouveau capitalisme* (Paris: Grasset, 1999).
46. Jean-François Lyotard, *La condition postmoderne: Rapport sur le savoir* (Paris: Éds. de Minuit, 1979).
47. Lyotard, *La condition postmoderne*, 7.
48. William E. Connolly, *Political Theory and Modernity* (Ithaca, NY: Cornell University Press, 1993), 10.
49. Of these postmodernists, *Grécistes* have been most sympathetic to Baudrillard and most critical of Derrida.
50. Gianni Vattimo, *The Transparent Society*, trans. David Webb (Baltimore: Johns Hopkins University Press, 1992), 94–95.
51. Wolfgang Welsch, *Unsere postmoderne Moderne* (Weinheim: VCH, 1987), 4.
52. Michel Maffesoli, *Le temps des tribus: Le déclin de l'individualisme dans les sociétés de masses* (Paris: Klincksieck, 1988), 17; Tomislav Sunic, "The Drug Store Culture," *The Scorpion* 10 (Autumn 1986). Cf. Simon Critchley and Peter Dews, eds., *Deconstructing Subjectivities* (Albany, NY: SUNY Press, 1996).
53. "Sous le signe de la reconquête identitaire," *Terre et peuple: La revue* 4 (Summer 2000).
54. Connolly, *Political Theory and Postmodernity*, 197. Also Zygmunt Bauman, *Intimations of Postmodernity* (London: Routledge, 1992), 36.
55. Vattimo, *The Transparent Society*, 70; Charles Champetier, "Implosions tribales et stratégies fatales," *Éléments* 101 (May 2001). Cf. Julia Kristeva, *Strangers to Ourselves*, trans. Leon S. Roudiez (New York: Columbia University Press, 1991).
56. Jean Baudrillard, *The Illusion of the End*, trans. Chris Turner (Stanford, CA: Stanford University Press, 1994), 107.
57. Alain de Benoist, "Minima moralia (2)," *Krisis* 8 (April 1991).
58. Malcolm Waters, *Globalization* (London: Routledge, 1995), 63.
59. Alain de Benoist and Tomislav Sunic, "Gemeinschaft and Gesellschaft: A Sociobiological View of the Decay of Modern Society," *Mankind Quarterly* 34:3 (Spring 1994).
60. The specific arguments Nietzsche and Heidegger make to support these claims and the appropriate documentary references are given in Chapter V.
61. Gianni Vattimo, *The End of Modernity: Nihilism and Hermeneutics in Postmodern Culture*, trans. Jon R. Snyder (Baltimore: Johns Hopkins University Press, 1988), 3; Daniel R. Ahern, *Nietzsche as Cultural Physician* (University Park: Pennsylvania State University Press, 1995), 4. For those postmodernists

who wish to salvage the Enlightenment's political project, but not its foundationalist philosophical premises, the *petits récits* are treated as social, not individual, narratives. For example, see Richard Rorty, "Postmodern Bourgeois Liberalism," *Journal of Philosophy* 80:10 (October 1983). Such postmodernists (R. Rorty, J. Squires, W. E. Connolly, *et al.*) insist on the embeddedness of subjectivity and thus the need for community and solidarity. In this, they resemble *Grécistes*, for they too reject a purely libidinal or anarchist notion of subjectivity. Yet, as liberals, they do so in order to reformulate the Enlightenment project, hoping in the process to rescue the notion of a freer, more rational world based on a self-consciousness relativism that affiliates with liberal values and a Deweyan pragmatism allegedly free of modernity's "bad" metaphysics. See Richard Rorty, "Cosmopolitanism without Emancipation," in *Modernity and Identity*, ed. Scott Lash and Jonathan Friedman (Oxford: Blackwell, 1992). Against this "weak" or "liberal" postmodernism, see Georges Charbonneau, "Les clowns du judéo-catholicisme," *Éléments* 57–58 (Spring 1986).

62. Postmodernists seem to suspect that narratives of any kind are sources of restraint, insofar as narrative is the medium through which a people makes sense of, defines, and lives in its world—and thus "limits" itself to certain "foundational postulates." See Arran Gare, "Narrative and Culture: The Role of Stories in Self-Creation," *Telos* 122 (Winter 2002).

63. Michel Foucault, *Discipline and Punish: The Birth of the Prison*, trans. Alan Sheridan (New York: Vintage, 1979).

64. Robert de Herte, "Faut-il être 'postmoderne'?," *Éléments* 60 (Fall 1986); Alain de Benoist, "Face à la mondialisation," in *Les grandes peurs de l'an 2000: Actes du XXXe colloque national du GRECE* (Paris: GRECE, 1997).

65. Armin Mohler, "Was Ist Postmoderne?," *Criticón* 96 (July–August 1986).

66. Henry de Lesquen, "L'idéologie dominante est-elle compatible avec la science?," in *Droite-Gauche: Un clivage dépassé?*, ed. Bernard Mazin (Paris: Éds. CDH, 1998); Jacques Monod, *Le Hasard et la nécessité: Essai sur la philosophie naturelle de la biologie moderne* (Paris: Seuil, 1970).

67. Robert de Herte, "Misère de l'humanisme," *Éléments* 97 (January 2000); Charles Champetier, "Voici l'ère néobiotique," *Éléments* 97 (January 2000). Because many of these new sciences contravene liberal postulates, whole fields of knowledge have been ignored or quarantined by the dominant ideology. Lysenkoism, censorship, and intellectual intimidation, it is thus salutary to note, were not solely Soviet pathologies, but remain still significant facets of American and European intellectual life. See Morton Hunt, *The New Know-Nothings: The Political Foes of the Scientific Study of Human Nature* (New Brunswick, NJ: Transaction Publishers, 2000); Ullica Segerstråle, *Defenders of the Truth: The Battle for Science in the Sociobiology Debate and Beyond* (New York: Oxford University Press, 2000); Alain de Benoist, *Vu de Droite: Anthologie critique des idées contemporaines*, 5th ed. (Paris: Copernic, 1979), 140–46; Alain de Benoist, "Différent, mais inégaux," *Éléments* 27 (Winter 1978); Odile de Madre, "Du progrès scientifique à la dictature idéologique," *Réfléchir et agir* 11 (Spring 2002).

68. The GRECE's Left-wing critics charge that such arguments stem from its members' earlier association with the far Right, insinuating, in effect, that biology

and the life sciences are inherently "fascist." Since the late seventies, the GRECE has stopped emphasizing the anti-egalitarian implications of the life sciences and downplays its earlier "biological realism." Yet allegations of "racism" and "fascism" are still routinely made to discredit it. While such charges rhetorically aim to silence and intimidate, they nevertheless need to be addressed, because they close off rational inquiry. Like most Rightists, *Grécistes* accept that man's hereditary heritage (as potential, not actuality) is primary in predisposing him to "particular attitudes and modes of behavior." See Alain de Benoist, "Culture," *Nouvelle École* 27 (Winter 1974–75). They also accept the existence of ethnoracial identities, acknowledging the existence and significance of cultural and racial differences. They thus reject all abstract, leveling notions of human identity and all efforts to socially engineer the elimination of such differences. The recognition of such differences (which are everywhere accepted in the non-white world) is, however, now automatically assumed to be racist—as if racism were a form of differentialism and not an ideology of racial superiority. See Alain de Benoist, "Contre tous les racismes," *Éléments* 8–9 (November 1974–February 1975); Gilbert Destrées, "Différentialisme contre racisme: Des origines modernes du racisme," *Éléments* 77 (n.d. [c. Spring 1993]); cf. Frithjof Schuon, *Castes and Races*, trans. Marco Pallis and Macleod Matheson (Bedfont, UK: Perennial Books, 1982). More fundamentally, the GRECE's recognition of biological and racial differences stems from its anti-liberal rejection of egalitarian ideology, whether this ideology takes the form of racial equality, sexual equality, class equality, status equality, or any other type of equality endeavoring to level and homogenize in the name of world betterment. An anti-egalitarian emphasis on difference, *Grécistes* insist, has nothing to do with imputations of "inferiority." This, however, is difficult for Leftists to accept, for notions of culture, identity, and particularity are alien to the egalitarianism and universalism of a modernist project that ostensively defends the "equality" of all races, yet refuses to acknowledge the differences distinguishing them. In this context, Claude Lévi-Strauss writes: "One cannot simultaneously lose oneself in the enjoyment of the Other, identify with him, and maintain oneself as different. Total, integral communication compromises . . . both one's fundamental integrity and that of the Other." Quoted in Alain de Benoist, "What is Racism?," *Telos* 114 (Winter 1999). In thus refusing to acknowledge the otherness of the Other, the Left simply reduces different peoples to their common humanity, treating their specific racial or cultural identities as insignificant, almost invisible. Yet, "by reducing the Other to the Same . . . [Leftists] are incapable of recognizing or respecting otherness for what it is." See Benoist, "What is Racism?" Not resistance to the homogenizing forces of liberal egalitarianism, as it attempts to "reduce everything to one and the same," but liberalism's universalist rejection of difference and particularity, *Grécistes* insist, is the real basis of racism. They, therefore, believe "racism" will be eradicated only when the Other is accepted "through a dialogical perspective of mutual enrichment," and not through an inquisitional denial of difference. See Benoist and Champetier, "The French New Right in the Year 2000"; Georges A. Heuse, "Race, racismes, antiracisme," *Nouvelle École* 29 (June 1976).

69. Throughout this study, I follow *Grécistes* in assuming that the "common bonds and feelings of community" that *are* Europe reach back beyond Caesar's Celtic-Roman creation to the earlier Indo-European invasion. See Jean-Claude Rivière, ed., *Georges Dumézil à la découverte des indo-européens* (Paris: Copernic, 1979). On the persistence of Indo-European themes in subsequent stages of European history, see Joël H. Grisward, *Archéologie de l'épopée médiévale* (Paris: Payot, 1981). On the cultural heritage linking the different European peoples, see Bronisław Geremek, *The Common Roots of Europe*, trans. Jan Aleksandrowicz et al. (Cambridge: Polity, 1996); Robert S. Lopez, *The Birth of Europe* (New York: M. Evans, 1967); Wulf Köpke and Bernd Schmelz, eds., *Das Gemeinsame Haus Europa* (Munich: Deutscher Taschenbuch Verlag, 1999); Anthony Pagden, ed., *The Idea of Europe: From Antiquity to the European Union* (Cambridge: Cambridge University Press, 2002); Venner, *Histoire et tradition des européens*. There is, of course, a large literature that sees "Europe" as simply an idea, a product of Enlightenment modernism, and not a distinct cultural or biocultural entity with an ancient lineage. For example, Brian Nelson, David Roberts, and Walter Veit, eds., *The Idea of Europe: Problems of National and Transnational Identity* (New York: Berg, 1992). While the GRECE opposes this current in emphasizing the primordial cultural and historical foundations of the European idea, it also acknowledges that *la nation européenne* is still to be realized.

70. In 1973, it became possible to speak of GRECE publications in the plural. *Éléments* was launched that year as a popular quarterly to complement the more theoretical *Nouvelle École*. A few years later, in 1976, a publishing house, Copernic, was established (later to be replaced by Le Labyrinthe). Several other reviews (*Études et recherches, Panorama des idées actuelles, Cartouches,* and *Krisis,* in addition to several internal bulletins and several newsletters aimed at teachers and servicemen) followed in subsequent years, though only *Krisis* would achieve the regularity of *Nouvelle École* and *Éléments*. By the time of its media discovery in the late seventies, the GRECE had become something of a publishing force on the anti-liberal Right.

71. On Rougier's influence, see Pierre Vial, "Notre ami de Louis Rougier," *Éléments* 44 (January 1983).

72. Alain de Benoist, "Giorgio Locchi," *Éléments* 76 (December 1992); Gennaro Malgieri, "Giorgio Locchi: Philosoph und Visionär," *Elemente der Metapolitik zur europäischen Neugeburt* 6 (1998).

73. Alain de Benoist, "Konrad Lorenz et l'éthologie moderne," *Nouvelle École* 25–26 (Winter 1974–75).

74. "Entretien avec Konrad Lorenz," *Nouvelle École* 25–26 (Winter 1974–75); Arnold Gehlen, "Philosophische Anthropologie und Verhaltensforschung" (1968), in *Gesamtausgabe* (Frankfurt am Main: Klostermann, 1978), vol. 4.

75. Benoist, *Les idées à l'endroit*, 93–100.

76. Louis Rougier, *Le conflit du christianisme primitif et de la civilisation antique* (Paris: Copernic, 1977); Louis Rougier, *Celse contre les chrétiens* (Paris: Le Labyrinthe, 1997).

77. Because this work is mainly concerned with the intellectual and programmatic rather than the organizational expressions of the New Right, the GRECE's

various dissident offshoots will be treated here as simply part of the larger New Right movement. Suffice it to say that the sharpest organizational divergences have occurred in the francophone world, where Robert Steuckers' Synergon movement and Pierre Vial's Terre et Peuple movement have come to constitute the principal rivals of Benoist's GRECE. In other European countries, the organizational fault lines are less clear-cut but nevertheless still present.

78. Quoted in Éric Werner, *L'après-démocratie* (Lausanne: L'Âge d'Homme, 2001), 11.
79. David Barney, Charles Champetier, and C. Lavirose, *La Nouvelle Inquisition: Ses acteurs, ses méthodes, ses victimes. Essai sur le terrorisme intellectuel et la police de la pensée* (Paris: Le Labyrinthe, 1993); Frank Adler, "Left Vigilance in France," *Telos* 98–99 (Winter 1993–Spring 1994). In one of the great reversals of modern history, virtually every European country identified with the former "Free World" has since adopted laws curtailing free speech, while the post-Communist Russian Duma, on three separate occasions, has resisted immense Zionist and US pressures to vote down similar laws attempting to muzzle whoever broaches issues that the established order considers sacrosanct. It seems hardly exaggerated, then, to claim that Russia, the former "Evil Empire," is today the "freest" country in the world.
80. Taguieff, *Sur le Nouvelle Droite*, 67–68.
81. Both the quantity (he generally produces at least a book and scores of articles every year) and the erudition (no major thinker of the postwar era has treated as many diverse issues with as much authority) of his literary productions have made Benoist the leading *Gréciste*. His relationship to the GRECE, however, remains ambiguous. He has asserted his autonomy *vis-à-vis* it (for example, in obtaining editorial independence for *Krisis*), but, at the same time, his intimate involvement in nearly every facet of its activities makes the GRECE incomprehensible without him. Part of this ambiguity resides in the fact that he refuses to assume the GRECE's official leadership. See Vial, *Une terre, un peuple*, 66.
82. In addition to these five currents, a sixth—geopolitics, specifically the Continental tradition of tellurocratic geopolitics—should be mentioned. See Chapter VIII.
83. Benoist, *Vu de Droite*, 15; Vial, *Une terre, un peuple*, 63.
84. "Seeing from the 'New Right': Derek Turner Interviews Alain de Benoist," *Right Now!* (April 1997).
85. For example, Jean Madiran, "Nouvelle Droite et délit d'opinion," *Itinéraires*, special number (October 1979).
86. On the Third Way, see Arnaud Imatz, *Par delà Droite et Gauche: Permanence et évolution des idées et des valeurs non conformistes* (Paris: Godefroy de Bouillon, 1995); also Jean Marc Vivenza, "Pour en finir avec la Troisième Voie!," at *Voxnr* (http://www.voxnr.com).
87. Benoist, *Les idées à l'endroit*, 20.
88. David Mata, "Trois auteurs pour être vaccinés," *Éléments* 65 (Spring 1989).
89. On the anti-positivist revolt, see Zeev Sternhell, *La Droite révolutionnaire, 1885–1914: Les origines françaises du fascisme* (Paris: Seuil, 1978); H. Stuart Hughes, *Consciousness and Society: The Reorientation of European Social Thought, 1890–1930* (New York: Harper and Row, 1958); Jean-Pierre Blanchard, *Aux*

*sources du national-populisme: Maurice Barrès, Georges Sorel* (Paris: L'Æncre, 1998).
90. For example, René Rémond, *Les Droites en France* (Paris: Aubier Montaigne, 1982). Maurras' association with the anti-positivist revolt was paradoxical in that formally (i.e., superficially) he considered himself a positivist. See Michael Sutton, *Nationalism, Positivism and Catholicism: The Politics of Charles Maurras and French Catholics, 1890–1914* (Cambridge: Cambridge University Press, 1982).
91. Jean Desperts, "Notre Maurras," *Éléments* 73 (Spring 1992).
92. Robert de Herte, "La révolution conservatrice," *Éléments* 20 (n.d. [c. 1977]); Armin Mohler, *Die Konservative Revolution in Deutschland, 1918–1932: Ein Handbuch*, 5th ed. (Graz: Leopold Stocker, 1999). Cf. Marieluise Christadler, "Die Nouvelle Droite: Zwischen revolutionärer Rechten und Konservativer Revolution," in *Konservatismus: Eine Gefahr für die Freiheit?*, ed. Eike Hennig and Richard Saage (Munich: Piper, 1983); also Denis Goedel, "Actualité de Moeller van den Bruck: Un néo-conservateur de la République de Weimar vu par les Droite française d'aujourd'hui," *Recherches germaniques* 11 (1981). While the Conservative Revolution ended with Hitler's *Machtergreifung* in 1933, it experienced a second breath in France during the thirties. See Jean-Louis Loubet del Bayle, *Les non-conformistes des années 30* (Paris: Seuil, 1969); Nicolas Kessler, *Histoire politique de la Jeune Droite (1929–1942): Une révolution conservatrice à la française* (Paris: L'Harmattan, 2001). In the US, certain Republicans have used the term "conservative revolution" to describe their various electoral successes—a usage derived from advertising and entirely remote to its European sense.
93. Quoted in Fritz Stern, *The Politics of Cultural Despair: A Study in the Rise of the Germanic Ideology* (Berkeley: University of California Press, 1961), 209.
94. Tomislav Sunic, *Against Democracy and Equality: The European New Right* (New York: Peter Lang, 1990), x. This is the first and only English-language monograph on the GRECE. Written by a California-trained Ph.D., who is a Croatian associate of Benoist, I became interested in his ideas in the early 1990s, when he wrote for the paleoconservative monthly *Chronicles*. His monograph is now somewhat dated, but it played a major role in introducing the *Nouvelle Droite* to the Anglo-American world. My own understanding of the GRECE is much indebted to it.

## Chapter II

# Metapolitics

In 1981, the French Right experienced an unexpected shock. For the first time in the history of the Fifth Republic, the Socialist Left, under the leadership of François Mitterrand and in coalition with the Communist party, took command of the state. While the professional politicians of the mainstream Right scrutinized polling returns for an explanation, Benoist probed the deeper sources of the Left victory.[1] As he saw it, there was nothing surprising in Mitterrand's victory. The electronic and print media, the universities and schools, the intelligentsia and the bureaucracy were all steeped in Left/liberal beliefs. Why, he asked, should Frenchmen support policies premised on self-reliance, discipline, patriotism, the cult of energy, and traditional values, when these conservative principles had become objects of derision? The Left's electoral triumph, he suggested, was accordingly less a matter of politics than of a culture which had changed the way Frenchmen looked at and lived in their world. This was especially worrisome to New Rightists in that most of the parliamentary Right shared the Left's cultural assumptions.[2] Valéry Giscard d'Estaing, the Right's presidential candidate, had, for example, governed France in the seventies not according to the nationalist and traditional principles of General de Gaulle, but according to Orleanist or market principles that subordinated the state to the economy and the nation to the multinationals.[3] Like other Right-wing politicians of the "corrupt, cosmopolitan oligarchy" (Le Pen), Giscard d'Estaing assumed that economics was primary, while culture was a mere accouterment—a sign, perhaps, of finesse—but nothing more consequential.[4]

Benoist, by contrast, reversed the relationship. It is not the political economy that determines a society's ideology (that is, the meaning-bearing way a people culturally understands itself), but ideology that dictates its politics.[5] As postmodernists would emphasize, culture is not power *per se*, but its sheath. How things are perceived, symbolized, and evaluated influence how society's agenda is set and how power is wielded.[6] If the anti-liberal forces were ever to regain control of the state, they would, Benoist concluded, first have to change the culture.

## The War of Position

Implicit in much traditionalist thought is the recognition not only of the significance of the cultural heritage, but of the culture/power relationship. The Counter-Enlightenment, for example, is hardly comprehensible without it.[7] The same holds for the German school of *Kulturkritik*, as it intellectually dissected capitalism's symbolic universe, as well as for the nineteenth-century English literary emphasis on tradition as the basis of the "good society."[8] The postwar Right, by contrast, entirely lost sight of this long-established relationship. Its fixation on anti-Communism, its economic liberalism, and its alliance with the United States tied it not just to the American political system, but to the subversions of Hollywood, Madison Avenue, and Tin Pan Alley—the pillars of America's Culture Industry.[9]

In the twentieth century, the notion that politics is an interwoven facet of culture's intricate web is one that has been most persuasively developed by the Communist theorist, Antonio Gramsci.[10] Gramsci's reflections on culture, which have had a formative influence on all New Right tendencies (as well as the New Left, whose present hegemony is owed in large part to his insights), appear mainly in his posthumously published *Prison Notebooks* (*Quaderni del Carcere*), composed during the thirties, while a prisoner in one of Mussolini's jails.[11] It was, though, the "Two Red Years" (*bienno rosso*) of 1919–20 that most shaped his understanding of its significance. Following the end of the First European Civil War, in a period of extreme crisis, Italy was convulsed by violent worker unrest, peasant land seizures, and institutional breakdown. These troubles reached their peak in September 1920, when trade unionists occupied Northern Italy's metal industry, the most advanced sector of the economy, and attempted to resume production under worker control. For a moment, it seemed as if Italy would follow Russia in making a revolutionary transition to a Soviet-style government. But this was not to be. The strikes soon subsided, the Left parties fractured, and within two years Mussolini's Fascists controlled the helm of state.

In his prison reflections, Gramsci repeatedly pondered the question of why, in a period when the dominant institutions were in disarray and the ruling class lacked the means of exercising power, the subaltern classes had failed to sustain a revolutionary course. The answer, he concluded, was ideology. Unlike his fellow Marxists, he thought the state's authority rested on more than its police and judicial powers. Trained in historical linguistics, Gramsci the scholar knew that because "the dominant speech community exerted prestige over contiguous subordinate communities," it was able to affect their use of language. Gramsci the revolutionary reached a similar conclusion about the role of culture. In his view, the political exercise of power depended on consent rather than coercion. Accordingly, the state was able to govern not because most people lived in fear of its repressive forces, but because they adhered to views—to a hegemonic ideology—that sanctioned its activities and made them seem "natural." From this, Gramsci was led to distinguish between civil society and political society, with the latter represented by the government and its various organs (the police, army, administration, judiciary, *et cetera*) and the former by the universities, the media, the Church, and the various cultural influences touching the general population. The effective use of state power, he believed, was thus contingent on maintaining an equilibrium between the political and civil realms.

In emphasizing the importance of civil society and the power of its cultural forms to generate consent, Gramsci's heterodox Marxism anticipated the postmodernist inversion of the base/superstructure model.[12] More immediately, his heterodoxy broke with Marx's crude materialism, which envisaged civil society as a secondary phenomena—or what the Rhinelander termed a "superstructural" outgrowth of the economic "base." For the founder of "scientific socialism," man was little more than a material substance, subject to the same "dialectical laws" governing nature. This made culture and society emanations, reflections, or reflexes of their economic base. Change this base, he argued, and the superstructural realm of civil society would change in a corresponding way. His economic reductionist view of the social world, however, mischaracterized not only the nature of cultural practice, as many neo-Marxists now acknowledge, it left the revolutionary process, particularly the growth of revolutionary class consciousness, dependent on the development of the economic forces.

It was against the "fatalism" implicit in Marx's determinism that V. I. Lenin would make his great contribution to revolutionary thought, for he, like Gramsci, recognized the power of ideas in history. In calling for a vanguard party to intervene in the historical process, his *What Is to Be Done?* (1902) sought to incorporate human will into the materialist theory of history. The revolution the Bolsheviks carried out in 1917 seemed, in fact, a brilliant confirmation of his theory.[13] But while Gramsci much admired Lenin's "voluntarist" conception of Marxism and unhesitantly rallied to his Communist International, he also realized that the Leninist model of revolution addressed a political system very unlike the European one. In contrast to the highly developed political systems of Western and Central Europe, Russia's imperial state system had itself been the principal source of its stability.[14] When it collapsed under the strain of war, nothing, as a consequence, stood between it and those who sought its capture. The foundations of the European state, on the other hand, were pre-eminently cultural and ideological, undergirded by a complex network of civil institutions and by a "common sense" that imbued it with reserves unknown to the Russian one. As long, then, as the reigning institutions, ideas, and mores—culture in the larger sense—remained those of the bourgeoisie, Gramsci was convinced the European ruling class would be able to "rule" over the subaltern classes, even in the absence of the state's coercive powers.[15] Since Lenin's voluntarism neglected these hegemonic supports, Gramsci thought his revolutionary theory had but limited application to Europe. To overthrow its more advanced capitalist order, he argued that revolutionaries would need not only to oppose its political system, but to conquer its civil society. A socialist revolution in Europe, in other words, would come about not through a frontal assault on the state, as Lenin advocated, but circuitously, as the workers' counter-hegemony gradually absorbed civil society and undermined the state's political society.

In what the Italian theorist described as "a war of position"—a war in which ideas, beliefs, and the various cultural practices they precipitate were the chief objects of contention—victory would depend on redefining the reigning values, creating alternative institutions, and subverting the spirit of the population. A spiritual or cultural revolution, in a word, would be requisite to a political revolution.[16] To wage this sort of revolutionary *Kulturkampf* (whose ground rules presupposed that man was a reflective being capable of acting on the basis of his reflections), intellectuals were needed. Those Gramsci called on to develop a counter-hegemonic culture were not the "traditional intellectuals" ensconced in the academy and print media, but rather "organic intellectuals"—practical men—whose knowledge and expertise were essential to the workaday world and to the "transmission of ideas" within civil society. By waging a cultural war to *supplement* the party's political activity, these organic intellectuals were to create within the popular classes the ideological and institutional foundations of a new order. Then, once their counter-hegemonic movement gained momentum in challenging the prevailing beliefs and values, Gramsci expected traditional intellectuals would rally to its ascending forces. A crisis in legitimacy would then ensue, undermining the existing state. The key to this war of position is not, therefore, political collapse, as the period 1919–20 had demonstrated, but the formation of "an intellectual/moral *bloc*" within civil society to challenge the existing order.

In the late sixties, when the GRECE's young founders abandoned the extra-parliamentary world of the far Right for the sake of their Gramscian cultural strategy—or metapolitics—it was with the recognition that the world is "a battlefield of ideas" and that culture is the most effective carrier of ideas.[17] This had been true in Gramsci's time, when the political system possessed greater authority than it presently does. It is, they hold, even truer today, as a depoliticized state allows politics to spill over into all the various domains of everyday life. As one critic put it, "it is no longer the gendarmes who patrol France, but culture."[18] To wage its own anti-liberal version of Gramsci's war of position, the GRECE's metapolitical strategy would set its sights on three long-range objectives. Through its publications, conferences, and various public engagements, it would endeavor to engage the ideas "that inspire and organize our age" (Madame de Staël), recuperating from them what it could for its own project. Secondly, it would seek to undermine the liberal order by discrediting its underlining tenets and affirming those traditional European ideas supportive of the identities and communities it champions. Finally, it aspired to cultural hegemony, if not within civil society as a whole, at least within the elite. From the beginning, then, its "Gramscianism of the Right" privileged culture, which was taken as the "infrastructural" basis of both civil society and the state.

## World-Openness and Will to Power

"What, though, is culture?" There is, of course, no single definitive answer to this question. But in seeking however partial a response, *Grécistes* look to philosophical anthropology, a discipline associated with the post-phenomenological works of Max Scheler (1874–1928).[19] Dissatisfied with Edmund Husserl's "idealist" examination of human consciousness, Scheler had sought to understand how the intellectual, institutional, and social facets of man's existence relate to the underlying structure of his biological being. It was, however, Arnold Gehlen (1904–76), a student of Scheler's colleague, Helmuth Plessner, and the most famed recent proponent of philosophical anthropology, who has had the greatest impact on the GRECE's understanding of culture.[20]

Following Scheler and Plessner, both of whom broke from a purely metaphysical concept of man in emphasizing his animal nature, Gehlen singles out man's culture-making capacity as his defining characteristic.[21] This capacity, he claims, developed as a consequence of man's "instinctual deficiencies." Although humans possess certain basic drives (such as self-preservation, aggression, territoriality, defense of the young, *et cetera*), these are few in number, limited in effect, and non-specific. If man had had only his few instincts on which to rely, he would not have long survived in nature—30,000 years ago when he lived under the open sky. To compensate for his instinctual deficiencies, he was compelled to draw on other faculties. For the evolutionary process that left him instinctually non-specific also imbued him with intelligence, self-consciousness, and an adaptable nature. By drawing on these faculties to cope with the natural exigencies of existence—exigencies resolved in animals by their "instinctual programming"—man "learned" to negotiate the environmental challenges of his world. In contrast, though, to animal instinct, this learning left him "world-open" (*Weltoffen*), for his responses to external stimuli were not automatically programmed by earlier responses, but based on reflection and hence open to change and revision. Biological laws might influence him, but only negatively, as a "framework and base."[22] In choosing, then, how to respond to nature's challenges, man had no alternative but to treat the world with care and foresight, to gain an overview of what had gone before and what was likely to happen in the future, to develop symbolic systems to communicate this knowledge, and, not least of all, to establish those institutions that would socially perpetuate the lessons of earlier responses.

The complex of habits, judgements, and techniques arising from man's world-open responses to his environment is, according to Gehlen, the fundament of his culture, insofar as this complex informs, disciplines, and stylizes all his subsequent responses to the world. Then, once this cultural complex becomes the unconscious frame of his behavior, it acquires the character of a "second nature" (*zweite Natur*), serving him somewhat in the way instinct serves animals. This second nature, his culture, is, however, neither automatic nor immutable, for man retains the capacity to make new choices and hence to modify his behavior.[23] This "condemns" him to endless choice-making and an ongoing process of becoming. Yet, even while subject to an endless process of development, his culture continues to be influenced by the legacy of earlier choices.[24] Like Heraclitus' river, whose waters are never stepped into twice, man's "cultural nature" remains the same, even as it constantly changes. That is, through various feedback processes based on an ever-widening accumulation of experience, it develops according to a "logic"—a vitality—distinctly its own, even though in developing it never mechanically replicates itself. On this basis, Gehlen characterizes culture as combining permanence and innovation, which makes man both its creature and its creator.[25]

Virtually every conscious realm of human activity, Gehlen holds, comes to be affected by culture. In his anthropology, it is virtually inseparable from man. For without it, and the role it plays in negotiating man's encounters with the world, man would be only an undifferentiated and still unrealizable facet of nature—unable, in fact, to survive in nature.[26] Contrary to a long tradition of rationalist thought (the anthropological structuralism of Claude Lévi-Strauss being the foremost recent example), there is no "natural man." Free of culture, man would be a cretin, unable even to speak.[27] Given the inescapable character of his culture, Gehlen argues that man is best described as a *biocultural* being: for although culture and nature are two distinct things, in him they form an indivisible unity.[28]

Since different families of men, in different times and environments, respond differently to the limitless choices posed by their world, their cultures grow in different ways. Evident in all that distinguishes a Californian from a man of Connemara, a Chinese from a Cameroon, such disparities account for the great diversity of human cultures, with their different valuations, different symbolic systems, different ways of making sense of and responding to the world.[29] As an organic unity with forms congruent with its distinct vitality, a culture, then, is understandable only in its own terms. For its essence lies neither in rationalist nor objectivist criteria, but in the conditioned behaviors and beliefs constituting the interrelated patterns and categories specific to it. There is consequently no single Culture, only different cultures, specific to the different peoples who engender them. An appeal to the universal or generic—to that which is not specific to a culture—can thus only be an appeal to its own negation. There can, it follows, never be a world culture, a single planetary consciousness, a single mode or distillation of life common to all men. For the heritage of choices that goes into making a culture and giving it its defining forms is distinct to every people, rooted in those cycles of growth and vitality distinct to it.[30]

Because man's "membership in humanity is mediated by his particular cultural belonging," the only universals he shares with those of another culture are those found in his animal nature (and even these are affected by different phylogenies).[31] This diversity of human cultures cannot, then, but imply diverse, if not incommensurable cultural perspectives, as different peoples define their interests, order their perceptions, and regulate their behaviors differently.[32] Similarly, all that a specific culture accepts as "objective" derives, in the last instance, from its particularistic valuations and vitality. This is not quite the same as subjectivism—unless a culture is in decline and overly self-conscious of its conventions—but it is testament to every culture's "relativist" character.[33]

Since all men are heirs to particular formations, without which they would not be men, even an individual seeking to individuate himself in a foreign culture is obliged to do so within a frame predetermined by his original heritage. As Gehlen argues, man can never be more than an individuated expression of his native culture. For it is through such an individualization that he realizes who he is and achieves his specific humanity.[34] All men may therefore possess the powers of cognition and the capacity to create culture, but because reason is informed by its specific concerns, it never—ultimately—transcends its specific subjectivity, even when drawing on objective and instrumentalist criteria to do so. A truly neutral reason without inherent cultural "bias" (as liberal modernity posits) would require a cultureless world—that is, a world without real human beings.

Just, then, as there is no single culture common to all men, there is no single definable reality in Gehlen's anthropology. The only reality man knows is informed by the intrinsically subjective and evolving tropes his specific heritage provides for making sense of it.[35] As Protagoras said 2,500 years ago, "man is the measure of all things." Given the world's different cultures, there is necessarily a plethora of different measures in the world. Conversely, an individual is never distinguishable from his culture and never independent of the "measures" he applies. He may be free to express his culture in his own way and a culture may permit an infinite number of individual variations and even considerable rebellion against it, but no culture is ever the sum of its parts nor is any individual independent of its encompassing attachments.[36] Culture alone imbues the individual with his distinct consciousness—and the consciousness of his distinctiveness. It is likewise more than a spiritual or mental state, for its supraindividual unity inevitably takes social, institutional, and demographic form. It is always, then, a people in its specificity, not a programmed abstraction labeled "humanity," that situates and shapes a culture.[37] Man's animal nature and his culture-making capacity may be universal, but his second nature is not. Once culture is "peeled away," the only "nature" remaining is animal or physiological. Ontologically, this implies not the primacy of objectivist abstractions, but of hermeneutical processes (culturally specific self-understandings) embedded in the history of a people's particular growth.

Similarly, different cultures, like the peoples animating them, are never arbitrary, but anchored in organically evolved ways of life that the reasoning mind may render into rational terms, but is nevertheless powerless to justify or explain. It is always culture that establishes the ground—the "objective" basis—upon which the individuals making it up are able to communicate, judge the meaning of things, and reach consensus. Without it, they would be unable to agree on common standards of truth and value—and thus live together. But more than establishing the basis of a people's existence, culture anticipates whatever a people will attempt in its future, for it endows its world with meaning—and hence direction.[38]

If healthy and self-confident, a culture takes into account man's world-open capacity, allowing him to make himself according to those of its norms and categories that best sustain him. Such an authentic or a "natural" enculturation has become, however, increasingly problematical in the modern age. As Giorgio Locchi (who played the greatest role in making Gehlen's anthropology central to the GRECE's cultural politics) argues, the traditional organic model of culture is now threatened by a "functional" one that jeopardizes the vitalistic basis of the enculturating process.[39]

Shaped by socioeconomic circumstances influencing both the micro and macro levels of existence, the functional model specific to present-day modern societies enculturates the individual according to systemic imperatives, which subordinate communal relations and individual subjectivities to large-scale social and institutional requirements. In the process, this model orients to man's sensuous and egoistical nature, leaving room only for the internalization of its generic ideals, which are experienced as either external imperatives or animal drives. Such a culture addresses men solely in their functional specificity or generic egoism, isolating them from those particularistic ways of life and behavior that have grown out of earlier forms of meaning. Swept along, then, by the macrostructures conditioning everyday existence and powerless to experience life according to imperatives based on a lived "fusion of purpose," the "other-directed" man of functional culture has no alternative, integrated as he is from the top down, but to rely on external stimuli for his direction. His life, therefore, is lived according to mechanical forms over which he has no control and which tie him to predetermined patterns of behavior. Nietzsche (an important influence on Gehlen) calls this sort of enculturation "subjective culture for outward barbarians"—for it leaves man's inner self dependent on outside forces for its direction, and hence susceptible to the most extreme forms of subjectivism and manipulation.[40]

By contrast, the second type of culture (organically emerging from historically formed and tradition-based communities) fosters an "inner-directed" individual possessing an internalized frame of reference congruent with his second nature, geared to a sociability that integrates individual and community into an interactive synthesis. Experienced as an inheritance bequeathed by "great ancestors," organic culture is lived as a project whose rhythms respond to the individual's distinct vitality, as that vitality is shaped by a stylization native to it. The individual, as such, does not consume culture, but applies it, for his behavior is less determined than inspired by it. This gives the man of organic culture, who encounters his world as an ongoing project, the freedom and confidence to realize his cultural ideal in face of the specific exigencies challenging him. Organic culture grows, accordingly, from the inside out, becoming a personalized expression of a collective way of life, and not an anonymously "consumed" commodity marketed to generic individuals situated in anonymous, indifferent social systems.[41]

For the last two centuries liberal societies have endeavored to impose their functional model on the whole world. Europeans, however, lived most of their history according to the organic model. The hero, the genius, and the great artist, all of whom have played exemplary roles in their civilizational epic, were emulated not because they rebelled against the prevailing culture, but because they succeeded in giving new form and vitality to it. Such a disposition for renewal was indeed inherent in their culture, for it was lived as a continuing response to an evolving world.

Late modern (or postmodern) society, subject to liberalism's market-driven functional culture, is, by contrast, virtually powerless to adapt its cultural identity or alter its relationship to the larger world, for individual adaptation is now subsumed to a mass-manufactured model responsive to systemic, not communal, personal, or vitalist imperatives. Thus, whenever this model becomes dysfunctional, so too does the cultural orientation of those situated within it, for its failures cannot but plunge the individual into a state of indeterminacy, away from established patterns of conduct and toward greater subjectivity. Unlike the hero of organic culture—who challenges the decomposition of his age for the sake of a conservative revolution that returns to first principles and allows the cultural ideal to be reasserted at a higher level—the other-directed man of functional culture tends to slip further and further into a state of formlessness, aimlessness, and inaction, vulnerable as he is to those external influences that leave his inner self uncultivated and subject his social persona to criteria alien to his felt needs.[42] From the perspective of Gehlen's philosophical anthropology, Locchi argues that the instrumentalist rationality of functional culture may have the capacity to undermine organic cultures and integrate man into impersonal macro-structures, but its generic dictates fail to generate those behaviors and beliefs compatible with man's second nature.

It is this context in which postmodernism needs to be situated. Against modernist claims to universality, which justify the worldwide imposition of a functional cultural model geared to faceless individuals situated in impersonal social structures, postmodernists highlight the pathologies that follow from the suppression of the lived and the particular. Postmodernists thus array themselves against modernity's homogenizing model of enculturation. Yet, while advocating a new cultural pluralism, they nevertheless dismiss, disparage, or ignore the significance of earlier organic cultures, often slipping into a pure relativism that mistakes man's second nature for a construct susceptible to endless—and arbitrary—reconstructions. Relatedly, they treat cultural particularisms as if they are akin to exchangeable market options and favor the widest variety of cultural formations. This causes them to advocate a free-floating subjectivity attuned to global markets and micro-groups, but resistant to specific organic formations, which are considered "totalizing" in the sense that the Great Narrative is.[43]

Although *Grécistes* ally with postmodernists in rejecting the instrumental dictates of modernity's functional culture, they take their distance from them in affirming the necessity, not the option, of organic cultures. For without such cultures, they claim an individual is powerless to negotiate the anonymous forces of contemporary society, with dysfunction, decadence, and alienation the inevitable (and already evident) consequence. To be at home in the world and in accord with one's own vitality, a people therefore needs not only to be free of functional restraints that alienate and distort, as postmodernists insist, it also needs a sense of belonging that anchors it in a meaningful reality. Belonging, however, comes only with the particular and the enrooted—and the particular and the enrooted cannot be discarded, deconstructed, or selectively re-appropriated, as postmodernists advocate, without risk of greater deculturation.[44]

This should not be taken to mean that New Rightists advocate a literal return to pre-modern cultural forms, whose naturalistic models are holistic and relatively simple. Complex societies cannot function in this way. Nevertheless, the traditional organic cultures[45] out of which present-day European societies have emerged need not, they argue, be rejected *in toto*, for even as a people evolves and assumes the need for certain functional forms, it retains a need for continuity, balance, and vitality, which can be meaningfully sustained only when rooted in the native soil of an enduring cultural identity. Tying vitality to one's native culture, New Rightists in this way endeavor to replenish all that has given life and form to the European idea over the ages, seeking to readapt Europe's organic culture to the complexities of contemporary social systems, fully conscious that its ongoing adaptation gives new meaning, as well as providing new depths to the culture as a whole.[46]

## The Identitarian Challenge to Liberal Modernity

More than political power is at stake in the New Right's metapolitics. If its understanding of culture is correct, the loss of Europe's traditional organic culture implies the loss of Europe itself. Indeed, the present globalist impetus of liberal ideology seems aimed at precisely this sort of annihilating deculturation, as the international system of acronyms (the UN, US, WTO, GATT, NAFTA, IMF, *et cetera*) forcibly channels the flow of money, goods, and services into markets favoring the integration of local cultures into a single global (in effect, Americanized) "culture" that takes functionalization to its ultimate extreme.[47] The whole, as a result, is turned into what some identitarians call a ZOA: a *zone d'occupation américaine*, where everything is subject to the cultural imperatives of Washington's "cosmo-capitalism."

In opposing the culturally "normalizing" forces of this process, the New Right rejects the principal constituents of contemporary Western life. One might wonder, though, what there is left to renew in the heritage it defends. And, more importantly, if it is even possible to pick and choose from existing legacies, designating some as authentic and others as distorting. In posing these questions, it bears emphasizing that the New Right does not reject modernity *per se*. Like Gehlen, it targets only those facets of modernity (or rather it targets only a particular liberal modernity) that seek to extirpate Europe's biocultural identity for the sake of its globalizing project. In this vein, the New Right holds that, in seeking to overcome an inferior or tainted past, "modernity" is not "modern" at all, but deeply rooted in the European soul.[48] Perhaps the most important identitarian theorist, Guillaume Faye, notes that: "The old European tradition was always modernist. . . . We don't stupidly revolt against contemporary Europe, but remain loyal to that which has always been part of Europe."[49] In this sense, the New Right allies with a "modernity" faithful to Europe's Faustian spirit—that is, to a modernity that frees Europeans from what is dead or life-denying in their culture. At the same time, though, it rejects whatever seeks growth not in Europe's expansive spirit, but in its negation—specifically in the functional—and ethnocidal—culture fostered by market societies intent on reducing everyone and everything to a marketable commodity.[50]

## Notes to Chapter II

1. Alain de Benoist, *Orientations pour des années décisives* (Paris: Le Labyrinthe, 1982), 5–10; Alain de Benoist, "Les causes culturelles du changement politique" (1981), in *La ligne de mire I: Discours aux citoyens européens, 1972–1987* (Paris: Le Labyrinthe, 1995).
2. Denis Lacorne, "Modernists and Protectionists: The 1970s," in *The Rise and Fall of Anti-Americanism: A Century of French Perception*, ed. Denis Lacorne, Jacques Rupnik, and Marie-France Toinet, trans. Gerald Turner (New York: St. Martin's Press, 1990). Cf. Raymond Aron, *Mémoires* (Paris: Presse Pocket, 1985), 2:979.
3. Pierre Vial, "L'Orléanisme n'est pas mort," *Éléments* 44 (January 1983).
4. Mikael Treguely, "Giscard d'Estaing: Un régionaliste européen," *Synergies Européennes: Service documentation* (November 2002).
5. Ideology is used here in the Dumézilian, not the Marxist, sense to indicate cultural outlook. See Georges Dumézil, *Mythe et épopée I: L'idéologie des trois fonctions* (Paris: Gallimard, 1968); Guillaume Faye, "Warum Wir Kämpfen," *Elemente für die europäische Wiedergeburt* 1 (July 1986).
6. Michel Foucault, *Power/Knowledge: Selected Interviews and Other Writings*, ed. Colin Gordon (New York: Pantheon, 1980).
7. For example, Joseph de Maistre, *Considérations sur la France* (Lyons: E. Vitte, 1924), 203–20.
8. Francis Mulhern, *Culture/Metaculture* (London: Routledge, 2000); Raymond Williams, *Culture and Society, 1780–1950* (New York: Harper and Row, 1966).
9. Jean Parvulesco, *Le soleil rouge de Raymond Abellio* (Paris: Guy Trédaniel, 1987), 16–17; Cercle Heraclite, "La France de Mickey," *Éléments* 57–58 (Spring 1986).
10. The best English-language biography is Alastair Davidson, *Antonio Gramsci: Towards an Intellectual Biography* (London: Merlin, 1977).
11. Antonio Gramsci, *Selections from the Prison Notebooks*, ed. and trans. Quentin Hoare and Geoffrey Nowell Smith (New York: International Publishers, 1971). An English translation of the complete notebooks is presently being undertaken by Columbia University Press, with the first volumes already in print. See also Antonio Gramsci, *Selections from Cultural Writings*, trans. William Boelhower (Cambridge, MA: Harvard University Press, 1985).
12. Richard Harland, *Superstructuralism: The Philosophy of Structuralism and Post-Structuralism* (London: Methuen, 1987), 1–2.
13. Gramsci hailed the Bolshevik seizure of power as a "revolution against *Capital*"—that is, as a rejection of Marx's economic determinism. See *History, Philosophy and Culture in the Young Gramsci*, ed. Pedro Cavalcanti and Paul Piccone (St. Louis, MO: Telos Press, 1975), 123–26.
14. Gramsci, *Selections from the Prison Notebooks*, 238. For why Russia differed, see Geoffrey Hosking, *Russia: People and Empire, 1552–1917* (Cambridge, MA: Harvard University Press, 1997).
15. Alain de Benoist, "Culture," *Nouvelle École* 25–26 (Winter 1974–75); Jean-Claude Valla, "Une communauté de travail et de pensée," in *Pour une renaissance culturelle: Le GRECE prend la parole*, ed. Pierre Vial (Paris: Copernic, 1979).

16. Alain de Benoist, "Le combat continue," *Éléments* 40 (Winter 1981–82).
17. Tomislav Sunic, *Against Democracy and Equality: The European New Right* (New York: Peter Lang, 1990), 29. Robert Dun (a crucial link to the interwar generation of revolutionary Europeanists) argues that metapolitics rests on several dubious presumptions, the most important of which is the belief that a movement against the liberal order needs to be based on a body of sophisticated ideas. Dun claims that all great revolutionary movements have been based on a small number of core ideas accessible to the common people. From this perspective, a counter-hegemonic movement has no specific need for a sophisticated "school of thought" like the GRECE, but rather for revolutionaries willing to rally the opposition around its core ideas. See his "Réflexions necéssaires sur un effondrement," *Réfléchir et agir* 9 (Summer 2001). In a similar vein, a group of Belgian revolutionary nationalists claims that 30 years of metapolitics in their country has produced "more disillusion than hope." See Ferg, "Ce que nous ne voulons plus," *Devenir* 15 (Winter 2000). For revolutionary traditionalists of the Evola school, who refuse to separate political from cultural struggle, it is no less problematical. See Georges Gondinet, "Les ambiguïtés du 'gramscianisme de droite,'" *Totalité: Révolution et Tradition* 10 (November–December 1979). The True Right even denies the possibility of meaningful change in liberal society. The Gramscian notion of cultural struggle has been subject to numerous other criticisms. Suffice it to say that metapolitics is not universally accepted on the anti-liberal Right.
18. Alain Paucard, *La crétinisation par la culture* (Paris: L'Âge d'Homme, 1998), 63.
19. H. O. Pappe, "On Philosophical Anthropology," *Australasian Journal of Philosophy* 39:1 (May 1961); Otto F. Bollnow, "Die philosophische Anthropologie und ihre methodischen Prinzipen," in *Philosophische Anthropologie Heute*, ed. Roman Rocek and Oskar Schatz (Munich: Beck, 1972); Arnold Gehlen, "Philosophische Anthropologie" (1971), in *Gesamtausgabe* (Frankfurt am Main: Klostermann, 1983), vol. 4.
20. On Gehlen, see Christian Thies, *Gehlen zur Einführung* (Hamburg: Junius, 2000); Karlheinz Weissmann, *Arnold Gehlen: Vordenker eines neuen Realismus* (Bad Vilbel: Antaios, 2000); Karlheinz Weissmann, "Arnold Gehlen: Von der Aktualität eines zu Unrecht Vergessen," *Criticón* 153 (January–March 1997).
21. Giovanni Monartra, "L'anthropologie philosophique d'Arnold Gehlen," *Nouvelle École* 45 (Winter 1988–89).
22. Alain de Benoist, "Racism and Totalitarianism," *National Democrat* 1 (Winter 1981–82).
23. Giorgio Locchi, "Éthologie et sciences sociales," *Nouvelle École* 33 (Summer 1979); Alain de Benoist, *Comment peut-on être païen?* (Paris: Albin Michel, 1981), 67.
24. Alain de Benoist, *Vu de Droite: Anthologie critique des idées contemporaines*, 5th ed. (Paris: Copernic, 1979), 171–73; Alain de Benoist, *Les idées à l'endroit* (Paris: Hallier, 1979), 95–97.
25. Arnold Gehlen, *Man: His Nature and Place in the World*, trans. Clare McMillan and Karl Pillemer (New York: Columbia University Press, 1988), 24–31. After his exchange with Lorenz, Gehlen was forced to modify his depiction of man's instinctual non-specificity (*Mängelwesen*). For a discussion of these later revisions to his theory of culture, see Thies, *Gehlen zur Einführung*, 35–104.

26. "Entretien avec Konrad Lorenz," *Nouvelle École* 25-26 (Winter 1974-75); Thies, *Gehlen zur Einführung*, 32.
27. Benoist, *Les idées à l'endroit*, 41.
28. Benoist, *Les idées à l'endroit*, 217. It is this emphasis on the culture-nature link that distinguishes Gehlen's anthropology from the "cultural determinism" of the Boas school, which ignores man's animal nature, posits an idealist concept of culture, and relies on a good deal of fraudulent research. See Derek Freeman, *Margaret Mead and Samoa: The Making and Unmaking of an Anthropological Myth* (Cambridge, MA: Harvard University Press, 1983). Typically, Franz Boas is feted in the American academy, but his culturalism is as "vulgar" as the biological or racial determinism he sought to refute. Much of contemporary research has, in fact, weighed in against Boas. For example, see Stephen Horigan, *Nature and Culture in Western Discourses* (London: Routledge, 1988).
29. Claude Lévi-Strauss, *Race et culture* (Paris: Denoël, 1987), 22-23; Benoist, *Les idées à l'endroit*, 216.
30. Alain de Benoist and Charles Champetier, "The French New Right in the Year 2000," *Telos* 115 (Spring 1999); Alain de Benoist, *Dernière année: Notes pour conclure le siècle* (Lausanne: L'Âge d'Homme, 2001), 88; Alain de Benoist, "Pour une déclaration du droit des peuples," in *La cause des peuples: Actes du XVe colloque national du GRECE* (Paris: Le Labyrinthe, 1982).
31. See John R. Baker, *Race* (Oxford: Oxford University Press, 1974), 468-529.
32. Friedrich Nietzsche: "No people could live without evaluating; but if it wishes to maintain itself it must not evaluate as its neighbor evaluates. Much that seems good to one people seems shame and disgrace to another . . . much that was called evil in one place was in another decked with purple honors." See *Thus Spoke Zarathustra*, trans. R. J. Hollingdale (London: Penguin, 1969), "Of the Thousand and One Goals."
33. Benoist, *Les idées à l'endroit*, 42, 101; Alain de Benoist, "L'ordre," *Études et recherches* 4-5 (January 1977).
34. Henri Gobard, *La guerre culturelle: Logique du désastre* (Paris: Copernic, 1979), 13.
35. Alain de Benoist, "Minima moralia (2)," *Krisis* 8 (April 1991).
36. Alain de Benoist, "Fondements nominalistes d'une attitude devant la vie," *Nouvelle École* 33 (Summer 1979).
37. Cf. Irenäus Eibl-Eibesfeldt, *Der Mensch—das riskierte Wesen. Zur Naturgeschichte menschlicher Unvernunft* (Munich: Piper, 1988).
38. Stefano Paltrinieri, "La théorie sociale d'Arnold Gehlen," *Nouvelle École* 46 (Fall 1990); Arnold Gehlen, *Man in the Age of Technology*, trans. Patricia Lipscomb (New York: Columbia University Press, 1980).
39. Locchi, "Éthologie et sciences sociales"; Alain de Benoist, "'Communauté' et 'société,'" *Éléments* 23 (September 1977).
40. Friedrich Nietzsche, *Untimely Meditations*, trans. R. J. Hollingdale (Cambridge: Cambridge University Press, 1983), 79; Guillaume Faye, "Le culture-gadget," *Éléments* 46 (Summer 1983).
41. Cf. Ferg, "Identité européenne et multiculture," *Devenir* 13 (Summer 2000).
42. Locchi, "Éthologie et sciences sociales."

43. Fredric Jameson, "Postmodernism, or the Cultural Logic of Late Capitalism" (1991), in *Postmodernism: A Reader*, ed. Thomas Docherty (New York: Columbia University Press, 1993).
44. The GRECE's defense of particularistic culture—a defense that makes no valuative differentiation between different cultures, but simply defends their specificity against the homogenizing impulses of liberal modernity—is seen by the Left as a sophisticated repackaging of traditional racism (insofar as culture is alleged to replace race as a criterion of exclusion). See Pierre-André Taguieff, "Le néo-racisme différentialiste: Sur l'ambiguïté d'une évidence commune et ses effets pervers," *Langage et société* 34 (December 1985). For a critique of this conflation of culturalism and racism, see Raymond Ruyer, *Les cents prochains siècles: Le destin historique de l'homme selon la Nouvelle Gnose américaine* (Paris: Fayard, 1977), 49–61. It is, in fact, the nature of authentic cultures to privilege their own imperatives. To the degree it remains authentic, every culture has no option but to "reject" other cultures (which may be "objectively" just as "good") because they are irrelevant to its own concerns. It is precisely this aspiration towards a self-sufficient unity in its representational modes that makes culture inherently "exclusive" and its members part of a living whole, distinct from others. See Benoist, "Culture"; Richard M. Weaver, *Visions of Order: The Cultural Crisis of Our Time* (Bryn Mawr, PA: Intercollegiate Studies, 1995), 3–21; Claude Lévi-Strauss, *Le regard éloigné* (Paris: Plon, 1983), 24–30. Finally, the New Right's identitarianism ought not to be confused with the Left's "identity politics," which is a radical form of liberal pluralism that seeks to validate the postmodern fragmentation of identity (usually of sexual and racial minorities). On the Left's identity politics, see Jonathan Rutherford, ed., *Identity: Community, Culture, Difference* (London: Lawrence and Wishart, 1990). "Identitarianism" is used herein to denote those tendencies defending traditionalist and anti-liberal—i.e. organic—concepts of identity.
45. This allusion to "traditional culture"—like all subsequent references to "traditional society," "traditional community," "traditional ideas," etc.—refers not to those primitive, tribal formations studied by anthropologists, but to the *premodern* Europe prior to the seventeenth century—that is, to the Greek, Roman, Celtic, Germanic, and medieval forms of the European civilizational heritage.
46. Cf. Nietzsche, *Untimely Meditations*, 83.
47. There are, admittedly, "many globalizations," with some peoples managing and others customizing the global forces of America's world order. This "diversity" does little, though, to diminish the ubiquity of globalism's normalizing effects. Cf. Peter L. Berger, "The Cultural Dynamics of Globalization," in *Many Globalizations: Cultural Diversity in the Contemporary World*, ed. Peter L. Berger and Samuel P. Huntington (Oxford: Oxford University Press, 2002).
48. Pierre Krebs, *Im Kampf um das Wesen* (Horn: Burkhart Weecke Verlag, 1997), 56.
49. Faye, *Nouvelle discours à la nation européenne*, 59. Cf. Mohler, "Was Ist Postmoderne?" Another identitarian describes the contemporary West as not modernist, but *gegenwartig*—i.e., presentist. See Krebs, *Im Kampf um das Wesen*, 56.
50. Pierre Krebs, *Die europäische Wiedergeburt* (Tübingen: Grabert, 1982), 62–71.

## Chapter III

# Liberalism's Reign of Quantity

Nothing defines the New Right's project as much as its opposition to the current cultural subversion. That liberalism is taken as the principal source of this subversion makes it primarily an anti-liberal project. But what does it mean by "liberalism"? Though lacking a coherent doctrine and clear genealogy, New Rightists consider it a modernist ideology, hostile to everything that cannot be counted, calculated, or bought.[1] Ascending with the market forces of the seventeenth and eighteenth centuries, liberalism emerged in opposition to the landed, still partially feudal interests of the old regime. Its demands for liberty—first, liberty of conscience; then, freedom of association and expression; and, most importantly, economic liberty and property rights—reflected the political concerns of those seeking to uncouple the economy from the authority of Church, state, and community. In this capacity, liberalism articulated the anti-traditionalist world view of the "rising bourgeoisie," as it sought to refashion state and society to accord with its contractual theory of politics, market model of social regulation, and individualistic anthropology.[2]

### The Quantitative Character of Political Rationalism

Just as the history of liberal modernity is largely the history of the world's progressive rationalization, the ideological core of liberal thought is a belief in the primacy of reason.[3] The source of this rationalism is often traced back to antiquity or to the late medieval appropriation of Aristotelian logic. Its trunk root, though, lies in the work of René Descartes (1596–1650), who stands at the base line of modern philosophy. Like the New Science of the seventeenth century, with its horological image of creation, Descartes' philosophy privileged the reasoning mind, as it endeavors to comprehend nature's mechanical, law-like properties. Because his philosophical project needed a principle of certainty on which to construct its rationalist model of the physical world—a principle expressible in a "universally valid and demonstrable form"—he was obliged to sweep away the "false" presuppositions of the existing heritage, for only then could he establish the clear, self-evident propositions that were to undergird his philosophical project.

In founding what was to be an indisputable epistemology, Descartes introduced a proposition that is today entirely in dispute: a proposition that assumes the world is a duality made up solely of material and conscious substances.[4] According to this dualistic schema, matter (*res extensa*) is an "extended, divisible, spatial" substance, distinct from and unrelated to mind, a conscious substance (*res cogitans*), which is "unextended, indivisible, and non-spatial." Human life thus comprises two distinct spheres: that of the individual's reasoning mind and that of the objective (or external) world associated with a field of unrelated material objects apprehensible through the human sensory apparatus. Instead, then, of envisaging reality as a holism with intertwining sensate and ideational dimensions, Descartes directed philosophy away from "the organic operation of the whole human being" and toward the epistemological concerns of subject-object (i.e., mind-matter) relations. From this, there would later emerge subjectivist and objectivist, idealist and materialist, rationalist and empiricist world views, each of which would have a formative influence on liberalism's development. It was, though, Descartes' focus on matter, as a homogeneous, ubiquitous, and quantifiable substance, that most affected the rationalist character of liberal thought.

In its quest for truth—epistemological truth—Descartes' project concentrated on the length, depth, breadth, and velocity of physical objects, for these alone enabled him to quantify "the empirical unity of the world" and render it into extensions whose measurements lent themselves to precise and predictable calculations. Through this emphasis on matter's quantitative facets, he hoped to avoid the plethora of qualitative attributes that had previously complicated scientific abstraction and arrive at "perfect, timeless truths" that might supplant the disputed truths of Catholic theology. His unprecedented success in reducing complex natural phenomena to simple mathematical explanations would, of course, do much to launch the career of modern science, but it came at a certain price. Besides reducing reality to a simple expanse of matter, "understood" in abstract mathematical terms that did little to enhance man's knowledge of his world and, in some cases, further estranged him from it, Descartes' quantifying reductionism had the effect of relegating the qualitative features of the European life—all those things associated with history and heritage—to a lower order of significance, as ecclesiastical authority was supplanted by the naturalistic rationalistic system of modern science.

Against this deculturating rationalism, New Rightists appeal to René Guénon (1886–1951), whose "philosophy of Tradition" has had a major influence on them. Guénon (who was also an accomplished mathematician) claims material quantities are the most ephemeral and insignificant facet of reality—and are not even purely quantitative.[5] Every quantitative substance, as Descartes himself acknowledged, has texture, smell, taste, color, form, and other qualitative features, which are meaningless only to the quantifying intelligence. Similarly, if the "objective world" were made up solely of material extensions, it would not only be an undifferentiated homogeneity, but unmeasurable, for measurement is a function of order and order a property of quality. To conceive of quantity without its qualitative features, he argues, is like conceiving of substance without its defining essence.[6] From this Guénonian perspective, quantification is seen as emptying the world not just of what makes it meaningful to man, but of what makes it human—insofar as it reduces the world's incomparable expressions to abstract calculations indifferent to all that is distinct to real life. Moreover, in denying any truth other than the self-validating ones of a mathematicized materiality, Cartesianism tends to confuse information about the lowest order of things—about empirical "facts" or details detached from their living connection to the larger world—with knowledge of the world, as if this decontextualized "information" conveys anything meaningful about the unity of being—or even about reality in the neutral sense of an empirical given.[7]

Besides bringing "everything down to an exclusively quantitative point of view" and "establishing a uniform criteria of truth and certainty based on the soulless world of numbers," Cartesianism oversimplified subjectivity (the mind), which was henceforth divorced from the material world and assimilated with pure intelligence. Pitting mind against matter in this way, the thinking substance (mind) was henceforth transformed into an uniform ethereal substance unrelated to the world it reflected and to all non-rational forms of thought. Aided by the scientific procedures of "methodological doubt," which were to free the mind of "prejudice and ignorance" (that is, to free it of cultural influence), the mind's principal task was to "mirror" (Rorty) the radically different substance of matter, with the assumption that truth was merely an accurate representation of the mind's reflections.[8] Everything, as a consequence, that failed to conform to the quantitative criteria of this correspondence theory of truth—the summer birdsongs enchanting man's world, the causes over which men fight and die, all the things in effect that make the world meaningful to man—were to be pushed into "the presumable swamp of the irrational" (Heidegger).

Along with detaching mind from the matter it allegedly reflects, Cartesianism detached reason from the time, place, and circumstance of its cognitions. Spatio-temporal realities (the domain of history and culture) were thus made irrelevant to its exercise, free as it allegedly was of those qualifying influences that might subject it to non-rational considerations. This, in turn, restricted reason to the theoretical, as the timeless mechanical properties of the material world were taken as the sole legitimate concern of human thought. Instead, then, of seeing the mind as conditioned by a highly particularized and not always rational field of determinants (such as Hume's "reason as slave of the passion"), Descartes' "incorporeal mind" dismissed the bonds linking inner and outer man, making one a subject, the other an object, and their detached relationship a mere epistemological matter.[9]

Analogously, his *cogito*, the thinking subject, ceased to be a being-in-the-world and became a purely disembodied subjectivity. To the degree Descartes even acknowledged the larger social and cultural realities situating his subject, they were treated as objects of a deterministic and instrumentalist logic, unconnected to the mind's involvement in the world and to the deeper springs of human meaning.[10] Hermeneutical notions of multiple interpretations, traditionalist concepts of transcendence, the higher values of life and personality, as well as the pragmatic dictates of biology and culture, all of which elude quantification, were similarly excluded from rationalist consideration. Above all, Cartesianism, and all the modern schools of thought influenced by it, have no room for history, whose dense encumbered particularities and attention to "local, timely, practical" issues arose not from bloodless epistemological concerns, but from man's culturally informed involvement in the particular life world into which he was "thrown" at birth. By contrast, Descartes' philosophy treats time as simply another form of quantity, to be geometrically rendered into a linear succession of "nows." As discussed below (Chapter V), this not only distorts the nature of human temporality in assuming that it is a forward progression, it has numerous pernicious implications for European culture. For by focusing on the world's purely quantitative, rather more complicated and defining qualitative facets, Cartesianism (and the rationalist/materialist world order it justified) assumed that reason's calculative faculties were all that were needed to generate substantial insights about the nature of the world and the meaning of life.[11]

Predictably, Descartes' philosophy caught the imagination of the early modern merchant class. As Guido de Ruggiero characterizes it, the bourgeoisie is "Cartesian in its cult of common sense, which is nothing but *la raison* in small change."[12] Spirit, soul, and subjective determinations, qualities unamenable to quantification and associated with the aristocracy's chivalric spirit, have always been tangential to the business of commerce. Just as Descartes' mathematical notion of reason ignores particularized patterns of human consciousness and higher metaphysical principles, the merchant's "counting mania" (Nietzsche) ignores everything irreducible to a monetary calculation, privileging, as it does, quantitative factors divorced from their qualifying context. Indeed, "rationality" to the merchant is little more than the possibility of calculation.[13]

Similarly, the merchant approaches the world's concrete properties not with the aim of understanding the spirit of the human enterprise, but for the sake of attaining the greatest number of his pecuniary objectives. In this spirit, he is wont to transform the world into an object—subject to his instrumental rationality, and dismissive of those "subjective" qualities that might obstruct his own enterprise. Not surprisingly, the affinity between the calculative sensibilities of the rising bourgeoisie and the quantitative impetus of Cartesian rationalism had a major impact on the modernist enterprise, for it authorized a decontextualized reason, oriented to the lowest material levels of existence, to play a revolutionary role in clearing away the historic heritage of European man.[14] It thus directed the modern mind toward technical routines favoring the manipulation of matter, rather than the cultivation of higher life forms. Rationalism's triumph could not, then, but imply a victory of quantity over quality in the realm of science, and of reason and money over culture and tradition. As one of Europe's greatest champions characterizes it, Cartesianism in the hands of the bourgeoisie helped bring about an era in which "metaphysics was to be a matter of weighing and measuring; government was to be a matter of counting noses; economy was to be entirely reduced to money-making; [and] the structure of society was to be a reflex of [monetary imperatives]."[15]

While the bourgeois appropriation of Cartesian rationalism would legitimate the subsequent liberal assault on culture and tradition, another of its offshoots influenced the way in which its rationalizing reforms were to be implemented. Because Descartes simply assumed the reliability of reason's representations—representations whose accuracy was crucial to his project—he offered a philosophically unsatisfactory account of how mind apprehends matter. In reaction, John Locke and the British empiricist school took up the alternative implicit in his mind-matter schema, emphasizing the sensate rather than the ideational foundations of knowledge. Henceforth, all that could not be seen, heard, touched, smelled, or experienced ceased to count, for the empiricist believed the senses alone were capable of establishing valid correspondences between the mind's subjective reflections and the objective reality they endeavored to reflect. Descartes' "clear and distinct" ideas were thus forced to cede to Locke's notion that ideas derived from sense impressions—that is, that mental phenomena were not mental in origin, but the result of sensations—and that the senses rather than the mind were primary in perceiving, and hence knowing, the objective world. Locke accordingly "sensualized all concepts of understanding" (Kant), somewhat in the way Descartes had previously conceptualized sensations.[16] Similarly, Locke viewed empirical reality (Descartes' world of extended substances) as a realm of inert matter, with "facts" neatly separated from one another. This made sense impressions primary, for they alone were treated as a reliable source of information about substantial matters. They were also taken as the principal determinant of man's nature, which was viewed as a *tabula rasa*, a blank slate, upon whose impressionable surface the formative effects of sense experience were to be imprinted.

From the above, it should be evident that empiricism constituted less a break with, than a variant of, rationalism, for both philosophies presumed the world was a duality, with consciousness located in the individual's mind, and concrete, spatial, and quantifiable objects—"external reality"—situated in a three-dimensional space outside the mind. Empiricism differed from rationalism mainly in turning the mind to the senses, rather than to itself, to disclose the nature of "external" reality. Analogously, Locke believed experiences entering the mind as sensations were sorted and reflected on by reason. As Descartes rejected "truths" not logically derived from clear, self-evident propositions, Locke banished whatever supposition empirical evidence failed to substantiate. Once the validity of an individual's sense impressions had been judged by the mind, reason, he thought, converted these impressions into simple ideas, as if ideas derived from bits of sense data. This "data-processing model of the mind" (Theodore Roszak) similarly followed Descartes in accepting that the natural world was rationally ordered, that the senses were a sort of mirror reflecting the objective reality outside them, and that nature's law-like properties were perceptible and thus accessible to reason. Finally, empiricists followed rationalists in treating truth as an object, rather than an "eventual phenomenon" unique to its interpretative encounter, and in imagining that all men reason and perceive in ways that were "everywhere and always the same."

When Cartesianism and its Lockean variant reached the eighteenth century, the emerging liberal consensus was prepared to anchor its project in the empirico-rationalist belief that nature was a set of mechanical objects governed by laws accessible to reason, that the individual was an environmentally shaped subject able to ascertain the truth of these laws, and that knowledge derived from evidence, experiment, and analysis was a panacea for all the foolish, unjust "irrationalities" of traditional society. On this basis, the Enlightenment's liberal theorists concluded that man no longer needed traditional, communal, or religious references to order his life: for in eliminating the error and ignorance embedded in tradition, scientific knowledge would suffice—as the "light of nature" replaced the "darkness of antiquity." Enlightenment thinkers thus called on reason to reconstruct man's social world and to do so in ways that made him the "legislator" of his existence. Religious toleration, constitutional government, and open markets, to dismantle traditional authorities and foster rational, self-interested behaviors, were all that was needed to refound the human community on a just and reasonable basis.

In the philosophical edifice of Immanuel Kant, representing the apotheosis of Enlightenment thought, a set of "synthetic *a priori*" judgements applicable to the phenomenal world sought to reconcile Cartesian rationalism and Lockean empiricism (mathematical reason and sensory experience) in a higher philosophical synthesis. For Kant, it was not objective (or noumenal) reality, as Locke thought, but the nature of the mind that held the key to the world's order. Time, space, and causality, he claimed, were mental categories, expressing the way man made sense of things (as they appeared to him) and not necessarily properties specific to the objective world (which was ultimately unknowable). From the perspective of Kant's "transcendental idealism," it was mind that conditioned man's relationship to his environment and enabled him to transcend the bounds of experience and thus of those "alien influences" that might prevent him, as a free moral being, from following the claims of his conscience. But if the phenomenological nature of the world's order derives from the mind, the mind (*pace* Descartes) is nevertheless obliged to observe its empirical character, for the mind alone, in its analytic capacity, can know nothing of its distinct spatio-temporal properties. By distinguishing between the world *für sich* and the world *in sich*, Kant would make man an autonomous moral agent capable of "legislating for himself" (of making rational moral choices irrespective of external influences), but nevertheless one obliged to acknowledge the causal constraints of phenomenal reality. So conceived, Kantian man was to determine himself according to reason's "universal standards" and, under these standards, to live in harmony with other autonomous beings, whose integrity required a condition of untrammeled freedom.

Because Kantian man was a "rational agent capable of reasoned choice," identities shaped by history, tradition, and race—implying collective and affective commitments of a pre-rational sort—were treated as potential threats to his reason and autonomy.[17] Indeed, the *Aufklärung* for Kant was precisely that stage in human development when the moral subject began to live in accord with its reason and not the "ignorance and superstition" of its heritage.

The loss, then, of those transcendent references—crystallized in tradition, sacramentalized in the Church, and worked out in history—were not seen as the beginning of modern nihilism, but as the adulthood of humanity, when morality and behavior were detached from "metaphysical fables" and refounded on secular rational principles. Kant, in this way, hoped to make the enlightened subject the leading actor in the liberal project and the "rational organization of everyday life" (Jürgen Habermas) its ultimate aim.[18] "Personal autonomy and societal rationality," philosophically premised on reason's power to legislate for itself, would accordingly influence all subsequent manifestations of liberal ideology, giving rise to a series of propositions whose implications have been nothing short of world-changing.

Foremost of these was that of individualism. In Enlightenment anthropology, the individual is posited as the primary constituent of the social world, constituting "an end in itself" (Kant). Like the Cartesian mind, whose unconditional claims lack contingency, the liberal individual is imbued with nature's timeless properties, for his rational essence is thought to pre-exist any contextualization or ontological determination. The practical, timely, and not necessarily reasonable demands of society, whose circumstantial impositions might influence the context affecting his development, are likewise believed to be tangential to his essence. Somewhat in the way early modern science took homogeneous matter to be the entirety of the world's extended substance, Enlightenment liberalism made its unencumbered individual society's basic component. His "I" was accordingly detached from his "we"—and hence from the people, the culture, the history, even the biological stock from which he "happened" to come.[19] As Guénon notes, "quantity can only separate," for it is "a principle of division."[20]

In contrast to ancient and medieval notions of man's inherent sociability, the liberal individual is conceived as a world unto himself, living with his fellows solely for convenience's sake. The notion that he might be part of a larger communal or natural order—situated in "the polluted stream of society in the irreversible flow of history"—was dismissed for the unprecedented view that in himself the individual constitutes a complete whole (even though he possesses no inherent qualities and no distinguishing attributes). Indeed, all that is positive in man's world is seen as coming from the rationality latent in his individuality.[21] Given, then, that cultural, historical, and biological qualities are "subjective" forms, subordinate to the individual's rational "essence," the liberal dismisses whatever influence they may have previously had on him. Temporally, this dismissal of supraindividual significations (i.e., man's decontextualization) reduces him to the "eternal now." Existentially, to his basic desires.

Because liberalism's quantitative optic was compelled to focus on the immediate and simplistic, with everything leveled down to choices between appetite and aversion, it lent itself to the myth of *Homo oeconomicus*—or, more accurately, was the premise upon which the myth historically arose. This myth has since become the paradigm for liberalism's quantitative model of individualization. In the story it tells, Guizot's *enrichissez-vous* constitutes the individual's chief existential concern, the competitive marketplace his natural niche, and commercial exchange the substance of his freedom. Accordingly, all that counts for the myth's capitalist protagonist are the forces of production, the laws of supply and demand, price mechanisms, market equilibrium, and the other "scientific" principles governing the quantitative realm associated with the economy.[22] This makes Economic Man a calculating "economic being" motivated by self-interest, and his society the arithmetical sum of all such beings.[23] The competitive and egotistic pursuit of individual self-interest is not seen, though, as leading to chaos (as one might expect), but to social mobility and "the greatest happiness for the greatest number." As for "the useless curiosities of history and the medieval lumber of tradition," which have regulated every former civilization, they never figure in the myth's narrative.[24]

In making Economic Man an autonomous being geared to the maximization of his options, liberalism sets itself against whatever impedes his self-sufficiency, including those common convictions and identities that go into making a people a living unity.[25] It tends, as a consequence, to associate individuality with the dissolution of traditional communal ties and to prize a monadic individualism, undifferentiated from one place, people, or era to another.[26] This prompts it to define freedom as the individual's right to "morally choose" his own ends—however incompatible these ends might be with his communal attachments.[27] One might even argue that liberal ideology is formed in opposition to the idea of community, for its underlying supposition is that the self-interested individual has no obligations other than the ones he contracts in the market.[28] Kant, for example, claimed that without the freedom to make rational choices between right and wrong, irrespective of the state of the real world, the individual would be neither autonomous nor moral. The right to make such choices—implying "the principle of unlimited self-regulation—indeed takes precedent in liberalism over every communal, cultural, or political imperative.[29]

In rejecting liberal individualism, New Rightists assume that the individual is never sufficient unto himself, but always an expression of larger affiliations, of which he is not the constituent element, only the function. The whole, as Aristotle says in reference to the human community, is necessarily anterior to its parts.[30] Failing to recognize the individual as a bearer of such larger attachments, liberal individualism is wont to rebuff those traditional or substantive values associated with family, *ethnos*, nation, and hence those identities constituent of social cohesion and the capacity to make history.[31] In the "open societies" of the Anglo-American world, for example, where "possessive individualism" has come to prevail over every other value, *Grécistes* point out that there is now no longer a term to denote those related individuals sharing the same blood, the same culture, and the same destiny, as was once conveyed in the term "folk." The modern English word "people"—the plural of "person"—has, instead, come to mean an indeterminate aggregate of not necessarily related individuals (the equivalent of the French *gens*, the Italian *persone*, or the German *Leute*). Notions of an organic body shaped by history and bound by certain transcendent attachments, such as still linger in the terms *peuple*, *populo*, or *Volk*, are today almost inexpressible in *the* language of trade and commerce.[32] Given, then, that the only thing factored into the liberal's individualistic calculus is the choice-making self, who rationally pursues his interests independent of larger considerations, the "people" has (or rather "have") been turned into the quantitative sum of the individuals making up "society." Liberalism, it follows, *c'est la mort du peuple*, for within its materialist universe human collaboration and solidarity are no longer based on a shared heritage or kinship, but on anonymous economic exchanges and self-interested behaviors.

By pitting its abstract individual against established communities, New Rightists claim liberalism makes man not only a wolf to his fellows, it creates a condition devoid of meaning and purpose. Meaning and purpose are, by definition, collective and contextual, for, as Wittgenstein once quipped, "one cannot play a language game by oneself."[33] Real individuals—always and everywhere—are embedded in specific cultures and communities, which alone possess the significations to define, motivate, and position them. A society that does not affirm its collective particularity and imbue its members with its specific cultural significance cannot, in their view, but leave the individual without a sense of purpose or identity—without even a meaningful sense of individuality. Just, then, as postmodernists see man as a facet of the sign systems and power networks situating him, New Rightists consider him a product of larger determinations, situated, to be sure, within a multi-generational communal context, but also inseparable from it.[34] An individual's life for them is thus necessarily communal—encompassing not simply the present, but past and future generations—for everything, they believe, is "constituted by its relations to everything else." This makes the self something greater than what the individual is "in himself."

Human communities, as such, are never mere clusters of abstract, interchangeable, and unrelated units of rational beings whose movements are understandable in the way physics understands the properties of inanimate material substances. They are, instead, organic hierarchies bound by time, place, and common purpose. Consider man in abstraction from these or reduce him to his elementary animal desires and you deprive him not just of what makes his life possible, but of those qualities that make him who he is. Whenever, then, it unhinges man from the immense chain of generations situating him, liberalism inevitably ends up privileging the elemental and subindividual in man, for it sweeps away all that is most human in him. This, in turn, reduces cultural specificity and communal attachment to mere "lifestyle" options.[35] Once such qualitative attachments are so discarded, so too is the human. This does not imply, of course, that New Rightists subscribe to the Marxist or socialist view that turns culture and community into fetishized abstractions justifying whatever collectivist imperative and centralized power that might threaten a person's or a people's distinct individuality. Against the liberal's atomizing individualism, as well as the Marxist's soulless collectivism, both of which rest on a purely quantitative understanding of the social world, they uphold the biocultural qualifications that distinguish one form of human life from another, as a people pursues what is inherent in its unique being.

Thus, when denigrating principles of community, liberalism ironically denigrates true individuality. For as quantity dominates quality in the natural sciences, so too does its anti-traditionalist rationalism dismiss those qualifications that distinguish one man from another. For once the social world becomes a collection of monadic individuals, inherent distinctions and supraindividual designations take on a secondary order of significance. What counts for liberalism is the basic zoological unit, which—ideally—is a self-contained rational being. The qualitative attributes of station, character, and breeding (not to mention race, culture, and history), whose importance has prevailed in every previous civilization, are thereby ignored, for the individual—any individual—is looked on as an "instance of humanity," worthy, in himself, of dignity. From this "naturalistic" notion of the individual, which denies everything in man that goes beyond his zoological nature, there emerges another of liberalism's defining doctrines—that of egalitarianism and the contention that all individuals, irrespective of their inherited or acquired qualities, are bearers of equal rights.[36]

Even though they knew little about heredity, early liberals did not actually believe men were equal in innate capacity. Against the hierarchical trappings of traditional society, they claimed man's common humanity dictated a condition in which all should be treated "fairly." In this sense, the initial liberal notion of equality implied a political condition in which government was envisaged as a form of social consent, with everyone equal in the eyes of the law and with duties subordinate to rights. From the beginning, however, this strictly political understanding of equality was criticized for its formality. More radical (and resentful) liberals have since emphasized the purely quantitative dimensions of environmental influences, seeking "equality of opportunity" to level the so-called playing field, and, when this fails to achieve equality (and fail it must), "equality of outcome."[37] Implicit in this expanding notion of "entitlement" is the belief that men are not simply morally equal (that is, "naturally good"), but potentially equal in general capacity, with the same malleable constitution. As John Dewey puts it: "Given a social medium in whose institutions the available knowledge, ideas, and art of humanity were incarnate, and the average individual would rise to undreamed heights of social and political intelligence."[38] For this sort of arithmetical egalitarianism, "human nature" is essentially uniform in potential and infinitely reformable, with individual differences attributable mainly to environmental factors.

Because such factors are taken as the principal source of human differences (that is, because liberalism assumes that with a bit of coaching Eliza Doolittle can be turned into My Fair Lady), inferior and superior individuals are viewed as either victimized or privilege. Against a traditionalism accepting difference as intrinsic to the nature of things and the human spirit as irreducible to materialist criteria, liberal egalitarianism holds that disparities are inherently unjust, derived from factors which are social, circumstantial—and hence reformable.[39] (This, incidentally, is a tacit admission that high culture is impossible, for it denies man's inherent disposition to strive beyond himself.)[40] The egalitarian fraternity liberalism advocates seeks, as a consequence, "to make equal what is unequal" (Nietzsche), which, of course, creates injustices of an even more irrational kind, as the innate differences of individuals, cultures, and races are ignored or repressed for the sake of a chimerical standard.[41]

The liberal and Marxist revolutions of the last two centuries represent the most bloody historical instances of these injustices, but their deleterious effects have spared no realm of modern experience. For example, if individual worth is independent of birth, accomplishment, and character, as egalitarians insist, and if the superior and the inferior owe everything to what the environment imprints on them, then such qualities are irrelevant in cases where one individual (or people or race), quantity that he (or it) is, comes into conflict with another. The "disorderly rule of the mob" comes thus to drown out the voice of the superior man, while the brain of a Goethe or a Gobineau is equated with that of a modern urban savage.[42] Any discrimination or distinction between men would otherwise violate the egalitarian principle, abjuring, as it does, notions of quality, hierarchy, and inherent human difference.

But more than flouting natural hierarchies, liberal egalitarians are wont to reverse them. Mother Teresa and Jeffrey Dahmer, the saint and the serial killer, assume for them a certain equivalence, for every man, however misbegotten, is considered as innately good as any other—virtue or attainment being simply another expression of unequal opportunities. On this count, the mugger and rapist, products of unhealthy social influences, rather than the mugged and raped, are treated as the real victims. Similarly, the educational system passes everyone and civil service exams are "normed" to ensure that "disadvantaged minorities" are not excluded, just as the strong, the noble, and the beautiful are chastised for their "advantages." Though egalitarianism's leveling impetus avoids the all-important economic realm of liberal society (conceived as a pre-political or private realm exempt from egalitarian principles and hence tolerant of the most ruthless social Darwinism), its ideological pervasiveness nevertheless does more than beguile electoral constituencies or justify New Class "planning": it legitimates a social order premised wholly on quantitative/economic criteria.

In endeavoring to equalize the conditions influencing individuals, liberals anticipate the worldwide extension—the universalization—of their egalitarian schemes, hoping thus to impose their uniform model of humanity on the entire planet. This universalist impetus stems from the same body of rationalist ideas as does individualism and egalitarianism. As *Telos* editor Paul Piccone describes it, "universalism" derives from an "identity logic" in which an "abstract concept redefines the concrete particular in its own image while delegitimating all that is left out."[43] Unlike the view that sees the world's multifarious expressions achieving coherence through the imposition of a specific cultural stylization, universalism assumes that the particular is an imperfect variant of the general, that behind the world's innumerable contingencies and differences there lies an ahistorical, transcultural essence linking them all, and that the universal is necessarily superior to the particular.

In this spirit, liberal universalists claim that non-Western peoples who have yet to embark on the course of modernization "are but temporarily prevented (by wicked leaders or severe crises or incomprehension) from pursuing Western pluralist democracy and adopting the Western way of life."[44] That is, they assume that liberal society embodies the universal ideal and that non-liberal societies are destined to adopt its allegedly rational forms. They thus refuse to accept that the world is composed of an array of diverse biocultural particularities, each with its own legitimacy, and, instead, promote a standardizing uniformity that seeks to eliminate national, racial, and historical differences for the sake of a borderless, color-blind order subject to one law, one market, and one humanitarian creed.

Like rationalism, universalism epistemologically corrupts notions of objectivity, refusing to accept realities diverging from the particularistic premises of its own narrative.[45] Anything, therefore, that separates the world's innumerable subjective forms from its notion of the general, the real person from its idealized notion of humanity—such as traditional communal institutions or thousands of years of evolutionary development—is treated as an aberration. Humanity as such is rendered into "man in general"—with the assumption that man is a quantitative unit, roughly equivalent to every other such unit.[46] Particularistic identities separating the individual from humanity, the part from the whole, are dismissed as transitory, bound to give way to "that which pertains to all," as men everywhere, however egoistic or unrelated, evolve into a single brotherhood affirming their common humanity—into what scholastics would have called "matter without form"—or into what today might be called a postmodern magna.

In refusing to accept the chimera of liberal universalism, New Rightists contend that there is no essence inherent in the order of things to frame the world's peoples into a single set of common coordinates to which mankind as a whole is destined to conform. Following postmodernists, they believe such essences derive from particularistic postulates that confuse a highly abstract generalization with an objective reality.[47] Like its generic individual, liberalism's universalist notion of humanity lacks actual substance, amounting to little more than a solipsistic projection of its own historically situated beliefs.[48] And since this projection renders human beings into terms compatible with a single mentality, informed by a single standardized way of life, liberalism rejects whatever human forms diverge from its standard (which explains something of liberalism's ultimate tendency toward totalitarianism). Racial, cultural, and historical differences are thus discarded and everything that is common to the different families of man—that is, their animal nature and the physical, sensual, comfort-loving desires of this nature—are privileged. The liberal's lofty ideals thus inevitably end up dismissing organic solidarities and cultural distinctions for the sake of all that is least human in man.[49]

Like equality and individualism, universalism assumes its most consequential form in the marketplace. Through the process of supply and demand and through the operation of price mechanisms that ignore qualitative designations, liberals believe self-interested individuals are able to engage one another on equal terms, as they search for advantage on the market's "level playing field." The more the self-interests of these individuals converge in this way, the more they allegedly contribute to the overall betterment of society, for in the process of harmonizing a totality of competing wills, the market allegedly establishes a general equilibrium of interests.[50] Yet, by making the market the principal arena of human intercourse, liberalism again orients to what is least elevated in human existence, for it forces "being" to submit to "having," confusing life with consumption and production. The market's compulsion to maximize profit, improve efficiency, rationalize behavior, and promote commerce cannot, then, but leave it indifferent, if not hostile, to those qualitative references that generate a sense of meaning, for profit, efficiency, and rationalization, the market's primary concerns, are rarely compatible with social solidarities, normative orders, or aesthetic principles resisting the domination of an unregulated quantification.[51]

In this vein, liberalism is wont to dismiss everything that renders life meaningful to man. In the name of free trade, for example, it will expose the nation's households to competitors in the world market, "where the strong always succeed in swallowing the weak." Similarly, its economic logic renders the nation's industrial base dependent on alien global forces, as it responds to financial imperatives, whose universal impetus ignores borders and causes it to export jobs, import coolie labor, and divert investments abroad. As the pre-eminent quantitative institution, the market, in fact, knows no homeland, only the great international exchanges, New York and London pre-eminently, where its monetary imperatives are encouraged to run roughshod over every qualitative consideration deterring its accumulations. It thus promotes the dissolution of peoples and the particularistic qualities that go into making them what they are—all for the sake of the most demeaning quantitative criteria: money.

Unlike the anti-capitalists of the far Left, New Rightists do not oppose the market or free enterprise *per se*, only a dog-eat-dog capitalism unaccountable to anything other than the bottom line.[52] As Benoist writes, "I would like to see a society with a market, but not a market society."[53] Against both the liberal creed of *laissez-faire* and the Left's statism, New Rightists favor an organic economic system in which market activity is geared to the general welfare. For this reason, they advocate a "recontextualization" of the economy within "life, society, politics, and ethics" in order to make it a means rather than simply an ends. Long-term development, innovation, and risk-taking enterprises (frowned on by the short-term profit concerns of anonymous managerial boards and institutional investors) would, they claim, actually benefit from a market subordinated to supraeconomic considerations, as such historical opponents of liberal capitalism as Bismarck's Germany, Henry Carey's America, Franco's Spain, or the present East Asian "tigers" demonstrate. Economic freedom and healthy enterprises, they add, cannot long be sustained in atomized, impersonal, and indifferent societies geared solely to economic interests, prone as they are to unrest, uncertainty, and the loss of commonly accepted beliefs.[54]

In rejecting liberalism's market dogmas, whose principal concern is financial speculation, the New Right by no means advocates a Soviet-style command economy (whose impetus, incidentally, was not sociocultural but economic). Guillaume Faye thus argues that while middle- and long-term economic objectives are rightfully the prerogative of the state, since they impinge on the welfare of the entire commonwealth, the execution of national economic strategies ought nevertheless to be in the hands of entrepreneurs free of bureaucratic micro-management. Unlike the present European situation, in which the economy is subject to the predatory *laissez-faire* forces of the global market, as well as to highly-regulatory, exorbitant-taxing domestic bureaucracies, identitarians propose a "liberal" functioning market, unhampered by unnecessary state controls, supportive of free initiative, protected from foreign interests, but nonetheless subordinate to the national interest.[55]

Similarly, New Rightists emphasize that the "good society" is not necessarily the wealthy one, for the ability to generate the means of existence is hardly the same as the generation of existential "meaning."[56] Markets may be ideal in facilitating certain kinds of exchanges, but in the higher realms they lack all relevance. A landscape painting sold in a supermarket, for example, may be "economically more efficient"—cheaper to make, easier to distribute, even aesthetically more appealing to the vulgar—than a canvas of John Constable or Claude Lorrain, but to what effect if one loves the real thing? It might likewise make perfect economic sense from a banker's or manager's perspective to downsize workforces, divert investments abroad, eliminate national tariffs, and open borders, but healthy communities, with stable tax bases, fairly paid workers, and secure living standards to support family life inevitably pay the price. Above all, the market's quantitative priorities, emphasizing profits accrued from exchange, rather than the productive needs of the nation, are not even "economically" viable. As Friedrich List, Karl Bücher, Othmar Spann, and certain other Central European economists have shown, liberal economies focused on exchange value are driven by profit and private gratification, not wealth creation. "The power to create wealth [, though,] is more important than wealth itself . . . [for] prosperity is not a matter of riches or exchanges . . . but of the degree to which the productive forces are developed."[57] Markets might therefore generate immense profits for multinational corporations, but, from a societal or national perspective, this has little to do with infrastructural developments, industrial innovations, the training of skilled workforces, or even efficient distribution systems. For once the well-being of individual investors and international financiers, not the productive forces of the nation, are taken as the "bottom line," the market's principal concern is no longer the economy, only the self-interest of those seeking to maximize their returns within it.

Historically, the liberal market, the private realm of individual competition, arose in tandem with the nation-state. Without it—and the role it played in removing particularistic obstructions to trade, disembedding individuals from traditional kin and communal obligations, establishing a common system of law, and commodifying labor—the market's rise would have been inconceivable.[58] Yet, once the early-modern nation-state made the market pivotal to civil society, the market sought to refashion the state in its own image. The great liberal revolutions of the late eighteenth and nineteenth centuries were the result.[59] The political philosophers preparing the conceptual platform of these modernist upheavals did so by advancing the idea that the state ought to be subordinate to society, serving to guarantee those relations under which a free market functions: because the state for these ideologues was the superstructural expression of civil society, just as civil society was the composite of individuals whose essence was pre-social and pre-political. In this view, the state's principal purpose is the removal of "obstacles to self-development."

Since liberals hold that the individual is an autonomous being and the state has no mandate to impose values and norms exterior to the private sphere, they advocate state neutrality "between different conceptions of the good life" (Charles Taylor), abjuring, in this way, any particularistic principle of identity or culture that might provoke the state's intervention in the economy or override their purely quantitative vision of market activity. The notion that the state transcends other associations, representing them not "as a whole, but as the aim and purpose of the whole" (Adam Müller), is thus entirely foreign to them. Against the traditional organic concept of the state—as a destining force rooted in a people's normative order and standing above competing social interests—liberals have sought to depoliticize it and restrict its powers, for they see it as addressing only the abstract individual, not the flesh-and-blood citizen embedded in the larger community.[60] Typically, Locke, the most important of the early ideologues of "liberty," envisaged the state as an association of landowners designed to protect their property rights—a sort of limited liability company based on contractual agreement.

Given that liberalism conceives of the state as primarily an administrative system subordinate to the economy, with the enforcement of individual "rights" taking priority over any collective sense of the public "good" and procedural processes substituting for established norms, it avoids the political. For normative "decisions" involving the application of power, constraint, and violence for a people's sake are, as Carl Schmitt argues, the inevitable basis of every organic political entity.[61] In Schmitt's view (which is that of the New Right), the state is inherently subjective, committed to a certain notion of the good, which, as Charles Maurras once noted, is found in "the order of things" rather than in material things.[62] This implies that the state is not the natural offshoot of family or civil society, as liberals (and Marxists) contend, but rather the extension of the ancient warrior bands and aristocracies, whose values of honor, courage, and loyalty manifested an order superior to clan or individual interests. Until the period of the Bourgeois Revolution (i.e., the late eighteenth century), the European state was indeed associated with a governing minority made up of dynastic and noble elements charged with upholding those collective and transcendent principles that went into making a state a state. The political system, as such, was considered neither a bureaucratic regulator of market relations nor a mediator of individual "interests," but an "order" anchored in history, culture, and blood.

In taking refuge in rationality and refusing to act as an autonomous authority that asserts its primacy over contending interests for the sake of a "community of destiny," the liberal state initially opted for a minimalist form ("the nightwatchman state"), whose role was limited to protecting "life, health, liberty, and property from violent assault." In this capacity, it was to intrude in civil life only to work out those compromises necessary for the maintenance of social harmony and economic exchange.[63] Its entire idea of the political was accordingly based on an economic model, as it approached political issues in terms that could be "negotiated"—somewhat in the way the market allows goods to be bargained and exchanged. The "open society" undergirding this state devoted to the interests of Economic Man was accordingly "incompatible with any idea of an all-encompassing state purpose"—insofar as such an idea might impinge on the individual's autonomy, hamper the market, or interfere with the state's ability to rationally adjudicate social conflicts. Yet, in refusing "purpose" in this sense, the liberals' allegedly neutral state not only ended up leaving society as a whole defenseless before those who had the economic means of influencing the state, it made the citizenry indifferent to the public sphere and to all those collective forces imbuing the "private citizen" with a sense of mutual consideration. It seems hardly coincidental, then, that the freedoms early liberals championed have grown with the growth of social anomie, the lost of existential meaning, and the economic domination of the state.

By contrast, the New Right's Schmittian notion of the state views politics as the art of decision-making, entailing the exercise of authority and the assertion of sovereignty on the basis of a normative, destining vocation arising from a particular form of group life and a particular group identity.[64] Unlike the liberal state, conceived as a rational instrument whose administrative pulleys and gears operate according to purely mechanical principles, the New Right's concept gives form and direction to a people's destiny by nurturing its vitalist imperatives and multigenerational heritage.[65] As Benoist puts it, "a people is governed, not managed."[66]

The distinction between purposeful government and rational management is, however, alien to virtually all forms of liberalism. Even in the late nineteenth century, when the "new liberals" in England and the "progressives" in the US began transforming the state into an instrument of social planning and "social justice," they retained an apolitical concept of "the political."[67] Characteristically, liberal theorists of all stripes continue to approach the state procedurally, deny its authority an ideal, conceive of society as a plurality of interests whose rivalries are to be impartially arbitrated, and treat individual self-realization, not the nation's blood and spirit, as the ultimate political goal. To them, the "essence of politics is dialogue, compromise, and mediation," not the existence, security, and destiny of a historically constituted people. Thus, whether the minimalist one of Locke or the interventionist one of the twentieth-century New

Class, the liberal state, on principle, abjures a national project, defining itself as the neutral instrument of the interests and individuals it "serves."[68]

With postmodernity, the evacuation of the political becomes especially pronounced. Where the modern order separated public and private spheres, formally acknowledging the primacy of the "public," the metanarrative collapse fosters a "public individualism" negating even this notion of the political. Without organic references and entirely other-directed, postmodernists look to public recognition for validation of their tribal identities. This, however, requires that the private self be treated as a public entity.[69] At the same time, it dictates a "personal politics" reliant on the most extreme individualist freedoms. In this spirit, postmodern politics eviscerates collective notions of territoriality, sovereignty, the public sphere, and virtually everything else comprising the traditional "language of the state." In the same stroke, it posits a "virtual" state diffused within informal networks of power that function more like a market than the institutions of the historic nation-state.[70] Indeed, postmodernists view the nation-state as an antiquated product of modernity (an "imagined community") and advocate a borderless world subject to the rule of international law.

Against this latest evacuation of the political, New Rightists argue that the political implies not simply social unity and cooperation, but the affirmation of such unity and cooperation. Historically, the political arose in opposition to the private, which excludes, individualizes, and separates. As former *Éléments* editor Charles Champetier notes, the root of "private," *privare*, means to separate, while "public," derived from *populus*, signifies "people" and hence that which connects a body of related individuals to a super-personal affiliation: the nation. The public accordingly refers to those common interests rising above private ones and constituting those links that bind its members as a national collectivity. Thus, whenever the concerns of private life supplant those of the political, the state turns from the collective to the individual, the public is rendered into the private, and individual interests are confused with those of the nation. There can, in sum, be no political without a public and no public without a people.[71]

The tribal logic of postmodernity's self-constituted micro-groups seems, however, to rule out even the possibility of defining, and hence defending, what unites a body of related individuals to a larger collective identity. It is not surprising, then, that, in endeavoring to realize their "global, cosmopolitan, democratic, egalitarian, classless, casteless society" (Rorty), postmodern political theorists privilege such conventional liberal issues as institutional access, inclusion, and representation, canonizing the procedural aspects of a rights-based politics focused on private identities. Likewise, the liberal modernist notion of the state as an adjunct of the market and of politics as an instrument of individuation are retained, while the irreparable link between the people and the political is rendered into a conceptual absurdity.[72]

Postmodernists are indeed not unlike modernists in resisting any concept of the "people"—and thus of the political. If society, though, is but a random collection of individuals (that is, if the private excludes the public), the "social contract" linking these individuals *qua* individuals, rather than their organic unity as a nation, becomes the ultimate political reference.[73] At this point, the state ceases to represent a people's "destining project" and ceases, in effect, to be a state. For only a political body transcending the private concerns of civil society and representing a collective or public purpose, New Rightists insist, deserves the appellation "state."[74] Given, therefore, that they view the metanarrative collapse not as justification for the tribalization of the social body, but as an opportunity to reanimate the European project, they advocate a revival of the political and the maintenance of a strong state, since the state alone has the capacity to fully realize Europe's historic destiny.[75]

In emphasizing the market-situated individual separated from larger ties, liberalism always appeals to the highest rational principles, but, as we have seen, inevitably ends up privileging what is basest in man—"dragging humanity towards the pit where pure quantity reigns."[76] That its reign of quantity has culminated in a de-Europeanizing *Gleichschaltung* should come thus as no surprise, for its impetus (in either its modern or postmodern form) has been to demote those cultural qualities that are the basis of human existence.[77] As the German identitarian Pierre Krebs observes, the Europe of the Greek gods, of the Germanic mysteries, of Roman law, of Celtic metaphysics has been overrun by the "Zombie Europe" of the merchants and managers, who have raised the market's quantitative principles above every transcendent expression of the European spirit.[78]

## Contemporary Measures

While the roots of liberal modernity reach back beyond the Reformation, it was not until 1789 that it began reshaping public institutions and not until the second half of the twentieth century that it eradicated the more tenacious vestiges of pre-modern life. As late as 1968, there existed areas of family, community, and religious activity still rooted in traditional ways. The last three decades, however, have witnessed a massive re-ordering of

European existence. In this period, encompassing the New Right's lifespan, European identity has changed more than in any comparable period of the last half millennium. Its effects have been especially acute in the realms of sex, race, and law.

As one of the most conspicuous expressions of contemporary liberalism, the application of individualistic, egalitarian, and universalist principles to the question of sex represents an unprecedented assault on tradition, specifically on customary sexual roles and the myths, values, and symbols historically undergirding them. Leading this assault, liberalism's feminist vanguard contends that there is no significant difference between men and women—"one is not born, but rather becomes a woman"—and that existing sexual roles are anything but natural, being the unjust constructs of a "patriarchy" bent on subjugating women. In the name of equality, feminists crusade to homogenize sexual identities on the basis of a quantitative model of humanity that is more categorical, and hence more absurd, than any previous liberalism. In this spirit, they reject conventional "gender relations," claiming that masculine and feminine "qualities" are irrelevant.[79] This causes them to challenge existing sexual roles, deny femininity, and argue for the "innate bisexuality of the human psyche." Perhaps the most influential of twentieth-century feminists, Simone de Beauvoir, defined the feminist movement as one to equalize male and female roles, making them interchangeable, with each "rational being" having the option of "choosing" his or her sexual identity.[80] Relatedly, Beauvoir's ideals were bisexuality, group marriage, and a new age of promiscuity. For such feminists, the biological foundations of sex are meaningless, based on "insignificant" anatomical differences without larger psychological or existential import.[81]

In denying culturally encoded notions of "femininity," most feminists end up inadvertently accepting a masculine model of human behavior, seeing women, in effect, as fallen men.[82] There is, however, a school of feminism ("the second wave") that takes the reverse track, extolling everything feminine, seeking to feminize men, and advocating expressive and maternal conceptions of the political. This school too resists sexual differences, but from the opposite perspective. Finally, there is an explicitly homosexual school of feminism which seeks the ultimate "liberation" of women. True to its liberal origins, no major school of feminism accepts sexual polarity and the indisputable fact that "humanity" has two sides.[83]

Against all these schools, the New Right affirms both the biological and cultural significance of sexual differences, arguing that they are not only inescapable but necessary facets of the human condition. In its view, women differ from men "in mind and function as yin differs from yang."

Their insistence on humanity's bipolarity, it needs stressing, makes no imputation of inferiority, just as the view that characterizes the two poles of electricity as positive and negative lacks such imputation. Each opposite reflects and complements the other. The suppression or distortion of one inevitably implies the suppression or distortion of the other. Against the anti-traditional, anti-biological impetus of liberal feminism, *Grécistes* advocate a "differentialist feminism" that recognizes and validates both the innate and culturally encoded character of sexual polarity.[84] In support of this view, they refer to the great biologist Alexis Carrel, who defined the good as that which best accords with one's nature—insofar as the good enhances life, propagates the species, and elevates the human spirit.[85] Nature created two distinct sexes and imbued them with differences that have served the human species since the dawn of time. To deny these differences, to see them as products of "oppression," or to turn them on their head can never be a source of emancipation, only of "evil" in Carrel's biological sense. It is, then, in assuming, not fleeing, their "nature," *Grécistes* argue, that the full realization of female identity—and freedom—is possible.

As heirs to the only people that never enslaved its women, New Rightists oppose all that falls under the category of misogyny. At the same time, they refuse the feminists' liberal explanation of it. They especially disagree with their analysis of the current situation. For West European and especially American women, both presently "empowered" by special laws and employment preferences, to speak of their oppression is not only exaggerated, it ignores the "gynocratic" tendency of the present global system.[86] Whatever oppresses women today, they point out, has little to do with a presumed "phallocracy," for the existing order grants them powers now denied men.[87] The New Class forces associated with postmodern society seem especially supportive of feminist egalitarianism, as well as homosexual and emasculating behaviors—for these anti-traditional practices readily lend themselves to a purely quantitative regime based solely on money and bureaucratic fiat.

While subjecting feminism to their anti-liberal critique, New Rightists by no means hypostatize existing sexual roles. They fully accept that these may change over time and differ from culture to culture. They do, however, argue that sex-specific roles complementing the innate biological differences between male and female are inherently healthy. In fact, such designated differences have always existed, because they express the differences found in nature. As Benoist eloquently phrases it, sexual roles are "a feature of culture grafted onto a feature of nature."[88] That men are aggressive, competitive, inclined to abstraction, and enterprising, and that women are nurturing, seducing, patient, and receptive is not, he insists, the result of a repressive patriarchal imposition or a misconceived process of socialization, but of an evolutionary process that balances and complements the difference of each sex, for without the feminine, a masculine society would be one-sided and dysfunctional, just as the opposite would be true. The feminist understanding of sexual relations, however, seems congenitally unable to grasp that masculine dominance is not a form of oppression, but an expression of nature. Mars and Venus, Dominique Venner points out, have always played antagonistic but complementary roles in European history.[89] To think that one seeks the exclusion or oppression of the other testifies only to the one-dimensionality of liberal thought.

Besides opposing feminists who deny the biological basis of sexual roles or treat them as inherently demeaning, New Rightists oppose those who believe such roles, and particularly family roles, are innate and immutable.[90] Conservatives (especially American conservatives) often react to feminism's contractual and anti-naturalist view of the family by extolling what they assume are traditional familial roles (but which are actually those of the nineteenth-century bourgeoisie), unconscious that several models of the family, with different sexual roles, appear in the historical record. Benoist, by contrast, contends that the family, however much it serves the biological and social needs of human reproduction, evolves in tandem with society, reflecting, thus, the health or disorder of the larger order.

Because contemporary society is so crisis-ridden, Benoist fully acknowledges the troubled state of the family. No longer serving as an economic household, educator, childminder, and, in some cases, careprovider, it now functions mainly as "a haven in a heartless world," addressing those emotional and security needs neglected by an atomized social system. As he sees it, the future well-being of the family lies neither in celebrating hopelessly lost forms nor in allowing New Class social engineers to redesign it. Rather, society itself needs to be revitalized so that the family will again have a meaningful function to perform. Europe, in fact, requires just such a revitalization, for the family remains the vital intermediary between the individual and the larger social order. Without it, there can be no meaningful transmission from one generation to the next, no lineage, no foundation for authority, and no privileged space in which to nurture the individual. There can, above all, be no reproduction of the people. Like sexual roles, the family is not dismissible: having existed in one form or another through all the ages, it continues to evolve.

The burning question today is obviously what form, if any, its future will take.[91]

If the fundamental division *within* a people is that between male and female, the fundamental division *between* peoples is biocultural. With American-style multiculturalism and human rights, liberalism now attempts to do for biocultural identity what feminism does for sexual relations: eliminate human difference in the name of an amorphous and standardizing quantity labeled "humanity." Liberal advocates of multiculturalism thus assert that peoples with different roots "can and should look across the frontiers of race, language, gender, and religion without prejudice or illusion, and learn to think against the background of a hybridized society." When championing culturally and racially mixed societies, which are inclusive but not assimilationist, these multiculturalists ostensibly celebrate the world's diversity. But in addition to venting a not so implicit hatred of all things European, Christian, and white, their cynical invocation of tolerance and pluralism opposes the very survival of the European race. In the name of tolerance and equality, multiculturalists thus insist on "the presence of other cultures, the mixing of populations, and the constitution of melting pots" (Jacques Robichez), seeking in this way to destroy the Continent's racial, cultural, and ethnic foundations. They endeavor, in effect, to impose a system in which Europeans are to be turned into an indifferent multiracial multitude, without roots or collective memories—programmed simply to consume.

This people-killing dogma represents, perhaps, the most noxious of liberalism's anti-European forms, for it legitimates the destruction of the European *ethnos*. The ethnocidal implications of this dogma are hardly ideological. In the last four decades, since 1962, when Africa breached Europe's southern frontier (Algeria), the Continent, and especially France, has been inundated by successive waves of Third World immigrants.[92] The amplitude of this inundation, involving masses and not individuals, is such that not a few demographers describe it as a "colonization."[93] If not soon halted, non-Europeans will come to comprise a majority of the Continent's population. French cities and towns will then resemble the bazaars of North Africa and its social life that of the occupied West Bank, while the Europid population which has occupied Eurasia's western extremities for the last 30,000 years will become a minority and those who previously failed to militarily conquer Europe will be allowed to take possession of its mutilated destiny, without a shot being fired.[94]

But more than promoting de-Europeanization and singling out certain non-white groups for special privileges, multiculturalists zealously demonize all who resist their ethnocidal practices. As *The Sunday Times* of London described it after "9/11," those doubting the desirability of multicultural society "have been cowed into silence for years, either by liberal guilt or through fear of the bullies of the race-relations industry."[95] In addition to preventing public discussion of their policies and fomenting a form of anti-white racism, multiculturalists have pressured European governments into passing an array of draconian laws to punish whoever criticizes immigration, resists the invasion of diverse, hostile peoples, or questions the race-mixing ideas undergirding their immigrationist ideology.[96] Unprecedented numbers of dissidents now, in fact, face heavy fines and imprisonment for defending their European identity.

The non-white *Völkerwanderung* multiculturalists promote is creating a highly explosive and untenable social situation, for France, like Europe as a whole, lacks the massive police apparatus and vast geographical expanses that have kept ethnoracial tensions "manageable" in the US. Typically, in urban areas, where neighborhoods have been lost to Muslim immigrants, Europeans have experienced not only escalating levels of violence and insecurity, they have quite literally lost control of their laws and institutions. There are presently 1,400 *zones de non-droit* in France (including eleven towns) and in nearly a hundred of these, republican jurisdiction has been supplanted by *sharia* (Islamic law).[97] Unlike the Little Italys and Germantowns of nineteenth- and early twentieth-century urban America, these *zones* have not the slightest intention of assimilating into the *dar-al-Harb* (the "impious" non-Islamic world, which Muslims view as the "world of war") and frequently, in small and increasingly not so small ways, assert their autonomy *vis-à-vis* it.[98]

As André Gandillon argues in his great book on the *lutte des peuples*, "the immigrant who refuses to assimilate adopts the attitude of the conqueror."[99] Hardly a week passes now without a newspaper report of a riot or bloody clash between police and Muslim gangs. Since 1990, French urban violence has grown 5 percent annually—since 2000, by 10 percent—as the fragmentation, violence, and disintegration associated with America's inner cities become an increasingly familiar European reality.[100] Other European countries with large immigrant colonies, especially Britain, Belgium, Italy, Greece, and Germany, are experiencing comparable problems, as their populations are polarized along similar ethnoracial lines. The lawlessness and fragmentation of such multiracial societies are now such that talk of a "return of the Middle Ages" (i.e., the breakdown of public order) is more and more to be heard.[101]

In face of this overwhelming threat to the existence of European peoples, the media, the academy, and the established "anti-racist" organizations (most dominated by Jews and Zionists) castigate whoever criticizes such changes, all the while making the term "multiculturalism" emblematic of the mobile postmodern society of optional values and fashionable identities that comes with globalization.[102] Emboldened by these self-flagellating exhibitions, the more militant members of France's Muslim community now openly contemplate a *jihad* against the "white cheese," using the language of war and genocide to frame their objectives.[103] Public authorities, though, persist in distinguishing between violent fundamentalists (who number perhaps 35,000) and the "peace-loving" Islamic community, unable or unwilling to acknowledge Islam's inherent hostility to Western secular society.[104] Yet, contrary to these official professions, Islam's history and teachings, as a large and growing identitarian literature documents, suggest that theocracy, violence, conquest, and a not so implicit hatred of the tolerant and inherently polytheistic nature of European peoples are pre-eminent—not incidental or aberrant—Muslim attributes. Between orthodox and fundamentalist Islam, there is, arguably, only a difference in temperament. And even this has been compromised by fundamentalist aggressions that enflame religious antagonisms.

In the view of not a few identitarians, Islam represents nothing less than a totalitarian creed, worse than Communism, for it regulates the entirety of a Muslim's life—from the way he wipes his backside to the way he wars on infidels.[105] Since the Hegira, Islam has consistently sought to impose its inflexible strictures not only on its own adherents, but on non-Muslims through an avowed policy of violence and conquest. Years before the "9/11" attack on the US, Islam had already begun its third great offensive against the *dar-al-Harb*, targeting Europe as a future Muslim homeland.[106] As Islamists set their sights on the Continent, multiculturalists busily prepare their way—in the spirit of their "criminal and exterminationist policies" (Robert Steuckers)—by denigrating the integrity of European culture, knowing full well that to demoralize a people is the best way of conquering it. It should come as no surprise, then, that a growing number of New Rightists believes the growth of European Islam constitutes nothing less than the opening salvo in what is likely to be a larger military struggle for the Continent's future.[107]

As Gehlen and others have demonstrated, infusions of "difference" are sources of wealth to a society only if there is a firm cultural core to assimilate them. To destroy this core by imposing a variety of cultural models, each with a different order of values, inevitably leads to the dissolution of established norms.[108] Multiculturalism, though, is more than anti-cultural; it is anti-democratic, for it realigns political, social, and cultural spheres in ways that dissolve ethnic cohesion and hence popular power, somewhat in the way the *millet* system of the former Ottoman empire did.[109] This anti-democratic effect has been especially destructive in the working class, where "cultural diversity" destroys those common memories, neighborhood solidarities, and organizational opportunities that once fostered European labor solidarity.[110] All strata of the European population, however, have been plagued by the breakdown of the dominant ethnocultural model, for the defense of their distinct interests now automatically risks the stigma of "racism."[111] Finally, in promoting the religious, cultural, and racial fragmentation of European society, multiculturalism enhances the power of the ruling liberal elites (*le parti américain*) by channeling rising levels of violence and insecurity into interconfessional or intercultural disputes that leave the system responsible for such conditions virtually unscathed.[112]

In contrast to liberalism's homogenized world of fractured cultures and peoples, New Rightists advocate a heterogeneous world of homogeneous peoples, each rooted in their own culture and soil.[113] Every people, they claim, has *le droit à la différence*: that is, the right to pursue their destiny in accord with the organic dictates of their distinct identity. They see, moreover, no convincing reason why Europeans should feel obliged to abandon their millennial heritage for the sake of certain dubious cosmopolitan fashions.

Recently, however, the GRECE's opposition to multiculturalism has undergone a significant shift. Until 1998, it opposed multiculturalist efforts to recognize immigrant communities as separate legal entities, for it claimed these efforts threatened the integrity of French identity.[114] Then, rather unexpectedly, it reversed course, adopting a "communitarian" position favoring the public recognition of non-French communities—so that immigrants would be able to "keep alive the structures of their collective cultural existence."[115] For some, this shift constituted nothing less than an identitarian betrayal, for others a recognition that Europe's enemy is not the immigrant *per se*, but the system responsible for the dissolution of meaningful identities.

For its critics, the New Right's communitarian turn highlights a major flaw in the GRECE's metapolitical project. Unlike Gramsci's notion of cultural struggle, which supplemented rather than replaced politics, the GRECE's metapolitics has always been more intellectual than political.[116] It initially conceived of its cultural interventions as part of a larger identitarian project to dislodge the ideological foundations of the postwar order for the sake of advancing the European idea—i.e., it saw itself as a metapolitical force. But in tending to emphasis the cultural to the exclusion of the political, it distorted what many consider the essence of metapolitics. Thus, while the existing far Right parties, particularly the National Front, absorbed certain of its ideas, using them to circumvent certain restraints imposed by the dominant discourse, the GRECE maintained no formal or informal links with this or other anti-system parties and, through its often "sharp" criticisms, burned its bridges to most of them. Even the extra-parliamentary world of revolutionary conservatives, radical nationalists, and post-fascists was kept at bay. This problem deepened in the late eighties, when many of the GRECE's founders departed the organization to affiliate with the National Front. As a younger, less politically experienced generation of intellectuals refilled its ranks, the GRECE's metapolitics increasingly gravitated to the rarefied and often navel-gazing world of high ideas or esoteric cultural figures.[117] By the early nineties, it was even prepared to acknowledge that its cultural role was simply to interpret, no longer to change, the world.[118] And here, noticeably, it began assuming positions inconsistent with its original *raison d'être*.[119]

When *Grécistes* initially sloganized *le droit à la différence*, they had sought to rebuff liberal efforts to stigmatize European identitarianism as a form of racism. At a certain point, however, their defense of cultural and ethnic difference took on a life of its own. From defending the French in France and Europeans in Europe, *le droit à la différence* gradually evolved into an abstract defense of identity. And this eventually led to a qualified multiculturalism, as the GRECE reversed much of its earlier argumentation and joined the liberal chorus demanding the institutional recognition of the immigrants' cultural identity—in the name of "difference." But the problem did not end there, for its defense of European identity has consistently been waged on the Left's cosmopolitan terrain—in that it fights not for the primacy of European peoples in Europe, but for the application of pluralistic standards to support Europeans in the defense of their heritage.

In assuming in this way the pluralistic ground of their adversaries, *Grécistes* inevitably compromised their identitarianism, for Europeans never needed—nor need now—to justify being European: more to the point, they were obliged to assert a monopoly in their own lands. *Le droit à la différence* ended up, then, parroting the ideology of liberal pluralist society and its relativist values.[120] Obviously, this augurs badly for the future of the GRECE's identitarianism, for it now tacitly acknowledges the right of non-Europeans to occupy and partition European lands. The mantle of European identitarianism, as a result, is beginning to pass from Benoist's organization to associations and concerns linked to a more steadfast, and racially conscious identitarianism, such as Robert Steuckers, Guillaume Faye, Pierre Vial, Pierre Krebs, and others, whose understanding of the New Right project, while still metapolitical, continues to aim at a revolutionary transformation of the state, rather than a compromising reconciliation with liberal policies promising their death as a people and civilization.

If *Grécistes* have perilously back-pedaled on multiculturalism, they have nevertheless remained steadfast in opposing human rights, its legal counterpart.[121] As a key component of the current globalizing process, the present world crusade for human rights originated with America's humiliation in Vietnam, after which the Carter Administration tried to revamp its morally tarnished foreign policy by cloaking itself in certain liberal ideals.[122] Human rights have since become not only a central ideological component of US policy, but "the moral horizon of our times" (Robert Badinter). As such, they form the cornerstone of what is often called the New World Order. That all men possess certain fundamental rights is, of course, a notion stemming from a longer liberal tradition (in which "natural rights," derived from man's humanity, are opposed to common rights, based on specific sociohistorical attachments). In place of the organic bonds regulating traditional society, human rights appeal to the rule of law—whose "unconditional" rationality allegedly resides in nature and whose basic intent is to protect "inalienable" liberties. Like earlier arguments for natural rights, such jerry-built rights presuppose an abstract humanity and make no reference to either the ethical consensus or cultural context to which common rights apply.[123] At the same time, such rights invoke numerous dubious principles, assuming the unity of mankind, the primacy of the individual, and the equality of all men.[124] The individualistic focus of human rights similarly takes no account of the society to which the individual belongs, according no right to group or collective entities.[125] They simply presume that rights pertinent to an Englishman coincide with those of an Eskimo—that such rights "are right and true and unchanging for all people everywhere" (George W. Bush). They are another abstraction derived from Cartesian rationality.

Given their liberal capitalist origins, Karl Marx and earlier generations of socialists were unrelenting in excoriating the advocates of human rights, pointing out that their universal principles were not just projections of their particular interests, but a means to promote the most naked class or imperialist interests. By contrast, the contemporary Left (in the form of what Germans call the *Ampelkoalition* of liberals, social democrats, and Greens) makes human rights a defining feature of its project.[126] Here again Marxist and liberal projects have converged. For once liberal modernity triumphed over its Soviet variant and demonstrated the superiority of its market, the socialist Left had nothing but the "inclusionary" potential of "bourgeois humanism" by which to define itself. In this spirit, it now identifies not only with the ideology of human rights, it enlists in many of the imperialist crusades waged under their banner. The 1991 war on Iraq and the murderous "humanitarian" assault on Christian Serbia in the civilizational wars of Bosnia and Kosovo, which every nineteenth-century socialist would have condemned as sordid, mercenary affairs, were, for this reason, nearly everywhere supported by it.[127] It seems hardly coincidental that the Left no longer struggles for a society without economic or class exploitation, but instead devotes itself to a world without nations, races, and religions, as it calls on all people to unite under the rainbow banner of the global market.

In opposing Washington's human rights crusade (which has virtually nothing to do with opposition to torture, brutality, or other objectionable practices), Benoist points out that if these rights inspired by the individualist principles of the liberal market were applied worldwide, they would justify the abolition of the Hindu caste system, Confucianism, Islam, and virtually every vestige of traditional culture—because traditional cultures refuse to privilege the individual at the expense of his community. These rights threaten historical forms of social solidarity. Max Scheler once noted that "the love of humanity [to which the human rights ideology appeals] emerged primarily as a protest against the love of the fatherland and consequently became a protest against every organized community."[128]

In this spirit, the liberal today loudly proclaims the "rights of man," but has not a word for the rights of communities, the rights of peoples, the rights of nations, the rights of states, or what Catholics once referred to as "the rights of God." Of these rights, whose integrity resists unregulated markets and the atomizing forces of bourgeois individualism, the liberal accords no recognition.[129] Like Jacobin or Soviet concepts of rights, the liberal's *Menschenrechtimperialismus* (Konrad Pingel) rejects every communal or particularist notion of a common particular good.[130] These rights, though, are not even a true "polytheism of values," for the only rights they actually acknowledge are those sanctioning activities favored by the global market.[131] Such classic liberties as freedom of speech, especially when linked to anti-liberal ideas, are not only not recognized, but often suppressed in their name. European liberties have, in fact, never been as compromised, as in this so-called age of human rights.[132]

## Virtual Totalities

In promoting feminism, multiculturalism, and human rights (in addition to individualism, equality, and universalism), liberalism portrays itself as an indomitable champion of liberty. Yet behind this self-representation lies a system of political domination that is arguably more intrusive than that of any former totalitarian regime. This at least is the opinion of the distinguished Soviet dissident, Alexander Zinoviev, who claims liberal societies now control their populations in ways that Hitler's Germany and Stalin's Russia never dreamt of.[133] The American-led West might have opposed Soviet tyranny during the Cold War, but to New Rightists, who share Zinoviev's view, the ostensible differences between the two rival hegemons were never as significant as their underlying similarities.[134]

Benoist claims totalitarianism (an admittedly disputed term) is characterized less by specific policies or formal characteristics than by a system of thought that ideologically reduces the whole of social reality to "a single truth, a single way of life, a single manifestation of good and evil."[135] Emerging in industrializing societies whose old social structures and norms had given way to ones infused with anomie and despair, classic totalitarianism addressed not simply the social problems distinct to liberal capitalist societies, but the existential void they inevitably created.[136] An important function of totalitarian ideology was to provide a secular belief system for masses experiencing a crippling loss of meaning.[137] In this spirit, classic totalitarianism called on a chosen people (the proletariat, the Aryan, Economic Man) to realize its "paradise on earth."

Though earlier theorists (such as Karl Popper, Hannah Arendt, Jacob Talmon, Carl J. Friedrich, Raymond Aron, and Zbigniew Brzezinski) assumed liberalism was inherently anti-totalitarian, Benoist argues that, historically, liberalism not only created conditions requiring totalitarian remedies, it today has the potential of becoming totalitarian whenever it succeeds in subordinating life's multiple dimensions to the quantitative logic of its economic system.[138] Another identitarian defines totalitarianism as having "nothing to do with method" and everything to do with systematizing "the totality of existence."[139]

From this perspective, Communism appears less alien to liberalism than the Cold Warriors made it out to be. Besides arising in response to liberal injustice, capitalist exploitation, and the market's unrelenting commodification of social relations, Communism's ideological roots lay in the same soil as liberalism, for both systems conceptually anchored themselves in Enlightenment ideas and shared similar technoeconomic models of the state (privileging optimum economic performance, higher living standards, egalitarian conditions, and a highly rationalized social order).[140] Because liberal regimes had difficulty fulfilling their promise of equality or regulating the unstable social aggregates their pulverization of traditional communities created, totalitarian alternatives often took on a certain attraction. A frustrated egalitarianism thus arose to demand drastic measures, including terror, to realize socioeconomic goals that moderate capitalist regimes had failed to achieve.[141] Through the forced mobilization of aggrieved populations, totalitarians endeavored, in effect, to accelerate developments that had taken decades, even centuries, to accomplish in the more advanced liberal societies. This dictated draconian methods, but less to enhance a tyrannical minority, as liberal individualists claim, than to create a tyranny of all against all for the sake of certain shared social aspirations.[142]

In traditional organic societies, the holistic yet hierarchical character of social life made such a monolithic system of controls impossible.[143] In classic liberal regimes, it was prevented by the separation of powers, as Church, state, and civil society competed with one another. However, with the end of the Second European Civil War, especially the end of the Cold War following it, Western societies have increasingly resorted to totalizing forms of rule, as they evolve into market-driven technocracies, whose cybernetic principles dominate almost the entire range of human existence, from the macro-structures of state and economy to the micro-personal realms of everyday life.[144] Since these technocracies no longer feel oblige to maintain the formal appearance of freedom, as was the case when their competition with the Soviets required it, everything obstructing the requirements of their totally administered world is now routinely repressed.

Contemporary totalitarianism, though, differs significantly from its classic forms. Given the available "cool" technologies (which have completed the Cartesian mathematicization of life), the "hard power" of earlier totalitarian regimes has ceded to a more efficient "soft power." Political control, in effect, no longer requires physical force, for the system targets the mind and the way individuals are "processed" to conform to its functional requirements. Through the "spectacular" organization of daily life, an asocial, self-referential consumerism (privileging individual gratification at the expense of communal loyalties) is now able to seduce credulous masses through an endless array of seductively packaged images that override critical self-reflection, program compliance, and render everything into the standardizing language of commerce.[145] As Jean Baudrillard observes, "muscled politics" is superfluous, for the system's digital manipulation of simulacra—what he calls its "ideology of technomorphic conditioning"—makes men desirous of their own servitude.[146]

Through image-based advertising, televisual narratives, and behavior manipulations appealing to the brain's right hemisphere, where information is emotionally processed, the system simulates a world of programmed images that only obliquely refers to real referents. Cut up, decontextualized, rearranged, reversed, looped and endlessly replayed, these images condition the way the individual perceives, and hence relates to, his environment. "Reality" is thus turned into a staged spectacle—a hyperreality—whose swirl of signs is little more than a program.[147] But once lived experience is lost to simulation in this way, the spectator is inevitably left ignorant, distracted, and psychologically dependent. One Russian identitarian notes: "We are quickly losing any general representation about the sense of life, about the logic of history, about the problems of man, about the destiny of the world."[148] This, moreover, is an increasingly necessary facet of market-driven technocracies, for individual estrangement from everyday existence is key to the individual's compulsion to live within its imaginary world.[149] Television, for example, allows liberalism's solitary individual to "consume as spectacle all those things which real life now denies: sex, luxury, adventure, travel, etc." (Benoist).

Along with depriving the individual of a sense of memory, place, and time, the controlled media creating this world of simulated spectacles fosters a psychological situation in which an ego isolated from collective realities is allowed to engage in any activity or indulge any fantasy—as long as it is devoid of meaningful social content.[150] The self (as in Aldous Huxley's dystopia) looks to the system to fulfill those narcissistic desires that the system itself fosters. Freedom is consequently redefined as the "absence of constraints and coercion"—that is, as indulgence—and ceases to be a "means of achieving an objective through social action."[151] (In Baudrillard's formulation, freedom ceases to be an "action" and becomes "a spiritual and consensual form of interaction.")[152] The system's highly touted "emancipation" and "empowerment" are similarly associated with consumerist forms of behavior and narcissistic identities, while the "good life" becomes a question of goods.

The system's totalitarian disposition is especially evident in its depoliticization. For once its regulatory logic assumes responsibility for order and its experts carry out the operations necessary to its maintenance, political questions are replaced by technical ones. Self-perpetuation then becomes the sole legitimating criteria for its continuing existence. Whatever or whoever threatens these criteria is treated, it follows, as a programming error. To debar whatever it finds distasteful, public discussion and other forms of discourse are conducted under the auspices of political correctness and "hate speech" laws.[153] Debate, dispute, and dissent are similarly programmed out of its "spectacular" conception of freedom, while thoughts and actions deviating from the reigning orthodoxies are deemed "phobic" and subject, as in the former Soviet Union, to clinical treatment, "sensitivity training," or ostracism.[154] Information, in fact, has become so managed that one American conservative now claims that US news accounts—what David Barsamian calls "nuzak"—must be read "in roughly the same way that Sovietologists used to read *Pravda*, scoring articles for little tell-tale facts buried deep within."[155] The few brave individuals still standing upright among the ruins of our former freedoms might not fear being sent to a "Gulag," but their books are not published, their access to public forums are denied, and their reputations discredited.[156]

Aleksandr Solzhenitsyn once said of his American exile that he had passed from a system in which one could say nothing (for everything had significance) to one where anything could be said without effect.[157] To New Rightists, this is key to the present totalitarian disposition of Western societies, for liberal freedoms have become largely meaningless in a world combining "perpetual surveillance with total indulgence." Thus, whenever the soft totalitarian regimes of the West speak of freedom, what they actually mean is the freedom to do business or engage in licentious behavior, not the freedom to participate in government, challenge the system's presuppositions, or pursue contrary options. Moral, aesthetic, and ideological opposition is likewise resisted, while "real cultural freedom encounters innumerable obstacles."[158] Such liberal managerial regimes may consequently look and act differently from earlier forms of totalitarianism and even legitimate themselves as desirable alternatives to them, but their means of control are, arguably, even more insidious and destructive.

## Notes to Chapter III

1. Alain de Benoist, *Orientations pour des années décisives* (Paris: Le Labyrinthe, 1982), 42–43. Although *Grécistes* distinguish between the different schools of liberalism, for simplicity's sake they are here conflated.
2. Alain de Benoist, "Le libéralisme contre les identités collectives," in *Aux sources de l'erreur libérale: Pour sortir de l'étatisme et du libéralisme*, ed. Benjamin Guillemand and Arnaud Guyot-Jeannin (Lausanne: L'Âge d'Homme, 1999); Thierry Maulnier, *Au-delà du nationalisme* (Paris: Les Grands Classiques de l'Homme de Droite, 1993), 127–41.
3. John A. Hall, *Liberalism: Politics, Ideology and the Market* (Chapel Hill: University of North Carolina Press, 1987), 9–32.
4. Anthony Kenny, *The Metaphysics of Mind* (Oxford: Oxford University Press, 1992). Certain neo-Cartesians have nonetheless sought to breathe new life into Descartes' scheme. For example, Paul M. Churchland, *Matter and Consciousness* (Cambridge, MA: MIT Press, 1984).

5. The key work criticizing modernity's quantifying essence is René Guénon, *The Reign of Quantity and the Signs of the Times*, trans. Lord Northbourne (Ghent, NY: Sophia Perennis, 1995). On Guénon, see Paul Sérant, *René Guénon* (Paris: Le Courrier du Livre, 1977); more generally, see Kenneth Oldmeadow, *Traditionalism: Religion in the Light of the Perennial Philosophy* (Colombo: Sri Lanka Institute of Traditional Studies, 2000); Raido, *Die Welt der Tradition*, trans. Martin Schwartz (Dresden: Verlag Zeitenwende, 1998). Also Robert de Herte, "Le règne de la quantité," *Éléments* 28–29 (March 1979); Arnaud Guyot-Jeannin, "Traditionalisme intégral et révolutionnaire en France," *Éléments* 74 (Spring 1992).
6. Louis de Bonald, *Pensées*, ed. Michel Toda (Paris: Perrin et Perrin, 1998), 24.
7. René Guénon, *The Crisis of the Modern World*, trans. Arthur Osborne (Ghent, NY: Sophia Perennis, 1996), 27.
8. Cf. Arnold Gehlen, "Die Bedeutung Descartes für eine Geschichte der Bewussstsein" (1937), in *Gesamtausgabe* (Frankfurt am Main: Klostermann, 1980), vol. 2.
9. Cf. Roberto Fondi, *La Révolution organiciste*, trans. Philippe Baillet (Paris: Le Labyrinthe, 1986).
10. Not coincidentally, all subsequent liberal reductions have followed on the same basis, for in taking reason's quantitative representations as the sole explicative source of worldly phenomena, human endeavors were hereafter viewed in terms of a few simple principles (such as self-interest, class struggle, the pleasure principle, etc.), which eliminated most realms of human experience from rational consideration. See Guillaume Faye, "Warum Wir Kämpfen," *Elemente für die europäische Wiedergeburt* 1 (July 1986).
11. Guénon, *The Reign of Quantity and the Signs of the Times*, 30–32.
12. Guido de Ruggiero, *The History of European Liberalism*, trans. R. G. Collingwood (Gloucester, MA: Peter Smith, 1981 [1925]), 21. Michael Oakeshott calls this substitution of method for substance a confusion of "technical knowledge" with "practical knowledge." For a critique of liberal rationalism overlapping part of the GRECE's (although one suffering from a suffocating abstractionism), see Oakeshott, "Rationalism in Politics" (1947), in *Rationalism in Politics and Other Essays* (Indianapolis: Liberty Fund, 1991). The other offshoot of Enlightenment liberalism, Marxism, is similarly Cartesian. Marx's labor theory of value, the pillar of his theoretical edifice, was, for example, based on a purely quantitative and rationalist concept of labor, alien to any artisanal or traditional concept. See Alain de Benoist, "Marx et le travail," *Krisis* 18 (November 1995).
13. Ludwig von Mises, *Liberalism in the Classical Tradition*, trans. Ralph Raico (San Francisco: Cobden Press, 1985 [1927]), 75.
14. Samuel Coleridge: "In all countries and in all ages, [the class of shopkeepers] has been, is now, and ever will be, the least patriotic and the least conservative of any." Extract from *Table Talk* (1832), in R. J. White, ed., *The Conservative Tradition* (New York: New York University Press, 1950), 156. Also Alain de Benoist, "Le bourgeois figure et domination," *Éléments* 72 (Winter 1991).
15. Francis Parker Yockey, *The Proclamation of London* (London: The Rising Press, 2001 [1949]), 5.

16. Richard Rorty, *Philosophy and the Mirror of Nature* (Princeton, NJ: Princeton University Press, 1979), 148.
17. Pierre Chassard, "De quelques morales négatives," *Krisis* 8 (April 1991). Kant was actually something of a "racist," though, revealingly, it was his "common human reason" that led him to think that people who lived like savages were "inferior" to those who lived in the complex societies of the white West.
18. Alain de Benoist, "Minima moralia," *Krisis* 7 (February 1991).
19. Alain de Benoist, "Comment le lien social a été rompu," *Éléments* 84 (February 1996).
20. Guénon, *The Reign of Quantity and the Signs of the Times*, 62.
21. Louis Rougier, *Du paradis à l'utopie* (Paris: Copernic, 1979), 194–95.
22. For a critique of the dominant economist illusions, see Michel Henochsberg, *Nous, nous sentions comme une sale espèce* (Paris: Denoël, 1999).
23. Alain de Benoist, *Les idées à l'endroit* (Paris: Hallier, 1979), 85.
24. Albert O. Hirschman, *The Passions and the Interests: Political Arguments for Capitalism Before Its Triumph* (Princeton, NJ: Princeton University Press, 1977).
25. Raymond Ruyer, *Les cent prochains siècles: Le destin historique de l'homme selon la Nouvelle Gnose américaine* (Paris: Fayard, 1977), 278. Cf. Friedrich A. Hayek, *The Constitution of Liberty* (Chicago: University of Chicago Press, 1960), 11–12.
26. Max Scheler, *On Feeling, Knowing, and Valuing: Selected Writings*, ed. Harold J. Bershady (Chicago: University of Chicago Press, 1992), 70. Cf. Ferdinand Tönnies, *Community and Society*, trans. C. P. Loomis (New York: Harper Torchbook, 1963 [1887]).
27. In the French Declaration of the Rights of Man (1789), article IV states: "Liberty consists essentially in being able to do whatever is not harmful to others; thus the exercise of the natural rights of each individual has no limits." See De Ruggiero, *The History of European Liberalism*, 67–68. Later liberals, like T. H. Green and L. T. Hobhouse, recognized that these rights were mere formalities as long as there were no educational system or social supports to prepare the individual for their exercise. In their various social engineering schemes, Left liberals today fully acknowledge the importance of social conditions for individualization. But like their predecessors, these social liberals still take individualization as their ideal, even if they see the bureaucratic agencies of the interventionist state as key to its realization. They likewise continue to think that the principal impetus to personal development comes from within the individual and not from society and culture.
28. Charles Champetier, "La Droite et la communauté," in *Aux sources de la Droite: Pour en finir avec les clichés*, ed. Arnaud Guyot-Jeannin (Lausanne: L'Âge d'Homme, 2000).
29. Alain de Benoist, "Le temps des hypocrites" (1992), in *L'écume et les galets, 1991–1999: Dix ans d'actualité vue d'ailleurs* (Paris: Le Labyrinthe, 2000).
30. Quoted in Alain de Benoist, "La liberté, la politique et la démocratie," *Éléments* 107 (December 2002).
31. Benoist, "Comment le lien social a été rompu"; Alain de Benoist, "Une philosophie impossible et inutile," *Éléments* 107 (December 2002). This emphasis on the social constituents of individualism by no means implies a hostility

to personalism or a penchant for a faceless collectivism. As the revolutionary conservative Hans Freyer puts it: "*In Wir wird die individuelle Verschiedenheit des einzelnen nicht ausgelöscht, sondern diese gehen mit ihrer Totalität, und das heisst mit ihren Unterschieden, in die Synthese des Wir ein.*" See *Soziologie als Wirklichkeitswissenschaft* (Leipzig: Teubner, 1930), 246.

32. Alain de Benoist, *Démocratie: Le problème* (Paris: Le Labyrinthe, 1985), 30. (The first chapter of this work has been translated into English in *Telos* 95 [Spring 1993] as "Democracy Revisited.")
33. Alain de Benoist, "Communautariens vs. Libéraux," *Krisis* 16 (June 1994); Alain de Benoist, "Carnets VI," *Études et recherches* 5 (Fall 1987); Jean Varenne, "Pourquoi la cause des peuples?," in *La cause des peuples: Actes du XVe colloque national du GRECE* (Paris: Le Labyrinthe, 1982). Cf. Hermann Keyserling, *Europe*, trans. Maurice Samuel (New York: Harcourt, Brace and Co., 1928), 392; Régis Debray, *Critique de la raison politique* (Paris: Gallimard, 1981), 48. Wittgenstein quoted in Gianni Vattimo, *The Transparent Society*, trans. David Webb (Baltimore: Johns Hopkins University Press, 1992), 18.
34. Pierre Le Vigan, "Clairière et sentiers de bûcherons," *Éléments* 74 (Spring 1992).
35. Alain de Benoist, "L'ennemi principal" (Part II), *Éléments* 41 (March–April 1982).
36. Jean Cau, *Discours de la décadence* (Paris: Copernic, 1978), 47; Arnold Gehlen, "Gleichheit" (1964), in *Gesamtausgabe* (Frankfurt am Main: Klostermann, 1978), vol. 7. Cf. John Locke, *Of Civil Government* (London: Everyman, 1943), 117.
37. Tomislav Sunic, *Against Democracy and Equality: The European New Right* (New York: Peter Lang, 1990), 97. Cf. J. Roland Pennock and J. W. Chapman, eds., *Equality* (New York: Atherton Press, 1967); Amy Gutmann, *Liberal Equality* (Cambridge: Cambridge University Press, 1980); Alex Callinicos, *Equality* (Cambridge: Polity, 2000).
38. John Dewey, *Liberalism and Social Action* (New York: G. P. Putnam's Sons, 1980), 69.
39. Cf. Norberto Bobbio, *Left and Right: The Significance of a Political Distinction*, trans. Allan Cameron (Chicago: University of Chicago Press, 1996), 67.
40. Arnold Gehlen, *Man: His Nature and Place in the World*, trans. Clare McMillan and Karl Pillemer (New York: Columbia University Press, 1988), 63.
41. Cf. Julius Evola and René Guénon, *Hiérarchie et démocratie* (Paris: Éds. de l'Homme Libre, 1999), 24; Jared Taylor, "Twelve Years of American Renaissance," *American Renaissance* 13:11 (November 2002).
42. Cf. Richard J. Herrnstein and Charles Murray, *The Bell Curve: Intelligence and Class Structure in American Life* (New York: The Free Press, 1994); Arthur R. Jensen, *The g Factor: The Science of Mental Ability* (Westport, CT: Praeger, 1998).
43. Paul Piccone, "Confronting the French New Right: Old Prejudices or a New Political Paradigm?," *Telos* 98–99 (Winter 1993–Spring 1994).
44. "Thème central: L'idée nominaliste," *Nouvelle École* 33 (Summer 1979); Aleksandr Solzhenitsyn, "A World Split Apart," Harvard discourse of June 8, 1978.
45. Robert de Herte, "Un instrument de domination," *Éléments* 107 (December 2002).

46. The absurdity of such thinking was perhaps most devastatingly rebuffed in Arthur Keith, *A New Theory of Evolution* (London: C. A. Watts, 1948), a work that earned this great thinker the crushing neglect of posterity.
47. Alain de Benoist, "Fondements nominalistes d'une attitude devant la vie," *Nouvelle École* 33 (Summer 1979).
48. Pierre Krebs, *Die europäische Wiedergeburt* (Tübingen: Grabert, 1982), 28–29.
49. Benoist, "L'ennemi principal" (Part II); Pierre Le Vigan, "Après le progrès, l'aventure continue," *Cartouches: L'actualité des idées* 3 (August 1997).
50. Benoist, "Le libéralisme contre les identités collectives." Cf. E. G. West, *Adam Smith: The Man and His Works* (Indianapolis: Liberty Fund, 1976), 14.
51. For example, George Soros, *The Crisis of Global Capitalism: Open Society Endangered* (New York: Public Affairs, 1998).
52. Guillaume Faye, *Contre l'économisme: Principes d'économie politique* (Paris: Le Labyrinthe, 1983), 61. Also Arnaud Guyot-Jeannin, "Le Droite et l'argent," in *Aux sources de la Droite: Pour en finir avec les clichés*, ed. Arnaud Guyot-Jeannin (Lausanne: L'Âge d'Homme, 2000).
53. Alain de Benoist, *Horizon 2000: Trois entretiens avec Alain de Benoist* (Paris: GRECE pamphlet, 1996). In this context, it is relevant to note that New Rightists in the National Front were instrumental in replacing the Front's former anti-trade union policies with a policy supportive of worker struggles, especially those against the globalizing forces of international capital. See Jacques Breitstein, "Offensive social du Front national," *Le Monde Diplomatique* (March 1997).
54. Othmar Spann, *The History of Economics*, trans. Eden and Cedar Paul (New York: Norton, 1930), 190.
55. Faye, *Contre l'économisme*, 23–24; Guillaume Faye, "La France s'appauvrit: Pourquoi?," *J'ai tout compris!* 12 (August 2001).
56. Benoist, *Horizon 2000*, 5–14. Against the neo-classical school of Smith and Ricardo, which continues to inform liberal economics, *Grécistes* and other New Rightists orient to the economic teachings of such anti-free trade theorists as Friedrich List and Othmar Spann, whose influence is still evident in Central Europe today. See Michel Sallon, "Friedrich List et son 'Système Nationale d'Économie Politique,'" and Alain de Benoist, "Sur List," *Nouvelle École* 45 (Winter 1988–89). Among contemporary economists, the French New Right is most influenced by François Perroux and Maurice Allais.
57. Quoted in Thierry Mudry, "Friedrich List: Une alternative au libéralisme," *Orientations* 5 (1988).
58. Karl Polanyi, *The Great Transformation: The Political and Economic Origins of Our Time* (Boston: Beacon Press, 1957).
59. Thomas Molnar, "Das Palast, der Tempel und die Zivilgesellschaft: Eine historische Kritik des Liberalismus," *Criticón* 135 (January 1993); Thomas Molnar, *L'hégémonie libérale* (Lausanne: L'Âge d'Homme, 1992). Cf. R. R. Palmer, *The Age of the Democratic Revolution: A Political History of Europe and America, 1760–1800*, 2 vols. (Princeton, NJ: Princeton University Press, 1959–64). The Roman concept of imperium dominated the post-medieval European state system, as it sought to restore the unity of the *res publica*, which had been weakened during the late Middle Ages. As theoretically elaborated by Machiavelli,

the modern state would represent the people or the nation, transcend the individual, and have sovereignty over society. It is this concept that eighteenth-century liberals attacked. See Alain de Benoist and Guillaume Faye, "Contre l'État-Providence," *Éléments* 44 (January 1983).

60. Benoist, *Orientations pour des années décisives*, 42–46; Guillaume Faye and Robert Steuckers, "La leçon de Carl Schmitt," *Éléments* 39 (Summer 1981).
61. Robert de Herte, "La politique retrouvée," *Éléments* 105 (June 2002); Julien Freund, "Que veut dire: prendre une décision?," *Nouvelle École* 41 (Fall 1984).
62. Cited in Yvan Blot, "L'identité française et son héritage antique," in *Les origines de la France*, ed. Jacques Robichez (Saint-Cloud: Éds. Nationales, n.d.).
63. Benoist and Faye, "Contre l'État-Providence."
64. John Chamberlain, *The Roots of Capitalism* (Indianapolis: Liberty Press, 1976), 67.
65. Carl Schmitt, *The Concept of the Political*, trans. George Schwab (Chicago: University of Chicago Press, 1996), 37; Alain de Benoist and Charles Champetier, "The French New Right in the Year 2000," *Telos* 115 (Spring 1999); Benoist, *Les idées à l'endroit*, 68.
66. Fabrice Laroche (Alain de Benoist), "Une nouvelle résistance," *Éléments* 16 (June 1976).
67. "Classical liberals," as well as contemporary libertarians, argue that this "statist" liberalism is liberal in name only, representing a form of socialism that in every respect is the opposite of all that liberalism originally entailed, especially in its assaults on private property. See Mises, *Liberalism in the Classical Tradition*. New Rightists, by contrast, see socialist statism not as the opposite, but the offshoot, of Enlightenment liberalism. Thus, while the "classical liberalism" of the nineteenth century differs from the "social liberalism" of the twentieth century, New Rightists see these differences as representing but a shift to bureaucratic interventionism, not a break with liberalism's underlying orientation to civil society and its economic, individualistic, and anti-traditional enterprises. For in both cases, the individual and the primacy of his rationally-motivated relations in the market remain central, with the classical liberal emphasizing the self-sufficiency of market mechanisms and the social liberal the necessity of state supports.
68. West, *Adam Smith*, 13.
69. Jonah Goldstein and Jeremy Rayner, "The Politics of Identity in Late Modern Society," *Theory and Society* 23:3 (June 1994); Alain de Benoist, "Un mot en quatre lettres," *Éléments* 95 (June 1999).
70. Peter van Ham, *European Integration and the Postmodern Condition: Governance, Democracy, Identity* (London: Routledge, 2001), 155–71.
71. Charles Champetier, "La res publica," *Éléments* 73 (Winter–Spring 1992).
72. See Zygmunt Bauman, *Intimations of Postmodernity* (London: Routledge, 1992), 199–203; Judith Squires, "In Different Voices: Deliberative Democracy and Aestheticist Politics," and Diana Coole, "Master Narratives and Feminist Subversions," in *The Politics of Postmodernity*, ed. James Good and Irving Velody (Cambridge: Cambridge University Press, 1998).
73. Guénon, *The Reign of Quantity and the Signs of the Times*, 3.

74. Alain de Benoist and Guillaume Faye, "Pour un État souverain," *Éléments* 44 (January 1983). It might be added that this has nothing to do with totalitarianism, which envisages the state not only as the representative of a people's collective self-interest, but as a force subordinating every social activity to its systemic needs.
75. On the GRECE's specific appropriation of Schmitt, see Alain de Benoist, *Vu de Droite: Anthologie critique des idées contemporaines*, 5th ed. (Paris: Copernic, 1979), 216-19; Alain de Benoist, "Préface," in Carl Schmitt, *Du politique*, ed. Alain de Benoist (Puiseaux: Pardès, 1990); Julien Freund, "Les lignes de force de la pensée politique de Carl Schmitt," *Nouvelle École* 44 (Spring 1987).
76. Guénon, *The Reign of Quantity and the Signs of the Times*, 77.
77. For an anti-liberal like James Burnham, whose *Suicide of the West: An Essay on the Meaning and Destiny of Liberalism* (Washington, DC: Regnery, 1964) represents perhaps the most important critique of liberalism to have been made by an American (after Yockey's *Imperium*), liberalism's de-Europeanizing thrust was sign that it was essentially an "ideology of Western suicide." In the name of certain mushy abstractions—equality, humanity, free enterprise, etc.—liberals, according to Burnham, not only refuse to defend the distinct qualities of their civilization, they justify policies that "corrupted the will and confounded the action" of Western peoples in their struggle against World Communism. New Rightists dispute not the descriptive character of Burnham's critique, but argue, instead, that he confused the symptoms of civilizational decline with its source. Instead of recognizing liberalism's quantitative spirit, which dismisses a civilization's cultural content and favors a generic culture, Burnham (the former Trotskyist) misread the nature of the liberal project, seeing it simply as a naive idealism rather than a culturally-hostile universalism. In a word, the real "suicide of the West" was not liberalism's susceptibility to Marxism, as Burnham unimaginatively claimed—but its indifference to its own civilizational heritage. That Burnham was a modernist, driven to anti-liberalism by anti-Communism, explains much of this. It also explains many of his mischaracterizations of the "world struggle" and the exaggerated character of his anti-Communism. On Burnham, see David Kelly, *James Burnham and the Struggle for the World: A Life* (Wilmington, DE: ISI Books, 2002). As a corrective to Kelly's neoconservative reading of Burnham, see Samuel Francis, "Burnham Agonistes," *Chronicles* (July 2002); also Samuel Francis, *Power and History: The Political Thought of James Burnham* (Lanham, MD: University Press of America, 1984).
78. Pierre Krebs, *Das Thule-Seminar: Geistesgegenwart der Zukunft in der Morgenröte des Ethnos* (Horn: Burkhart Weecke Verlag, 1994), 24.
79. Instead of "sex," feminists prefer the term "gender," arguing that the former designates the biological difference between males and females and the latter the "artificial" or socially constructed divisions between masculine and feminine roles. This terminological distinction implies that social construction is arbitrary and biological difference is a pretext, not the actual basis of social divisions. To accept the notion of "gender" is tantamount, then, to accepting the feminist contention that "gender differences" are purely social. As such, it is neither a neutral nor a scientific term. While New Rightists acknowledge that social roles are constructs and differ from one social order to another,

they nonetheless emphasize that they directly or indirectly relate to biological differences, which, contrary to feminist claims, are neither arbitrary nor insignificant.

80. Simone de Beauvoir, *The Second Sex*, trans. H. M. Parshley (New York: Vintage, 1952). On the aberrant character of feminist androgyny, see Guillaume Faye, *Sexe et idéologie* (Paris: Le Labyrinthe, 1984); Philippe Baillet, "Evola, la sexualité et le 'retour à la culture,'" *Études et recherches* 5 (Fall 1987); and Julius Evola, *Eros and the Metaphysics of Love* (Rochester, VT: Inner Traditions, 1983).
81. "Itinéraire," *Nouvelle École* 11 (January 1970); Benoist, *Vu de Droite*, 343-44; Yves Christen and Charles Champetier, "Biologie du beau sexe," *Éléments* 93 (October 1998); Yves Christen, *L'égalité des sexes* (Monaco: Rocher, 1987). Cf. James Dabbs, *Heroes, Rogues, and Lovers: Testosterone and Behavior* (New York: McGraw-Hill, 2000).
82. Cf. Julius Evola, "Feminismus und heroische Tradition," *Der Ring* (June 6, 1933).
83. Benoist, *Vu de Droite*, 364; Robert de Herte, "La preuve par deux," *Éléments* 93 (October 1998). Cf. Arnaud Guyot-Jeannin, ed., *Aux sources de l'éternel féminin: Pour en terminer avec tous les conformismes* (Lausanne: L'Âge d'Homme, 2001); Luce Irigaray, *Je, tu, nous: Pour une culture de la différence* (Paris: Grasset, 1990); Geneviève Fraisse, *La différence des sexes* (Paris: PUF, 1996).
84. Benoist, *Vu de Droite*, 346.
85. Quoted in "Itinéraire," *Nouvelle École* 11 (January 1970).
86. Laurence Terry, "Libérez les hommes!," *Éléments* 20 (February 1977).
87. Henri Gobard, *La guerre culturelle: Logique du désatre* (Paris: Copernic, 1979), 48-63; Charles Champetier, "La nouvelle cause des femmes," *Éléments* 93 (October 1998).
88. Robert de Herte, "Masculine/Féminine," *Éléments* 14-15 (March 1976).
89. Dominique Venner, *Histoire et tradition des européens: 30,000 ans d'identité* (Paris: Rocher, 2002), 186-88.
90. Alain de Benoist, *Famille et société: Origines, Histoire, Actualité* (Paris: Le Labyrinthe, 1996), 11.
91. Robert de Herte, "Réconcilier famille et société," *Éléments* 83 (October 1983); Benoist, *Famille et société*, 18-22.
92. Jean-Marie Le Pen: "*L'Algéria française aurait été le fer de lance de cette Europe en Afrique. Notre défaite* [in 1962] *a . . . laissé les portes ouvertes aux 'Barbares' qui affluent chez nous.*" Quoted in Grégory Pons, *Les rats noirs* (Paris: Jean-Claude Simoën, 1977), 50.
93. Alain Griotteray, *Immigration: Le choc* (Paris: Plon, 1984); Valéry Giscard d'Estaing, "Immigration ou invasion?," *Le Figaro Magazine* (August 21, 1991); Michel Massenet, *Sauvage immigration* (Paris: Rocher, 1994). One French identitarian notes that it is now no longer necessary to purchase an airplane ticket to encounter exotic civilizations: a visit to any one of Paris' 80 metro stations suffices. See Jean-Claude Rolinat, "En France comme ailleurs," *Terre et peuple: La revue* 7-8 (Summer 2001).
94. Cf. Theodore Dalrymple, "The Barbarians at the Gates of Paris," *City Journal* 12:4 (Autumn 2002). The number of non-Europeans in France is not officially known. The cited figure is the estimate of one of France's leading demographers.

See "L'avenir démographique: Entretien avec Jacques Dupâquier," *Krisis* 20-21 (November 1997). Another academic (Jean-Paul Gourévitch) claims it is closer to 9 million. Some put the figure as high as 14 million, while the media usually refer to 5 or 6 million. In Europe as a whole, there are an estimated 26 million. But qualitatively more alarming than these figures is the fact that one-third of the population under 30 is now of non-European origin and has a birth rate many times higher than the European one.

95. *The Sunday Times* (February 10, 2002), reprinted in *World Press Review* (April 2002).
96. Laurent Gouteron, "Le désordre juridique, miroir du désordre politique et morale," *Relève politique* 2 (Spring 2002).
97. Jeremy Rennher, "L'Occident ligoté par l'imposture antiraciste," *Écrits de Paris* 640 (February 2002). Even the politically correct editor of *Violence en France* (Paris: Seuil, 1999), Michel Wieviorka, acknowledges that the explosion of violence and criminality since 1990 is an outgrowth of Islamic power. Because the French government keeps most data on immigrant crime and racial terror securely under wraps, the little that is known has been surreptitiously leaked by frustrated officials. The publication with the best access to these leaks is the monthly *J'ai tout compris! Lettre de désintoxication*, edited by Guillaume Faye.
98. Jean-Raphaël de Sourel, *La fin de l'Europe et sa civilisation humaniste* (Paris: Éds. des Écrivains, 1999), 161-68.
99. André Gandillon, *Les fondements du XXIe siècle* (Paris: Éds. Roudil, 1992), 1:367.
100. *Le Figaro* (June 18, 2001); Xavier Raufer, *L'explosion criminelle* (Paris: Valmonde, 2001).
101. Lucien Robin, "La sécurité, un droit pour tous," *Écrits de Paris* 639 (January 2002); "L'implosion de l'état républicain français," *J'ai tout compris!* 16 (December 2001).
102. Robert Dun, "Réflexions d'un homme d'extrême-droite" (1993), in *Une vie de combat: Cartouches intellectuelles* (Saint-Étienne: Crève-Tabous, 2000).
103. *Inter alia*, see *Le Monde* (January 7, 1990, and January 30, 1990); *Le Matin de Paris* (November 9, 1986); *Le Figaro* (October 12, 2000); *InfoMatin* (December 18, 1995). Cf. Hans-Peter Raddatz, *Von Gott zu Allah? Christentum und Islam in der liberalen Fortschrittsgesellschaft* (Munich: Herbig, 2001); Christian Jelen, *La guerre des rues: La violence et "les jeunes"* (Paris: Plon, 2000).
104. "Les décombres," *Réfléchir et agir* 10 (Winter 2001). For Samuel P. Huntington, it is precisely this unwillingness to acknowledge cultural, religious, and civilizational sources of dispute that poses "the underlying problem for the West." See *The Clash of Civilizations and the Remaking of World Order* (New York: Simon and Schuster, 1996), 217.
105. For example, Guillaume Faye, *Avant-Guerre: Chronique d'un cataclysme annoncé* (Paris: L'Æncre, 2002), 15-18.
106. The first Arab wave of the seventh century brought the Muslims to Poitiers and the second Turkish wave of the twelfth to seventeenth centuries led to the destruction of Christian Byzantium, the occupation of the Balkans, and the storming of Vienna. The third wave, in the form of the present colonization, is more stealthy in character, but potentially more catastrophic.

107. Arnaud Menu, "L'islam et l'Europe: Deux visions du monde inconciliables," *Terre et peuple: La revue* 10 (Winter 2001). Identitarians increasingly evoke the need for a new *reconquista*. This is especially evident in Philippe Randa's novel *Poitiers demain* (Paris: Denoël, 2000) and the album *Reconquista* by the group Fraction on Heretik Records.
108. Guillaume Faye, "La société multiraciale en question," *Éléments* 48–49 (Winter 1983–84). Cf. John Gray, *Enlightenment's Wake: Politics and Culture at the Close of the Modern Age* (London: Routledge, 1995), 23–24.
109. On the *millet* system, see Sarkis Atamian, *The Armenian Community: The Historical Development of a Social and Ideological Conflict* (New York: Philosophical Library, 1955); H. A. R. Gibb and Harold Bowen, *Islamic Society and the West*, 2 vols. (London: Oxford University Press, 1950–57), especially volume 1. Cf. Tatu Vanhanen, *Ethnic Conflicts Explained by Ethnic Nepotism* (Stamford, CT: JAI Press, 1999).
110. Patrice Gros-Suaudeau, "Le règne du nouvel Ordre Mondial," *Écrits de Paris* 615 (November 1999).
111. For those inclined to believe that this is simply an unfortunate offshoot of generally well-intended policies and not their intended consequence, they might consult Éric Werner, *L'avant-guerre civile* (Lausanne: L'Âge d'Homme, 1998), or E. Michael Jones, *The Slaughter of Cities: Urban Renewal and Ethnic Cleansing* (South Bend, IN: St. Augustine's Press, 2002).
112. Cf. Samuel Francis, "Nations within Nations," *Chronicles* (January 1999).
113. Krebs, *Das Thule-Seminar*, 47–52.
114. Faye, "La société multiraciale en question."
115. Charles Champetier, "Multiculturalisme: La force des différences," *Éléments* 91 (March 1998); Benoist and Champetier, "The French New Right in the Year 2000." (The multicultural turn probably owed a good deal to the influence on Benoist of Piccone's "federal populist" crowd at *Telos* and of that of American communitarians, like Michael Sandel.)
116. Édouard Rix, "Gramsci, théoricien du pouvoir culturel," *Réfléchir et agir* 9 (Summer 2001).
117. The generational turnover has also led to a certain "softening" of the GRECE's anti-liberalism and a weakening of its ties to the revolutionary Right. This, I believe, relates to the growing depoliticization of its project and its increased emphasis on issues that, in seeking to engage the Left intelligentsia on its own turf, grants far too much to the ideas it seeks to subvert. For a characteristic example of this softening, see "Three Interviews with Alain de Benoist," *Telos* 98–99 (Winter 1993–Spring 1994).
118. "Présentation," *Éléments* 77 (n.d. [c. 1993]).
119. In tandem with its embrace of multiculturalism, the GRECE has also recently abandoned its Gramscian concept of metapolitics. A key document by Alain de Benoist and Charles Champetier now claims that: "Metapolitics is not politics by other means. It is neither a 'strategy' to impose intellectual hegemony, nor an attempt to discredit other possible attitudes or agendas. It rests solely on the premise that ideas play a fundamental role in the collective consciousness and, more generally, in history." See "The French New Right in the Year 2000"; also Charles Champetier, "Sur l'archéofuturisme," *Éléments* 95 (June 1999).

This redefinition, however, seems to make nonsense of the GRECE's cultural project, for such a concept of cultural activity ceases to be metapolitical — — in no longer seeking to reshape civil society for the sake of a political conquest. In repudiating the "political" and hence the link between theory and practice, its project consequently becomes purely "intellectual" — and indifferent. This contrasts with the revolutionary strategy to which it initially adhered — and to which many non-GRECE New Rightists still adhere. See "Entretien avec Jean-Claude Valla," *Éléments* 6 (July 1974); Benoist, *Vu de Droite*, 456–60; Pierre Vial, *Une terre, un peuple* (Villeurbanne: Terre et Peuple, 2000), 52–54.

120. For a perspicacious critique of the GRECE from an identitarian perspective, see "Cinq questions à Robert Steuckers sur la Nouvelle Droite," at *Archivio Eurasia* (http://utenti.tripod.it/ArchivEurasia). Also Guillaume Faye, *L'Archéofuturisme* (Paris: L'Æncre, 1998), 19–49.

121. Alain de Benoist, *Europe, Tiers monde, même combat* (Paris: Robert Laffont, 1986), 73.

122. Robert de Herte, "L'idéologie du troisième âge," *Éléments* 37 (January 1981).

123. Alain de Benoist and Guillaume Faye, "La religion des droits de l'homme," *Éléments* 37 (January 1981). Human rights, it might be added, are advanced as metaphysical postulates, as if rights were not the creation and conquest of real men. Cf. John Finnis, *Natural Law and Natural Rights* (Oxford: Oxford University Press, 1980). Behind the lofty idealism of human rights, it is important to stress that such rights have had little effect on the US practice of carpet-bombing civilians, organizing death squads, torturing prisoners, or contracting foreign agents to carry out assassinations, destabilize governments, and engage in drug trafficking.

124. Pierre Krebs, *Im Kampf das Wesen* (Horn: Burkhart Weecke Verlag, 1997), 26.

125. Charles Champetier, "Reflections on Human Rights," *Telos* 118 (Winter 2000).

126. Marx was unsparing in lambasting the bourgeois hypocrisy of human rights, which made grand humanitarian appeals camouflaging capital's "private interests and caprice." See, for example, "On the Jewish Question" (1843), in *Karl Marx: Early Texts*, trans. and ed. David McLellan (Oxford: Blackwell, 1972). (Does it mean anything that *Le Droit Humain* is the name of Masonry's Global Order?)

127. That the Left resisted Bush II's Iraqi war in 2003 testifies less to a change of heart than to its discomfort with his crude, bullying, and bellicose unilateralism, which discarded the rhetoric of human rights for those old-fashioned imperialist methods that human rights had made obsolete.

128. Quoted in Sunic, *Against Democracy and Equality*, 108. Cf. Charles Conant Josey, *The Philosophy of Nationalism* (Washington, DC: Scott-Townsend Publishers, 1995), 2.

129. Benoist, *Orientations pour des années décisives*, 39.

130. Benoist and Champetier, "The French New Right in the Year 2000."

131. Alain de Benoist, *Communisme et nazisme: 25 réflexions sur le totalitarisme* (Paris: Le Labyrinthe, 1998), 137–39.

132. Philippe de Saint-Robert, "Droits de l'homme, droits des peuples et langue de bois," *Éléments* 71 (Fall 1991).

133. Alexandre Zinoviev, *La grande rupture: Sociologie d'un monde bouleversé*, trans. Slobodan Despot (Lausanne: L'Âge d'Homme, 1999), 94, 102; Alain de Benoist, "Le système des médias," in *Critiques-Théoriques* (Lausanne: L'Âge d'Homme, 2002). Relatedly, many Russians think Westerners are far less conscious of—and resistant to—the "brainwashing" techniques of their own states than were the citizens of the former USSR. See Victor Loupan, *Le défi russe* (Paris: Éds. des Syrtes, 2000), 127.
134. Cf. Alex Delfini and Paul Piccone, "Modernity, Libertarianism and Critical Theory: Reply to Pellicani," *Telos* 112 (Summer 1998).
135. Faye, *Contre l'économisme*; Michael Walker, "Against All Totalitarianisms," *The Scorpion* 10 (Autumn 1986); Alain de Benoist, "Fortschritt in Grauen," *Junge Freiheit* (October 12, 2001).
136. Julien Freund, "Le conflit dans la société industrielle," *Nouvelle École* 45 (Winter 1988–89). Cf. Robert Nisbet, *The Quest for Community: A Study in the Ethics of Order and Freedom*, 3rd ed. (San Francisco: ICS Press, 1990).
137. Benoist, *Communisme et nazisme*, 99.
138. Claude Polin, *Le totalitarisme* (Paris: PUF, 1983). Cf. Hans-Dietrich Sander, "Die Charaktermasken des totalitären Liberalismus," *Staatsbriefe* (August 1996).
139. Today, for example, whenever the West asserts the primacy of human rights, these rights assume the same unreflective and authoritarian status as Marxist-Leninist principles did in the former Soviet Union, for their dogmatic assertion refuses all discussion outside their framework. See Walker, "Against All Totalitarianisms"; Alain de Benoist, "Introduction," in *L'écume et les galets, 1991–1999: Dix ans d'actualité vue d'ailleurs* (Paris: Le Labyrinthe, 2000).
140. Cf. J. L. Talmon, *The Origins of Totalitarian Democracy* (London: Secker and Warburg, 1952).
141. Benoist, *Les idées à l'endroit*, 159–62; Benoist, *Communisme et nazisme*, 127; Alain de Benoist, "Un totalitarisme peut en cacher un autre," *Éléments* 46 (Summer 1983). Cf. Eugen Weber, *Varieties of Fascism* (Princeton, NJ: Van Nostrand, 1964), 38, 54–56, 139.
142. Polin, *Le totalitarisme*, 33. Cf. Alexandre Zinoviev, *Homo Sovieticus*, trans. Jacques Michaut (Paris: Julliard/L'Âge d'Homme, 1982).
143. Liberalism is wont to see the organic holism of traditional societies as an incipient totalitarianism, but as the work of Louis Dumont demonstrates, such societies are its exact antithesis. See his *Homo Hierarchicus: The Caste System and Its Implications*, trans. Mark Sainsbury et al. (Chicago: University of Chicago Press, 1980).
144. Jacques Ellul, *The Technological Society*, trans. John Wilkinson (New York: Vintage, 1964); Alain Touraine, *La société postindustrielle* (Paris: Denoël, 1969); Daniel Bell, *The Coming of Post-Industrial Society* (New York: Basic Books, 1973); François-Bernard Huyghe and Pierre Barbès, *La soft-idéologie* (Paris: Robert Laffont, 1987); Herbert Marcuse, *One-Dimensional Man* (Boston: Beacon Press, 1964); Augusto Del Noce, *L'époque de la sécularisation*, trans. Philippe Baillet (Paris: Éds. des Syrtes, 2001).

145. Cf. Vladimir Volkoff, *Petite histoire de la désinformation* (Paris: Rocher, 1999); Guy Debord, *Society of the Spectacle*, trans. Fredy Perlman and John Supak (Detroit: Black and Red, 1977).

146. Alain de Benoist, "Spectacles et simulacres," *Nouvelle École* 37 (Spring 1982); Charles Champetier, "Implosions tribales et stratégies fatales," *Éléments* 101 (May 2001); Guillaume Faye and Patrick Rizzi, "Vers le médiatisation totale," *Nouvelle École* 39 (Fall 1982); Jean Baudrillard, *Simulations*, trans. Phil Beitchman, Paul Foss, and Paul Patton (New York: Semiotext[e], 1983), 30–37; Jean Baudrillard, *La Gauche divine* (Paris: Grasset, 1985), 148–53. Cf. Edward S. Herman and Noam Chomsky, *Manufacturing Consent: The Political Economy of the Mass Media* (New York: Pantheon, 1988).

147. Champetier, "La nouvelle cause des femmes."

148. A. G. Dugin, "Eurasia Above All: Manifesto of the Eurasian Movement," at *Arctogaia* (http://www.arctogaia.com).

149. Arnold Gehlen, *Man in the Age of Technology*, trans. Patricia Lipscomb (New York: Columbia University Press, 1980), 55.

150. "Three Interviews with Alain de Benoist." Cf. Christopher Lasch, *The Culture of Narcissism: American Life in an Age of Diminishing Expectations* (New York: Norton, 1978).

151. Alain de Benoist, "Hayek: A Critique," *Telos* 110 (Winter 1998); Philippe Baillet, *Julius Evola ou La sexualité dans tous ses "états"* (Chalon-sur-Saône: Hérode, 1994), 61–67.

152. Jean Baudrillard, *The Illusion of the End*, trans. Chris Turner (Stanford, CA: Stanford University Press, 1994), 30.

153. Alain de Benoist, "La pensée unique" (1996), in *L'écume et les galets*; Charles Bonneau, "Le totalitarisme post-démocratique," *Éléments* 73 (Spring 1992).

154. Charles Champetier, "Notes sur la liberté d'expression," *Lien express: Bulletin de liaison des membres du GRECE* 2 (December 2000). In September 2000, *Le Figaro* published a series of interviews on the theme: "Is debate still possible in France?" Almost all the personalities interviewed for the piece answered in the negative.

155. William J. Corliss in *Chronicles* (July 1998), 45.

156. Éric Werner, *L'après-démocratie* (Lausanne: L'Âge d'Homme, 2001), 8–10; Sander, "Die Charaktermasken des totalitären Liberalismus"; Benoist, *Orientations pour des années décisives*, 60; Alain de Benoist, "Démocratie virtuelle" (1996), in *L'écume et les galets*; Günther Maschke, "Allemagne: L'éternelle année zéro," in *Non à la censure! De la police de la pensée à la Nouvelle Inquisition. Actes du XXXIe colloque national du GRECE* (Paris: GRECE, 1998); Klaus J. Groth, *Die Diktatur der Guten: Political Correctness* (Munich: Herbig, 1999). The British *National Journal* 60 reports that between 1994 and 2000, more than 52,000 Germans were prosecuted for opinions allegedly at odds with the country's Basic Law. All the major European countries now criminalize "hate speech" and prohibit the discussion of certain taboo issues. In some countries it is even a crime to refer to scientifically or historically recognized "facts" in defense of forbidden views. It is perhaps not coincidental that France's Gayssot Law, designed to silence and criminalize anti-liberal dissent, was authored by one of the leading contemporary representatives of Marxist-Leninist thought, the

PCF's Jean-Claude Gayssot. The links between Soviet totalitarianism and the new liberal forms of ideological control were thus formally—or, at least, symbolically—codified. For this reason, some Europeans claim the fall of the Soviet empire signaled the fall of Western free thought, for the rules of civilized discourse have since been effectively suspended. Pornographers, rappers, Zionists, homosexual activists, and Communists have experienced not the slightest abridgement of their "rights." Cf. Robert Faurisson, "Revisionists Hunted in Europe," at *The Heretical Press* (http://www.heretical.org/main.html).

157. Alain de Benoist, "L'engrenage de l'égalitarisme," *Éléments* 24–25 (Winter 1977–78).

158. Thomas Molnar, *The Emerging Atlantic Culture* (New Brunswick, NJ: Transaction Publishers, 1994), 97. Robert Dun points out that not only liberals like Benedetto Croce, but anarchists like Errico Malatesta and Camillo Berneri, were free to write, speak, and teach in Fascist Italy, while today in republican France "revisionist" historians like Robert Faurisson and Vincent Reynouard have been dismissed from their tenured university posts and penalized with crippling fines for having the courage to resist the manufactured consent of the Jewish Lobby. See "Les Tartufes de la liberté contre la liberté" (1997), in *Une vie de combat*.

## Chapter IV

# Twilight of the Gods

The New Right's identitarian project is premised on the notion that the refusal to be oneself—a condition Martin Heidegger calls "inauthenticity"—leads to both existential and civilizational disorder. As suggested above, the most consequential threats to European authenticity come from liberalism and its various offshoots, such as feminism, multiculturalism, and human rights, all of which invert indigenous references for the sake of certain decontextualized ones. Yet liberalism, New Rightists contend, is but the culmination—the modernization—of an earlier, more primordial threat: Christianity.[1] In contravening the Continent's Greco-Roman, Celtic, and Germanic pagan heritage they allege that this religion of Semitic origin has estranged Europeans from their native spirituality, provoking the single most damaging cultural distortion (pseudomorphosis) of their identity.[2]

### Christianity

Historically, Christianity was not an organic offshoot of the European spirit, but a plebeian encroachment of Rome's "cosmopolitan and disarticulated masses."[3] In Ernst Bloch's formulation: "*Im Christentum steckt die Revolte*"—a revolt which vented both the masses' class hatred and their hostility to the Roman imperium.[4] The ascending Church was thus allegedly imbued with an ontology informed by the Jews' *ressentiment* of the gentile kingdoms and a herd morality that sought to pull down all that was strong and noble in the imperial tradition. Its persecuted messiah especially appealed to the empire's "corrupt Chandala classes."

By contrast, among the homogeneous and still vigorous peoples of Northern Europe, this dubious Judaic heresy encountered innumerable obstacles.[5] Even with its Roman and Hellenic accretions, its Oriental essence seemed perverse, for notions of original sin, pacifism, self-abnegation, guilt, and monotheism could only repel those valuing strength and honor, loyalty and courage, balance, restraint, and respect for life's multiplicity. Of the numerous early manifestation of the Jesus movement, Arian (not Aryan) Christianity alone attracted them. Yet, in denying Christ's divinity and accommodating pagan belief, this heterodox Christological tendency was entirely compatible with a culture whose martial standards scorned the servile ones of Christian love.[6] While Northern Europeans did eventually succumbed to the Nicene Christianity of the Catholic Church, it was not through any elective affinity with its beliefs, but rather because the Holy See had convinced their "long-haired kings" of the diplomatic advantage of doing so, or, as in Ireland, its sophisticated Roman forms gave new life to native Gaelic culture, or else, they were forced at sword point. Typically, these pagan "converts" saw Christ as a victor over death, not the suffering redeemer, whose mission was to expiate human sinfulness.[7] The Church's consolidation in the centuries following the empire's fall also depended on an accommodation with paganism, whose influence persisted long after the Continent's "conversion." The historian James C. Russell characterizes this accommodation (in which pagan elements were "Christianized") as the "Germanization of early medieval Christianity," for Catholicism was compelled to make so many concessions to paganism that it ended up transforming itself from "a universal salvation religion [into] a Germanic, and eventually European, folk religion."[8]

While Protestantism, particularly its Calvinist wing, later attempted to undo this accommodation by re-rooting North Europeans in the Hebraic forms of the early Church, it succeeded only in undermining Christianity, for the secularizing forces it unleashed shattered the old Biblical myths, dislodged transcendental references, and discredited Christianity among the European masses, most of whom today remain Christian in name only. This, though, did not mark the end of Christian influence. Its most distinct beliefs, *Grécistes* claim, have since been profaned and incorporated into the modernist project. Liberalism, for example, secularized the Church's universalism, egalitarianism, and individualism, in the process reformulating Christian charity as humanitarianism, hope as progress, and redemption as abundance. Though the churches are now empty, Europe allegedly has never been as saturated with Christian sentiment, for its principles prevail in the guise of the regnant liberalism.[9]

The cultural distortion that came with Christianity took many forms. At the most fundamental level, New Rightists share Nietzsche's contention that Christianity was a "slave revolt" against aristocratic ideals.[10] By this score, its gospel of love and salvation was little more than a plebeian *nein-sagen*, venting an instinctive hatred of ascending life.[11] It accordingly leveled, standardized, and devitalized life's higher forms, crushing "every feeling of reverence and distance between man and man." It catered, as such, to the weak, the sickly, and the mediocre, jeopardizing the very survival of those it ensnared. In abiding Christianity, and its subsequent secular offshoots, Europeans supposedly compromised the aristocratic basis of their civilizational project. This did not mean that their Faustian aspirations for the infinite would go unasserted after their conversion. In the various traditions of the Grail Quest, in the conquest of the world's great oceans, and in the splitting of the atom, they lived on—but were henceforth impaired by an inner doubting tension that was at cross-purposes with Europe's native spirit—or, at least, so *Grécistes* claim.[12]

Equally consequential in its pseudomorphosis was the dogmatic mindset that came with Christianity. In contrast to the pagan tradition, its monotheism was an inexhaustible source of rigidity and fanaticism. Positing the unquestionable supremacy of its teachings, the Church zealously persecuted all who opposed it. It pitted Jerusalem against Athens (that is, revelation against reason), tore down pagan temples (including many architectural treasures of the ancient world), burned pagan books, and executed thousands of Druids.[13] Early Christian literature, Benoist writes, is one long hateful cry of prohibition, destruction, and pillage.[14] Yet, it was not monotheism *per se* that most distinguished Christianity from Europe's primordial religious heritage, but the dualistic ontology upon which it rested. This dualism held that an unbridgeable gap separated God the Creator from man the creation. As such, the natural world for it ceased to be the body of the gods, infused with the sacred, and became, instead, a creation called forth out of nothing by a transcendent Creator, who stood outside and above it. The various manifestations of earthy existence were thus denigrated—for true life was allegedly not of this world, but of the next.[15]

Along with subordinating man's world to God's celestial order, Christianity's dualistic ontology conceived of the world in terms of the divine rationality ordering it (*logos*). As in Platonism (from which the Church borrowed much), the world became a pale reflection of a higher order. The immediate real was thus taken as incomplete, given that the true sources of being lay elsewhere. This allegedly led early Christians to turn their backs on the everyday world, refuse civic rites, and disparage social commitments. And since all worldly events, despite their apparent incoherence and antagonism, were considered expressions of the *logos*, Christianity was obliged to emphasize the rationalist aspects of belief, for only its "prescriptions, laws, and interdictions" were thought to harmonize with the divine.[16] By replacing the sacred, mythic elements of pagan Europe with the *logos*' ubiquitous rationality and conceiving of divinity in other-worldly terms, Christianity could not but desacralize the cosmos, objectify nature, and devalue creation.[17]

Apart from God's occasional intervention, the world for it became a "vale of tears." As Nietzsche put it, "With the 'Beyond' one kills life."[18] The Christians' other-worldly references also supposedly disparaged the significance of national and cultural particularisms—for the "universal soul" of this Jewish heresy did not differ from one race or nation to another or from one individual to another. In the words of one New Testament scholar: "To accept the Christian religion, people have always had to adjust their thinking to the very unusual notion of belonging to a people and a history that was not really their own."[19] In this spirit, the Church's "new covenant" was made between God and humanity. Christians came thus to see themselves as God's children, indifferent to, if not contemptuous of, the various ethnonationalist ascriptions dividing men and obstructing the spread of His word.[20] As Louis Pauwels described it, Christians have no *patrie*, only God's Promised Land.[21] Against paganism's affirmation of communal attachments, Christianity focused on individual salvation and did so at the group's expense, repudiating in this way the ancient synthesis of spirituality and civicism.[22]

For nearly 15 centuries Christianity dominated the Continent. In disenchanting the world, associating faith with reason, and fostering individual subjectivity, Benoist claims it prepared the present "eclipse of the sacred." Europeans as a result now lack the spiritual references—the transcendent certainties—that once inspired them, for a post-Christian world, in which science or liberal ideology has been substituted for the Church's discredited teachings, is a world that knows only life's material properties and the existential groundlessness that dooms the individual to impotence. Spiritually adrift, Europeans now seem to have dissipated even their instinct for survival, as ethnomasochism becomes foremost in their hierarchy of values and effeminacy renders them defenseless before larger dangers.[23] Faced with the nihilism born of this void, New Rightists call for "a return to ourselves"—and to the primal sources of their heritage—advocated not for the sake of some pre-Christian Golden Age, but as a means of reigniting the European project—and hence Europe's will to power.

## Paganism

Only the deities of ancient Europe, they claim, offer a spiritual recourse to the present malaise.[24] The guilt, the fear, the narrow petty bourgeois obsession with well-being, and the self-hating love of the Other that leaves Europeans defenseless before liberal market values: this disposition is native not to the *Rig Veda*, the *Iliad*, or the *Edda*, but to Christianity's

Near Eastern belief system (which, from the beginning, constituted an antipode to Greco-European thought and sensibility). To surmount the debilities brought about by this suppression of their native spirit, New Rightists claim Europeans need to replenish their spirit at the font of their being. Free of Yahweh, an alien desert god, the sacral sense still vibrant in the Continent's forests and holy places holds out the single possible alternative to the present soul-killing desacralization.[25] As Ernst Jünger warns, only a return of the old gods can save us from the impending chaos.[26]

In appealing to the pagan heritage, New Rightists do not actually seek an actual restoration of ancient pagan practices, just as they distance themselves from New Age pagans, whose eclectic mix of ancient cults and postmodern hedonism are no less anti-identitarian than the Christian/modernist practices they oppose.[27] Instead, their paganism strives to resuscitate Europe's ancestral concept of the cosmos, its classical ethical principles, its notion of time and history, and its affirmation of community. In this, it seeks to affirm the integrity of the European project and "all the inscrutable creative powers manifested in their nature," rejecting, in the process, a "misanthropic" religion that leaves man begging forgiveness from a god forged in the image of a Near Eastern despot.

Above all, the New Right's paganism aims at transvaluating the Judeo-Christian values that have inverted all that is strong and noble in their heritage. This makes its paganism a philosophical disposition, rather than an actual effort to re-institutionalize old religious practices. This, however, is not without spiritual significance. Though the Olympian deities no longer occupy the existing pantheons, the ideals they personify have persisted in folklore, customs, literature, and the popular *mentalité*—which suggests that the pagan spirit still lives in the recesses of the European soul.[28]

New Rightists consequently see their task as making others conscious of its lingering presence. They are not so naive as to believe that after the Christian millennia paganism will ever be what it once was: but this is not their intent. In appealing to the old gods, they invoke the original being that made them who they are. From this heritage that promises them a meaningful future, their *ja-sagen* affirms all that is vital in their heritage. "The revolution of the twenty-first century," one identitarian predicts, is likely to be religious: in reuniting Europeans with their inmost spirit, a pagan cultural revival holds out the prospect that they too will be part of this ascension.[29]

In either its ancient or contemporary form, paganism affronts Christian/liberal principles. This is especially evident in the antinomies dividing Christian monotheism from pagan polytheism. Just as the Abrahamic tradition reduced the multifaceted expressions of the divine to a single godhead, its monotheism posits a single truth, a single spirit, and a single humanity. It tends, as a consequence, to be one-dimensional and single-minded, with rigid polarities, fixed categories, and an either/or logic that, in Descartes' (unconsciously revealing) words, condemns "the forest of errors" for the desert's self-evident truths.[30]

Pre-Christian polytheism, by contrast, emerged from sacred groves and mythopoetic sensibilities full of nuance and liberality. In this vein, the renowned French Celticist Jean Markale points out that ancient Celtic thought lacked the black-and-white register of Judeo-Christian theology.[31] For the worshippers of Lugh and Bridgit, whose temples were the then untamed forest of Western Europe, there were no absolutes. Monotheism's principle of identity (that a = a) did not exist for them. Between good and evil, right and wrong, sharp and precise boundaries were entirely lacking. The Celtic world existed in a spirit of paradox. What was right in one situation was likely to be wrong in another, what was a nightmare for one might be a dream for another. Just as the line they drew between man and god was blurred, the spirits governing the Celtic world resided in man as much as they did in their gods. These spirits were contradictory yet complementary. Man's goal was not to reject or deny, but to order them for the sake of harmony and measure—for, as Heraclitus observes, "the cosmos works by harmony of tension, like the lyre and bow" (Haxton translation). In distinction to monotheism's univocal logic (or liberalism's demobilizing relativism), Celtic polytheism held that there were varied shades of truth and being, because its world was an open one, with nuanced meanings and conflicting attractions. The idea of a universal prescription, such as came with the Christian's alien *logos*, seemed an absurdity to Europe's root peoples, for such a dogmatic assertion negated life's world-open, self-determining character. Early Europeans simply took it for granted that many stories were needed to get at the whole truth, just as this truth was knowable only through its numerous variations.

This textured understanding of truth rested on the most quintessential of pagan principles: that life has no purpose other than itself.[32] As Homer, Hesiod, and Heraclitus portrayed it, life is struggle, nothing more. It is neither good nor bad. In a world without inherent purpose, the weak perish, while the strong forge their values into a body of life-affirming principles—and thrive. Those who put their fate in the hands of others (whether those of a heavenly patriarch or of the liberals' nanny state) are easily thrown down and crushed. Believing life has no aim other than to complete itself, the ancients thought life concealed no higher meaning: man alone creates it. Every human form—individual or communal—unconsciously seeks a higher level of being. This is nature's law. In Homer's world, there were, for instance, heroes fated to die young (like Achilles) and others who would enjoy a long, eventful existence (such as Odysseus). Unlike Judeo-Christians, Europe's greatest poet made no moral distinction between them. In face of an impersonal reality, it is not right or wrong, good or evil, long life or short that counts, but honor and dishonor, beauty and ugliness, courage and cowardice. Only those imposing themselves and their style on the primordial chaos—drawing the sublime from the setbacks and triumphs that inevitably accompany their struggles—survive and achieve a meaningful life. By affirming the innocence of being and the inevitable normative influences at work in every human community, the tragic, heroic spirit of pagan Europe endeavored to shape existence according to its forms. This made paganism a religion of works, not faith.[33]

The monotheistic truths of the Abrahamic tradition, like those of liberal rationalism, are, by contrast, universal, grasping the world in forms applicable to everyone, everywhere, at every time.[34] Infused with an intolerance and rigidity native to Semitic religions, the early Church hoped to reorganize the world on the basis of its indisputable truths. Liberalism would later seek the same, only with a secular concept of *logos*. In either case, the *logos* was addressed through the individual's spirit or reason, not the community's destining project. Pagans, by contrast, felt no compulsion to dismiss the immediate real for an allegedly higher reality, even though they, unlike modern men, felt the eternal presence of the transcendent. The sacred—that which is greater than man—was indeed thought to envelope the profane, giving it meaning and significance.[35] As the old Nordic adage describes it: "The divine sleeps in the rock, breathes in the plant, dreams in the animal, and wakes in man."[36] Such a notion made the divine integral to the pagans' world, part of the continuum linking man, being, and cosmos. Pagans thus identified with its particularisms—rather than reified them, like Christians, or incessantly reformed them, like liberals.

The pre-Christian world was what it was, not what the truths of a putative *logos* deemed it to be. Within the pagan's mythic cosmology, there was no divinity—no higher reality—superior to life. Man and god were of the same substance as the world, for the world was a manifestation of the divine. Although this made the divine and the human, the higher and lower life forms consubstantial with the world, the gods nevertheless governed man, and man dominated the lower life forms, for the sense of the transcendent was also one of the strictest hierarchy. Indeed, it was because the pagan accepted that the world lacked an *a priori* meaning that he was free to impose his order upon it, to turn the chaos threatening him into a cosmos affirming him. Outside this order, beyond the web of significations spun by his culture, there was no higher power, no objectivity, no immutable truths. The gods of his polytheistic pantheon reflected life's manifold possibilities, subject as they were to time, chance, and contingency. The Greeks, for example, did not prostrate themselves before their deities, as if they were masters who needed appeasing, but rather treated them as projections of "the most successful specimens of their own caste."[37] The difference between them was, accordingly, one of degree, not kind, which meant that every time a pagan surpassed himself in overcoming his egoism and achieving tragic grandeur, he came to resemble his gods.[38]

Inseparable from his world, the pagan was also inseparable from his people. Even as "possessors of divine energy," his gods did not lay down universal laws, for they were themselves creatures of their universe and spoke only to those who believed in them. Because different peoples implied different gods, pagan thought was specific to its place—and hence to its communal context.[39] In accepting that real men, situated in specific environments, gave shape and meaning to their world, the pagan was free to encounter life on its own terms and mold it according to his culturally informed notion of what it meant. He felt no need of holy book or prophet, pope or inquisitor, to decode its multiple manifestations.[40] Contrary to Judeo-Christian strictures, which devalue the Other, impose a single model of belief, and demand a unilateral relation to God, the pagan found traces of the divine in all things. As the sole creator of meaning, he alone defined the divine, which was not simply his highest reference, but what he himself aspired to be. Just as all men had religion because they had community, pagan rites and spiritual devotions were entirely specific to their community, representing its collective aspirations. "I," the bearer of an Gaelic oath pledged, "swear by the gods by whom my people swear."[41]

No universality of belief was thus possible in the pagan world. Julius Evola observes that the etymological root of the word "religion" (the Latin *religio*) means "to link" or "to unify"—that is, to link or unify the religious practitioner with the spiritual community to which he belongs, consecrating the social bonds that bind him to it and to the spirit which he himself is bound.[42] Paganism was consequently indistinguishable from the pagan's civic life, which was the bedrock of his "morality."[43] Only through the faithful exercise of civic rites and sacrifices to the local gods was it possible for him to rise above the common lot and achieve a higher spiritual status.[44] Indeed, the only true piety was civic, reflected in the pagan's deference to his ancestors, his line, and his "city."[45] Ancient virtue was defined, in a word, by what the community held highest—and not by the gods, who were hardly models of morality.[46]

## Myth

For New Rightists, it is the difference between *mythos* and *logos* that best illustrates the spiritual divide separating the open-ended holism of ancient European paganism from Judeo-Christian dualism and its liberal offshoots.[47] In siding with *mythos*, whose metaphoric images evoke perspectival "truths" unfathomable to analytic or dialectical methods, these identitarians take their stand with what they consider the more cogent tradition. Though both Christianity and liberalism brand myth the fictitious projection of pagan superstition and irrationality, they argue that its truth claims (which are not to be confused with mythology) are no less compelling than those of *logos*—whose rationalist procedures of thought (logic) are "an invention of schoolteachers, not philosophers."[48] As Paul Veyne in his study of Greek myth contends, "There are different programs of truth.... The difference between fiction and reality is not objective and does not pertain to the thing itself. It resides in us."[49] Truth here is not "the product of some natural illumination," but of an experience of the world, as it is culturally, subjectively, and imaginatively signified.

Benoist points out that *logos* was itself originally another of *mythos*' expressions, for the image of the idea precedes and is frequently more pregnant than its discursive formulation.[50] Moreover, as logical proposition, with its universalist implication ignoring the perspectival nature of truth, *logos* implies nothing about the meaning of the world. *Logos* may be a more logically, analytically, and clearly developed form of thought, but cognitively it is not necessarily superior to *mythos* and often less suggestive and encompassing. More important still, *logos*—especially in its modern form—empties the world of those truths that once constituted the essence and meaning of the European project. Against this "disenchantment," which leaves the European powerless before the great spiritual challenges confronting him, a revival of Europe's mythic heritage alone holds out the prospect that the true sources of his being might also be recovered and the European project reborn.

Contrary to Christian and liberal claims, GRECE-inspired New Rightists hold that myth has little to do with a fantasized past in which the origins of the cosmos, the coming into being of the gods, or the heroic deeds of the founding generation are recounted and memorialized. Rather, its principal function has always been to supply models of meaningful behavior for the present. The "beginnings" it allegorically evokes accordingly designate how the chaos inherent in the world became the cosmos of a specific cultural tradition (*kosmos* being Greek for "order") and thus what this order requires to sustain itself. But more than the story of a people's origin, myth is the narrative basis of all that makes a people what it is—and, by implication, what it can be. In this sense, it is situated beyond the true and the false, beyond confirmation or denial. Its main function, as such, is to "encode" those "exemplary precedents," however encrusted with legend and poetry, that once occurred and reoccurs whenever a people responds to the creative promptings of its unique life force to impose itself—its cosmos—upon the world.[51]

In memorializing these primordial forces, myth offers gestures that are to be imitated and repeated because they demand what is highest in a people. Thus, however fictitious, myth expresses "truths" eluding analytic or discursive proposition, based, as it is, on a culture's interpretative encounter with its world and its "cosmological vision of the future" (Locchi). Through the mythic inscription of these truths and the heritage they found, the fundament of a culturally-defined existence is created, perpetuated, and perpetually recreated. And like postmodern discourse, the truths of myth are internal, dependent not on its mimetic and universal properties, but on its capacity to arouse the commitment of those who "believe" them. Myth, thus, makes little distinction between inner and outer, subject and object, mind and matter, but treats these polarities as multiple expressions of life's embracing holism, for it is a relationship to the world before it is a system of signs about the world. Only when it and the life sustaining it die—that is, only when it ceases to be a vital relationship to the world—does myth become merely a body of fantastic and imaginary beliefs, without social or existential significance.[52]

In establishing the narrative boundaries defining the people adhering to it, myth perpetuates a certain order of being that expresses a will to life. In postmodern fashion, New Rightists accept that this order's foundations are products of a cultural construction and not the direct and faithful reflection of an objective reality—even though its "constructs" help create the basis for such a reality.[53] Myth renders man's encounter with the world into a living heritage, turning discontinuity and innovation into a coherent tradition. As Mircea Eliade explains, myth is "creative and exemplary," revealing how things come to be, defining their underlying structures, and suggesting the multiple modalities of being they imply.[54] It does not describe reality "objectively," but roots it in a cultural heritage of significance that affirms it as a manifestation of original being. At the same time, myth creates this reality. By projecting a certain relation between an image and an idea, it unveils (creates) dimensions of "truth" inaccessible to rationality.[55] (This, of course, does not mean that it flouts the "laws" of nature, only that these laws are recognized in its own terms—unlike Christian/liberal efforts to escape them by substituting some sort of divine/rational ideal.) Intuitively grasped by its believers, myth's allegorical tenets enable man to engage his world, participate in its re-creation, and make present what is absent. Its truths, as such, are existentialist, not essentialist. They cannot be refuted, only rejected.[56]

For this reason, Benoist argues that the behavior our beliefs inspire are more important than the beliefs themselves.[57] Myth has little to do with rationalist notions of truth (*verum*), for its power resides not in its correspondence to an object's "noumena," but in its aesthetic accordance with a state of soul, in its power to evoke certain emotions or effects, and in its capacity to inspire man's being with *certum*.[58] In this sense, the mythic revelations of the *Voluspá* or the *Táin Bó Cuailnge* are as cogent as the scientific verities of *The Origin of Species* or the *Principia Mathematica*. Both as existential postulate and as "child of the imagination," myth apprehends those certitudes which tradition accepts as true. It is, Benoist writes, what justifies our existence.[59]

Given that myth's paradigmatic principles generate those unquestioned presuppositions legitimating a people's historical vocation, it is prescriptive, providing its believers with a normative framework that lends coherence—meaning—to their activities, their laws, and their world view.[60] Its certitudes are accordingly summoned whenever a people attempts to re-create its world and hence itself. If there is no myth to preserve the particular truth of its original being—the particular truth (or belief) that allows it to overcome the world's chaos and live according to the transcendent principles sustaining its will to power—there can be no re-creation. And if there is no re-creation, there can be no destiny—and no people.[61] As Martin Heidegger puts it, myth "expresses what is to be said before all else . . . [It is] what shows itself in advance and in everything as that which presences in all 'presence.'"[62] Through myth, a people affirms, as well as creates, its specific "reason" to live. Without it, "every culture loses the healthy natural power of its creativity," for it is myth's exemplary force that prompts a people to forge their common values into a destiny that presses "upon its experiences the stamp of the eternal."[63] Mythic time is correspondingly reversible, as the origins it recounts are repeated in each subsequent gesture of renewal.[64] Indeed, myth is "free" of time. Unlike the Christian or the liberal, who disenchants the world by conceiving of it in terms of an abstract logocentrism, the man of myth takes his possibilities from a spiritual-poetic world which constantly regenerates itself. Whenever he affirms the paradigmatic act inscribed in myth, he thereby re-centers himself at his source, commencing a new beginning.

Myth, finally, seeks to preserve this primordial source as a force for change, for it is what enables man to escape profane, chronological time and enter the sacred time in which creation occurs and reoccurs. In disclosing a people's truth—not as *logos*, with its narrow pre-constituted determinisms, but as the possibility that is both prior and posterior to the present—myth knows no immutable truth, even as it serves as a source of meaning and certitude in an otherwise meaningless and uncertain world.[65] With the advent of modernity and its narrow rationalist understanding of the world, Europe's pagan myths may have passed from view, but, for New Rightists, the mythic *patrie* latent in the Continent's ancient forests and temples, where the sources of life are deeply rooted, still has the power to resuscitate new "truths"—new myths—to sustain their civilizational project.[66]

## Tradition

New Right identitarians believe a people is a living organism. As such, it can die. To guard against this, a people needs a common heritage to define itself and maintain its will to live together. In this sense, tradition serves as the scaffolding around which a people constitutes itself. If there is no heritage—no transmission (*traditio*) from one generation to another—a people has nothing to live for and no reason to remain together.[67] It is, then, as the horizon against which a people's existence is worked out that tradition imparts purpose to its common endeavors. As Gehlen writes, "without it one can keep restlessly active . . . and yet lack any inner sense that all this busyness carries any moral significance."[68] This is why identitarians believe Europe's pagan, mythic traditions are essential to its renaissance.

The revival of these traditions, however, faces an awesome array of countervailing forces, for the modern order is premised not only on the belief that reflexive reason frees man from tradition and hence from the need to root his identity in it, but that the rapidly accelerating rate of change and innovation characteristic of modernity, especially late modernity or postmodernity, deprives traditional meanings and practices of their former relevance.[69] Against this dismissive rationalism, New Rightists hold that tradition is the basis of, not an obstacle, to all that man can achieve in the present. This was true 30,000 years ago; it is, they claim, still true today.

Like the larger culture, of which they are an integral part, traditions embody the habits and beliefs of the people who uphold them. They are thus part of a living presence—and not simply vestiges of the past. And because they arise organically, as experience, habit, and value, and because they unconsciously shape what are culturally acceptable and individually satisfying modes of behavior, no amount of reason or theoretical modeling can substitute for them. As such, traditions arise and are sustained by a vitality distinct to those who uphold them. A people in this sense no more chooses its traditions than "it chooses the color of its hair or eyes" (Gustave Le Bon). On this count, Benoist describes tradition as that historically formed structure reflecting the perennial in a people's culture.[70] This situates it beyond time, representing the imperishable in a people's orientation to the world. Tradition serves thus to encode those defining principles that maintain a people in its timelessness, establishing the frame of its collective consciousness and the order of its collective being. At the same time, it conditions a people's view of its world, giving permanence to its abiding values and shaping the growth of its identity, as it is subject to the forces of time and change. Its loss can thus never be a step forward, but only backwards, toward devitalization and decline.

The existential centrality of tradition is especially evident in the fact that many, especially the most important, European traditions share a common origin, reaching back to the crucible of "Indo-European civilization" (subject of the next chapter). While varying in detail among the different European families, many of these traditions express a common relationship to the larger world, linking the Continent's different national families through rituals, customs, and norms which speak to kindred sensibilities and common origins. As the greatest of its identitarian historians, Dominique Venner, writes: "To live according to tradition is to conform to the ideal it incarnates, to cultivate excellence according to its standard, to rediscover its roots, to transmit its heritage, to be in solidarity with the people who uphold it."[71] Without tradition, there would, in truth, be no Europe, for the historical, cultural, and genetic bonds Europeans share with their ancestors would otherwise be impossible to sustain.

Tradition in this sense has little to do with "traditionalism"—which freezes "eternal" truths in sterile, lifeless forms. Nor is it necessarily the same as traditions. "*Tradure*," its Latin root, means to "translate" and in this sense tradition is the means by which innovation is rendered into an idiom conversant with the larger heritage.[72] Russell Kirk aptly describes it as the vital force that influences the future in filtering out all that is mistaken in innovation and doing so in a way that reaffirms whatever is viable in the past.[73]

This understanding makes tradition compatible with modern reflectivity, in that thought and action are constantly refracted back upon one another. But more than its reflective function, tradition creates a sense of continuity, which permits the discontinuity of events to appear as aspects of a single meaningful experience. It denotes, as such, not the past, but that which stands outside of and beyond time. All healthy societies tend thus to balance tradition and innovation, for with only tradition, a society would ossify, losing its capacity to adapt to altering conditions; with only innovation, it risks anarchy, with nothing allowed to settle or take effect. The opposite of tradition, Venner notes, is not modernity, but nihilism.[74] (The primitive, disoriented behaviors characteristic of contemporary society, identitarians contend, are indeed one obvious consequence of its loss.)

The meanings and identities forged in the past and perpetuated in tradition need, however, to be reaffirmed in every generation. For tradition exists only in the living and remains vital only in its renewal.[75] The New Right's effort to revive the forces of tradition and make Europeans conscious of their shared origins has taken several forms. Early on, Benoist and the GRECE's *Commission des Traditions* undertook a study of European first names, determining which were native to Europe and which were imports, what they signify, and what importance should be attached to them. Because naming positions a child "as the referent in the story recounted by those around him," it is a cultural practice of considerable significance. Benoist and the historian Pierre Vial have also produced a book-length study on the all-important but reluctantly discussed issue of death, examining the ways Europeans have thought of, mourned, and reconciled themselves with it. Other *Grécistes* have produced monographs on traditional rites (such as those associated with Christmas and the solstice), on legends and mythology, on totem figures (like horses and wolves), and on various holidays and customs. But the most important facet of the GRECE's effort in this field occurred between 1975 and 1983 in an irregular bulletin titled *GRECE/Tradition* and later published as a single massive volume, *Les traditions d'Europe*. These studies attempted a synoptic history of those popular traditions associated with the seasonal cycles that once governed the rhythms of European life. Although centuries or even millennia old, these traditions are presently on the verge of disappearing, as the modern world renders the seasons, days, and hours homogeneous and interchangeable.[76]

In rescuing such traditions from oblivion, the GRECE, like other New Right organizations, pursues several goals. Many of the most important traditions tend to be trans-European. Though varying in detail from nation to nation, their common elements indicate that, in addition to Europe's high culture, the Continent's popular culture possesses a genuinely European dimension. Their study also reveals the larger significance, often of pagan or mythic origins, of the most fundamental facets of European life: of holidays and festivals, Christmas cards and Easter eggs, Christian rites, important religious heresies and literary movements, May Day and Mothers' Day, artistic styles, and innumerable other cultural practices. And because these traditions frequently allude to a pre-Christian past, having grown out of the beliefs of the Continent's Indo-European founders, *Grécistes* emphasize the degree to which they illuminate the depth of Europe's primordial culture.[77] In reviving these traditions, they seek therefore to reacquaint Europeans with the premodern sensibility still latent in their heritage. This is especially evident in the New Right's philosophy of time and history.

## Notes to Chapter IV

1. Against the conventional view identifying the Right with Christianity, see Gerd-Klaus Kaltenbrunner, ed., *Antichristliche Konservative: Religionkritik von Rechts* (Munich: Herderbücherei, 1982). Also Armin Mohler, *Die Konservative Revolution in Deutschland, 1918–1932: Ein Handbuch*, 5th ed. (Graz: Leopold Stocker, 1999), 117–21.
2. Alain de Benoist, "La religion de l'Europe," *Éléments* 36 (Fall 1980); Louis Rougier, *Celse contre les chrétiens* (Paris: Le Labyrinthe, 1997).
3. Alain de Benoist, *Les idées à l'endroit* (Paris: Hallier, 1979), 167–84. Cf. Anne Bernet, *Les chrétiens dans l'empire: Des persécutions à la conversion* (Paris: Perrin, 2003). A good deal of modern scholarship, however, discounts the view that Christianity first took root among the lower orders of the ancient world; see Rodney Stark, *The Rise of Christianity* (Princeton, NJ: Princeton University Press, 1996), 29–48.
4. Quoted in Kaltenbrunner, *Antichristliche Konservative*, 11.
5. Prudence Jones and Nigel Pennick, *A History of Pagan Europe* (New York: Barnes and Noble, 1999), 59–77.
6. Roland H. Baintain, *Christianity* (Boston: Houghton Mifflin, 1964), 127–39.
7. Baintain, *Christianity*, 182.
8. James C. Russell, *The Germanization of Early Medieval Christianity: A Sociohistorical Approach to Religious Transformation* (New York: Oxford University Press, 1994), 39. While *Grécistes* acknowledge Christianity's syncretic character, they also emphasize that it never fully conquered Europe, and that the greatest European achievements, whether in the form of the Gothic cathedrals, the music of Bach, or the chivalric ethic, were essentially expressions

of Celtic and Germanic paganism. See Patrick de Plunkett, "Analyses," *Nouvelle École* 27–28 (January 1976); Pierluigi Locchi, "La musique, le mythe, Wagner et moi," in *Études et recherches* 3 (June 1976). Cf. Julius Evola, *Revolt Against the Modern World*, trans. Guido Stucco (Rochester, VT: Inner Traditions, 1995), 287–301.

9. Alain de Benoist, *Comment peut-on être païen?* (Paris: Albin Michel, 1981), 273. Cf. Arnold Gehlen, "Die Säkularisierung des Fortschritts" (1967), in *Gesamtausgabe* (Frankfurt am Main: Klostermann, 1978), vol. 7.

10. Friedrich Nietzsche, *On the Genealogy of Morals*, trans. Walter Kaufmann and R. J. Hollingdale (New York: Vintage, 1967), Essay I, § 7; Benoist, *Les idées à l'endroit*, 167–84; Benoist, *Comment peut-on être païen?*, 87–88. Julian, Rome's last pagan emperor, is reputed to have said: "If the Christians triumph, then in 2,000 years the world will be Jewish." Quoted in Eugène Krampon, "Mourir pour Jérusalem?," *Réfléchir et agir* 9 (Summer 2001). When Pope John Paul II called Judaism "our elder brother in the Faith," giving it primacy over Christianity, he, in effect, acknowledged the perspicacity of Julian's admonition. This allegedly "conservative" pope, it is worth adding, has "kissed the Koran [and] watched as the Crucifix was removed from a Catholic altar and replaced with a statue of Buddha"—discrediting, in effect, the authority of the Christian faith. See letter of William Winterbauer, *Culture Wars* 21:3 (February 2002).

11. Friedrich Nietzsche, *Ecce Homo*, trans. Walter Kaufmann (New York: Vintage, 1969), 271–72.

12. Thomas Molnar and Alain de Benoist, *L'éclipse du sacré: Discours et réponses* (Paris: La Table Ronde, 1986), 241. While the GRECE is best known for its paganism, it remains a polymorphic organization with divergent currents. Against the paganism of Benoist and the GRECE majority, there is the Catholic traditionalism of Arnaud Guyot-Jeannin, Christophe Levalois, and Claude Rousseau, as well as pagan elements, once represented by Pierre Vial, who emphasize those Christian legacies compatible with traditionalism and paganism. See Arnaud Guyot-Jeannin, *Révolution spirituelle contre le monde moderne: Essai d'analyse chrétienne* (Neuilly-sur-Seine: Cercle Sol Invictus, 2000), and Pierre Vial, "Réflexions pour un débat," *Études et recherches* 5 (Fall 1987). Elsewhere, generalizations are more difficult to make. In some European countries, Spain, for example, Catholicism dominates the New Right, and pagans are the minority; in Slavic countries, where the pagan tradition is weaker, Orthodoxy is dominant; in Germany, Catholicism influences *Junge Freiheit*, while paganism dominates the Thule-Netz of Pierre Krebs.

13. Alexandre Gryf, "La persécution contre les païens 312–565," *Nouvelle École* 52 (2001).

14. Alain de Benoist, "Christianisme," *Nouvelle École* 52 (2001).

15. Sigrid Hunke, "Was Trägt über den Untergang des Zeitalters?," *Elemente für die europäische Wiedergeburt* 1 (July 1986); Alain de Benoist, "Sacré païen et désacralisation judéo-chrétienne du monde," in *Quelle religion pour l'Europe?*, ed. Démètre Théraios (Paris: Georg, 1990).

16. Tomislav Sunic, *Against Democracy and Equality: The European New Right* (New York: Peter Lang, 1990), 74; Pierre Le Vigan, "Le Christianisme et les religions du livre," *Nouvelle École* 52 (2001). Arguing for Christian identitarians,

Robert Barrot insists that the notion of a "Judeo-Christian heritage" is a fabrication, that Jesus' Jewish origins are spiritually refuted in New Testament doctrine, and that Christianity's essence is Greco-Roman, not Hebraic. See his *Il est trop tard* (Paris: Godefroy de Bouillon, 2001), 23–26.

17. Molnar and Benoist, *L'éclipse du sacré*, 131–47; Hunke, "Was Trägt über den Untergang des Zeitalters?"
18. Friedrich Nietzsche, *The Anti-Christ*, trans. R. J. Hollingdale (Harmondsworth, UK: Penguin, 1968), § 58.
19. Burton L. Mack, *Who Wrote the New Testament? The Making of the Christian Myth* (San Francisco: Harper Collins, 1995), 294.
20. For a Christian identitarian rebuttal, see Jean-Pierre Blanchard, *Mythes et races: Précis de sociologie identitaire* (Paris: Éds. Detérna, 2000), 103–12.
21. Louis Pauwels, *Comment devient-on ce que l'on est?* (Paris: Stock, 1978), 145. Cf. Richard Fletcher, *The Barbarian Conversion: From Paganism to Christianity* (New York: Henry Holt, 1997), 30–31; Egon Haffner, *Der "Humanitarismus" und die Versuch seiner Überwindung bei Nietzsche, Scheler und Gehlen* (Würzburg: Konigshausen und Neumann, 1988), 75.
22. Guillaume Faye, "La problématique moderne de la raison ou la querelle de la rationalité," *Nouvelle École* 41 (November 1984); Louis Rougier, *Du paradis à l'utopie* (Paris: Copernic, 1979), 60; Louis Dumont, "La genèse chrétienne de l'individualisme moderne," *Le Débat* 8:15 (September 1981); Pierre Bérard, "Louis Dumont: Anthropologie et modernité," *Nouvelle École* 39 (Fall 1982).
23. Michael Walker, "Les enjeux culturels de l'Europe," in *Crépuscule des blocs, aurore des peuples: Actes du XXIIIe colloque national du GRECE* (Paris: GRECE, 1990). As Le Bon writes, "A people rarely survives the death of its gods." See Alice Widener, ed., *Gustave Le Bon: The Man and His Works* (Indianapolis: Liberty Press, 1979), 284.
24. Jacques Marlaud, *La renouveau païen dans la pensée française* (Paris: Le Labyrinthe, 1986), 64–66.
25. Marlaud, *La renouveau païen dans la pensée française*, 132. Cf. Bernard Rio, *L'arbre philosophal* (Lausanne: L'Âge d'Homme, 2001).
26. Quoted in Robert de Herte, "Le retour des dieux," *Éléments* 27 (Winter 1978).
27. Christian Bouchet, *Néo-paganisme* (Puiseaux: Pardès, 2001). Cf. Julius Evola, *Masques et visages du spiritualisme contemporain*, trans. Philippe Baillet (Puiseaux: Pardès, 1991).
28. Benoist, *Comment peut-on être païen?*, 18–25.
29. Vial, "Réflexions pour un débat." As Kierkegaard writes, "Everything that passes for politics today will be unmasked as religion tomorrow." Quoted in Irving Kristol, *Reflections of a Neoconservative* (New York: Basic Books, 1983), vi.
30. Benoist, *Comment peut-on être païen?*, 157–74.
31. Jean Markale, *The Celts: Uncovering the Mythic and Historic Origins of Western Culture*, trans. Christine Hauch (Rochester, VT: Inner Traditions, 1993), 297. Cf. Thorleif Boman, *Hebrew Thought Compared with Greek*, trans. Jules L. Moreau (New York: Norton, 1970 [1960]).
32. Faye, "La problématique moderne de la raison ou la querelle de la rationalité"; Marlaud, *Le renouveau païen dans la pensée française*, 68–71; Dominique

Venner, *Histoire et tradition des européens: 30,000 ans d'identité* (Paris: Rocher, 2002), 108.
33. Marlaud, *Le renouveau païen dans la pensée française*, 49.
34. Sigrid Hunke, *Von Untergang des Abendlands zum Aufgang Europas* (Rosenheim: Horizonte, 1989), 296.
35. Benoist, *Comment peut-on être païen?*, 34.
36. Quoted in Robert Dun, "Confidences d'un loup-garou," in *Païen!*, ed. Pierre Vial (Saint-Jean-des-Vignes: Éds. de la Forêt, 2001).
37. Friedrich Nietzsche, *Human, All Too Human*, trans. Marion Faber (Lincoln: University of Nebraska Press, 1984), § 114.
38. Alain de Benoist, "L'ordre," *Études et recherches* 4–5 (January 1977); Benoist, *Comment peut-on être païen?*, 56; Walter F. Otto, *Die Götter Griechenland* (Frankfurt am Main: Klostermann, 1987), 15–20.
39. Bernard Marillier, *Indo-Européens* (Puiseaux: Pardès, 1998), 61.
40. Alain de Benoist, *Les idées à l'endroit* (Paris: Hallier, 1979), 185; Christopher Gérard, *Parcours païen* (Lausanne: L'Âge d'Homme, 2000), 20.
41. "Entretien avec Alain de Benoist: Comment peut-on être païen?," *Éléments* 89 (July 1997); Jean Haudry, "Aux sources indo-européennes de notre paganisme" in *Païen!*, ed. Pierre Vial (Saint-Jean-des-Vignes: Éds. de la Forêt, 2001); Marie-Louise Sjoestedt, *Gods and Heroes of the Celts*, trans. Myles Dillon (Berkeley, CA: Turtle Island Foundation, 1982), 29.
42. Jean Mabire, ed., *Julius Evola: Le visionnaire foudroyé* (Paris: Copernic, 1977), 20; Gérard, *Parcours païen*, 15; Pierre Le Vigan, "L'Europe et son identité religieuse," *Éléments* 72 (Winter 1991).
43. Benoist, *Comment peut-on être païen?*, 213–15.
44. Benoist, *Les idées à l'endroit*, 46.
45. Benoist, *Les idées à l'endroit*, 54.
46. Rougier, *Du paradis à l'utopie*, 38.
47. Alain de Benoist, *L'empire intérieur* (Paris: Fata Morgana, 1995), 9; Marlaud, *Le renouveau païen dans la pensée française*, 24; Giorgio Locchi, "Die Zeit der Geschichte," *Elemente für die europäische Wiedergeburt* 1 (July 1986); Benoist, *Comment peut-on être païen?*, 18–19.
48. So claims not only the "numinous" school of comparative mythology (Mircea Eliade, Walter F. Otto, Jean-Pierre Vernant et al., to which the GRECE is close), but also structuralists around Claude Lévi-Strauss and neo-Kantians associated with Ernst Cassirer. See Kurt Hübner, "La recherche sur le mythe: Une révolution encore méconnue," *Krisis* 6 (October 1990). On logic's "unphilosophical" character and its problematic "principle of identity," see Martin Heidegger, *Introduction to Metaphysics*, trans. Ralph Manheim (New Haven, CT: Yale University Press, 1953), 21–36, 170–79; Friedrich Nietzsche, *The Gay Science*, trans. Walter Kaufmann (New York: Vintage, 1974), § 111; and Alain de Benoist, "Les fausses alternatives" (1983), in *La ligne de mire I: Discours aux citoyens européens, 1972–1987* (Paris: Le Labyrinthe, 1995).
49. Paul Veyne, *Did the Greeks Believe in Their Myths? An Essay on the Constitutive Imagination*, trans. Paula Wissing (Chicago: University of Chicago Press, 1988), 21.

50. "Itinéraire," *Nouvelle École* 19 (September 1969); Veyne, *Did the Greeks Believe in Their Myths?*; Nietzsche, *The Gay Science*, § 344. Even science, whose knowledge of nature is similarly mediated, is a form, however sophisticated, of mythic thought. See Thomas S. Kuhn, *The Structure of Scientific Revolutions*, 3rd ed. (Chicago: University of Chicago Press, 1996), in which the problem of competing scientific paradigms is posed ultimately as an aesthetic one, based less on the procedures of normal science than on culturally-informed preferences. Revealingly, *mythos* and *logos* were originally interchangeable terms. See Benoist, *L'empire intérieur*, 9, 54.
51. Roger Caillois, *L'homme et le sacré*, 2nd ed. (Paris: Gallimard, 1950), 132–36; H. R. Ellis Davidson, *Gods and Myths of Northern Europe* (Harmondsworth, UK: Penguin, 1964), 9–10.
52. Giorgio Locchi, "Mythe et communauté" (1979), at *Voxnr* (http://www.voxnr.com).
53. Jean-François Lyotard claims modernity emerged once the *grand récit* of Christian redemption was secularized and used to legitimate the primacy of scientific reason. In rejecting metanarrative notions of universalism, objective reason, and determinism, postmodernism bears a certain kinship to pre-Christian paganism. Not coincidentally, Lyotard went through a pagan phase, in which he sought out its *petits récits* as an alternative to Christianity's "logocentric" narrative. He failed, however, to pursue his paganism to its logical end. Not only did he end up rejecting its mythic sense of the sacred, he rejected its pillars of blood, community, tradition, and history. He turned instead to the "minority groups" and "libidinal flows" of the present global order for his *petits récits*, as if these, and not historical communities whose organic cultures thrive on myth and poetry, could possibly resist the modern narrative. New Rightists may follow Lyotard in accepting that the postmodern subject must look to itself for certainty, but they take their distance from him in defining the subject not in terms of libidinal subjectivities, but according to those mythic "verities" rooted in the distant reaches of Europe's primordial heritage.
54. Mircea Eliade, *Myths, Dreams and Mysteries*, trans. Philip Mairet (New York: Harper and Row, 1960), 14–15.
55. Kurt Hübner, *Die Wahrheit des Mythos* (Munich: Beck, 1985), 257–70; Alain de Benoist, "Un mot en quatre lettres," *Éléments* 95 (June 1999).
56. Alain de Benoist, "Les mythes européens" (1984), in *Le grain de sable: Jalons pour une fin de siècle* (Paris: Le Labyrinthe, 1994); Benoist, *Les idées à l'endroit*, 115–21.
57. Robert de Herte, "La question religieuse," *Éléments* 17–18 (September 1976); Benoist, *Les idées à l'endroit*, 51.
58. Gilbert Durand, *Les structures anthropologiques de l'imaginaire* (Paris: Dunod, 1984), 323–24; Julien Freund, "Une interprétation de Georges Sorel," *Nouvelle École* 35 (Winter 1979–80).
59. Benoist, *L'empire intérieur*, 14–15. Cf. José Ortega y Gasset, *Historical Reason*, trans. Philip W. Silver (New York: Norton, 1984), 17–21.
60. Alain de Benoist, "Réflexions sur l'identité nationale," in *Une certaine idée de la France: Actes du XIXe colloque national du GRECE* (Paris: Le Labyrinthe,

1985). Cf. Georges Sorel, *Reflections on Violence*, trans. T. E. Hulme and J. Roth (Glencoe, IL: The Free Press, 1950), 48–53.
61. Marlaud, *Le renouveau païen dans la pensée française*, 30; Pierre Vial, "Servir la cause des peuples," in *La cause des peuples: Actes du XVe colloque national du GRECE* (Paris: Le Labyrinthe, 1982).
62. Martin Heidegger, *Parmenides*, trans. André Schuwer and Richard Rojcewicz (Bloomington: Indiana University Press, 1992), 60.
63. Friedrich Nietzsche, *The Birth of Tragedy*, trans. Walter Kaufmann (New York: Vintage, 1967), § 23; Marlaud, *Le renouveau païen dans la pensée française*, 29; Richard Eichler, "Die Geburt der Kunst aus dem Mythos," *Elemente der Metapolitik zur europäischen Neugeburt* 4 (1990).
64. Mircea Eliade, *The Sacred and the Profane: The Nature of Religion*, trans. Willard R. Trask (San Diego: Harcourt Brace Jovanovich, 1956), 68. Also Nietzsche, *Human, All Too Human*, § 96.
65. Veyne, *Did the Greeks Believe in Their Myths?*, 3, 14–15; "Les Grecs croyaient à leurs mythes: Entretien avec Jean-Pierre Vernant," *Krisis* 6 (October 1990).
66. Benoist, "Les mythes européens."
67. Friedrich Nietzsche: "Tradition arose without regard for good or evil or any immanent categorical imperative, but above all in order to preserve a community, a people." See *Human, All Too Human*, § 6. Also Gianni Vattimo, *The End of Modernity: Nihilism and Hermeneutics in Postmodern Culture*, trans. Jon R. Snyder (Baltimore: Johns Hopkins University Press, 1988), 120–21, 132.
68. Arnold Gehlen, *Man in the Age of Technology*, trans. Patricia Lipscomb (New York: Columbia University Press, 1980), 68.
69. Even while accepting that the "reflectivity" of modern social life entails ongoing change and that knowledge depends on new information and new perceptions, New Rightists stress that meaning and identity are only weakly tied to reflectivity. Modernity may have freed man from the customs and traditions that once shaped his behavioral modes, but no amount of self-reflectivity can substitute for those non-rational facets of history and culture that define man's innermost identity or sustain the meanings infusing his life with significance. Only an abstract, decontextualized concept of man—the self as a purely reflexive project—renders tradition entirely superfluous.
70. Benoist, *Les idées à l'endroit*, 115.
71. Venner, *Histoire et tradition des européens*, 49. Also Dominique Venner, "La tradition, une idée d'avenir," *Relève politique* 2 (Spring 2002).
72. Herte, "La question religieuse."
73. Russell Kirk, "The Question of Tradition" (1989), in *The Paleoconservatives: New Voices of the Old Right*, ed. Joseph Scotchie (New Brunswick, NJ: Transaction Publishers, 1999), 61.
74. Venner, *Histoire et tradition des européens*, 17; Alain de Benoist, *Vu de Droite: Anthologie critique des idées contemporaines*, 5th ed. (Paris: Copernic, 1979), 156.
75. Xavier Saint-Delphin and Luc Saint-Etienne, "La Droite et la religion," in *Aux sources de la Droite: Pour en finir avec les clichés*, ed. Arnaud Guyot-Jeannin (Lausanne: L'Âge d'Homme, 2000).

76. Alain de Benoist, *Les traditions d'Europe*, 2nd ed. (Paris: Le Labyrinthe, 1996); Alain de Benoist, *Le guide pratique des prénoms* (Paris: Enfants Magazine, 1979); Alain de Benoist and Pierre Vial, *Le Mort: Traditions populaires, histoire et actualité* (Paris: Le Labyrinthe, 1983); Alain de Benoist, *Fêter Noël* (Paris: Atlas-Edena, 1982); Jean Mabire and Pierre Vial, *Les solstices: Histoire et actualité* (Paris: GRECE, 1975); Jean Mabire, *Les dieux maudits: Récits de mythologie nordique* (Paris: Copernic, 1978). Most of the GRECE's work on tradition is to be found in *Éléments* and *Nouvelle École* and is too numerous to cite.
77. Cf. Jérémie Benoit, *Le paganisme indo-européen* (Lausanne: L'Âge d'Homme, 2001).

## Chapter V

# Archeofuturism

Without a memory of its collective past and the foundational myths defining and distinguishing it from others—without, that is, the encompassing cultural forces that bind a multiple of related individuals to a larger identity—a people, *Grécistes* argue, ceases to be a people.[1] The anti-identitarian contravention of these forces is especially prominent in the Christian/modernist concept of history, which disparages a people's origin and seeks deliverance from time's linear progression. Against Christians/modernists, New Rightists contrapose an "archeofuturist" concept, which holds that a people's greatest accomplishments arise from the most primordial impulses of its heritage. Lacking such an appropriation, they believe a meaningful future is all but impossible.

### The Christian/Modernist Concept of Time

Since history begins with man's original sin, Christians consider it a tale of his fallen state.[2] This directs their gaze beyond the "vale of tears," to the end of time, when man, or at least the saved among men, are to be returned to God's grace.[3] From this finalist (or eschatological) historical vision—whose culmination is to be the Last Judgement, Genesis' antipode—there arises the linear concept of time, in which the present issues from a former determination and the future follows the "path of time" to something better. Within the frame of this irreversible progression—running from the fall to salvation, from the particular to the redeeming universal—time ceases to function as a recurring cycle (as Thucydides, Vico, or Oswald Spengler thought) and becomes a vector, which ascends from creation (occurring but once) to Moses, to Jesus, to the Resurrection, and finally to the world's end. With events situated at different stages in salvation's progression along this ascent, each stage represents a present ("the now") distinct from a past ("the no-longer-now") and a future ("the not-yet-now"). Time is homogenized in this way into a sequence of successive now-points, each of which is roughly analogous to the other.[4] The linear series formed by this succession of now-points becomes, in turn, part of a "dynamic process in which the divine purpose is realized" (Christopher Dawson). Its emphasis on the teleological or culminant outcome of the historical process has a similar effect of embalming the past for the sake of a future repudiating all that precedes it.[5] In John Milton's phrase, history's mono-directional progression is a "Race of time / Till time stand fixt"—and man escapes it.[6]

Because it presupposes a rational necessity underlying time's irreversible course, New Rightists believe Christianity's linear concept of history has the ontological effect of locking man into an abstract temporal continuum whose single desired outcome—salvation—corrupts "the innocence of becoming" (Nietzsche).[7] Modernity also gives this concept a messianic cast, for Christianity's secular offshoots, liberalism and Marxism, share a similar *"telos* of redemption"—framed in managerial rather than spiritual terms, with the GNP replacing "the grace of Christ," happiness salvation, and reason faith, but nevertheless one in which history progresses beyond the past's errant legacy, as each new stage surmounts the previous one in "a continuous process of liberation."[8] Modernists refuse Christian transcendence, in effect, only to re-establish it as an immanent progression in which divine revelation gives way to the light of reason and the logic of history.[9] This secularized version of linearity makes time a process governed not by life, but by a metaphysics seeking deliverance in what lies ahead—specifically, "the global triumph of economic rationality," which offers its universal solution to every social, moral, and political "problem" bequeathed by the past.[10] In either its Christian or modernist form, then, the linear concept of history implies a directional, uniform, causal, and moral progression that anticipates the future as an "overcoming" of the past.[11]

Notwithstanding the rational necessity linking the beginning and end of history, the linear concept devalues the actual substance of history. As Paul Hazard describes it, the modernist views history as "a large sheet of paper covered with creases which need to be ironed out."[12] Just as the Christian believes history begins with original sin and man's exile from paradise, the liberal sees it as starting with the social contract that leads the individual out of the natural state of freedom and into the constraints imposed by society, and the Marxist assumes it commences with the end of primitive communism and the advent of class society. In all these variants, history is viewed as a progression leading beyond the "thralldom of the past"—that is, as a process that irons out the historical "creases." The soul's salvation, the market's progress, class struggle: each endeavors to overcome an original fall as the historical process strives to regain a pristine origin. They each, in a word, look to escape history, conceived as a detour between paradise lost and paradise regained.[13]

## The Longest Memory

Against the Christian/modernist concept of history, which "dialectically" negates an erring past in the name of an expiating future, New Rightists adopt the perspective of *la longue durée*, evoking from the Continent's primordial origins its longest memory—which "rises up in us whenever we become 'serious.'"[14] Through the "immemorial" (Nietzsche) in Europe's past, rather than through a future redemption, the longest memory summons the distant recesses of time, where the inmost sources of European existence lie.[15] From these, they claim, Europeans derive their identity, their modes of action, their governing ethic, and, above all, their means of shaping the future and ensuring their survival as a people. Without a firm anchorage in this memory, a people, they believe, lacks the means to survive.

The critic will ask, though: how cogent is it to think of Europe as comprising such a community of memory? Scholarly convention has long held that the ancient Near East prepared the seedbed of European culture and that European civilization owes its existence not to itself, but to another. The GRECE predictably rejects this *ex oriente lux* (light from the East) thesis, claiming it reflects the deracinating impulse of Christian/modernist universalism and its hostility to Europe's pre-Christian origins.[16] Against the diffusionist view situating Europe's roots in the Euphrates River valley, New Rightists argue for the integrity of European origins: "We come from the people of the *Iliad* and the *Edda*, not the *Bible*."[17] And in this, their historiographical apostasy, they have been especially fortunate in not having to await the vindication of another Schliemann or Evans. For the archeological advances of the last few decades, particularly the radiocarbon dating of Colin Renfrew and his team at Cambridge, have now uncovered a large body of evidence for the autochthonic origins of European civilization. This, in turn, has provoked a major revision in prehistoric studies, reframing them in terms more closely akin to the New Right's "Eurocentrism."[18] While this revision detracts not in the least from Near Eastern achievements, it does alter the conventional view of the Continent's "barbarian" origins and its alleged debt to non-European sources.[19]

New Rightists further contend that the historiographical disparaging of archaic Europe, with its culturally negative implications, pales in comparison with the indifference and disdain usually accorded to her

Indo-European progenitors.[20] Despite their pivotal role in "prehistory" and the popular interest they continue to generate, the history and study of the Indo-Europeans rarely makes it into the university curriculum. Stigmatized by their association with the Nazis' Aryan cult, their study since the war has been limited to a few academic institutions, and there to the margins of what are already marginalized disciplines. Yet, the Indo-Europeans, especially their Greco-Roman, Celtic, and Germanic offshoots, are the ones, New Rightists claim, who are Europe's founders. This emphasis on the Continent's "Aryan" heritage has predictably armed their critics, adept at *reductio ad Hitlerum*, with potentially explosive charges.[21] But the longest memory they invoke is motivated by biocultural rather then mere racialist concerns.[22] For better or worse, Europe's identitarian roots are those of the people who conquered its lands in the third and second millennia B.C., establishing not merely the basis of its languages, culture, and destiny, but its distinct biological constitution.

Besides rekindling the compromising associations German National Socialism brought to Indo-European studies, the New Right's interest in them commits identitarians to an intellectually daunting enterprise. When the GRECE first took up its metapolitical strategy in the late 1960s, Indo-European studies were a *terra incognita* within the intelligentsia, even though France was home to one of the world's greatest Indo-Europeanists.[23] Moreover, for the longest time (and still today), Indo-European studies have been mainly philological, unamenable to the sort of cultural project the GRECE hoped to pursue. Only with the work Georges Dumézil began producing in the late 1930s—largely neglected until *Grécistes* unearthed it—did it become possible to infer anything significant about the biocultural character of Europe's root peoples and challenge the prevailing *ex oriente lux* thesis.[24]

Working with a knowledge of 20 Indo-European languages and employing methods that had up to then been reserved for historical linguistics, Dumézil spent his entire academic life comparing the literary remains of the different Indo-European peoples. In these comparative studies, embracing 60 books and several hundred scholarly articles, he related details gleaned from the *Rig Veda*, the Homeric epics, the Irish tales of Cúchulainn, the Norse sagas, and other Indo-European literatures to patterns or configurations that seemed to make up shared wholes and point to a common origin (or to what Claude Lévi-Strauss, in his decontextualized and ahistorical adaptation of Dumézil's approach, called "structures").[25] Unlike previous students of comparative mythology (such as James G. Frazer), Dumézil did not assume the existence of a universal or archetypal reason, with cultural differences between peoples attributable to their different stage in the same evolutionary course of development. In accepting that one culture was irreducible to another, that the world languages had not a single, but a variety of origins, that the most primitive of the world's peoples, the pygmies of the Congo or the aborigines of Australia, did not represent the most archaic of cultural forms, he warned of the misunderstanding that inevitably comes when comparing the apparent similarities of disparate cultures. Only related elements from kindred cultures and peoples, he insisted, can be compared without distorting their inherent meaning.[26] Benoist writes: "Cultures, like *mentalités*, cannot be reduced to one another. They create their [own] universes and behave according to their own properties."[27]

The most culturally significant implication of Dumézil's vast *opus* came with the discovery of what he called the "tripartite ideology."[28] This ideology (or world view) allegedly influenced the way Indo-Europeans organized their societies, ordered their values, and envisaged their religious pantheons. As such, its discovery suggested that the Indo-Europeans were not merely a language group, but also a culture.[29] Central to this ideology and the culture animating it were society's division into three broad castes or "functions": sages, warriors, and producers. In addition to dividing labor and regulating social relations, these functions formalized what was most distinct to the Indo-European cultural style and hence to what would most influence the different national families succeeding them.[30] Although features of the tripartite ideology have been found among certain other peoples (the Japanese pre-eminently), Dumézil stressed that it was institutionalized and assumed conscious articulation primarily among Indo-Europeans. This makes it the defining element of their culture and, by implication, the essence of Europe's "living past."[31]

As New Rightists read Dumézil, the tripartite ideology sanctioned principles that not only established the basis of European culture, it allowed the highest representatives of their people to govern—that is, the wise men and priests who performed the sacred rituals and remembered the old stories, and the warrior aristocrats upon whose courage and self-sacrifice the community's survival depended. By contrast, farmers, stock-herders, craftsmen, traders—the producers—were relegated to the lowest social order (the "third function") and refused sovereign authority. Economic activity, as such, was justified only to the degree it was "necessary for ensuring the dignity of an existence conforming to one's own estate, without the lower instincts of self-interest or profit coming first."[32] In so conditioning the European *mentalité*, tripartition made wisdom and courage more important than economic-reproductive functions, even though the three functions formed a unity and could not be separated. Tripartition also gave culture, its high symbols and the power of its defining ideals, pride of place above other pursuits, unlike the modernist inversion of these values, which turns Europeans away from their solar traditions and toward the darkened realm of baser concerns.

Whenever New Rightists appeal to the longest memory or refer to Europe's Indo-European origins, they evoke, then, not simply the primordial stirrings of their people's being, but those ancient warrior and priestly virtues rebuking the shekel-counting mania of the modern *Geist*.[33]

## The Wellspring of Being

The first major thinker to inform the GRECE's philosophy of history—and theoretically validate Europe's longest memory—was Friedrich Nietzsche, for his rejection of modernist metaphysics and his embrace of the old Greek myths to counter the bloodless rationalism of Christian or modernist "dialecticians" anticipated the New Right's identitarian project. Moreover, in appealing to "we good Europeans," his philosophical project addressed "historiological" issues bearing specifically on the problems of historical fatigue and cultural renewal. From this, there has emerged the most radical of his ideas—the thought of Eternal Return—which is pivotal to the New Right's anti-liberal philosophy of history.[34]

As Giorgio Locchi interpreted it, the Nietzschean notion of Eternal Return does not imply a literal repetition of the past. It is an axiological rather than a cosmological principle. It represents, as such, a will to metamorphosis in a world that is itself in endless metamorphosis, serving as a principle of becoming that knows neither end nor beginning, only the process of life perpetually returning to itself. It thus affirms man's "world-open" nature, subject as he is to ongoing transformations and transvaluations.[35] Against the determinism implicit in modernity's progressive narrative, Nietzsche's Eternal Return exalts the old noble virtues that forged life's ascending instincts into a heroically subjective culture. Homer's Greeks might be dead and gone, yet, whenever "the eternal hourglass of existence is turned upside down," "opening" the future to the past, Nietzsche thought the epic spirit, as that which bears returning, might again be roused and lead to something analogous.[36]

Life, he argued, is not a timeless essence inscribed with a predetermined *telos*. As being, it is becoming, and becoming is will to power. Eternal Return here represents the affirmation of man's original being, the assertion of his difference from others, and, in its infinite repertoire of exemplary past actions, the anticipation of whatever his future might hold. Its recurring past functions thus as a "selective thought" that puts memory's endless assortment of experience in service to life. As Vattimo characterizes it, the past is "an always available reserve of future positions."[37] Man has only to envisage a future similar to some select facet of what has gone before to initiate its return.[38] The past, then, is not a point on a line, a duration measurable in mechanical clock time, understandable as an onward succession of consecutive "nows." Rather, it recurs as a "genealogical" differential whose origin inheres in its willful assertion. This makes it recoverable for futural re-enactments that endeavor to continue life's adventure.[39] Just as the pagan gods live forever and the end of one cycle commences another, the past of Nietzsche's Eternal Return recurs in every successive affirmation of will, in every conscious exertion of memory, in each instant when will and memory become interchangeable. It is consequently reversible, repeatable, and recoverable.

This past is also of a whole with other temporalities. I can never be younger, but as time advances, the future recedes. In the present, these temporalities meet. The human sense of time comes in this way to encompass an infinity of temporalities, as past, present, and future converge in each passing moment. Since this infinity is all of a piece, containing all the dimensions of time, as well as all the acts of man, affirmed in their entirety "whenever we affirm a single moment of it," the present functions as an intersection, not a division, between past and future.[40] Within this polychronous totality, man's will is free to access an expanse of time, in which there is no prescribed end, only possibility. As to historical teleology or finality, they are for Nietzsche mere derivatives of the Christian/modernist indifference to life's temporal play. Against this indifference, he stresses that it is man's participation in the eternal recurrence of his original affirmation that imposes order on the world's underlying chaos and hence it is man who shapes the future—not a supra-human force that goes by the name of God, Progress, or the laws of Historical Materialism.[41] In the spirit of the ancient Hellenes, who treated life's transience as the conjuncture of the actual and the eternal, of men and gods, Nietzsche's Eternal Return testifies to both the absence of a preordained historical meaning and the completeness of the present moment.[42]

Nietzsche's refusal of linear temporality infuses man with the idea that he always has the option of living the thought of Eternal Return. Just as every past was once a prefiguration of a sought-after future, every future arises from a past anticipation—that can be anticipated again. "The impossible," as teleologically decreed, "is not possible."[43] Indeed, only in seeking to overcome that which resists is life's will to power manifested. His *Übermensch*, the antithesis of modern man stuck in the one-dimensional world of the present, is steeped in the longest memory not because he bears the accumulated wisdom of the past, but because he rejects the weariness of those governed by an imagined necessity and instead imposes his will, as an assertion of his being, upon the vagaries of time.[44] Memory here is synonymous with will.

In this context, Mircea Eliade reminds us that in ancient Aryan myth, the gods fall from the heavens whenever their memories fail them. Those who remember, however, are immutable.[45] In Greek legend, the goddess Mnemosyne, the personification of memory and the mother of the Muses, is omniscient because she recalls everything. The poets the muses inspire draw on Mnemosyne's knowledge to return to the font of their being and to what is most originating in them.[46] Unlike the Christian/modernist approach to history, which sees the past as working out a divine or immanent *logos*, early Greek thought searched for the laws of becoming, the exemplary models, that would open man to primordial time—where culture, cosmos, and myth were at play.[47] Eternal Return, as such, has nothing to do with repeating the same thing endlessly, but of enabling man to create himself again and again, in a world where time—and possibility—are eternally open. It replicates in this way the mythic process, reinvigorating the images that have the potential to save Western man from his nihilism.[48]

Nietzsche's identification of being with becoming should not be taken to mean that the genealogical spirit of mythic origins—the spirit of an eternally open and purposeless world subject solely to the active force of will—gives man the liberty to do whatever he pleases. The limits he faces remain those posed by the conditions of his epoch and by nature. In the language of social science, Nietzsche fully acknowledges the inescapable constraints of structures, systemic forces, or what Auguste Comte called "social statics." Yet, within these limits, all that is possible is possible, for man's activities are always prospectively open to the possibilities inherent in the moment, whenever these are appropriated according to his own determinations: that is, whenever man engages the ceaseless struggle that is his life. "Necessity," he argues, "is not a fact, but an interpretation."[49] History does not reflect the divine will or the market's logic, but the struggle between men over the historical images they choose for themselves. What ultimately conditions existence in this view is less what acts on man from the outside ("objectivity") than on what emanates from the inside (will), as he "evaluates" the forces affecting him. Nature, history, and the world may therefore affect the way man lives, but they do so not as "mechanical necessities."

Given this rejection of both immanent and transcendental forms of determinism, Nietzsche's concept of history is far from being a literal recapitulation of the primitive cyclical concept of time. According to Eliade, the Eternal Return of archaic societies implies an endless repetition of time, that is, another sort of "line" (a circle).[50] By contrast, Nietzsche eschews time's automatic repetition, seeing Eternal Return in non-cyclical, as well as non-linear terms. The eternity of the past and the eternity of the future, he posits, necessitate the eternity of the present and the eternity of the present cannot but mean that whatever has happened or will happen is always at hand in thought, ready to be potentialized.[51] Just as being is becoming, chance the verso of necessity, and will the force countering as well as partaking in the forces of chaos, the eternity of the Nietzschean past reverberates in the eternity of the future, doing so in a manner that opens the present to its possibilities.[52] The past of Eternal Return is thus nostalgic not for the past, as it is with primitive man, but for the future. History, Locchi notes, only has meaning when one tries to surpass it.[53]

Neither linear nor cyclical, Nietzsche's concept of time is spherical. In the "eternally recurring noontide," the different temporal dimensions of man's mind form a "sphere" in which thoughts of past, present, and future revolve around one another, taking on new significance as each of their moments becomes a center in relation to the others. Within this polychronous swirl, the past does not occur but once and then freeze behind us, nor does the future follow according to determinants situated along a sequential succession of linear developments. Rather, past, present, and future inhere in every moment, never definitively superseded, never left entirely behind.[54] "O my soul," his Zarathustra exclaims, "I taught you to say 'today' as well as 'one day' and 'formerly' and to dance your dance over every Here and There and Over-There."[55] Existentially, the simultaneity of these tenses enables man to overcome the inertia of duration or succession. There is no finality, no obstacle to freedom. Whenever the Janus-headed present alters its view of the different temporalities situating it, its vision of past and future similarly changes. The way one stands in the present consequently determines how everything recurs.[56] And since every exemplary past was once the prefiguration of a sought-after future, these different temporalities have the potential of coming into new alignment, as they phenomenologically flow back and forth into one another.

Recollected from memory and anticipated in will, the past, like the future, is always at hand, ready to be actualized.[57] Whenever this happens and a particular past is "redeemed" from the Heraclitean flux to forge a particular future, the "it was" becomes a "thus I willed it."[58] In this fashion, time functions like a sphere that rolls forward, toward a future anticipated in one's willful image of the past.[59] Existence, it follows, "begins in every instant; the ball There rolls around every Here. The middle [i.e., the present] is everywhere. The path of eternity is crooked [i.e., non-linear]."[60] This recurrence, moreover, goes beyond mere repetition, for the re-enactment of an archaic configuration is invariably transfigured by its altered context. The conventional opposition between past and future likewise gives way before it, as the past, conceived as a dimension of the polycentric present, becomes a harbinger of the future and the future a recurrence of the past. The present consequently ceases to be a point on a line and becomes a crossroad, where the totality of the past and the infinite potential of the future intersect. This means history has no direction, except that which man gives it. He alone is the master of his destiny. And this destiny, like history, bears a multitude of possible significations. As in pagan cosmology, the world is a *polemos*, a field of perpetual struggle, a chaos of unequal forces, where movement, submission, and domination rule. As such, it knows only particular finalities, but no universal goal. Becoming is eternal—and the eternal contains all possibility.[61]

Whenever the man of Eternal Return rejects the *ressentiment* and bad conscience of the teleologists and steps fully into his moment, Nietzsche counsels: *Werde das, was Du bist!* [62] He does not advocate the Marxist-Hegelian *Aufhebung*, liberal progress, or Christian salvation, but a heroic assertion that imbues man with the archaic confidence to forge a future true to his higher, life-affirming self. Becoming what you are implies here both a return and an overcoming. Through Eternal Return, man—"whose horizon encompasses thousands of years past and future"—returns to and hence transvalues the spirit of those foundational acts that marked his ancestors' triumph over the world's chaos. This first historical act, which myth attributes to the gods, involved choosing one's culture, one's second nature. All else follows on its basis—not through reproduction, though, but through the making of new choices posed by the original act. There is, indeed, no authentic identity other than this perpetual process of self-realization.

In effecting man's sense of history, Eternal Return overcomes the resentment that dissipates his will, the bad conscience that leaves him adrift in the random stream of becoming, the conformist pressures that subject him to the determinations of the modern narrative. Instead, as will to power, it compels man to confront what he believes are the essential and eternal in life, and they, in turn, impart something of the essential and eternal to the "marvelous uncertainty" of his own finite existence, as he goes beyond himself in being himself. The willful becoming of Eternal Return functions thus, as a means of defining man's higher self, as the return of the essential and eternal validates both his origins and the values—the mode of existence—he proposes for his future.

Since such a disposition is framed in the genealogical context of a primordial origin, Eternal Return (*pace* Foucault and the postmodernists) fosters not an atomized, discontinuous duration in which becoming is out of joint with being, but a self-justifying coherence uniting individual fate and collective destiny in a higher creativity—even if this "coherence" is premised on the belief that the world lacks an inherent meaning or purpose.[63] Every individual act becomes in this sense inseparable from its historical world, just as the historical world, product of multiple individual valuations, pervades each individual act. "Every great human being," Nietzsche writes, "exerts a retroactive force: for his sake all of history is placed in the balance again."[64] Whenever, then, the thought of Eternal Return puts the past and future in the balance, as the present casts its altering light on them, it re-establishes "the innocence of becoming," enabling the active man to decide his fate—in contrast to the life-denigrating man of mechanical or teleological necessity, whose past is fixed and whose future is foreordained.[65]

The final, and today most important, component of the GRECE's historical philosophy comes from Martin Heidegger, whose anti-modernist thought began to influence its metapolitical project, and supplant that of Nietzsche, in the early 1980s.[66] Like the author of *Thus Spoke Zarathustra*, Heidegger rejects Christian/modernist metaphysics, viewing man and history, being and becoming, as inseparable and incomplete. The past, he argues, may have passed, but its significance is neither left behind nor ever permanently fixed. When experienced as authentic historicity, it "is anything but what is past. It is something to which I can return again and again."[67] Thus, while the past belongs "irretrievably to an earlier time," Heidegger believes it continues to exist in the form of a heritage or an identity that is able to "determine 'a future' in the present."[68] In this spirit, he claims "the original essence of being is time."[69]

Unlike other species of sentient life, Heideggerian man (like Nietzschean and Gehlenian man) has no predetermined ontological foundation: he alone is responsible for his being. Indeed, he is that being whose "being is itself an issue," for his existence is never fixed or complete, but open and unfinished.[70] It is he who leads his life and is, *ipso facto*, what he becomes. Man in Heidegger's understanding of the world is compelled thus to "make something of himself" and this entails that he "care" about his *Dasein* (his "being-there" as situated human existence). Inseparable from its specific historical-cultural context, *Dasein* is experienced as an ongoing possibility (inner rather than contingent) that projects itself toward a future that is "not yet actual."

The possibility man seeks in the world into which he is "thrown" is similarly conditioned by temporality, for time is not only the horizon against which he is thrown, it is the ground on which he realizes himself. Given, then, that time "draws everything into its motion," the possibility man seeks in the future (his project) is conditioned by the present situating him and the past affecting his sense of possibility. Possibility is thus not any imagined possibility (as postmodernists are wont to believe), but a historically specific option that is both inherited and chosen. *Dasein*'s projection cannot, as a consequence, but come "toward itself in such a way that it comes back," anticipating its possibility as something that "has been" and is still present at hand.[71]

The three temporal dimensions (or ecstases) of man's consciousness are, for this reason, elicited whenever some latent potential is pursued.[72] Birth and death, along with everything in between, inhere in all his moments, for *Dasein* equally possesses and equally temporalizes past, present, and future, conceived not as fleeting, sequentially ordered now-points, but as simultaneous dimensions of mindful existence.[73] Therefore, even though it occurs "in time," *Dasein*'s experience of time (temporality) is incomparable with ordinary clock or calendar time, which moves progressively from past to present to future, as the flow of "nows" arrive and disappear. Instead, for Heidegger *Dasein*'s temporality (i.e., the time consciousness distinct to man in his specificity) proceeds from the anticipated future (whose ultimate possibility is death), through the inheritance of the past, to the lived present. *Dasein*'s time is hence not durational, in the quantitative, uniform way it is for natural science or "common sense," but existential, ecstatically experienced as the present thought of an anticipated future is "recollected" and made meaningful in terms of past references.

History in this sense never ends. It has multiple subjective dimensions that cannot be objectified in the way science objectifies nature. It is constantly in play. As Benoist writes, the historical "past" is a dimension, a perspective, implicit in every given moment.[74] Each present contains it. The Battle of Tours is long past, but its meaning never dies and always changes—as long as there are Europeans who remember it. The past, thus, is latent in existence and can always be revived. Because the "what has been, what is about to be, and the presence" (i.e., the "ecstatical unity of temporality") reach out to one another in every conscious moment and influence the way man lives his life, *Dasein* exists in all time's different dimensions. Its history, though, has little to do with the sum of momentary actualities which historians fabricate into their flattened narratives. Rather, it is "an acting and being acted upon which passes through the *present*, is determined from out of the future, and takes over the past."[75] When man chooses a possibility, he makes present, then, what he will be through a resolute appropriation of what he has been.[76] There is, moreover, nothing arbitrary in this appropriation, for it arises from the very process that allows him to open himself to and "belong to the truth of being," as that truth is revealed in its ecstatical unity. For the same reason, the present and future are not "dominated" by the past, for the appropriation of the past is made to free thought—and life—from the inertia of what has already been thought and lived. This makes history both subversive and creative, as it ceaselessly metamorphizes the sense of things.[77]

Man's project consequently has little to do with causal factors acting on his existence from the "outside" (what in conventional history writing is the purely factual or "scientific" account of past events) and everything to do with the complex ecstatical consciousness shaping his view of possibility (that is, with the ontological basis of human temporality, which "stretches" *Dasein* through the past, present, and future, as *Dasein* is "constituted in advance").[78] Because this ecstatical consciousness allows man to anticipate his future, *Dasein* is constantly in play, never frozen in an world of archetypes or bound to the linearity of subject-object relations. As such, the events historically situating it do not happen "just once for all nor are they something universal," but represent past possibilities which are potentially recuperable for futural endeavors.

For Heidegger, the notion of an irretrievable past makes no sense, for it is always at hand. Its thought and reality are therefore linked in that its meaning is inseparable from man, part of his world, and invariably changes as his project and hence his perspective changes. The past, then, cannot be seen in the way a scientist observes his data. It is not something independent of belief or perspective that can be grasped *wie es eigentlich gewesen* (Leopold von Ranke). Its significance (even its "factual" depiction) is mediated and undergoes ceaseless revision as man lives and reflects on his lived condition.[79] This frames historical understanding in existential terms, with the "facts" of past events becoming meaningful to the degree they belong to his "story"—that is to say, to the degree that what "has been" is still "is" and "can be." In Heidegger's language, "projection" is premised on "thrownness." And while such an anti-substantialist understanding of history—which sees the past achieving meaning only in relationship to the present—is likely to appear fictitious to those viewing it from the outside, "objectively," without participating in the subjective possibilities undergirding it, Heidegger argues that all history is experienced in this way, for what "has been" can be meaningful only when it is recuperable for the future.

As long, therefore, as the promise of the past remains something still living, still to come, it is not a disinterested aspect of something no longer present. Neither is it mere prologue, a path leading the way to a more rational future. It is, rather, something with which we have to identify if we are to resolve the challenges posed by our project—for only knowledge of who we have been enables us to realize the possibility of who we are.[80] Indeed, it is precisely modern man's refusal to realize his inner possibility and use those freedoms that "could ensure him a supra-natural value" that accounts for his "revolutionary, individualistic, and humanistic destruction of Tradition."[81]

Like Nietzsche, Heidegger believes that whenever *Dasein* "runs ahead towards the past," the "not yet actual" opens to the inexhaustible possibilities of what "has been" and what "can be." Based on this notion of temporality, both Heidegger and Nietzsche reject the abstract universalism of teleological becoming (suitable for measuring matter in motion or the Spirit's progression towards the Absolute), just as they dismiss decontextualized concepts of being (whether they take the form of the Christian soul, the Cartesian *cogito*, or liberalism's disembodied individual). Heidegger, however, differs from Nietzsche in making being, not will, the key to temporality. The often unbalanced sage of Sils-Maria, he claims, neither fully rejected the metaphysical tradition he opposed nor saw beyond beings to being.[82] Thus, while Nietzsche rejected modernity's faith in progress and perpetual overcoming (the *Aufhebung* which implies not only the transcendence but the leaving behind), his "will to power" allegedly perpetuated modernity's transcendental impulse by positing a subjectivity that is not "enowned" by being. As a possible corrective to this assumed failing, Heidegger privileges notions of *Andenken* (the recollection which recovers and renews tradition) and *Verwindung* (which is a going beyond that, unlike *Aufhebung*, is also an acceptance and a deepening)—notions implying not simply the inseparability of being and becoming, but becoming's role in the unfolding, rather than the transcendence, of being.[83]

Despite these significant differences, the anti-modernist aims Nietzsche and Heidegger share allies each of them to the GRECE's philosophical project. This is especially evident in the importance they both attribute to becoming and to origins. Heidegger thus argues that whenever being is separated from becoming and deprived of temporality, as it is in the Christian/modernist *logos*, then being—in this case, abstract being rather than being-in-the-world—is identified with the present, a now-point, subject to the determinisms governing Descartes' world of material substances.[84] This causes the prevailing philosophical tradition to "forget" that being exists in time, as well as space.[85] By rethinking being temporally and restoring it to becoming, Heidegger, like Nietzsche, makes time the horizon of all existence—freeing it from the quantitative causal properties of space and matter.

Because it is inseparable from becoming and because becoming occurs in a world-with-others, being is always embedded in a "context of significance" saturated with history and tradition. For as man pursues his project in terms of the worldly concerns affecting him, both his project and his world are informed by interpretations stemming from a longer history of interpretation. His future-directed project, in fact, is conceivable solely in terms of the world into which he is "thrown." Thus, while he alone makes his history, he does so as a "bearer of meaning," whose convictions, beliefs, and representations have been bestowed by a collective past.[86] Being, as such, is never a matter of mere facticity, but specific to the heritage (context) situating it. (Hence, the inescapable link between ontology and hermeneutics.) It is, moreover, this meaning-laden context that constitutes the "t/here" (*da*) in *Dasein*, without which being (*qua* being-in-the-world) is inconceivable.[87] And because there can be no *Sein* without a *da*, no existence without a specific framework of meaning and purpose, man, in his ownmost nature as being, is inseparable from the context that "makes possible what has been projected."[88] Being is possible then only in "the enowning of the grounding of the t/here."[89]

Unlike Cartesian reason, with its unfiltered perception of objective reality, Heidegger sees all thought as self-referential, informed by historical antecedents that are inescapable because they inhere to the only world *Dasein* knows. This leads him to deny rationalism's natural, timeless, ahistorical truths. Like being, truth is necessarily historical. Heidegger consequently rejects modernity's Cartesian metaphysics, which posits the existence of a rational order outside history. By reconnecting subject and object in their given temporality, he seeks to deconstruct modernity's allegedly objective cognitive order. "Every age," as R. G. Collingwood contends, "must write its own history afresh," just as every man is compelled to engage his existence in light of what has been handed down to him.[90]

In contrast to inauthentic *Dasein*—that "temporalizes itself in the mode of a making-present which does not await but forgets," accepting what is as an existentialist imperative (but which, situated as it is in "now time," is usually a corrupted or sclerotic transmission confusing the present's self-absorption with the primordial sources of life)—authentic *Dasein* "dredges" its heritage in order to "remember" or retrieve the truth of its possibility and "make it productively its own."[91] The more authentically the potential of this "inexhaustible wellspring" is brought to light, the more profoundly man becomes "what he is."[92] In this sense, authentic historicity "understands history as the 'recurrence' of the possible."[93] And here the "possible" is "what does not pass," what remains, what lasts, what is deeply rooted in oneself, one's people, one's world—in sum, it is the heritage of historical meaning that preserves what has been posited in the beginning and what will be true in the future.[94]

"I know," Heidegger said in 1966, "that everything essential and everything great originated from the fact that man . . . was rooted in a tradition."[95] In disclosing what has been handed down as a historically determined project, tradition discloses what is possible and what is innermost to man's being. The beginning of a heritage is thus never "behind us as something long past, but stands before us . . . as the distant decree that orders us to recapture its greatness."[96] The archaic force of origins, where being exists in its unconcealed fullness, is present, though, only when *Dasein* resolutely chooses the historically-specific possibility inherent in the heritage it inherits. In Benoist's formulation, "in matters of historical becoming, there are no established metaphysical truths. That which is true is that which is disposed to exist and endure."[97] This notion of historicity highlights not merely the openness of past and future, but the inevitable circularity of their representations.

The Christian/modernist concept of linear history, in deriving the sense of things from the future, inevitably deprives the detemporalized man of liberal thought of the means of rising above his necessarily impoverished because isolated self, cutting him off from the creative force of his original being and whatever "greatness"—truth—it portends. Conversely, whenever Heideggerian man is "great" and rises to the possibilities latent in his existence, he invariably returns to his autochthonous source, resuming there a heritage that is not to be confused with the causal properties of his thrown condition, but with a being whose authenticity is manifested in becoming what it is. Being in this sense "proclaims destiny, and hence control of tradition."[98] Again concurring with Nietzsche, Heidegger links man's existence with the "essential swaying of meaning" that occurred *ab origine*, when his forefathers created the possibilities that remain open for him to realize. From this original being, in which "quality, spirituality, living tradition, and race prevail" (Evola), man is existentially sustained and authenticated—just as a tree thrives in its native soil.[99] As Raymond

Ruyer writes, "one defends the future only by defending the past," for it is in the past that we discover new possibilities in ourselves.[100]

Though a self-conscious appropriation of origins hardly resolves the problems posed by the human condition, it nevertheless frees man from present-minded fixations on the inauthentic.[101] His "first beginning" also brings other beginnings into play—for it is the ground of all subsequent groundings.[102] Without a "reconquest" of *Dasein*'s original commencement (impossible in the linear conception, with its irreversible and deracinating progressions), Heidegger argues that there can never be another commencement.[103] Only in reappropriating the monumental impetus of a heritage, whose beginning is already a completion, does man come back to himself, achieve authenticity, and inscribe himself in the world of his own time. Indeed, only from the store of possibility intrinsic to his originary genesis, never from the empty abstractions postulated by a universal reason transcending historicity, does he approach the finite, historically-situated tasks "demanded" of him and open himself to the possibility of his world. Commencement, accordingly, lies in front of, not behind, him, for the initial revelation of being is necessarily anticipated in each new beginning, as each new beginning draws on its source, accessing there what has been preserved for posterity. Because the "truth of being" found in origins informs *Dasein*'s project and causes it to "come back to itself," what is prior invariably prefigures what is posterior. The past in this sense is future, for it functions as a return backwards, to foundations, where future possibility is ripest.

This makes origins—"the breakout of being"—all-important. They are never mere antecedent or *causa prima*, as modernity's inorganic logic holds, but "that from which and by which something is what it is and as it is. . . . [They are] the source of its essence" [i.e., its ownmost particularity] and the way truth "comes into being . . . [and] becomes historical."[104] As Benoist puts it, the "original" (unlike modernity's *novum*) is not that which comes once and for all, but that which comes and is repeated every time being unfolds in its authenticity.[105] In this sense, Heideggerian origins represent the primordial unity of existence and essence that myth affirms, for its memorialization of the primordial act suggests the gestures that can be repeated. Therefore, whenever this occurs—whenever myth's "horizon of expectation" is brought into view—concrete time is transformed into a sacred time, in which the determinants of the mundane world are suspended and man is free to imitate his gods.[106]

Given that origins, as "enowned" being, denote possibility, not the purely "factual" or "momentary" environment affecting its framework, human *Dasein* achieves self-constancy (authenticity) only when projected on the basis of its original inheritance—for *Dasein* is able to "come toward itself" only in anticipating its end as an extension of its beginning.[107] Origins, here, designate identity and destiny, not causation (the "wherein," not the "wherefrom"). Likewise, they are not "out there," but part of us and who we are, preserving what "has been" and providing the basis for what "continues to be." This makes them the ground of all existence, "gathering into the present what is always essential."[108]

The original repose of being that rescues authentic man from the "bustle of mere events and machinations" is not, however, easily accessed. To return *Dasein* to its ground and "recapture the beginning of historical-spiritual existence in order to transform it into a new beginning" is possible only through "an anticipatory resoluteness" that turns against the present's mindless routines.[109] Such an engagement—and here Heidegger's "revolutionary conservative" opposition to the established philosophical tradition is categorical—entails a fundamental questioning of the "rootless and self-seeking freedoms" concealing the truth of being: a questioning that draws "its necessity from the deepest history of man."[110] For this reason, Heidegger (like New Rightists) sees history as a "choice for heroes," demanding the firmest resolve and the greatest risk, as man, in anxious confrontation with his heritage, seeks to realize an indwelling possibility in face of an amnesic or obscurant conventionality.[111] This heroic choice (constituting the only authentic choice possible for man) ought not, however, to be confused with the subjectivist propensities of liberal individualism. A heroic conception of history demands action based on what is "original" and renewing in tradition, not on what is arbitrary or willful. Similarly, this conception is anything but reactionary, for its appropriation of origins "does not abandon itself to that which is past," but privileges the most radical opening of being.[112]

This existential reaching forward that, at the same time, reaches back affirms the significance of what Heidegger calls "fate."[113] Like Nietzsche's *amor fati*, fate in his view is not submission to the inevitable, but the "enowning" embrace of the heritage of culture and history into which man is thrown at birth. In embracing this heritage—in taking over the unchosen circumstances of his community and generation—man identifies with the collective destiny of his people, as he grounds his *Dasein* in the truth of his "ownmost particular historical facticity."[114]

Truth, in this sense, reflects not an objective reflection of reality, but a forthright response to destiny—to "the unfolding of a knowledge in which existence is already thrown" (Vattimo). The "I" of *Dasein* becomes in this way the "we" of a destining project. Against the detemporalized, deracinated individual of liberal thought, "liberated" from organic ties and conceived as a phenomenological "inside" separated from an illusive "outside," Heideggerian man achieves authenticity through a resolute appropriation of the multi-temporal, interdependent ties he shares with his people. In affirming these ties, Heidegger simultaneously affirms man's mindful involvement in the time and space of his own destined existence. Indeed, Heideggerian man cannot but cherish, for himself and his people, the opportunity to do battle with the forces of *fortuna*, for in doing so he realizes the only possibility available to him, becoming in the process the master of his "thrownness"—of his historical specificity. The community of one's people, "being-with-others" (*Mitsein*), becomes, then, "the *in* which, *out of* which, and *for* which history happens."[115] *Dasein*'s pursuit of possibility is hence necessarily a "co-historicizing" with a community, a co-historicizing that converts the communal legacy of the far-distant past into the basis of a meaningful future.[116] History for Heidegger is indeed possible only because *Dasein*'s individual fate—its inner "necessity"—connects with a larger sociocultural "necessity," as a people struggles against the perennial forces of decay and dissolution in order "to take history back unto itself."[117]

## The Future of the Past

In the present, the past and future coexist—as memory or tradition, anticipation or project. It is up to man to determine how to relate to these different temporalities. From pagan myth and the works of Nietzsche and Heidegger, *Grécistes* propound a historical philosophy that endeavors to free Europeans from the deculturating determinisms of the Christian/modernist project. Following Guillaume Faye, I call this philosophy "archeofuturism," for it posits that there can be no destining future without an original predestination.[118] If ever, then, Europeans are to regain the creative spirit of their being and play a historical role again, archeofuturism holds that they have no alternative but to rediscover "the original essence of their identity." This obliges them to reappropriate their longest memories, as they approach the future with the conviction of their ancestral lineage. If they continue, however, to pursue the liberal modernist principles that cause them to forget their origins and repress their inner vitality, archeofuturists fear they are likely to succumb to the "end of history," where the past ceases to return and the future folds in on an "eternal now."[119]

An archeofuturist emphasis on origins, to reiterate, does not imply that Europeans are bound to repeating the foundational acts of their forebears, such as occurs in "cold societies" (that is, in those primitive communities whose synchronic principles play a commanding role among anti-historical thinkers like Lévi-Strauss).[120] Instead of nostalgically perpetuating the identitarian vestiges of a former Golden Age, archeofuturists seek the original impetus of archaic possibilities so as to create new ones. As Benoist puts it, they are "nostalgic for what will be."[121] Indeed, for them the quest for a European identity is real only when under construction, deconstruction, or reconstruction. "We," he writes, "assume a heritage in order to continue it or refound it."[122] Identity here is neither rationale for present conditions nor occasion for a folkloric revival, but requisite to a meaningful future.[123]

The New Right's archeofuturism posits for this reason an unfolding of identity on the basis of the history and culture situating it. For unlike the denizens of Lévi-Strauss' "cold societies" or those of modern consumer societies, Europeans attuned to their heritage are true to themselves whenever they make choices endeavoring to begin the beginning again—"with all the strangeness, darkness, insecurity that attend a true beginning."[124] This makes the archeofuturist past "a permanent dimension of all lived moments." In this spirit, New Rightists feel Europeans do justice to whom they are only when they look forward, providing their heritage another opening to the future. "Remembrance of [our] inception," Heidegger writes, "is not a flight into the past, but readiness for what is to come."[125]

Heirs to the Indo-Europeans, the revolutionary forces gathered under the New Right banner today appeal to the Continent's longest memories because there the future is disclosed in its fullness and because there, where causality cedes to destiny, being commences anew. Every great revolution, Benoist reminds us, envisages its project as a return to origins.[126]

## Notes to Chapter V

1. Jean Varenne, "L'héritage indo-européen," *Éléments* 40 (Winter 1982); Alain de Benoist, *Orientations pour des années décisives* (Paris: Le Labyrinthe, 1982), 52–53; Pierre Krebs, *Im Kampf um das Wesen* (Horn: Burkhard Weecke Verlag, 1997), 16–20; Guillaume Faye, *Le système à tuer les peuples* (Paris: Copernic, 1981), 164–77; Friedrich Nietzsche, *Untimely Meditations*, trans. R. J. Hollingdale (Cambridge: Cambridge University Press, 1983), 63; Hellmut Diwald, *Mut zur Geschichte* (Bergisch Gladbach: Lübbe Verlag, 1983), 8. Cf. Christopher Dawson, "The Christian View of History," *Blackfriars* 32 (July 1951).
2. Sigrid Hunke, *Europas andere Religion: Die Überwindung der religiösen Krise* (Düsseldorf: Econ Verlag, 1969), 27–39. Cf. D. H. Lawrence, *Apocalypse* (New York: Viking, 1931), 59.

3. Alain de Benoist, *L'empire intérieur* (Paris: Fata Morgana, 1995), 31.
4. Alain de Benoist, "Sacré païen et désacralisation judéo-chrétienne du monde," in *Quelle religion pour l'Europe?*, ed. Démètre Théraios (Paris: Georg, 1990); Alain de Benoist, *Comment peut-on être païen?* (Paris: Albin Michel, 1981), 101–10. In Catholicism, especially among its former peasant adherents, this progressive sense was mitigated by "liturgical time," whose sacred calendar cyclically (i.e., annually) repeated the historical time of Jesus. Like other pagan encrustations, however, liturgical time has been largely eliminated in the "Novus Ordo Church" of Vatican II. See Alain de Benoist, "Le nouvelle calendrier liturgique," *Nouvelle École* 12 (March–April 1970).
5. Mircea Eliade, *Myth and Reality*, trans. Willard R. Trask (New York: Harper and Row, 1963), 134–35. Cf. Karl Löwith, *Meaning in History* (Chicago: University of Chicago Press, 1949); Oscar Cullmann, *Christ and Time: The Primitive Christian Conception of Time and History*, trans. Floyd V. Filson (New York: Harper and Row, 1967). The teleological is by no means foreign to the ancients; it is, for example, central to Aristotle's thought. But Aristotle, like Plato and Socrates before him, anticipated the Christian/modernist metaphysics opposed by *Grécistes*—Christianity being, in Nietzsche's phrase, a "Platonism of the masses." The Indo-European world view that has been lost and is lamented here, to use Greek examples, refers to the age of Homer, the pre-Socratics, and the tragedians.
6. John Milton, *Paradise Lost*, book 12, lines 554–55.
7. Alain de Benoist, "Recours au paganisme," in *Dieu est-il mort en Occident?*, ed. Danièle Masson (Paris: Guy Trédaniel, 1998).
8. Louis Rougier, *Du paradis à l'utopie* (Paris: Copernic, 1979), 125; Pierre Chassard, *La philosophie de l'histoire dans la philosophie de Nietzsche* (Paris: GRECE, 1975), 26–40. See also Carl Schmitt, *Political Theology*, trans. George Schwab (Cambridge, MA: MIT Press, 1985), 36–52; Martin Heidegger, *Hegel's Phenomenology of Spirit*, trans. Parvis Emad and Kenneth Maly (Bloomington: Indiana University Press, 1994), §§ 10a, 13b.
9. Martin Heidegger, *Contributions to Philosophy (From Enowning)*, trans. Parvis Emad and Kenneth Maly (Bloomington: Indiana University Press, 1999), § 7. Cf. Georges Sorel, *The Illusions of Progress*, trans. John and Charlotte Stanley (Berkeley: University of California Press, 1969).
10. "The social revolution ... cannot draw its poetry from the past, but only from the future." See Karl Marx, *The Eighteenth Brumaire of Louis Bonaparte* (1852), in *Selected Works* (Moscow: Progress Publishers, 1969), 1:400. Like those adhering to the Biblical, liberal, and Freudian traditions, Marxists conceive of origins in purely negative terms: the "long detour" that began with the abandonment of "primitive communism" (analogous to the expulsion from Eden/the end of the natural state/the patricidal act). Hence, the Marxist effort to "escape history." On the progressive impulse of liberal historiography, see Herbert Butterfield, *The Whig Interpretation of History* (New York: Norton, 1965).
11. Alain de Benoist, "Une brève histoire de l'idée de progrès," *Nouvelle École* 51 (2000); Alain de Benoist, *Les idées à l'endroit* (Paris: Hallier, 1979), 35–38. For a powerful critique of modern historicism that has much influenced the

New Right, see Julius Evola, *Les hommes au milieu des ruines* (Paris: Les Sept Couleurs, 1972), 109-18.
12. Paul Hazard, *The European Mind, 1680-1715*, trans. J. Lewis May (Cleveland: Meridian, 1963), 154; Alain de Benoist, "Comment le lien social a été rompu," *Éléments* 84 (February 1996).
13. Giorgio Locchi, "Die Zeit der Geschichte," *Elemente für die europäische Wiedergeburt* 1 (July 1986).
14. Friedrich Nietzsche, *On the Genealogy of Morals*, trans. Walter Kaufmann and R. J. Hollingdale (New York: Vintage, 1967), Essay I, § 3. "Grèce," it might be noted, is French for "Greece."
15. Pierre Vial, "Servir la cause des peuples," in *La cause des peuples: Actes du XVe colloque national du GRECE* (Paris: Le Labyrinthe, 1982), 67; Guillaume Faye, "Warum Wir Kämpfen," *Elemente für die europäische Wiedergeburt* 1 (July 1986).
16. Pierre Vial, "Aux sources de l'Europe," *Éléments* 50 (Spring 1984); Christian Lahalle, "Le peuplement de la Grèce et du basin égéen aux hautes époques," *Nouvelle École* 43 (December 1985). The most prominent recent, though dilettantish, variant of the *ex oriente lux* thesis is Martin Bernal, *Black Athena: The Afroasiatic Roots of Classical Civilization*, 2 vols. (New Brunswick, NJ: Rutgers University Press, 1987-91).
17. "Thème central," *Nouvelle École* 17 (March-April 1972); Pierre Krebs, *Das Thule-Seminar: Geistesgegenwart der Zukunft in der Morgenröte des Ethnos* (Horn: Burkhart Weecke Verlag, 1994), 88.
18. Vial, "Aux sources de l'Europe"; André Cherpillod, "L'écriture en Europe à l'époque préhistorique," *Nouvelle École* 50 (1998). Also Colin Renfrew, *Before Civilization: The Radiocarbon Revolution and Prehistoric Europe* (New York: Cambridge University Press, 1979); Alexander Marshack, *The Roots of Civilization: The Cognitive Beginnings of Man's First Art, Symbol and Notation* (New York: McGraw-Hill, 1972); Marija Gimbutas, *The Goddesses and Gods of Old Europe, 6500-3500 B.C.* (London: Thames and Hudson, 1982); Richard Rudgley, *The Lost Civilizations of the Stone Age* (New York: The Free Press, 1998); Barry Cunliffe, ed., *Prehistoric Europe: An Illustrated History* (Oxford: Oxford University Press, 1994). These discoveries had long been suspected; see Geoffrey Bibby, *The Testimony of the Spade* (New York: Merton, 1957). Recent archeological digs in the south of France now indicate that both writing and agriculture may, in fact, have originated in Europe several millennia before they are thought to have developed in the Near East. See Michael Bradley, "A Cradle in the Wrong Place," *National Post* (Canada) (July 5, 2000).
19. The evidence should, but has not discredited the old diffusionist view. In a characteristic display of the *ex oriente lux* influence among "Anglo-Saxon" historians, J. M. Roberts acknowledges the recent evidence that puts Europe's civilizational origins on a par with Near Eastern ones, yet nevertheless roots Europe's identity in the "Holy Lands." See *A History of Europe* (New York: Allen Lane, 1996), 12-20, 54.
20. This is evident in the work of such ideologically inspired historians of the ancient world as Moses Finley and Pierre Vidal-Naquet, both of whom view the world of Homer and the Myceneans in terms of their supposed Near Eastern

filiations. See Alain de Benoist, *Vu de Droite: Anthologie critique des idées contemporaires*, 5th ed. (Paris: Copernic, 1979), 45. For a brief but first-rate overview of Indo-European studies, see Bernard Marillier, *Indo-Européens* (Puiseaux: Pardès, 1998); also John V. Day, "In Quest of Our Linguistic Ancestors: The Elusive Origins of the Indo-Europeans," *The Occidental Quarterly: A Journal of Western Thought and Opinion* 2:3 (Fall 2002).

21. David Barney, "Le stade pipi-caca de la pensée," *Éléments* 42 (June 1982).

22. "Itinéraire," *Nouvelle École* 21-22 (Winter 1972-73); Marco Tarchi, "Prolégomènes à l'unification de l'Europe," in *Crépuscule des blocs, aurore des peuples: XXIIIe colloque national du GRECE* (Paris: GRECE, 1990); Charles Champetier, "Anti-utilitarisme: des nouveau clivages," *Éléments* 74 (Spring 1992); Alain de Benoist, "Les Indo-Européens: à la recherche du foyer d'origine," *Nouvelle École* 49 (1997). *Grécistes* do not view the Indo-Europeans as a racial group, but as a linguistic-cultural one. Contrary to the claims of their critics, the question of race is irrelevant here, for all the peoples of archaic Europe, whether Indo-European or non-Indo-European, were Europid ("white"), descendants of the Cro-Magnons. What is at stake is biocultural identity, not race, though liberal universalists (with their abstract concept of humanity) have trouble following the logic of this distinction. See Benoist, *Comment peut-on être païen?*, 174; Claude Lévi-Strauss, *Race et histoire* (Paris: Denoël, 1987), 23; Oswald Spengler, *The Decline of the West*, trans. Charles Francis Atkinson (New York: Knopf, 1989), 1:21. Moreover, given the GRECE's opposition to the former Soviet Union and its ongoing opposition to the US, it rejects notions of "racial unity" with the so-called "white world." See Guillaume Faye, "Il n'y a pas de 'Monde Blanc,'" *Éléments* 34 (April 1980). This, arguably, concedes too much to the dominant ideology. For a trenchant critique of the implicit (and racially unconscious) egalitarianism undergirding the GRECE's culturalism, see Guillaume Faye, *La colonisation de l'Europe: Discours vrai sur l'immigration et l'Islam* (Paris: L'Æncre, 2000), 74-84, a work that revises Faye's earlier position in stressing the biocultural rather than the merely cultural basis of identity.

23. Benoist, "Les Indo-Européens." In this context, it is relevant to note that the young Dumézil was forced to find employment outside France because, as his mentor told him, there was "no place" for him in the French university system. See Marco V. Garcia Quintela, *Dumézil: Une introduction*, trans. Marie-Pierre Bouyssou (Crozon: Éds. Armeline, 2001), 25.

24. On Georges Dumézil, see C. Scott Littleton, *The New Comparative Mythology: An Anthropological Assessment of the Theories of Georges Dumézil*, 3rd ed. (Berkeley: University of California Press, 1982); Garcia Quintela, *Dumézil*. See also Jean-Claude Rivière, ed., *Georges Dumézil à la découverte des Indo-Européens* (Paris: Copernic, 1979); Jean Varenne, "L'héritage de Georges Dumézil," *Éléments* 62 (Spring 1987). For a critique of his work, see Wouter W. Belier, *Decayed Gods: Origin and Development of Georges Dumézil's "Idéologie Tripartite"* (Leiden: Brill, 1991).

25. C. Scott Littleton, "'Je ne suis pas . . . structuraliste': Some Fundamental Differences between Dumézil and Lévi-Strauss," *Journal of Asian Studies* 34:1 (November 1974); Georges Dumézil, *Mythe et épopée III: Histoires romaines* (Paris: Gallimard, 1973), 14-15. Relatedly, it is worth noting that Dumézil has

had a formative influence on one of the great postmodernists: see Didier Eribon, *Michel Foucault et ses contemporains* (Paris: Fayard, 1994), 161.
26. Jean-Claude Rivière, "Pour un lecture de Dumézil," *Nouvelle École* 21–22 (Winter 1972–73).
27. Alain de Benoist, "Introduction," in Louis Rougier, *Le conflit du christianisme primitif et de la civilisation antique* (Paris: Copernic, 1977), 15.
28. On the tripartite ideology, see Georges Dumézil, *L'idéologie tripartite des Indo-Européens* (Brussels: Latomus, 1958); Jean Haudry, *La religion cosmique des Indo-Européens* (Milan: Arché, 1987); J. P. Mallory, *In Search of the Indo-Europeans: Language, Archaeology and Myth* (London: Thames and Hudson, 1989), 130–34.
29. Rivière, "Pour un lecture de Dumézil"; Jean Mabire, *Les dieux maudits: Récits de mythologie nordique* (Paris: Copernic, 1978), 21–27; Friedrich Nietzsche, *The Anti-Christ*, trans. R. J. Hollingdale (Harmondsworth, UK: Penguin, 1968), § 57.
30. J. H. Grisward, "Trois perspectives médiévales," *Nouvelle École* 21–22 (Winter 1972–73); Jean-Claude Rivière, "Archéologie de l'épopée médiévale," *Nouvelle École* 46 (Fall 1990). Cf. Georges Duby, *The Three Orders: Feudal Society Imagined*, trans. Arthur Goldhammer (Chicago: University of Chicago Press, 1980).
31. Dumézil, *Mythe et épopée III*, 341–42; "Georges Dumézil répond aux questions de Nouvelle École," *Nouvelle École* 10 (September 1969); "Itinéraire," *Nouvelle École* 21–22; Jean Haudry, "Die indoeuropäische Tradition als Wurzel unserer Identität," in *Mut zur Identität: Alternative zum Prinzip der Gleichheit*, ed. Pierre Krebs (Struckum: Verlag für Ganzheitliche Forschung und Kultur, 1988). The non-political Dumézil would pay dearly for his discoveries. In the 1980s, a full-scale witch-hunt was launched against him, initiated by the Italian-Jewish UCLA historian Carlo Ginzburg, who, in "Mythologie germanique et nazisme: Sur un ancien livre de Georges Dumézil," *Annales ESC* 40:4 (July–August 1985), accused him, in so many words, of Nazism. The charge was then taken up by the Left-wing daily *Libération* and made the rounds of several politically correct Parisian journals. The falseness of the charge and the readiness of certain intellectuals to use it to smear one of the century's great scholars, because his work happened to lend credence to certain nonconformist ideas, has been fully documented in Didier Eribon, *Faut-il brûler Dumézil? Mythologie, science et politique* (Paris: Flammarion, 1992); also Garcia Quintela, *Dumézil*, 123–98. On the "fascist" epithet as a political ploy for discrediting new ideas, see Hans-Helmuth Knütter, *Die Faschismus Keule: Das letzte Aufgebot der deutschen Linken* (Frankfurt am Main: Ullstein, 1993). On the "living past," see R. G. Collingwood, *An Autobiography* (Oxford: Oxford University Press, 1978), 96–98.
32. Julius Evola, *Revolt Against the Modern World*, trans. Guido Stucco (Rochester, VT: Inner Traditions, 1995), 98.
33. "Itinéraire," *Nouvelle École* 21–22. In contrast to ancient Indo-European society, where the sovereign function of politics determined the modalities of productive-reproductive activity, and hence their value and significance, modern society subordinates politics (the first function) to social-economic interests

(the third function). With this, the aspirations of the masses—by definition, base and uncultured—take command of the civilizational order. Similarly, merchants and producers impose themselves on warriors and sages. Work consequently ceases to be a service and is commodified, as great masses "are condemned to perform shallow, impersonal, automatic jobs" (Evola) for the sake of certain dubious materialist values. Likewise, land—in the form of farmstead or manor—that once represented a lineage becomes exchangeable for money; education is replaced by training, honor by guilt, aristocracy by elite, community by society, justice by social service. As the feminine principles associated with the third function take precedent over masculine ones, the father likewise ceases to be a patriarch and becomes a figure of good-natured ridicule. Universal rights are similarly granted without qualification, social functions lose their equilibrium, and rank becomes a matter of monetary standing. This, in turn, fosters an ethic of skepticism and relativism, as norms and established moralities are viewed as mere conventions to be flouted. Not coincidentally, the modernist inversion of the tripartite hierarchy makes traditional roles a mockery, organic consensus unattainable, true order an impossibility. As the spiritual poverty of this inversion spreads, so too does the enormous wealth and unmediated power of the third function presiding over this inverted hierarchy, in which the "inferior" dominates the "superior." See Benoist, "L'ordre." Nietzsche's characterization of this inversion is especially severe: "What is womanish, what stems from slavishness and especially from the mob hotchpotch: *that* now wants to become master of mankind's entire destiny." See *Thus Spoke Zarathustra*, trans. R. J. Hollingdale (London: Penguin, 1969), "Of the Higher Man."

34. Friedrich Nietzsche, *Beyond Good and Evil*, trans. Walter Kaufmann (New York: Vintage, 1966), § 56; Friedrich Nietzsche, *The Gay Science*, trans. Walter Kaufmann (New York: Vintage, 1974), §§ 285, 341; Nietzsche, *Thus Spoke Zarathustra*, "The Vision and the Riddle" and "The Convalescent." Also Philippe Granarolo, *L'individu éternel: L'expérience nietzschéenne de l'éternité* (Paris: Vrin, 1993), 37. Cf. M. C. Sterling, "Recent Discussions of Eternal Recurrence: Some Critical Comments," *Nietzsche-Studien* 6 (1977).
35. Eugen Fink, *Nietzsches Philosophie* (Stuttgart: Kohlhammer, 1960), 91.
36. Friedrich Nietzsche, *Human, All Too Human*, trans. Marion Faber (Lincoln: University of Nebraska Press, 1984), § 24; Benoist, *Les idées à l'endroit*, 74; Armin Mohler, "Devant l'histoire," *Nouvelle École* 27-28 (Winter 1974-75).
37. Gianni Vattimo, *The End of Modernity: Nihilism and Hermeneutics in Postmodern Culture*, trans. Jon R. Snyder (Baltimore: Johns Hopkins University Press, 1985), 82.
38. Pierre Chassard, *Nietzsche: Finalisme et histoire* (Paris: Copernic, 1977), 174; Clément Rosset, *La force majeure* (Paris: Minuit, 1983), 87-89; Jean-Pierre Martin, "Mythe et cosmologie," *Krisis* 6 (October 1990).
39. Granarolo, *L'individu éternel*, 34-52.
40. Friedrich Nietzsche, *The Will to Power*, trans. Walter Kaufmann and R. J. Hollingdale (New York: Vintage, 1967), § 1032.
41. Nietzsche, *The Will to Power*, § 706; Chassard, *La philosophie de l'histoire dans la philosophie de Nietzsche*, 114-18.
42. Fink, *Nietzsches Philosophie*, 75-92.

43. Nietzsche, *The Will to Power*, § 639.
44. Nietzsche, *Thus Spoke Zarathustra*, "Of the Vision and the Riddle." "Origins" for Nietzsche do not bear the timeless essence of things, but rather the unencumbered expression of their original being, the *Herkunft* that serves as *Erbschaft*. See Nietzsche, *On the Genealogy of Morals*, Essay II, § 12; *The Gay Science*, § 83. Cf. Michel Foucault, "Nietzsche, Genealogy, History," in *Language, Countermemory, Practice: Selected Essays and Interviews*, trans. Donald F. Bouchard and Sherry Simon (Ithaca, NY: Cornell University Press, 1977).
45. Eliade, *Myth and Reality*, 115–20.
46. J. P. Vernant, "Aspects mythiques de la mémoire en Grèce," *Journal de Psychologie* 56 (1959).
47. Eliade, *Myth and Reality*, 134–38.
48. Granarolo, *L'individu éternel*, 47–52.
49. Nietzsche, *The Will to Power*, § 552, also § 70; Giorgio Locchi, "Éthologie et sciences sociales," *Nouvelle École* 33 (Summer 1979).
50. Mircea Eliade, *The Myth of the Eternal Return; or, Cosmos and History*, trans. Willard R. Trask (Princeton, NJ: Princeton University Press, 1965), 36, 85–86, 117; also Mircea Eliade, *The Sacred and the Profane: The Nature of Religion*, trans. Willard R. Trask (San Diego: Harcourt Brace Jovanovich, 1959), 108–10.
51. Chassard, *La philosophie de l'histoire dans la philosophie de Nietzsche*, 121–22.
52. Nietzsche, *The Gay Science*, § 109.
53. Giorgio Locchi, "L'histoire," *Nouvelle École* 27–28 (January 1976).
54. Benoist, *Vu de droite*, 298–99.
55. Nietzsche, *Thus Spoke Zarathustra*, "Of the Great Longing." (Translation modified.)
56. Nietzsche, *The Gay Science*, § 233; Martin Heidegger, *Nietzsche: The Eternal Recurrence of the Same*, trans. David Farrell Krell (San Francisco: Harper and Row, 1984), 245; Benoist, *Les idées à l'endroit*, 38–40.
57. Alain de Benoist, "Fondements nominalistes d'une attitude devant la vie," *Nouvelle École* 33 (June 1979); "Itinéraire," *Nouvelle École* 24 (Winter 1973–74).
58. Nietzsche, *Thus Spoke Zarathustra*, "Of Redemption."
59. Locchi, "L'histoire"; and, from the same author, *Nietzsche, Wagner e il mito sovrumanista* (Rome: Akropolis, 1982).
60. Nietzsche, *Thus Spoke Zarathustra*, "The Convalescent."
61. Jacques Marlaud, *Le renouveau païen dans la pensée française* (Paris: Le Labyrinthe, 1986), 25; Chassard, *La philosophie de l'histoire dans la philosophie de Nietzsche*, 112–15; Benoist, *Vu de Droite*, 85–87.
62. Nietzsche, *Thus Spoke Zarathustra*, "The Honey Offering." The admonition—"Become that which you are"—is native to all traditional cultures. See Heinrich Jordis von Lohausen, *Denken in Völkern: Die Kraft von Sprache und Raum in der Kultur- und Weltgeschichte* (Graz: Stocker, 2001), 12–15.
63. In passing, it might be noted that postmodernists reject the linear concept for a flattened history that turns the past into a palimpsest whose significance is capricious and best ignored. Cf. Susan D. Ermarth, *Sequel to History: Postmodernism and the Crisis of Representational Time* (Princeton, NJ: Princeton University Press, 1992); Keith Jenkins, *Why History? Ethics and Postmodernity* (London: Routledge, 1999).

64. Nietzsche, *The Gay Science*, § 34.
65. Granarolo, *L'individu éternel*, 133-44; "Itinéraire," *Nouvelle École* 15 (March-April 1971).
66. "Lectures de Heidegger," *Nouvelle École* 37 (April 1982).
67. Martin Heidegger, *The Concept of Time*, trans. William McNeill (Oxford: Blackwell, 1992), 19.
68. Martin Heidegger, *Being and Time*, trans. John Macquarrie and Edward Robinson (New York: Harper and Row, 1962), § 79.
69. Heidegger, *Hegel's Phenomenology of Spirit*, § 13b.
70. Heidegger, *Being and Time*, § 79; Benoist, "Un mot en quatre lettres."
71. Heidegger, *Being and Time*, § 65.
72. Heidegger, *Being and Time*, §§ 69, 72; Benoist, *Comment peut-on être païen?*, 26.
73. Martin Heidegger, *On Time and Being*, trans. Joan Stambaugh (New York: Harper and Row, 1972), 11-15; Alain de Benoist, "La religion de l'Europe," *Éléments* 36 (Fall 1980).
74. Benoist, "La religion de l'Europe."
75. Martin Heidegger, *Introduction to Metaphysics*, trans. Ralph Manheim (New Haven, CT: Yale University Press, 1953), 44.
76. Heidegger, *Being and Time*, § 65.
77. This, incidentally, is why much contemporary history writing is so ahistorical—for it examines the past only to celebrate or criticize the present, treating it as a stepping stone, a determinant, perhaps a "place" to visit, but not as a lived dimension of the present and rarely as a herald of what is possible.
78. Heidegger, *Being and Time*, §§ 72, 76, and 79. The distinction between the "selective" character of memory, in its function as a people's cult of remembrance, and the scientific impulse of historical research, as it breaks with moral or ideological judgements, is emphasized in Alain de Benoist's *Communisme et nazisme: 25 réflexions sur le totalitarisme au XXe siècle* (Paris: Le Labyrinthe, 1998), 9-13. In stressing that memory demands affiliation and history distance, Benoist sides with "history" whenever the argument turns on the "facts"—the "objective truth"—of an issue. This, however, is a point whose problematic relation to an identitarian philosophy of history *Grécistes* have failed to clarify. As Heidegger argues, the "objective truth" of the professional historian is usually an evasion of historical understanding insofar as truth based on scientific methods and rules of procedures is mainly an expression of modernity's calculative logic: the factual explanation of "what is" being not necessarily the same as a knowing understanding of it. Although Heidegger's distinction between correctness (in the sense of correspondence) and truth (as enowning being) is relatively unambivalent (see *Contributions to Philosophy*, § 76), Benoist often marshals the "facts" against the selective memory of those with whom he polemicizes, assuming that memory based on distortion, ignorance, or repression is, *ipso facto*, at odds with history, and that "facts" and "history" ought to be understood in the conventional, i.e., epistemological, sense. While this suggest that the GRECE's historical philosophy is not to be confused with an identitarian solipsism, it still leaves unanswered the question of how "truth" relates to fact. Heidegger, for example, holds that truth, expressing being, which is neither subjective nor objective but a "happening unfolding" in the world, alone orders

"fact." Benoist, though, seems to hedge his argument here, conflating fact and truth in ways that would be unacceptable to Heidegger. This is especially evident in the articles devoted to "Mémoire et histoire" in *L'écume et les galets, 1991-1999: Dix ans d'actualité vue d'ailleurs* (Paris: Le Labyrinthe, 2000); also Alain de Benoist, *Dernière année: Notes pour conclure le siècle* (Lausanne: L'Âge d'Homme, 2001), 127-28. For an identitarian effort to resolve this problem, see Dominique Venner, *Histoire et tradition des européens: 30,000 ans d'identité* (Paris: Rocher, 2002), 264-65.

79. Robert Steuckers, "Conception de l'homme et Révolution conservatrice: Heidegger et son temps," *Nouvelle École* 37 (April 1982); Charles Champetier, *Homo Consumans: Archéologie du don et de la dépense* (Paris: Le Labyrinthe, 1994), 98.
80. Benoist, *Comment peut-on être païen?*, 26-27.
81. Julius Evola, "Über das Geheimnis des Verfalls," *Deutsches Volkstum* 14 (1938).
82. Martin Heidegger, "The Word of Nietzsche," in *The Question Concerning Technology and Other Essays*, trans. William Lovitt (New York: Harper and Row, 1977).
83. Vattimo, *The End of Modernity*, 51-64.
84. Heidegger, *Being and Time*, § 5; David L. Miller, *The New Polytheism: Rebirth of the Gods and Goddesses* (New York: Harper and Row, 1974), 48.
85. Heidegger, *The Concept of Time*, 12-13; Guillaume Faye and Patrick Rizzi, "Pour en finir avec le nihilisme," *Nouvelle École* 37 (Spring 1982).
86. Heidegger, *Being and Time*, § 5.
87. Heidegger, *Being and Time*, § 29; Heidegger, *Contributions to Philosophy*, § 120 and § 255. To see *Dasein* as pure existence, "stripped of all security and standing," causes many commentators to misread Heidegger. For example, Karl Löwith, "The Political Implications of Heidegger's Existentialism" (1946), *New German Critique* 45 (Fall 1988).
88. Heidegger, *Being and Time*, § 65.
89. Heidegger, *Contributions to Philosophy*, § 92.
90. R. G. Collingwood, "The Philosophy of History" (1930), in *Essays in the Philosophy of History*, ed. William Debbins (New York: Garland, 1985), 138. Heidegger, though, goes a step further than Collingwood: each generation must not only confront the heritage of its past, but appropriate what it finds "essential" in it in order to establish the "upon which" it projects its being. See Heidegger, *Being and Time*, § 65.
91. Heidegger, *Being and Time*, § 6 and § 79.
92. Heidegger, *Being and Time*, § 74; "Itinéraire," *Nouvelle École* 17 (March-April 1972).
93. Heidegger, *Being and Time*, § 75.
94. "What 'is' is not current events and neither is it what is present right now. What 'is' is what approaches from what has-been and, as this, is what approaches." Heidegger's claims that the inability to discern this difference between "now" and "what is" stems from the present era's "flight from history." See Martin Heidegger, *The Principle of Reason*, trans. Reginald Lilly (Bloomington: Indiana University Press, 1991), 80-81. Relatedly, the development of modern historical studies, which has immensely expanded our knowledge of the past, occurs in

a period that has almost entirely divested the past of "real" meaning and made a hedonistic cult out of the moment. Because the past is dead to our age, the great contemporary works of historical scholarship bear a greater resemblance to archeological studies than to "history" in the classic sense. In *Thus Spoke Zarathustra*, "The Home-Coming," Nietzsche appropriately calls the modern historian a "gravedigger."

95. "'Only a God Can Save Us': *Der Spiegel* Interview with Martin Heidegger" (1966), in *The Heidegger Controversy: A Critical Reader*, ed. Richard Wolin (Cambridge, MA: MIT Press, 1993), 106; also Heidegger, *Being and Time*, § 74. Cf. Benoist, *Vu de Droite*, 37.
96. Martin Heidegger, "The Self-Assertion of the German University" (1933), in *The Heidegger Controversy: A Critical Reader*, ed. Richard Wolin (Cambridge, MA: MIT Press, 1993).
97. Benoist, *Vu de Droite*, 23.
98. Martin Heidegger, "The Onto-theo-logical Nature of Metaphysics" (1957), in *Essays in Metaphysics*, trans. Kurt F. Leidecker (New York: Philosophical Library, 1960), 44; Heidegger, *Contributions to Philosophy*, § 91.
99. Eliade, *Myth and Reality*, 92.
100. Raymond Ruyer, *Les cents prochains siècles: Le destin historique de l'homme selon la Nouvelle Gnose américaine* (Paris: Fayard, 1977), 323.
101. Heidegger, *Being and Time*, § 76.
102. Heidegger, *Contributions to Philosophy*, §§ 3, 20.
103. Heidegger, *Introduction to Metaphysics*, 191; Benoist, *Comment peut-on être païen?*, 28.
104. Martin Heidegger, "The Origin of the Work of Art" (1935), in *Basic Writings*, ed. David Farrell Krell (New York: Harper and Row, 1977), 149, 187; Thomas Molnar and Alain de Benoist, *L'éclipse du sacré: Discours et réponses* (Paris: La Table Ronde, 1986), 215. In Hellmut Diwald's epic history of the German nation, the "narrative" begins with the Yalta Conference of 1945, which sealed the fate of the Third Reich, and "runs backwards" to the founding of the first *Reich*, in what is undoubtedly the most extraordinary historiographical illustration of this key Heideggerian idea. See his *Geschichte der Deutschen* (Frankfurt am Main: Ullstein, 1978).
105. Benoist, *L'empire intérieur*, 18.
106. Eliade, *The Myth of the Eternal Return*, 28–36.
107. Heidegger, *Being and Time*, § 65; Benoist, *L'empire intérieur*, 17.
108. Martin Heidegger, "The Anaximander Fragment" (1946), in *Early Greek Thinking*, trans. David Farrell Krell and Frank A. Capuzzi (San Francisco: Harper Collins, 1984), 18; Benoist, "La religion de l'Europe."
109. Heidegger, *Introduction to Metaphysics*, 39; Eliade, *The Sacred and the Profane*, 31, 95; Benoist, "La religion de l'Europe."
110. Heidegger, *Introduction to Metaphysics*, 6; Heidegger, *Contributions to Philosophy*, §§ 117, 184.
111. Faye, *Les nouveaux enjeux idéologiques*, 68, 78; Heidegger, *Being and Time*, § 74; Vial, "Servir la cause des peuples."
112. Heidegger, *Being and Time*, § 74.
113. Heidegger, *Being and Time*, § 74.

114. Heidegger, *Contributions to Philosophy*, § 11.
115. Heidegger, *Introduction to Metaphysics*, 152.
116. Heidegger, *Being and Time*, § 74.
117. Heidegger, *Being and Time*, § 74; Benoist, *L'empire intérieur*, 23–26; Steuckers, "Conception de l'homme et Révolution conservatrice." It might be noted that this merger of individual fate and collective destiny intends not the sublation of the ego, but its enrootment and growth.
118. "Archeofuturism" is a term coined by Guillaume Faye and now part of the general identitarian vocabulary, although *Grécistes* have yet to embrace it. See Guillaume Faye, *L'Archéofuturisme* (Paris: L'Æncre, 1998).
119. Nietzsche, *Thus Spoke Zarathustra*, "Prologue," § 5; cf. Francis Fukuyama, "The End of History?," *The National Interest* 16 (Summer 1989).
120. Claude Lévi-Strauss, *Anthropologie structurale* (Paris: Plon, 1973), chap. 2. Cf. Giorgio Locchi, "Histoire et société: critique de Lévi-Strauss," *Nouvelle École* 17 (March 1972). Benoist has accordingly called America, the model of modernity, a "cold society," frozen in an "eternal present," without a past or a future. See Robert de Herte (Alain de Benoist) and Hans-Jürgen Nigra (Giorgio Locchi), "Il était un fois l'Amérique," *Nouvelle École* 27–28 (Fall–Winter 1975).
121. Quoted in Frédéric Julien, "Droite, Gauche, et troisième voie," *Études et recherches* 5 (Fall 1987).
122. Benoist, *Les idées à l'endroit*, 41; Robert de Herte, "Le retour des dieux," *Éléments* 27 (Winter 1978).
123. Benoist, "Recours au paganisme." In a related vein, Michel Marmin points out that Yeats, Joyce, Synge, and other luminaries of the Celtic Twilight—arguably the greatest of identitarian movements—attempted no return to Eden or recourse to provincialism. For example, "in replenishing Irish roots . . . [Joyce] sought to nurture such thick and prodigious forests in Ireland that their shadows would be cast upon the whole world." See Michel Marmin, "Les piège des folklore," in *La cause des peuples: Actes du XVe colloque national du GRECE* (Paris: Le Labyrinthe, 1982). Cf. Ulick O'Connor, *All the Olympians: A Biographical Portrait of the Irish Literary Renaissance* (New York: Henry Holt, 1987).
124. Alain de Benoist, *Horizon 2000: Trois entretiens avec Alain de Benoist* (Paris: GRECE pamphlet, 1996), 15; Heidegger, *Introduction to Metaphysics*, 39; Heidegger, *Contributions to Philosophy*, § 5.
125. Martin Heidegger, *Basic Concepts*, trans. Gary E. Aylesworth (Bloomington: Indiana University Press, 1993), 17; "Entretien avec Alain de Benoist," *Éléments* 56 (Winter 1985). Cf. Russell Kirk, "The Question of Tradition" (1989), in *The Paleoconservatives: New Voices of the Old Right*, ed. Joseph Scotchie (New Brunswick, NJ: Transaction Publishers, 1999).
126. Maiastra, *Renaissance de l'Occident?* (Paris: Plon, 1979), 295. The GRECE's recent qualified support of multiculturalism would seem to render this conclusion purely rhetorical. Yet, if *Grécistes* have begun to imbibe the universalism of the dominant ideology and retreat from the political implications of their historical philosophy, opposed in principle to any Balkanization of the lands their forefathers settled, archeofuturism has nevertheless become part of the intellectual arsenal of other, more steadfast identitarians.

Chapter VI

# Anti-Europe

On January 21, 1991, as an Arctic cold front swept over Northern Europe, more than 100,000 Parisians gathered in the Place de la Bastille to protest America's planned attack on Saddam Hussein's Iraq. Orchestrated by the Communist party, the protest attracted mainly trade union and far Left opponents of what would be the first war of America's New World Order. To the organizers' surprise, it was learned that among the demonstrators, standing shoulder to shoulder with the various Leftists and unionists, was the GRECE's founder, Alain de Benoist. Conventional wisdom had it that the Right identified with US policy—and by this count, *Grécistes* had no place at the protest.

In point of fact, much of the traditional Right had always viewed the US as a greater threat to European civilization than Communist Russia. As early as the 1920s, Julius Evola, Oswald Spengler, and Count Keyserling had worked out critiques of US civilization that sought to warn Europeans of its dangers. With the advent of the Cold War, the American *Vabanquespieler*, Francis Parker Yockey, and the brother-in-law of the martyred Robert Brasillach, Maurice Bardèche, reformulated these critiques in view of America's world hegemony.[1] The Right's anti-Americanism was compromised, however, by its strident anti-Communism.[2] Then, after the US bogged down in Vietnam, it was overshadowed by Left-wing opposition to American policy. Yet, from the beginning of the American experiment, it was the anti-liberal Right, already opposed to its own bourgeoisie, that was the "new nation's" most severe critic, not the Left.[3]

## Europe and America

Like Conservative Revolutionaries, National Bolsheviks, revolutionary Europeanists, etc., New Rightists consider the United States an anti-Europe. Born of the Old World's "detritus," its people long harbored a certain hatred of Europe and a latent desire to take revenge on her.[4] Beginning with the Pilgrim Fathers, their North American wilderness was conceived as a New Israel, a pure land uncorrupted by the Babylon they had fled. In Puritan hagiography, John Winthrop, the first New England governor, was portrayed as a Moses-like figure, who had led the "visible saints" out of Egypt to the Promised Land, where their City on the Hill was to be a beacon to "the rest of the world."[5] Designating themselves "His redeemed and world-redeeming remnant," these latter-day Israelites (whom C. Northcote Parkinson describes as having "all the deep conviction, all the austerity, all the devotion and all the intolerance of the modern Communist") hoped to create "godly-wise commonwealths" free of Old World perfidy.[6] The country's settlement was seen thus as representing the antithesis of the civilization they had left behind.[7]

From the start, America's Judaizing settlers (as the self-designated successors of the ancient Israelites and thus as "the destined lord of the world") would define themselves in rejecting the Old World, which the New World was to supplant. Because civilizations stem from particular biocultural forms, American was founded on the fantasy that it could create an ideal world "from nothing," as its settlers repudiated who they were for the sake of a "religious" illusion designating them as something other than European. America in this way condemned itself not just to rootlessness, but to sterility—for no colony has ever superseded, let alone replaced, the mother culture from which it received life.

The same holds for America's "Christian" religion. Despite "living more perfectly in the spirit," the Calvinist instigators of the American enterprise had little actual interest in the inner life of the soul. Their main concern was to live in accordance with "spiritually hygienic formulas" that reduced morality to a rule or technique and helped multiply their worldly successes ("moral achievements") in the here and now.[8]

Concerned, then, with maintaining a pious but this-worldly existence in their Promised Land, they thought the important thing was to minimize the individual's inner life, where the snares of evil might lodge, and concentrate on uplifting activities, such as those sanctioned by their capitalist work ethic. Combined with the promises of the new land (this "field of exploitation"), the rules and formulas they devised commended the country's settlers to activities that were assumed to lack the normal limitations of human nature, given that their project was carried out under the guidance of God Himself.[9] The moral good resulting from their worldly successes (in contrast with the "vices of poverty") imbued American Protestants (like later New Age apostles) with a distinctly optimistic faith in the sensate here and now. One historian of early America concludes that the country's churches exercised "more influence on the social and political than the spiritual lives of their communicants."[10] With its anti-traditionalist, Judaic "religiosity" and its moralist obsession with individual behavior, the Puritan notion of Christian life privileged the material opportunities of the new land, just as prosperity was assumed to denote election and irreligion was assumed to be incompatible with success.

Rejecting that "sense of destiny and tragedy that had chastened Europeans over the centuries" and refusing to accept the legitimate differences between the Old World and the New, *New* England's pious founders took it for granted that behaviors based on European antecedents were immoral or unenlightened, while those conducive to thriving New World enterprises were good—even if this risked confusing acquisitiveness with virtue.[11]

Such an ethic would make the American a man of action, diligent in business, as Nietzsche noted, but one simultaneously "indolent in spirit."[12] From the perspective of the European religious tradition, American Protestants seemed, in fact, to lack spiritual depth of any sort. Similarly, their "plain style" churches resembled town halls rather than the Druids' sacred groves or the Gothic masterworks of medieval Catholicism, just as their clergymen preached the proper moral formulas and practiced no sacred rites.

The Biblical (i.e., Hebraic) Christianity of America's founding generation actually bore little relationship to its European counterpart and, in not a few cases, "fought against the orthodoxy of Protestant Europe." Some scholars contend that the American religious tradition most resembles that of Judaism, with its materialist emphasis on worldly matters—or on what most religions consider the essence of irreligion.[13] US Protestantism would subsequently play a leading role in spurring the country's modernization, while European modernization encountered stiff religious opposition. One identitarian argues that American Christianity was always "a matter more of a way of life than a genuine faith."[14] Similarly, the term "Americanism" entered the major European languages as a Roman Catholic critique of religious modernism and the poet Charles Baudelaire coined the term "*américaniser*" to stigmatize materialistic lifestyles based on American values.[15]

As a "form of Jewish fundamentalism" (Reinhold Oberlercher), US Protestantism (this "religion of immanence") might even be characterized as *the* religion of liberal modernity, for its principal aim has been to uplift the "Israelites" in their modern Canaan. Even today, when the churches in this country "founded" by "Calvin the Judaizer" no longer monopolize the Sunday mornings of the country's population, its secular institutions (particularly the government, the favored universities, and the "press") still see America as God's kingdom and its history as the march of the divine through the world.[16] Without the slightest embarrassment, one prominent Left-wing academic boasts that "other nations thought of themselves as hymns to the glory of God, [while] we [Americans] redefine God as our future selves"—a self, characteristically, which confuses material achievement with moral rectitude.[17] That US Protestantism (like its later Novus Ordo Catholic analogue) masks a spiritual void, persists in an era when Europeans have abandoned it, and accommodates the profanities of late modernity, seems, in view of its initial Calvinist despiritualization, anything but paradoxical, for it has always been more attuned to the behavioral needs of liberal capitalism than to the medieval religious ideals it sought to "reform."

Regarding "Europe with the most ignorant chauvinism and contempt" (Mark Twain), New England Puritans hoped to spare themselves the scourge of Old World ways by spurning liturgical religion, the aristocracy, the fine arts, the humanist traditions of the Renaissance and the aesthetic hedonism of the Baroque, the quasi-pagan customs of the European common people, the patriarchal family, and the regalian authority of the monarchical or imperial state. Having "no crumbling castles, no dark ruins, no useless memories and vain quarrels to trouble them" (Goethe), these expatriated Calvinists on "the outer borderlands of European civilization" readily embraced the rationalizing principles of quantity, whose leveling impulse already represented a rejection of Europe. Despite its Old World ties, America, then, embarked on a different course. Against Europe's strong state and established Church, its organizing ideal would be rooted in the workaday routines of Dumézil's "third function." The "masculine principles" Europeans pursued in art, war, and statecraft would subsequently cede to the "feminine principles" of nourishment and security, just as its religious life revolved around this-worldly, sensate concerns.

But more than inverting Europe's traditional hierarchy, Americans (like Jews) thought themselves superior for having done so. The lands of their morally tarnished kinsmen were thus quickly forgotten, as European life became a "matter of ignorance, indifference, and contempt" (Thomas Molnar).[18] Their prosperous country henceforth sufficed in itself, being the moral exception to the tragedy-laden human condition they had fled. Even in the present globalist age, for which they are largely responsible, Americans continue to ignore the outside world, whose periodic intrusions seem only to confirm the error or perversion to which they associate it. What is good for America—a virgin land conceived in opposition to Europe's corrupt moral order—is, conversely, good for the "Rest of the

World." "The vocation of the human race," it follows, "is American."[19] Their struggle against imperial taxation at the end of the eighteenth century was accordingly waged not as a colonial dispute with the Mother Country, but as a world crusade against "the traditional ethnic, religious, and tribal loyalties of the Old World" (Gordon S. Wood). "The cause of America," the famous English ideologue of liberty, Thomas Paine, claimed, "is the cause of all mankind."[20]

With similar modesty, their endeavor in 1776 "to begin the world anew" was thought to be guided by divine purpose, just as every step toward independence was thought to be "distinguished by some token of providential agency" (George Washington). The moral "exceptionalism" of this self-designated Elect affected even the American sense of time—for Utopia is not only "nowhere," it is "timeless." From the moment the Puritans set foot on the "new" continent, they were convinced that they had beaten history—that they had avoided the failings of other peoples and discovered the secret of happiness. Their time would be not that of fallen man—of profane history—but of the saved, just as the passions impelling history's turbulent course elsewhere would find no course in their Adamic wilderness. To safeguard this *novus ordo seclorum*, James Monroe's declaration of 1823 officially ordered the Old World out of the New.

Like many earlier anti-liberals, New Rightists see America as "a commonwealth of third-rate men." With horizons limited to "money, liberty, and God," there seems little to recommend its people—in that money is the province of the Golden Calf, liberty the ruse of a community-killing individualism, and the Old Testament God an unappealing manifestation of the Levantine spirit. Americans remind *Grécistes*, as they did Stendhal, of the "small shopkeepers of Rouen or Lyons, miserly and unimaginative" in their relations to the larger world.[21] Though acknowledging the exceptions to the philistine in American life, they argue that these only affirm the rule. A flourishing mercantile society in a land blessed by nature presented Americans with innumerable occasions to "sin." Both avarice and self-righteousness would thus assume prominent roles early in their national narrative.

Some Europeans have suggested that America secretes its own homeopathic remedies, pointing to figures like Jack London, Edgar Allan Poe, T. S. Eliot, Ezra Pound, Francis Parker Yockey, James Burnham, Thorstein Veblen, Henry James, Lothrop Stoddard, and other standard-bearers of high culture. *Grécistes*, though, consider these figures "prophets without honor."[22] It would be a mistake, they argue, to expect a deracinated people, in an ahistorical land, adhering to a Puritanical conception of the world and fixated on economic ideals, to be capable of correcting its errors or outgrowing its limitations, for its failings are not incidental to whom they are as a "people." Americans may have their exceptional men (they are of European stock, after all), but for their identitarian critics the telling fact is that these great figures never occupied the country's pantheon or animated its collective project.

The introduction of Irish Catholics early in the nineteenth century and the subsequent demographic transformation would do little to mitigate the Puritan heritage, only further secularize it. For however problematic their integration, immigrants readily assimilated the belief that the Atlantic crossing had put an ocean between themselves and the sins of the Old World. When the "Irish-American" John O'Sullivan called on "the nation of nations" to expand its "empire of liberty," he offered a rationale for America's Manifest Destiny that was every bit as self-righteous as anything the Puritans had proclaimed. The key to successful assimilation would be the assimilation of the original Puritan ideal. American morals might change their cadence now and then (shifting from chastity to promiscuity, from prohibition to transgression, from bigotry to licentious tolerance), but the reigning institutions always have a formula to sell and justify it.

Since God and nature favored America, it seemed only natural that its way of acting and thinking was the one right way. Immigrants were not to worry about the country's oscillating moral cycles (about the various pilgrimages back and forth between "Las Vegas and Salt Lake City"), only to devote themselves to the profane spirit of American enterprise. With Calvinist insistence, they were called on to forget the "popish" Babylon they had fled and join the chorus celebrating the country's exceptionalism.[23] Whether native born or recently arrived, everyone in this new land was to focus on the endless possibilities of making money—which would spare them the vicissitudes of Europe's tragic sense. The entire culture, the paleoconservative editor of *Chronicles* laments, "has been devoted to getting and spending."[24]

Beyond the varied stocks and sects contributing to its settlement, America's economic opportunities united everyone in a common endeavor. Consensus was accordingly in individualistic economic terms, not history, heritage, or religion. "We are who we are," one American feminist writes, "independent of our specific communal associations."[25] For such a people, religious, ethnic, or even communal identity is simply a private matter (like the Protestant conscience). Its ideology of "individual merit" and hard work and its society of self-made men had, in fact, little need of "impractical" cultural identities, only formulas to keep its people free and prosperous. The disparate, not always compatible "segments" of America's sprawling, Balkanized society would meld—to the degree they could—in their common quest for material well-being, which was assumed to confer certain moral virtues.

In this "business-obsessed and culturally stunted society" (Burnham), numerous segments of American life were naturally left outside the governing consensus. Even the English-speaking Irish assimilated only to the degree they conformed to the prevailing entrepreneurial ethos. Such was also the case for many Southerners, whose High Church and gentry ways—like the "Scotch-Irish backcountry," with its warrior ethic and "border idea of natural liberty" (David Hackett Fischer)—ill-fit the Puritan narrative. Business also imposed rules of public behavior that restricted differences (ethnocultural or otherwise) to the private realm, just as these differences were dispersed over distances and segmented into specialized communities. It was, in fact, only with the great social engineering projects of the New Deal state and its self-serving world war that most European immigrants and Southerners finally succumbed to "Americanization."[26]

Benoist characterizes "Americanism" as an "ideology based on a "'universal republic' . . . whose heterogeneity leaves room for consensus only at a material level."[27] Just as the American state came to rest on a rationalist document (the Constitution) and not an "American identity," newcomers were expected to define themselves in American terms, keep their lingering Old World identities to themselves, embrace the country's business ideology, and get to work. The creedal notion of national identity (in which blood gave way to ideology) could not but make America "the living negation of all specificity."[28] The country consequently became "something like a boardinghouse, where visitors could come and stay as long as they like."[29]

At no point in American history is it possible to talk of its "people" as a distinct ethnic or national entity, for in rejecting the qualitative standards of the Old World for the quantitative ones of the New, individualistic ideals, institutionalized on the basis of radical Protestant or Enlightenment principles, overwhelmed those of a biocultural identity. Nathaniel Hawthorne wrote: "Americans have no country—at least, none in the sense an Englishman has a country."[30] The reserves of national sentiment affecting a European simply did not exist in the United States, whose people were not actually a "people," only a population devoted to a common economic endeavor, sanctioned by its democratic ideology. The United States, as a result, lacked those deeper values or bonds—associated with an organic *telos*—that might have knitted its inhabitants into a cohesive national body.

In an acultural society of disparate individuals, money alone serves as a measure of a man's worth.[31] Like Max Weber's Puritan, the American seeks salvation in amassing wealth. There has been no other socially validating standard. Money has ruled America from the beginning, motivating its settlement, organizing its social hierarchy, educating its citizenry, and defining its moral order. There has, indeed, never been a higher sense of life in this new land, for what counts above all is not who you are, but what you have. "Getting more" is simply more important than "being more." Notions of self-sacrifice, duty, and patrimony, second nature to feudal aristocracies created on the field of battle, are entirely foreign to "elites" recruited from the business class. And since money is without quality, potentially anyone can have it—which, of course, is never true of culture or history or blood. This makes money the great equalizer.[32]

America (at least the modern America arising from its Calvinist crucible) may be the only Western country never to have known an aristocracy, titled or otherwise, that promoted a "higher kind of man" valuing character as a good and an end in itself. The Puritan/liberal notion that an individual's merit is synonymous with his material success is alien to the European spirit: the aristocrat, whose standards still inspire, values that which does not have a price.[33] The priest, the magistrate, the scholar, the artist, the man of letters—all of whom figured in the upper ranks of European society (at least until a generation ago)—are formed by spirit, not industry, commerce, or intellectual specialization.

Typically, qualities reflecting breeding or culture are deeply suspect to Americans. A semi-literate basketball player will be rewarded, for example, as if he were a prince, while a gifted classical scholar might end up driving a taxi. The novelist Walker Percy says: "Ours is the only civilization which has enshrined mediocrity as its national ideal."[34] Americans as such have no love of "the superior man," only "winners"—and only as long as they succeed without ceasing to be like everyone else. For in a society "of many scrambling, ordinary, and insignificant people, the power of genius and great-souled men," one historian writes, "no longer seemed to matter."[35] The greatest trial in American history, the most searing and transformative of its national experiences, was not the War Between the States, with its exorbitant toll of blood and destruction, but the Great Depression of the thirties, which discredited the market and hence the American Dream of economic well-being.

The US is by no means devoid of European high culture. Not all the British folkways contributing to the country's formation bore the same anti-European impetus as those of New England—although New England became the country's hegemonic section. It might even be argued that there has always existed "an ethnic and separatist America implicitly at odds with the existence of the United States." Its Puritan character nevertheless suggests that the country's grain runs against its European identity.[36] Similarly, its autonomous self-interested subject, *Homo oeconomicus*, oriented to market exchanges and contractual relations, has long defined its *demos*. Americans tend, as a result, to substitute mercantile conventions for tradition, identify themselves in economic terms, and elevate the monadic principles of "Life, Liberty, and the Pursuit of Happiness," rather than the blood and traditions of their forefathers, to the pinnacle of their concerns. Notions of a "people," an *ethnos*, a particularistic cultural organism imbued with a historically shaped destiny or an original spiritual quality has, in principle, been alien to a "national" project devoted to commercial enterprise and the abstractions of its founding documents.[37] Whatever culture Americans have known has been limited mainly to an anthropological one: a folkloric structure of everyday existence, compatible with market activity and open institutions, but without historical roots or cultivated offshoots.[38]

## The Homeland of Modernity

As an anti-Europe, the United States represents the pre-eminent exemplar of liberal modernity. Nowhere else, *Grécistes* argue, were the Enlightenment principles—of equality, rationalism, universalism, individualism, economism, and developmentalism—more thoroughly realized than in this new land "liberated from the dead hand of the European past."[39] The country's constitutional Framers, it follows, were steeped in Enlightenment liberalism—which "blended with the earlier ecclesiastical culture of New England" and with the later Emersonian ideals of individualism and self-reliance. This led them to adopt a political system whose ideological underpinnings rested on rationalist abstractions exalting the individual rather than the history and traditions of its people. In this spirit, the federal state was conceived not as an instrument of its people's destiny—nationality in the European sense did not exist in America—but as a *cosmopolis*, potentially open to all humanity.[40]

Contrary to the contention of certain paleoconservatives, as well as the arguments of those historians associated with the school of "civic republicanism," this propositional notion of the American state was not the invention of latter-day Jacobins, like William Jefferson Clinton and George W. Bush, but inherent to the country's original constitutional project (as defined by its Northeastern elites).[41] The US Declaration of Independence (like the founding documents of the later Soviet Union) appealed to "certain inalienable Rights," rather than the nation, just as the "We the People" of the Constitution invoked the security and welfare of a multitude of individuals and corporate entities (the thirteen states), but not a specific people or *ethnos*. The formation of the United States—this "most liberal . . . most democratic . . . most commercially minded and . . . most modern [country] in the world" (Gordon S. Wood)—had, indeed, little to do with its people's willful desire to pursue a national destiny, but simply with its desire to be free of taxes and British meddling in what was then still part of the British empire. As Albert Jay Nock said of Thomas Jefferson, he believed, "as most of the colonialists did, that if they could get a working measure of economic independence, political independence was not worth the cost of a quarrel."[42] One of the country's greatest historians similarly argues that the Republic's constitutional foundations were designed to protect and promote the self-interests of its mercantile elite.[43]

The American state was dedicated to a contractual theory of government based on individual liberty and market freedoms—not to a people, a tradition, or a destiny.[44] Practically, this entailed "independence" not just from the English Crown, but from the "bonds of blood, family, and personal influence." Relatedly, the liberty to which Americans ("foes of the impious Canaanites") dedicated their republican enterprise was "not the sort of liberty for which the Spartans had died at Thermopylae" (Santayana), but simply the freedom to do business and to live unhampered by dependencies based on heritage, community, or established authorities. The American political tradition accordingly makes no reference to a *patrie* or a *Vaterland* (concepts foreign to its experience), only to certain nebulous ideals embodied in the founding documents, the Old Testament, and the liberal economy—all of which reject the sinful accretions of the Old World. Ironically, this creedal notion of identity has since turned against those who created it. One identitarian points out that "the principles upon which the United States [were] established contained the logistics of the destruction of the [British] identity of the people who promulgated them."[45] That European America is presently in retreat before Black, Hispanic, and Jewish America seems, from this perspective, less a matter of a misinterpreted or abused constitution than of a state based on abstract modernist principles indifferent to racial, ethnic, religious, or national identities. (Is it coincidental, then, that America has always supported "racial admixtures which most countries would think incongruous or comic" [G. K. Chesterton]?)

Just as the Puritans viewed mundane institutions as potential sources of evil, so too did the Framers view their new state—a necessary evil, perhaps, but nevertheless one with the potential to threaten one's goods and divert the individual from the "inner light" and full application of his energy. Their "procedural republic" (Michael Sandel) would thus privilege individual autonomy and natural rights, while the state's powers were divided and balanced for the sake of a multitude of conflicting interests.[46] Even when political parties emerged after George Washington's Administration, breaking with the purely individualistic conception bequeathed by the Founders, they continued to represent coalitions of interest groups, not coherent formations with contending notions of the national idea. One party was thus expected to administer the government, the other to form the watchful opposition; changes in government might affect power sharing and influence peddling, but not the state's character, just as electoral promises to the electorate were routinely ignored for the sake of upholding the economic interests of those who "filled the party's coffers." These parties have rarely differed in principle—being more like "a one-party system with two main factions" (Benoist). Politics, in fact, has always taken a back seat to the state's legal-institutional activities. Even in the early years of the Republic, when the federal government hardly existed, the Constitution was practically worshipped.[47] In the popular mind, it was synonymous with state and union. Not coincidentally, the constitutional guarantees of American civil society took precedent over the government, as real power in America fell into the hands of judges and financiers, and constitutional principles mingled with those of the market and the court.[48]

Dismissing the European notion that the state is the ultimate expression of the nation's will and thus the executor of its destiny, the American model rested on nomocratic principles, whose "Laws of Nature and Nature's God" sought to circumvent the political for the sake of the legal. Like the Enlightenment's confusion of juristic and scientific law, this nomocratic model of the state stemmed from the illusion that the law's detachment from any specific body of cultural values (incarnating as the law allegedly does a "cold impartiality") made it able to adjudicate conflicting claims on the basis of strictly neutral criteria.[49] Characteristically, American jurisprudence approaches the law as if it were the expression of reason itself, objective and ubiquitous in its affirmation of human rights—and not the product of America's particularistic concept of right and wrong. (Relatedly, common law is frequently taken as an expression of natural law, just as judicial review is apt to usurp the political process.)

Against the legal rationalism of US jurisprudence, New Rightists hold that laws are never rational abstractions based on natural rights, but rather the codification of norms, whose origins are pre-eminently cultural and whose purpose is the defense of the national organism rather than the free-floating individual.[50] But because the law is "sovereign" in the American system and the rule of reason overrides case law, judges making rulings on the basis of rationalist criteria tend to ignore not just existing norms and precedents, but the democratic will itself. Not infrequently, this sort of jurisprudence—"independent of Heaven itself"—ends up contradicting the unwritten moral law of legitimacy, as opinion is disregarded in favor of "reason" and legislative law in favor of individual conscience.[51]

The absurdity of such a "government by judiciary" is perhaps most strikingly evident in the recent application of "constitutional rights" to illegal Mexican immigrants, as the universalism inherent in the US nomocracy reduces its own citizens to the same legal status as aliens.[52] For implicit in the country's constitutional order is the notion that a law can be just without conforming to the specific values of those it is designed to serve.[53] (Emmanuel Todd notes that the US "treats conquered peoples like ordinary citizens and ordinary citizens like conquered peoples.")[54] A state, though, that refuses to distinguish between its own citizens and foreigners effectively abandons its *raison d'être*.[55] By this token, the "dictatorship of law" decreed by the Constitution rises above those the law is designed to serve, as Americans are rendered into a generic humanity. The Chinaman, the Mexican, and the Negro are thus imbued with the same rights of citizenship as Americans of European extraction, as if they all belong to the same organic body.

If law reflects the rationality of the natural order, it must also reflect a higher morality to which the state is obliged to conform. A nomocratic state accordingly reduces the political to the judicial. But once constitutional principles are substituted for a political concept of its people's will and individual rights take precedent over communal norms, the state's main function becomes the arbitration of domestic conflicts on the basis of "the supreme law of the land"—not the defense of a specific national ontology grounded in tradition and culture.[56] As a result, American liberal thought has trouble accepting that the political entails not simply the application of abstract legal principles to isolated individuals, but the culturally partisan art of distinguishing between those orders that are the state's friend and those that are its enemy.[57] Such a rationalist concept of the political (or rather, such a rationalist evasion of the political) also explains why the Framers shied away from making the Republic an instrument of its people's destiny—and for a moment thought of adopting German as the official language to obscure the country's British origins.

Related to this nomocratic flight from the political is the belief that war, politics' ultimate expression, is not simply a regrettable distraction from civil and social engagements, but something inherently unnatural. In principle, Americans refuse to accept that conflict is endemic to a nation's life, or that violence, not reason, is often the only possible or honorable recourse in cases when states collide.[58] Yet far from being an atavistic exception, war, *Grécistes* insist, is integral to the state's "natural history." ("*La paix, pour chaque nation*," as De Maistre observes, "*n'est qu'un répit.*")[59] A state, though, based on a constitutional system and material way of life, rather than a people, inevitably views war—"the virile side of existence" (Venner)—as something of a dilemma, not simply because there is no collective identity to defend, but also because there is no higher will to self-sacrifice. Contrary to the reveries of their court historians (Stephen Ambrose pre-eminently), modern Americans are typically terrible soldiers: they rarely have a commitment to what they are fighting for, nor, in cases where their overwhelming technological superiority fails, have they the slightest predilection for heroics.[60]

Even with the largest arsenal in world history, a "Hebraic confidence in their mission" (Brogan), and a propensity for using their military might to impose their will on the international community, Americans remain one of the least militaristic of peoples, incapable of fighting all but the most inept and debilitated powers.[61] Quite naturally, one does not take life-threatening risks for a Constitution or a Universal Republic. Against the political soldier of the pajama-clad Vietcong, Somali gangsters determined to defend their turf, or German boy scouts ready to turn their small arms against an armored division (Teutoburg Forest, February 1945), the American is likely to run—literally from the field of battle, metaphorically into something analogous to the smoke-filled relief of the hemp leaf. Unlike a French, Russian, or German soldier, who fights for his *patrie*—that is, for the land of his fathers, with all its emotive associations of "blood and soil"—the American has only a creedal identity to defend.[62] It seems hardly coincidental that the soldier-gangsters of the *Dirty Dozen* and the cowering draftees of *Saving Private Ryan* have been immortalized in the country's mythology, while real heroes, like Jim Bowie, William Travis, or Davy Crockett, are now relegated to the rogues' gallery of the politically incorrect.

Whenever, though, the Republic's technological might does prevail, the vanquished quite literally have hell to pay, for America wages war not to defeat an enemy, the very concept of which is foreign to its Puritan/

liberal view of the world, but to vindicate humanity.[63] Whoever stands in its way, therefore, deserves to be crushed, for every means is legitimate when fighting for humanity's survival. It was the country's first Caesar, Abraham Lincoln, in unleashing the Republic's industrial might against the vastly outnumbered Confederate Army (half of which would perish) and its looting, raping soldiers against the South's women and children (as if they were Vietnamese villagers), who contrived the modern notion of total war, in which the enemy is not simply a threatening rival (wearing a uniform), but an ideological evil embodied in a people that has to be exterminated.[64] Unlike the older European tradition of war, which accepted conflict as an unavoidable facet of international relations and fought limited wars to defeat, not annihilate, an opponent worthy of human dignity, Americans fight in the name of eradicating "evil": they "war against war." In this spirit, the country's chief twentieth-century Caesar declared that: "There has never been—and there can never be—[a] successful compromise between good and evil. Only total victory [which destroys, as well as defeats the enemy] can reward the champions of tolerance, and decency, and faith."[65]

As all its modern engagements demonstrate, Americans wage their "humanitarian" crusades in good conscience, justifying the horrors they commit in the name of the highest moral principles.[66] The terrors they inflicted on German, Italian, Japanese, Korean, Vietnamese, Cambodian, Iraqi, and Serbian civilians in the last half century, comparable in scope only to the horrors of Genghis Khan, have, however, rarely been inspired by a Mongol love of cruelty. Instead, they stemmed from the country's Hebraic-Puritanical righteousness, for as Jeremiah said to the Old Testament God: "In your goodness destroy my enemies."[67]

This coupling of nomocratic and moralistic principles has spawned a progressive world view that is among the most subversive in history. Progressivism might even be described as the country's civil religion, for it animates its institutions, its political discourse, and its intellectual forms. Having begun their history by scrapping Europe's tragic vision for Calvinist, Hebraic, and Enlightenment notions of happiness, progress, and material well-being, Americans have since remained indifferent to any organic sense of culture or heritage, for a way of life geared to animal comforts and business imperatives suffices on the basis of quantitative and utilitarian standards alone.[68] This has influenced not only the breadth but also the depths of American life. For example, the ardent "environmentalism" (in the Lockean sense) undergirding its inorganic standards means that ethological thinkers like Konrad Lorenz, rejecting the *tabula rasa* character of man's nature, or traditionalists, extolling the perennial, have usually gotten a cold reception in the US. By contrast, behaviorism, pragmatism, and technoscience, marshalling hordes of "facts" against first principles and focusing on quantitative abstractions indifferent to blood and spirit, dominate the country's intellectual life. And this follows not simply from their usefulness in advertising and mass marketing, but, above all, from their affinity with the environmentalist animus of American progressivism—and the belief that "the struggle for social justice [which is usually taken to mean the pursuit of rational social organization and material well-being] is central to their moral identity" (Rorty).

Given such a disposition, the prototypical American is a technician of some sort: mechanic, computer programmer, service provider, academic specialist. Without refinement or high culture, he thrives in a fix-it-up realm, where attention to detail compensates for the absence of higher references. Like mathematical truths, technical ones are self-evident, appealing to a rationality requiring little in the way of cultural formation. As Keyserling notes, cultureless people are necessarily more receptive to new technology than the cultured.[69] For it is not just America's mass men, but naked primitives in remote rainforests, who readily assimilate satellite dishes and electronic gadgets. It seems hardly coincidental, then, that the most culturally deficient of Western peoples is also the most technically advanced and the most politically progressive. Similarly, the main enemy of America's technoeconomic civilization, with its incessant emphasis on "noise, toys, and technology," has always been cultural specificity—which resists instrumentalization, standardization, and automation. Ironically, the country's lack of a genuine cultural dimension—and thus a philosophic temperament able to "scientifically conceptualize causality" (which is as necessary to science as pure technics)—makes its incessant technological innovations dependent on the import of foreign (mainly European) scientists.

## Planet of the Clowns

The journal *Terre et peuple*, one of a number of "revolutionary nationalist" or *völkisch* publications born of GRECE-style identitarianism, recently devoted an issue to "The Planet of the Clowns," in which it highlighted the more preposterous expressions of American life. The hypocrisy of US imperialism and the cretinism of its mass culture have, of course, been frequent targets of European ridicule. But New Right tendencies akin to the GRECE, as evidenced in this issue, delight in emphasizing the absurdity of *Homo americanus*. From that part of the population claiming to have been abducted by aliens, to creationist accounts of human origins, to a president claiming fellatio by a student aide ought not to be considered a "sexual relation," they have had a field day. Their acerbic treatment of American folkways, however, is less to mock than to unmask and discredit the authority of America's global leadership.

In this spirit, they target the great American myths for deconstruction. Because few of these excite the popular imagination as much as the "frontier," having inspired so many "novels, films, television programs, and advertising images," few have been as often lambasted by them. In contrast to the European world, where the frontier represented a border with a potentially hostile state and thus an area in which one's political destiny had to be reaffirmed, the American frontier was a wilderness, a vacuum to be filled.[70] This would have a formative affect on the American psyche, for it allowed the founding event to be repeated over and over in the course of its development, serving as another Promised Land, where there was no civilization, no social hierarchy, no settled ways to obstruct the flourishing of its Puritan version of the Hebraic fable. "Look to the West," George Washington counseled, "that is where our destiny lies. Europe is the past."[71]

The "winning of the West," the defining event in the country's history, was, however, not quite the epic struggle John Ford celebrated in his classic films, but more like a seedy Jim Thompson pulp about an unprecedented real estate bargain, which was there for the taking.[72] Similar to GIs who fight wars won in advance, the country's "pioneering nomads" triumphed over a negligible enemy. The American population grew thus in the great empty spaces of this second Eden with only a minimum of traditional culture, repeating and reinvigorating the founding myth. Lacking a common past and common allegiances, their ways would become those of a perpetual uprooting and mutation. The ongoing land grab of the western expansion, the speculative fevers it set off, the new corporate and financial powers it "enfranchised," and the continual demographic migrations it provoked, broke apart families and communities, accelerated the forces of change — allowing little to settle and solidify, especially in the way of fixed hierarchies, social customs, and a learned culture. Neither peasant nor aristocrat, but market-oriented farmer, the countries' nineteenth-century settlers felt little obligation to the heritage that had spawned them and no desire to root themselves in the soil they worked. Hurrying to exploit the new land, they thought it best to keep "their institutions loose and their traditions light."[73] What Ernst von Salomon said of the German peasant could never have been said of them, for the land the German husbanded "was something more than money and stock; it was inheritance and race, family and tradition and honor, past, present, and future."[74] Severed from the sensibilities of those who had tamed the great forests and plains of Eurasia, the American homesteader cared little for his culture's spread, only its economically lucrative abandonment. As a result, whatever European form and order lingered along the Eastern seaboard tended to be dissipated in the sprawl West, where the deracinated, deculturated, and highly mobile frontiersman reveled in his "freedom." California, the far Far West, has long been the brightest beacon of the American Dream.

With the frontier, there also came the outlaw. Whether backwoodsman, cowboy, or modern-day gangster, the outlaw occupies a special place in the American imagination, functioning as the anti-hero who fills the breach in the wall of Puritan restraint. In this capacity, he exemplifies the exception that proves the rule, justifying the taboos he inevitably breaks. As depicted in Hollywood productions and teenage "canticles," his antisociety inversely reflects the routinized existence of most Americans. The line between society and anti-society, however, is never quite fixed. The hold-ups, rackets, and frauds in which the outlaw specializes are formally condemned, but condemnation is usually nuanced with admiration, for he is, after all, a self-made man—even if he takes legally prohibited "shortcuts." Though expected to be caught in the end, he nevertheless serves the system by clarifying what the rules are and what the game is all about.[75]

In Europe, the outlaw (not to be confused with the social bandit) is a negative and usually menacing figure. That he plays a pivotal role in American popular thinking seems due to the raw, quantitative character of the American mind, with its uncultured fixation on "making it." The American's lack of high culture has consequently left him without a sense of superiority or uniqueness, causing him to look to the plebeian exemplars of his "cultureless civilization" for guidance. He thus typically avoids singularity, deprecates refinement, and is mass minded. From the earliest age, he is taught to "get along" and "not rock the boat." The "tyranny of opinion" especially struck Alexis de Tocqueville, who claimed to have known no country where there was "less independence of spirit and less real freedom of discussion" than the United States.[76] In a similar vein, Count Keyserling thought "the land of liberty cares little for freedom of thought."[77] In fact, uniformity and conformity seemed programmed into American life, which is not surprising, considering that a society of nomadic individuals, cut off from rooted identities, necessitates a mechanical cohesiveness. Individualism might be universally acclaimed, but everyone is apt to buy the same unnecessary consumer products, watch the same TV shows, think in terms of the same bumper stickers, and wear the same T-shirts, Levis, and ball caps. Without a real culture, a sense of place, or a historical identity, the other-directed American has only the bustle distinct to his way of life by which to fill his inner void: moving every few years, routinely changing jobs, hunting down sales for the sake of shopping. Those finding no escape in such quintessential facets of the national experience always have the therapist's couch or an array of psychopharmaceuticals. "Whoever thinks otherwise goes voluntarily into the madhouse."[78]

A quantifying standardization dominates the physical as well as the psychic environment of American life. Unlike the medieval and baroque cores of European cities and the Continent's manicured countryside and historical landscapes, thick with memory and distinction, America impresses with its sheer enormity. In Werner Sombart's view, Americans "mistake bigness for greatness."[79] One American city accordingly resembles another in its towering glass and concrete forests, its cancerous suburbs, its labyrinthine malls, its endless streets of gasoline stations and fast food joints, and, above all, in its lack of scale and harmony. "Built in a style suitable for pillboxes, airplanes, and refrigerators" (Jünger), these monotonous, eye-offending metropolises are indeed "little more than networks of endless, unreal circulations . . . of fabulous proportions, without space or dimension."[80] The only way it is even possible to "tell you are leaving one . . . and entering another is when the franchises start repeating and you spot another 7-Eleven, another Wendy's, another Costco, another Home Depot."[81] The immensity and assortment of these "poured-concrete gulags" testify, to be sure, to great energy and often organizational talent, but they also aver an absence of grace and style.[82] Monumental sculptures and public memorials, grand boulevards, palatial government buildings, and great cathedrals, such as imperial Spain built between Mexico City and Buenos Aires, have had little appeal to a people disparaging greatness and grandeur. The barren quality of American cityscapes is such that one might be tempted to say: *c'est Descartes descendre dans la rue* (Robert Aron). Indeed, the structures they tear down and rebuild every generation, perhaps better than anything else, reflect the "throwaway, transient aspect" of a society indifferent to a sense of time or place—that is, to a society out of harmony with itself, its history, and its surroundings.

Despite the possibilities bequeathed by their great natural wealth, Americans have never overcome their initial dearth of culture. According to the former Harvard philosopher George Santayana, "their culture was half a pious survival [of the Europe they rejected], half an intentional acquirement; it was not the inevitable flowering of a fresh experience."[83] In nearly four centuries, it has produced no major school of art (comic strips and commercial art aside), no world-class painter or sculptor, no notable style of architecture, not even a middling composer. However inventive, Americans are not creative. "If ever art were wanted, one could easily buy it."[84] Their "religion of praxis and productivity" has, in truth, left them unreceptive to any appreciation of the transcendent or the sublime. Typically, their well-endowed museums are filled with imported works, but few indigenous creations. Their National Endowment for the Arts similarly judges Andres Serrano's "Piss Christ"—a crucifix in a jar of urine—a creation worthy of funding and exhibition. Their "libido for the ugly" (H. L. Mencken) is notorious, even in the "elite." For example, Bill Clinton's tenor saxophone epitomized not merely the course demimonde of America's jazz world—"the clearest sign of the age's deep-seated predilection for barbarism" (Richard Weaver)—but also the proletarianized aesthetics of its ruling class. In this vein Henry Miller argues in *The Air-Conditioned Nightmare* (1946) that "there's no real life for an artist in America—only a living death."

While the American mind excels in technical and economic matters, in other ways it rarely rises above the tawdry. The enormous mass appeal of its literature and film thus captivates through their primitive fascination with violence and action, their slick descriptive powers devoid of mystery, subtlety, and depth, their morbid interest in the reactions of a hero "to whom things are done"—but not through an exploration of the abiding existential themes.[85] The country's true greatness has obviously not been in the realms of high culture, but rather in its practical feats of technoscience and in the vast quantities of steel, concrete, celluloid, and plastic it has worked, while its "noblest" achievement is arguably "that fabulous bathroom which the economist and the sociologist vie in praising."[86] One notorious anti-American is reputed to have said that: "There is more culture in a single Beethoven sympathy than in 300 years of American history."[87]

This New World is animated by facts and statistics, which orient more to the quantitative facets of space than to the identity-producing ones of time. When Jean Baudrillard first visited the US in the early 1970s, it was, he relates, as if he had left behind an aristocratic culture, steeped in history, and suddenly entered another dimension, more spatial than temporal, where there was no lived culture, only the simulation of one.[88] In settling their ahistorical wilderness, Americans thus rarely referred to the past, just as today they think nothing of rewriting their history to suit the sensibilities of various racial minorities or legislative mandates. They seem not even to want a history, just as they shy away from having a destiny. Lacking a historical sense, their self-understanding is typically one-dimensional.[89] The only time they seem comfortable with is the "eternal now" of Nietzsche's Last Man, who replaces history with the ongoing flow of "current events."[90] As Benoist writes, the general aspiration "in a country where the Constitution makes the pursuit of happiness the common goal can only be a permanent state of ahistorical prosperity."[91] Even their materialism seems stuck in the present, for Americans are generally less interested in possessing than spending money. Consumption, as such, becomes an end in itself. The notion of a patrimony, of an inheritance to be nurtured and passed on to successive generations, is similarly alien to a people that has always been "weary of the past" and, by implication, of the future. Seeing themselves as self-made men, created out of nothing, Americans expect the same of others.[92]

Given their want of ecstatical consciousness, the inhabitants of these "United States of Amnesia" (Gore Vidal) tend to live fast, unconcerned with what will follow in their wake. This has given Americans an enormous capacity for change, but also a lack of depth and a propensity for destruction. They accordingly rely on environmental modifications to compensate for the deficiencies they might discern in their uncultivated interiors. Nowhere in the world, in fact, has as much money and effort been invested in "education" and self-improvement—as if it is possible to "fix" whatever they happen to lack.[93] Their public schools, though, graduate semi-illiterates and their universities, with the best libraries and the biggest endowments in the world, neglect general culture, produce specialists and technicians who are otherwise uneducated, have students reluctant to read books, and professors more concerned with getting ahead than getting at the truth. It seems hardly surprising, then, that the fabulous facilities of American higher education have never produced a pure science or generated a paradigmatic idea—only "a harvest of leaves." Their fixation on exterior technical factors to compensate for individual deficiencies testifies to "a mental atrophy of all [their] higher interests" (Evola).[94]

Because their prosperity, success, and optimism have made life so easy for them, twentieth-century Americans are inclined to a puerile character structure. Theirs, indeed, is "a land where the 'kid,' brash, unsophisticated, spoilt and demanding, rules supreme."[95] The father in this *Kinderland*, where no one bows to authority, is expected to be a "buddy" to his children and a companion to his wife, while the mother, personifying the feminine values of love, comfort, and security, the dominant American values, is alone imbued with moral weight. But even having children and forming families is increasingly taken as a threat to the present-minded culture of self-gratification. In the character-diminishing spirit of its "expanding, polluting, noisy society of tract homes, subdivisions, shopping malls, freeways, junior colleges, state colleges, and universities for all" (W. I. Thompson), personal relations are routinely entered into without formality, popularity comes to define personality, and personality is treated as if it were synonymous with character. "Nice guys," Americans are notorious for their lack of critical spirit, their desire to get along and do the "right thing." Analogously, they have no patience with analysis or argument and a preference for distractions, such as televised sports and computer games. They will champion Larry Flynt's right to publish his pornographic *Hustler*, but think nothing of censoring a nonconformist historian like David Irving. Their elites are often as "dumbed down": they rarely speak foreign languages and usually cannot find on the map the countries they presume to instruct. In the spirit of such self-righteous crusaders as Woodrow Wilson or Bush the Younger, they will readily rearrange the world without having the slightest compunction to know what they are doing.

For New Rightists, an uprooted people—with a child's present-mindedness, indifferent to quality, and addicted to reality-distorting fables that make no distinction between "hype and life"—is a people without a future. American enterprise and technology may have made the US dominant in today's world, but its ultramodern civilization of "low kitsch and high tech" lacks a destining vision—and hence the possibility of a meaningful destiny. Fated to repeat the eternal present, America for Benoist is a "cold society" (*à la* Lévi-Strauss)—an ultramodern Borneo—with ribbons of multi-lane highways and forests of high-rise buildings, but without the transcendent features that have made other civilizations great in their time. Prisoner of the fast life, America, he predicts, will likely die as swiftly and brutally as it was born.[96]

The Planet of the Clowns is a caricature, to be sure, but the nature of caricature, however absurd, is to exaggerate its subject's distinctive features.

## Toward Zion

God chose America. This Promised Land with a Biblical mandate (that persists even after the death of God) assumes its norms and practices are those mandated by mankind. Once world power was achieved in 1945, it immediately sought to "reform" the international arena in its own image. Ironically, the other great extra-European power born of Enlightenment rationalism, Communist Russia, was driven by a similar missionary zeal. During the Cold War (1947–89), these two modernist hegemons locked horns in a tectonic struggle for world supremacy. Since the Soviet collapse, America has had the field entirely to itself and the full extend of its universalizing mission—as it goes "abroad in search of monsters to destroy"—is now glaringly evident.

Every great nation thinks of itself as the center of the universe: this is perfectly natural. What is not "natural" is the self-righteous manner in which Americans seek to universalize their national interests. In the spirit of their Puritan forefathers (first cousin to the Jacobin and Bolshevik), they assume that their values and institutions represent humanity's highest aspirations. Quite typically, Robert Kennedy spoke of America's "right to the spiritual direction of the planet" and Bush the Elder of the "inexorability" of America's global leadership.[97] Whoever opposes its sanctimonious unilateralism is simply dismissed as an enemy of humanity. America, thus, does not openly fight to maintain its access to the oil regions of the Persian Gulf (which might be justified in terms of *Realpolitik*): instead, whenever "the Promised Land becomes the Crusader State" (which is most of the time), it fights under the moral banner of resisting dictators, punishing aggressors, liberating oppressed peoples, or preventing the spread of "weapons of mass destruction." At one level, of course, this is simply eyewash—American leaders are not so naive as to believe that morality prompts their predatory crusades. Yet, because its elites are steeped in the opiate of American exceptionalism, with its lack of historical depth, they usually have trouble distinguishing between their Sunday school homilies and their mercenary objectives, compelled as they are to justify their foreign ventures in ways that inevitably conflate the two.[98] The result is a messianic compulsion to impose its standards on the Rest of the World.

René Guénon once prophesied that "in the name of 'liberty' . . . [Americans] would force the whole world to imitate them."[99] Spurred by its unique blend of Old Testament and modernist beliefs, US-sponsored schemes for global order presume that cultural and political differences are transitory, that the course of unilinear development is toward a single universal (to wit, American-centric) world community, and that the realization of its "planetary suprasociety" cannot but entail a superior level of well-being for all men. Just as its original Calvinist architects saw America as "a light to the nations," today America's Jewish policymakers identify their "Hebraizing" interests with those of humanity, expecting the world's peoples to remake themselves in the democratic, capitalist, and culturally barren image of the United States. In the words of one American conservative, the "faith-based imperialism" of the present scripture-quoting Evangelical in the White House (Bush II) is "brazen in the implicit assumption that the President of the United States and his lieutenants are morally entitled to run the planet."[100]

Though it long posed as a bastion of anti-imperialism, the US today has come to represent the world's foremost imperialist power. Friends and foes have often and emphatically said as much.[101] But it should be noted, as New Rightists do, that American imperialism differs from its European antecedents in being more economic than political. Its imperial model originated in Latin America, where the US typically assumed control of a country's economy without having to occupy its territory or take control of its state apparatus. If occupation were necessary, the Marines were sent in only as long as it took to secure the key economic sectors and broker agreements with local elites. (When longer engagements were necessary, such as in the Philippines, Vietnam, or Iraq, it has simply proved itself inadequate to the task.) Today, through globalization, which enables its capital, symbols, and way of life to achieve a broader dimension, the US pursues a similar "Latin American strategy," extending its Monroe Doctrine to Europe, the Persian Gulf, and other regions it considers part of its *Lebensraum*. As it does, it "mobilizes its massive political and economic power to deregulate the world economy, open foreign markets to American investment, gain access for its enterprises to all their economies, raw materials, and workforces, and does so for the sake of generalizing a free trade system that functions according to American rules and to the profit of American interests."[102]

To sustain these imperial ambitions, the IMF, World Bank, GATT, WTO, UN, and other US-created bodies provide the necessary administrative and organizational supports for its world market empire. Once a nation succumbs to the global system of vassalage such bodies impose, US loans and aid bring its agricultural and industrial policies into line with American models. Native patterns of social regulation are then dissolved and made to accord with the norms and interests of its market.[103] Finally, and perhaps most importantly, its Culture Industry supplants indigenous systems of symbolization, establishing Basic English as the *lingua franca* and its deculturated, denatured, and pathogenic foods, clothes, and lifestyles as the universal standard. Those refusing to be so vassalized—Iraq, Iran, Serbia, Cuba, Nicaragua, Libya, Sudan, Afghanistan, North Korea—the so-called "rogue states"—are identified with Hitler's Third Reich and treated accordingly.

In highlighting the distinctive Latin American character of US imperialism, New Rightists stress the flimsy moral grounds on which Jefferson's "universal nation" asserts its sanctimonious claim to world leadership. One *Gréciste* writes that "the Calvinist foundation of American policy

... makes it unable to think of interstate relations in other than messianic terms."[104] As such, it arrogantly runs roughshod over the Rest of the World, belying all the lofty principles with which it formally identifies. The United States, for example, portrays itself as the pillar of a democratic, law-abiding world order based on peaceful economic transactions and human rights, but it consistently ignores international conventions and readily resorts to unilateral military solutions whenever it suits its needs. It poses as the world's chief moral exemplar, yet its highest social forms privilege narcissism and materialism. It professes a hatred of war and makes a fetish of the Jews' "Holocaust industry" (Norman Finkelstein), yet dropped two atomic bombs on civilian targets, fire-bombed the cultural capitals of Central Europe, surreptitiously radiated segments of its own population, and conducted every one of its modern engagements with a cold technological inhumanity unknown in history. No less hypocritically, it stands in the forefront of globalist demands for liberal democracy, yet thinks nothing of unseating democratically elected governments that displease it. It similarly champions the rights of oppressed peoples, yet, in tactically arming and advising Turkey, it has been more than complicit in the murder of 40,000 Kurds.

Though it waged a holy war on Iraq in 1991 (because of its invasion of what was a former Iraqi province), it had not a word of protest for its allies' even more murderous occupations of Lebanon, Cypress, the West Bank, East Timor, Gaza, or Northern Ireland. And now, since the World Trade Center attack of 2001, it wages an international crusade against Islamic terrorists, ignoring in the process not only that these terrorists got their start as CIA operatives in the Soviet-Afghan war, the anti-Russian Chechen insurgency, and the Bosnian and Kosovo interventions against Christian Serbia, but that the massive loss of life on 9/11 was a direct offshoot of US policy (whether it was a "black op" or not).[105]

American duplicity has not been limited to the international arena. Though the country obsessively portrays itself as a model society, New Rightists point out that Americans themselves are increasingly disturbed by life in their plutocratic *cosmopolis*. However cretinized by TV and distracted by nagging bills, all sections of the population harbor deep suspicions of the government and are prepared to believe the worse about it. There is a pervasive feeling that the political process is out of touch with the people, that the moral fabric of their communities has unraveled, that the middle class, the country's pride, is threatened by a rapacious overclass and a murderous non-white underclass.[106]

Since the "Civil Rights Revolution" of the sixties, which imposed an onerous system of racial discrimination on white males, the country has been racked by unprecedented levels of crime and incarceration (ten times the rate of Europe). At the same time, its white majority has been subjected to a de-Europeanization campaign that has destroyed the integrity of its schools, neighborhoods, and former way of life. A large part of the population is also sedated with illegal narcotics or psycho-pharmaceuticals (4 million of whom are schoolchildren on the amphetamine "Ritalin"). Income discrepancies have come to resemble those of the Third World, with the top 1 percent of the population owning 40 percent of the country's wealth (1995 figures).[107] Even before the recent downturn, its much touted high employment and booming economy masked structural underemployment, wage stagnation, low productivity, and an excessive money supply that portends a bear market more devastating that that of the thirties. Trade deficits remain unmanageable, federal budgetary deficits continue to grow, the Social Security and Medicare systems hover on the brink of insolvency, parasitic government employees outnumber manufacturing workers (21 million to 18 million), domestic saving rates are among the lowest in the world, credit expansion and borrowing exceed growth and accumulation (just as consumption massively exceeds production), and the whole system depends on foreigners being compelled to buy the US debt.[108] Even the country's "new economy," associated with the "high-tech" sector, is largely a creation of hype and speculation, inferior in import to the great technoeconomic breakthroughs of the last century.[109]

But even more damning than their corruption and mismanagement, American elites have shown not the slightest interest in the survival of European America and, through their Third World immigration policies, have demonstrated their willingness to import a replacement population. With these criminal policies, there has come a meltdown of the family, declining white natality, the "proliferation of every kind of sexual aberration," unprecedented marriage failures, mothers forced into labor markets, small children exiled to day-care centers, and the elderly removed to sanitized warehouses. At a time when the "knowledge society" is trumpeted from every bully pulpit, American schools, the worse in the industrial world, no longer educate, literacy rates have fallen below 75 percent, and university scholars are routinely denied tenure for nonconformist opinions or grading systems unamenable to quota considerations.[110]

Not a few indicators (IQ tests, SAT scores, US Army entrance exams) suggest that the population's mean intelligence is in conspicuous decline. One liberal critic estimates that "the number of genuinely literate adults in the US amounts to fewer than 5 million people—that is, less than 3 percent of the total population."[111] The country's transition to a so-called "knowledge economy" comes, though, not just at the cost of an educated citizenry, but "of poor public services, low social standards, weak communities, rising violence, and high poverty" (Peter Hain). The socially aberrant character of American life has been further exacerbated by guerrilla skirmishes between conservative and progressive cultural forces, a general Balkanization of the social order, the virtualization of the public sphere, low-intensity race war in the inner cities, homicidal outrages by disgruntled employees and alienated schoolchildren, and the virtual collapse of commonly accepted moral standards.

For New Rightists, America is not just a "planet of the clowns," absurd in its pretenses. It stands as a menacing affront to everything they value in the European heritage. Little wonder that they view its New World Order as the greatest threat to their Old World.

## Notes to Chapter VI

1. Maurice Bardèche, *L'œuf de Christophe Colomb* (Paris: Les Sept Couleurs, 1951); Francis Parker Yockey, *The Enemy of Europe*, trans. Thomas Francis (Reedy, WV: Liberty Bell, 1985).
2. On the difficulty of the term "anti-Americanism," see Marie-France Toinet, "Does Anti-Americanism Exist?," in *The Rise and Fall of Anti-Americanism: A Century of French Perception*, ed. Denis Lacorne, Jacques Rupnik, and Marie-France Toinet, trans. Gerald Turner (New York: St. Martin's Press, 1990). For its historical development, see Philippe Roger, *L'ennemi américain: Généalogie de l'anti-américanisme français* (Paris: Seuil, 2002). For an identitarian definition, see Guillaume Faye, *Pourquoi nous combattons: Manifeste de la Résistance européenne* (Paris: L'Æncre, 2001), 55–57. For its relationship to European antimodernism, see Peter Wagner, "The Resistance That Modernity Constantly Provokes: Europe, America and Social Theory," *Thesis Eleven* 58 (August 1999).
3. As one revolutionary nationalist puts it: "*La superpuissance américaine incarne tout ce monde modern que nous vomissons.*" Quoted in Christian Bouchet, *Les nouveaux nationalistes* (Paris: Éds. Déterna, 2001), 103. Revealingly, all the nationalists Bouchet interviewed for this work expressed similar sentiments.
4. Robert de Herte (Alain de Benoist) and Hans-Jürgen Nigra (Giorgio Locchi), "Il était une fois l'Amérique," *Nouvelle École* 27–28 (Fall–Winter 1975); Alain de Benoist, "C'est encore loin, l'Amérique," in *La ligne de mire II: Discours aux citoyens européens, 1988–1995* (Paris: Le Labyrinthe, 1996). Also Robert Steuckers, "La menace culturelle américaine," at *Archivio Eurasia* (http://utenti.tripod.it/ArchivEurasia/index.html); Reinhold Oberlercher, "Wesen und Verfall Amerikas," at *Dr. Reinhold Oberlercher* (http://www.deutsches-kolleg.org). It might be added that the New Right view of America's "peopling" addresses only the official narrative. Irish immigrants, for example, saw themselves as "exiles" in America and never lost their love for "the proud old woman" they left behind—indeed, her brave sons would save and struggle to free her from her

bondage (only to have the bourgeois "democratic dictator," Seán Lemass and his Celtic Tiger crowd, give it back—in spades).
5. Sacvan Bercovitch, *The Puritan Origins of the American Self* (New Haven, CT: Yale University Press, 1975), 5, 46–47, 63, 113.
6. C. Northcote Parkinson, *The Evolution of Political Thought* (London: University of London Press, 1958), 166.
7. Michael Walker, "Auf der Suche nach dem verlorenen Amerika," *Elemente für die europäische Wiedergeburt* 1 (June 1986). Cf. Jean Plumyène, *Les nations romantiques: Histoire du nationalism, le XIXe siècle* (Paris: Fayard, 1979), 101–5. By contrast, the American South, closer to the legacy of the English gentry than New England's Puritan merchants, was far more European in character. Its gentlemen slaveholders, Anglican churches, and Ciceronian educational tradition gave "Southern civilization" a character very unlike the bourgeois North. Without the Northern War of Aggression (which Yockey called the "war between quantity and quality"), the US would undoubtedly have retained more of its Old World heritage. In a characteristic expression of anti-liberal disdain for the North's "anti-culture," Maurice Bardèche describes Sherman's terrorist assault on Atlanta and the subsequent crushing of Southern civilization as nothing less than a "barbarian victory"—concluding that the term "Yankee," unlike that of "Confederate" (*Sudiste*), is itself synonymous with "barbarism." See *Sparte et les Sudistes* (Paris: Les Sept Couleurs, 1969), 130.
8. Thomas Molnar, *The Emerging Atlantic Culture* (New Brunswick, NJ: Transaction Publishers, 1994), 37; Thomas Molnar, *L'américanologie: Triomphe d'un modèle planétaire?* (Lausanne: L'Âge d'Homme, 1991), 32–34.
9. Thomas Molnar, "Pour l'américanologie," in *États-Unis: Danger. Actes du XXVe colloque national du GRECE* (Paris: Le Labyrinthe, 1992).
10. Carl and Jessica Bridenbaugh, *Rebels and Gentlemen: Philadelphia in the Age of Franklin* (New York: Oxford University Press, 1962), 18.
11. Oswald Spengler, *The Hour of Decision*, trans. Charles Francis Atkinson (New York: Knopf, 1934), 68.
12. Friedrich Nietzsche, *Daybreak: Thoughts on the Prejudices of Morality*, trans. R. J. Hollingdale (Cambridge: Cambridge University Press, 1997), § 186.
13. D. W. Brogan, *The American Character* (New York: Time, 1962), 83.
14. Michael Walker, "Our America: Lost and Found," *The Scorpion* 7 (Summer 1984).
15. Jean-Baptiste Duroselle, *France and the United States: From the Beginnings to the Present*, trans. Derek Coltman (Chicago: University of Chicago Press, 1978), 62.
16. François Labeaume and Charles Champetier, "A l'Ouest rien de nouveau?," *Cartouches: L'actualité des idées* 3 (August 1997).
17. Richard Rorty, *Achieving Our Country: Leftist Thought in Twentieth-Century America* (Cambridge, MA: Harvard University Press, 1998), 22–24.
18. Alain de Benoist, "États-Unis: Le maintien d'une puissance," *Éléments* 70 (Spring 1991).
19. Molnar, *The Emerging Atlantic Culture*, 22.
20. Quoted in Edmund S. Morgan, *The Birth of the Republic, 1763–89*, 2nd ed. (Chicago: University of Chicago Press, 1977), 75.

21. "Stendhal et les États-Unis d'Amérique," *Études et recherches* 4–5 (January 1977).
22. Jean Mabire, "Faut-il brûler Jack London?," *Éléments* 35 (Summer 1980).
23. Duroselle, *France and the United States*, 79.
24. Thomas Fleming, "Free Greeks, Servile Americans," *Chronicles* (February 2001).
25. Martha A. Ackelsberg, "Identity Politics, Political Identities: Thoughts Toward a Multicultural Politics," *Frontiers: A Journal of Women Studies* 16:1 (1996).
26. Cf. E. Michael Jones, *The Slaughter of Cities: Urban Renewal as Ethnic Cleansing* (South Bend, IN: St. Augustine's Press, 2002).
27. Alain de Benoist, "Racism and Totalitarianism," *National Democrat* 1 (Winter 1981–82); Pierre Krebs, *Im Kampf um das Wesen* (Horn: Burkhart Weecke Verlag, 1997), 71.
28. Alain de Benoist, *Les idées à l'endroit* (Paris: Hallier, 1979), 267.
29. J. G. Jatras, "Rainbow Fascism at Home and Abroad," *Chronicles* (June 1998).
30. Quoted in Robert H. Wiebe, *The Segmented Society: An Introduction to the Meaning of America* (New York: Oxford University Press, 1975), 90; Plumyène, *Les nations romantiques*, 101.
31. Cf. Raymonde Carroll, *Cultural Misunderstandings: The French-American Experience*, trans. Carol Volk (Chicago: University of Chicago Press, 1987), 129–31.
32. Herte and Nigra, "Il était une fois l'Amérique"; Hermann Keyserling, *Europe*, trans. Maurice Samuel (New York: Harcourt, Brace, and Co., 1928), 209–10. Cf. Mark A. Noll, ed., *God and Mammon: Protestants, Money, and the Market, 1790–1860* (Oxford: Oxford University Press, 2001).
33. Keyserling, *Europe*, 192.
34. Walker Percy, *The Moviegoer* (New York: Knopf, 1980), 223.
35. Alain de Benoist, *Vu de Droite: Anthologie critique des idées contemporaines*, 5th ed. (Paris: Copernic, 1979), 398–401; Gordon S. Wood, *The Radicalism of the American Revolution* (New York: Vintage Books, 1991), 359.
36. Walker, "Our America."
37. Alain de Benoist, *Démocratie: Le problème* (Paris: Le Labyrinthe, 1985), 30, 40; and Herte and Nigra, "Il était une fois l'Amérique." Cf. Jacob Burckhardt, *Reflections on History*, trans. M. D. Hottinger (Indianapolis: Liberty Classics, 1979), 39.
38. Liberal nationalists like Michael Lind would dispute this. But, revealingly, they define a "nation" not as an ethnocultural community bound by history and high culture, but as a community with "a common language, common folkways, and a common vernacular culture"—which describes a bowling team or a postmodern tribe, but not a nation in the European sense—for a "way of life," with its emphasis on the physical requirements of existence, bears only a refracted relationship to a "culture" representing the existential distillation of a people's timeless beliefs and creations. See Michael Lind, *The Next American Nation: The New Nationalism and the Fourth American Nation* (New York: The Free Press, 1995), 5.
39. Although New Rightists acknowledge the European roots of modernity, they claim European modernity lacks the universal impulse which Americans

(former colonials shallowly rooted in the European, especially the Continental and Catholic tradition) have imparted to it. See Guillaume Faye, *Les nouveaux enjeux idéologiques* (Paris: Le Labyrinthe, 1985), 56. Jean Baudrillard quips: "America is the original version of modernity. We [Europeans] are the dubbed or subtitled version." See *America*, trans. Chris Turner (London: Verso, 1988), 76.

40. Even if one agrees with Donald W. Livingston that behind the rationalist language of the founding documents there lies the "corporate identity" of the 13 original states, it still does not alter the fact that the Declaration of Independence and the Constitution expressed principles that spoke to the interests of individuals and corporations, but not to those of a historically formed, self-conscious people. See his "Dedicated to the Proposition," *Chronicles* (June 2001). More credibly, Roger Scruton describes the Founding Fathers as having propagated "the myth of a 'new constitution' while enjoying the privileges of an established order"—that is, of not acknowledging the British roots of America's constitutional arrangement. He also suggests that the abstract formulas of a "written constitution," like those of the US, are inherently prone to the sort of liberal reinterpretations that have turned the twentieth-century American state into a devouring Leviathan. See his *The Meaning of Conservatism*, 2nd ed. (London: Macmillan, 1984), 46–47.
41. Michael Oakeshott, "Rationalism in Politics" (1947), in *Rationalism in Politics and Other Essays* (Indianapolis: Liberty Fund, 1991). Even a so-called traditionalist like Russell Kirk defends America as an "idea." See *The American Cause*, 3rd ed. (Wilmington, DE: ISI Books, 2002), 50. New Rightists are also inclined to reject the argument that the American Revolution was a conservative one, with the colonialists defending British constitutional principles and not abstract natural rights born of Enlightenment liberalism.
42. Albert Jay Nock, *Mr. Jefferson* (Tampa, FL: Hallberg Publishing Company, 1983), 64. On Jefferson's affinity with Adam Smith and the Whig economic tradition, see John Chamberlain, *The Roots of Capitalism* (Indianapolis: Liberty Press, 1976), 15–20.
43. Charles A. Beard, *An Economic Interpretation of the Constitution* (New York: Macmillan, 1960).
44. Cf. Michael P. Zuckert, *The Natural Rights Republic: Studies in the Foundations of the American Political Tradition* (Notre Dame: University of Notre Dame Press, 1996). Robert H. Wiebe, in *Self-Rule: A Cultural History of American Democracy* (Chicago: University of Chicago Press, 1995), argues that mass participation in frequently held elections created "unity out of the diversity of American life." These "marching and huzzahing" electoral pastimes may have indeed invigorated the Early Republic—they did not last much beyond the Civil War—but, again, they testify to the political or ideological foundations of the American experiment, not its national, ethnic, or even historical basis. Wiebe also ignores the fact that it was the racial homogeneity of the white, mainly Nordic, population that undergirded the socially integrative impact of American electoral democracy. The loss of this homogeneity in the postbellum period, as much as the industrialization of the economy, seems to have played a

no less significant role in the subsequent "metamorphosis" of American electoralism into the present media spectacle.
45. Walker, "Our America." Cf. Julius Evola, "Le déclin de l'Orient," in *Explorations: Hommes et problèmes*, trans. Philippe Baillet (Puiseaux: Pardès, 1989).
46. "The negation of the political, which is inherent in every consistent individualism, leads necessarily to a political practice of distrust toward all conceivable political forces and forms of state. . . . The systematic theory of liberalism concerns almost solely the internal struggle against the powers of the state. For the purpose of protecting individual freedom and private property, liberalism provokes a series of methods for hindering and controlling the state's and government's power." See Carl Schmitt, *The Concept of the Political*, trans. George Schwab (Chicago: University of Chicago Press, 1996), 70.
47. Brogan, *The American Character*, 16.
48. "Federal populists," such as those associated with the journal *Telos*, would argue that the American constitutional concept of the state expressed the country's original commitment to federalism and federalism's intended defense of Protestant particularism. The problem with this argument is that "state governments" reflected the same general anti-political impetus as the federal government, and the various forms of particularism that federation was intended to defend have since been emptied of all religious content. What Paul Piccone calls the "terminally heterogeneous" character of the US seems to testify less to its population's resistance to New Class homogenization (which is not at all adverse to the most extreme forms of racial/cultural diversity) than to the multicultural character of postmodern society and the American individualist tradition. If the historical and anthropological records are any guide, only culturally homogeneous peoples, with coherent and well-anchored moral, cultural, and social orders, possess the means to resist the standardizing impetus of a "bureaucratically administered society." Cf. Barry A. Shain, *The Myth of American Individualism: The Protestant Origins of American Political Thought* (Princeton, NJ: Princeton University Press, 1994).
49. Benoist, *Les idées à l'endroit*, 268.
50. Cf. Robert Barrot, *Il est trop tard* (Paris: Godefroy de Bouillon, 2001), 148–91.
51. Alain de Benoist, "Antigone? Légalité et légitimité" (1997), in *L'écume et les galets, 1991-1999: Dix ans d'actualité vue d'ailleurs* (Paris: Le Labyrinthe, 2000). Cf. John Gray, *Enlightenment's Wake: Politics and Culture at the End of the Modern Age* (London: Routledge, 1995), 64–85.
52. As evidenced in the Supreme Court's argument for annulling California's Proposition 187, a 1994 ballot initiative aimed at keeping illegal immigrants off the welfare rolls.
53. Alain de Benoist and Guillaume Faye, "La religion des droits de l'homme," *Éléments* 37 (January–April 1981). Cf. Michael J. Sandel, *Democracy's Discontent: America in Search of a Public Philosophy* (Cambridge, MA: Belknap Press, 1996), 4.
54. Emmanuel Todd, *Après Empire: Essai sur la décomposition du système américain* (Paris: Gallimard, 2002), 95.
55. Carl Schmitt, *Du politique*, ed. Alain de Benoist (Puiseaux: Pardès, 1990), xxiii.

56. Tomislav Sunic, "Liberalism or Democracy? Carl Schmitt and Apolitical Democracy," at *Synthesis* (http://www.rosenoire.org).
57. Cf. Hans-Dietrich Sander, "Die Ermordung der Politik durch die Justiz," *Staatsbriefe* (January 2000).
58. Alain de Benoist, "Ni fraîche, ni joyeuse," *Éléments* 41 (March–April 1982); Alain de Benoist, "L'enigma soviétique dans le miroir de l'Occident," *Nouvelle École* 38 (Summer 1982). When the Muslim fanatics under Osama bin Laden launched their holy war on the US in September 2001, the born-again Methodist occupying the White House, prompted by his Jewish handlers, responded in the same crude fundamentalist terms, resorting to the simplistic dichotomies of the Abrahamic tradition to call on Americans to crusade against "evil"—instead of calling on them to fight a threatening enemy. See Pierre Vial, "Ni Jihad, ni McWorld: Europe liberté," *Terre et peuple: La revue* 10 (Winter 2001).
59. Even more remote to the American sensibility is an understanding of war's role in forging the national character. As Joseph de Maistre put it: *"Les véritable fruits de la nature humaine, les arts, les sciences, les grandes entreprises, les hautes conceptions, les vertus mâles tiennent surtout à l'état de guerre. On sait que les nations ne parviennent jamais au plus haut point de grandeur dont elles sont susceptibles, qu'après de longue et sanglantes guerre."* See *Considérations sur la France* (Lyons: E. Vitte, 1924), 36. Also Alain de Benoist, "Minima moralia," *Krisis* 7 (February 1991). America's Puritanical view of war persists despite the fact that the country was "made by war" and that its history resembles *une succession d'actes de brigandage* (Pierre-Antoine Cousteau). Cf. Geoffrey Perret, *A Country Made by War: From the Revolution to Vietnam—the Story of America's Rise to Power* (New York: Random House, 1989).
60. The armies of the Revolution and, later, the Rebel South were, an obvious expression of the warrior spirit native to men of Indo-European origin. The above statement applies to postbellum America and the "weak-willed, self-interested, pleasure-mad morons that Hollywood has tried so desperately to make them" (Yockey).
61. Guillaume Faye, "L'audace de la puissance," *Éléments* 56 (Winter 1985). Revealingly, the American South, the one-time antithesis of the North, is the one region where the soldier is respected and military values are still evident.
62. Herte and Nigra, "Il était une fois l'Amérique"; Benoist, *Les idées à l'endroit*, 263–66.
63. Schmitt, *The Concept of the Political*, 41. On America's Calvinist view of war, see Jean-Paul Mayer, *Dieu de colère: La stratégie américaine sous l'influence du puritanisme* (Paris: ADDIM, 1996); also Oswald Spengler, *Preussentum und Sozialismus* (Munich: Beck, 1919), § 14.
64. Cf. Thomas J. DiLorenzo, *The Real Lincoln: A New Look at Abraham Lincoln, His Agenda, and an Unnecessary War* (New York: Prima, 2002).
65. Quoted in Thomas Fleming, *The New Dealers' War: Franklin D. Roosevelt and the War Within the War* (New York: Basic Books, 2001), 181.
66. Faye, "L'audace de la puissance"; Robert Steuckers, "Pourquoi faut-il être anti-américain?," in *Bréviaire anti-américain* (Paris: GRECE pamphlet, n.d.).
67. Robert Poulet, *J'accuse la bourgeoisie* (Paris: Copernic, 1978), 206. Cf. Maximilian Czesany, *Europa im Bombenkrieg, 1939–1945* (Graz: Stocker, 1998);

Jean-Claude Valla, *La France sous les bombes américaines* (Paris: Librairie Nationale, 2001).
68. Benoist, *Vu de Droite*, 398–99. Cf. Louis Hartz, "The Coming of Age of America," *The American Political Science Review* 51:2 (June 1957).
69. Hermann Keyserling, *The World in the Making*, trans. Maurice Samuel (New York: Harcourt, Brace and Co., 1927), 128–29.
70. Konrad Pingel, "Der amerikanische Globalismus und die geostrategischen Imperative," *Staatsbriefe* (May–June 2001).
71. Quoted in Patrick J. Buchanan, *A Republic, Not an Empire: Reclaiming America's Destiny* (Washington, DC: Regnery, 1999), 53.
72. Herte and Nigra, "Il était une fois l'Amérique." Herte and Nigra (pen names of Benoist and Locchi) are obviously off target here. Not only was the conquest of the American West one of the great chapters in the "march of the white race," it was opposed and criticized by the same liberals who have always resisted the great and heroic in the name of "equality, toleration, and treason." Only Russia's conquest of Siberia and Alaska in the seventeenth century had more importance to the growth of the European race in the modern period.
73. Wiebe, *The Segmented Society*, 4.
74. Ernst von Salomon, *It Cannot Be Stormed*, trans. M. S. Stephens (London: Jonathan Cape, 1935), 12.
75. Herte and Nigra, "Il était une fois l'Amérique."
76. Cited in Benoist, *Démocratie*, 66.
77. Hermann Keyserling, *America Set Free* (New York: Harper and Brothers, 1929), 77.
78. Friedrich Nietzsche, *Thus Spoke Zarathustra*, trans. R. J. Hollingdale (London: Penguin, 1969), "Prologue."
79. Quoted in Julius Evola, *L'arc et la massue*, trans. Philippe Baillet (Paris: Pardès, 1983), 35.
80. Jean Baudrillard, *Simulations*, trans. Phil Beitchman, Paul Foss, and Paul Patton (New York: Semiotext[e], 1983), 26.
81. Tom Wolfe, *A Man in Full* (New York: Farrar, Straus and Giroux, 1998), 171. (Tenses modified.)
82. Michel Marmin, "Faut-il détruire le Center Beaubourg?," *Éléments* 20 (n.d. [c. 1977]).
83. George Santayana, *Character and Opinion in the United States* (New York: Doubleday Anchor Books, 1956), 1.
84. Nock, *Mr. Jefferson*, 172.
85. Herte and Nigra, "Il était une fois l'Amérique."
86. Georges Duhamel, *America the Menace: Scenes from the Life of the Future*, trans Charles Miner Thompson (London: George Allen and Unwin, 1931), 177.
87. Quoted in Walter Laqueur, *Black Hundred: The Rise of the Extreme Right in Russia* (New York: Harper Perennial, 1993), 145.
88. Jean Baudrillard, "L'Amérique, de l'imaginaire au virtuel," in *L'Amérique des français*, ed. Christine Fauré and Tom Bishop (Paris: Éds. François Bourin, 1992). If Baudrillard were a product of the present-day rather than the older, pre-Americanized France (he was born in 1929), such a judgement would

almost certainly have eluded him, for the deculturation of postwar Europe is increasingly making it resemble the US.
89. Armin Mohler, "Devant l'histoire," *Nouvelle École* 27–28 (Fall–Winter 1975).
90. Christine Fauré and Tom Bishop, "L'Amérique des français," in *L'Amérique des français*, ed. Christine Fauré and Tom Bishop (Paris: Éds. François Bourin, 1992).
91. Benoist, *Les idées à l'endroit*, 268.
92. Marco Tarchi, "La colonisation subtile," in *Le défi de Disneyland: Actes du XXe colloque national de la revue "Éléments"* (Paris: Le Labyrinthe, 1986). From the perspective of European traditionalism, the "self-made man" is an abomination, for it holds that man is inseparable from what nurtures his spirit and informs his existence. He is not to be judged thus by his accumulations, but by what he transmits from his origins to his progeny. Accomplishment here is a matter of internal (spiritual) realization, not external (material) possession.
93. François Ryssen, "Généalogie de l'antiaméricanisme français," at *Voxnr* (http://www.voxnr.com).
94. Benoist, *Vu de Droite*, 346.
95. Michael Walker, "The Lotus Eaters," *National Democrat* 2 (Spring–Summer 1982).
96. Herte and Nigra, "Il était une fois l'Amérique."
97. Quoted respectively in Claude Julien, *America's Empire*, trans. Renaud Bruce (New York: Pantheon, 1971), 31, and Pierre-Marie Gallois, *Le soleil d'Allah aveugle l'Occident* (Lausanne: L'Âge d'Homme, 1995), 25. The prize for American self-righteousness has to go to the foreign-born former Secretary of State, the "hormonally challenged" Madeleine Albright: "If we have to use force, it is because we are America. We are the indispensable nation. We stand tall. We see farther into the future." Quoted in Chalmers Johnson, *Blowback: The Costs and Consequences of American Empire* (New York: Henry Holt, 2000), 217.
98. Donald William, *Le choc des temps: Géopolitiques* (Montreal: Éds. Sciences et Culture, 2000), 30.
99. René Guénon, *East and West*, trans. Martin Lings (Ghent, NY: Sophia Perennis, 1995), 44.
100. Robert Higgs, "George Bush's Faith-Based Foreign Policy," *San Francisco Chronicle* (February 13, 2003).
101. Samuel P. Huntington, *The Clash of Civilizations and the Remaking of World Order* (New York: Simon and Schuster, 1996), 185; Kai-Alexander Schlevogt, "Wachauf, Amerika!," *Junge Freiheit* (October 12, 2001). Cf. Tony Smith, *America's Mission: The United States and the Worldwide Struggle for Democracy in the Twentieth Century* (Princeton, NJ: Princeton University Press, 1994); Johnson, *Blowback*.
102. Alain de Benoist, quoted in Lionel Placet, "Les rencontres de la pensée rebelle," *Résistance: Le mensuel du réseau radical NR et solidariste* 5 (February 2003).
103. Pierre Krebs, "Eine Epoche in der Krisis," *Elemente der Metapolitik zur europäischen Neugeburt* 4 (1990).
104. Louis Montgrenies, "Du messianisme à la guerre totale," *Éléments* 69 (Fall 1990).
105. Benoist observed shortly after the events that "the American people are currently suffering . . . the consequences of an international policy . . . [that] has

produced in the world so great a sum of misery, unhappiness, and disaster that one part of the world has interpreted American policy as a declaration of war upon itself." See "Jihad vs. McWorld: An Interview with Alain de Benoist," originally in *Padania* (September 19, 2001), translated at *Australian Nationalist Archive* (http://www.alphalink.com.au/~radnat). (Translation modified.)

106. Thomas Molnar, "Fin de millénaire aux États-Unis," *Krisis* 20–21 (November 1997). Cf. Sandel, *Democracy's Discontent*, 3; Patrick J. Buchanan, *The Great Betrayal: How American Sovereignty and Social Justice Are Being Sacrificed to the Gods of the Global Economy* (Boston: Little, Brown, 1998), 19.

107. *New York Times* (April 17, 1995). The 1995 figures compare with 21 percent for 1949. Cf. Kevin Phillips, *Wealth and Democracy: A Political History of the American Rich* (New York: Broadway Books, 2002); John Cassidy, "Who Killed the Middle Class?," *The New Yorker* (October 16, 1995).

108. Jean-Louis Gombeaud and Maurice Décaillot, *Le retour de la très grande Dépression* (Paris: Economica, 1997). If qualitative rather than monetary measurements (that is, if health, happiness, well-being, vibrant families, connectedness, and creativity, instead of material wealth) are used to evaluate the American economy, rather than being foremost in the industrial world, it hovers near the bottom. See Amartya Sen, *Choice, Welfare, and Measurement* (Cambridge, MA: Harvard University Press, 1997). The work of the following major economic theorists all reflect badly on US economic health: Serge-Christophe Kolm, Maurice Allais, Nicholas Georgescu-Roegen, Michel Aglietta, Frédérique Leroux, and Amitai Etzioni. On the specific social and economic problems presently threatening US economic hegemony, see John Gray, *False Dawn: The Delusions of Global Capitalism* (New York: The New Press, 1998); Jean Heffer, "Il n'y a pas de miracle économique!," *L'Histoire* (April 2000); Guy Millière, *L'Amérique monde: Les derniers jours de l'empire américain* (Paris: François-Xavier de Guibert, 2000); Pierre Biarrès, *Le XXIe siècle ne sera pas américain* (Paris: Rocher, 1998); Michael A. Bernstein and David E. Adler, eds., *Understanding American Economic Decline* (Cambridge: Cambridge University Press, 1995). On the US propensity to assert its military prowess as compensation for its economic or social inferiority, see Robert W. Tucker and David C. Hendrickson, *The Imperial Temptation: The New World Order and American Purpose* (New York: Council of Foreign Relations Press, 1992). Finally, few informed commentators (as opposed to neocon ideologues) take the country's present hegemony as anything but temporary. For example, see Charles A. Kupchan, *The End of the American Era: U.S. Foreign Policy and the Geopolitics of the Twenty-first Century* (New York: Knopf, 2002).

109. Guillaume Faye, "L'imposture de la 'nouvelle économie,'" *Terre et peuple: La revue* 6 (Winter 2000).

110. Alain de Benoist, "Vers l'indépendance! Pour une Europe souveraine" (1983), in *La ligne de mire I: Discours aux citoyens européens, 1972–1987* (Paris: Le Labyrinthe, 1995).

111. Morris Berman, *The Twilight of American Culture* (New York: Norton, 2000), 42.

Chapter VII

# The West Against Europe

For nearly a half century, the most salient feature of the world order was the Cold War between the two extra-European superpowers. In this clash of Soviet Communism and American liberalism, the entire international community was polarized around one or the other of the two camps. Given its ideological nature, this polarization has been subject to considerable dispute. From the liberal perspective, it was a struggle between a "free world" based on civil rights, Christianity, and the Western heritage—and a godless, "totalitarian" slave state antithetical to all the West represented. Marxists, on the other hand, considered it a class battle between a truly egalitarian and rational project championing the highest values of the Western humanist tradition and an oppressive system cynically exploiting individual freedoms for the sake of wage slavery, imperialism, and class privilege. But however it was interpreted, the Cold War converged on Europe, dominating virtually every facet of Continental life, even when the battlefields lay elsewhere. Not every observer, however, took this standoff seriously. From their Continental perspective, *Grécistes* saw it less as a genuine enmity than a convenient justification for the *condominium américo-soviétique* then usurping European sovereignty.

## The Cold War Condominium

Even before the Battle of Berlin, Europe's fate had been decided. During the various wartime conferences, but especially at Yalta, American and Soviet leaders worked out how they would rearrange the postwar world.[1] While Franklin Roosevelt—America's "president for life"—assumed his alliance with the Soviet dictator would continue after the armistice, he also expected him to serve as a junior partner in his Great Powers consortium. Stalin's unwillingness to play this role (along with the economic needs of America's armament sector to maintain wartime levels of production) accounts for the subsequent rift in US-SU relations.[2] Revealingly, the threatening rivalries and local flashpoints that followed never interfered with their condominium for the postwar world.[3] In fact, at one level, the Cold War—this ideological struggle between "the state capitalism of the Soviet East and the private capitalism of the liberal West" (Hermann Rufer)—seemed designed to justify Europe's subjugation to the extra-Europeans. For despite their occasional frictions, an actual nuclear exchange remained a remote possibility, although the perceived threat of such helped drive all humanity into one of the two nominally opposed sheep pens.[4] But more than legitimating the Continent's subjugation to the extra-Europeans, the Cold War detracted Europeans from their civilizational project, forcing them to accept imperatives alien to their specific geopolitical interests.[5] As a consequence, the United States and the Soviet Union each had a stake in perpetuating a conflict that ensured their control of the world's epicenter.[6]

The underlying similarities of the rival *blocs* would do much to facilitate their collusion. This is not to suggest an international conspiracy between American liberalism and Russian Communism. But the two powers were more than ready to cooperate whenever their interests overlapped. While *Grécistes* had greater reservations about the US version of technoeconomic civilization, they fully agreed with Martin Heidegger's contention that "from a metaphysical point of view, Russia and America are the same."[7]

In this optic, the conflict between liberalism and Communism revolved around secondary issues. Both ideological systems, for example, believed that "economy is destiny," both subscribed to an inorganic materialism shirking life's tragic dimension and both promoted a "democratic" leveling suppressing every healthy expression of authority and superiority.[8] They likewise shared similar bureaucratic systems of apolitical governance, adhered to Enlightenment notions of individuality and equality, and incessantly sought to mechanize the various facets of human existence. Finally, they both extolled a non-European notion of liberty—for one, the individual freedom to accumulate limitless wealth, for the other, the economic security to realize individual freedoms. Neither, on this account, had the slightest interest in the most fundamental freedom of all: the collective liberty of a people or nation to pursue its destiny, as it takes cultural, historical, and biological rather than merely economic form.[9]

In many respects, the US and the SU were fruits of the same tree—but, *Grécistes* insist, poisonous fruits. The heritage of eighteenth-century rationalism had had, of course, a formative impact on Europe and since 1945 been everywhere institutionalized under the auspices of *le parti américain*. Nevertheless, the Enlightenment played a far different role on the Continent than it did in the two extra-European powers. In the first place, it was balanced by a Counter-Enlightenment and by traditions, hierarchies, and aristocracies that curbed its plebeian effects. Secondly, its extra-European expressions assumed a different tenor: in the East, the libertarian socialism derived from Enlightenment principles took on a terrorist and totalitarian character foreign to European sentiment, while in the West, market capitalism was turned into a massifying productionism alien to Continental practices. Finally, Europe possessed a cultural legacy, institutions, and a complex identity that mitigated the Enlightenment's soulless materialism, while the SU and the US were artificial civilizations based on rationalist principles hostile to the imperatives of blood and spirit.[10] For this reason, New Rightists believed the affinities linking Europe and the two superpowers were ones Europeans had no stake in nurturing.[11]

Despite their similarity, *Grécistes* thought the American, rather than the Russian, system posed the greater threat to Europe. Not only were Americans consistently more universalist, cosmopolitan, and egalitarian than Communists, they employed a more sophisticated system of social control.[12] To maintain their totalitarian empire, the Russians took to breaking the bodies of those opposing them, while the pioneers of Hollywood and Madison Avenue knew how to destroy their souls and hence their will to resist. That there were concerted rebellions against the Soviets, but none against the Americans (at least none in Europe), *Grécistes* believed, was sign not of the latter's beneficence, but of their greater subversion—and insidiousness.[13] Between the Soviet and liberal systems, *Grécistes* went on record favoring the former, because Communism's murderous despotism did not annihilate a people's will to survive in the way Americanization did.[14]

Given this view of the Cold War, *Grécistes* refused to stand with the flag-waving anti-Communists of the mainstream Right. This would occasionally earn them the epithet of "pro-Soviet." Yet, what *Grécistes* found objectionable in the American experiment was no less objectionable than what they found in Soviet Communism.[15] Their opposition to the Atlantic alliance had, though, another, more compelling motive. As Jean Cau put it: "It is in not being American today that we have the best chance of not being Russian tomorrow." That is, only in remaining autonomous *vis-à-vis* one *bloc* would Europeans be able to remain independent *vis-à-vis* the other.[16] Not coincidentally, the anti-Communism of the postwar Right helped justify the Americanization of Europe, recuperating, in effect, the anti-liberal forces for the sake of US interests.

The New Right's refusal to be drawn into the Cold War's anti-Communist politics did not, then, make it pro-Communist. In its view, Soviet Russia (*l'Amérique inversée*) was a pathological product of the Enlightenment project, criminal in the great numbers of people it killed—"the worst case of political carnage in history" (Martin Malia)—and detestable in the way it inculcated a spirit of mediocrity and servility in the Russian people.[17] They opposed it on principle, but as their secondary enemy, after the US. They also followed Ernst Nolte in seeing Communism as an international party of civil war, responsible for many of Europe's great catastrophes in the twentieth century.[18] Finally, they opposed the Soviet Union because it militarily threatened Europe and deflected Europeans from their own civilizational project. In no case, however, were they prepared to make Russia's subjugation of Eastern Europe a justification for submitting to the even more menacing threat posed by America's liberal market empire.

According to *Grécistes*, America's antipathy to Europe—which usually bears the guise of Germanophobia, anti-militarism, anti-fascism, and (since the "re-education" or de-Germanization of the Germans), Francophobia—long preceded the Cold War.[19] It was not until the twentieth century, though, that its anti-Europeanism acquired a meaningful political form. Beginning with the Versailles Peace Conference of 1919, Woodrow Wilson (in collusion with Continental radicals) endeavored to impose America's "impartial justice" on the Old World. Under the tutelage of this "anti-Metternich," who lacked the slightest understanding of Europe's ethno-historical contours and believed God had created the United States to lead the world's nations onto "the path of liberty," the Romanov, Hapsburg, Ottoman, and Hohenzollern empires were formally dissolved and liberal democratic states, without the slightest viability or legitimacy, set up in their place. Instead of his vaunted "peace without victors," the former Princeton professor dictated an extraordinarily punitive settlement, in the process giving birth to Adolf Hitler and the inevitability of another world war. He succeeded, in a word, in wrecking the old European state system and "imperiling the whole white race."[20] As a matter of course, his anti-European crusade to make "the world safe for democracy" (that is, to make the "world safe for the policies of the American *Lebensraum*") has been replicated by virtually every subsequent American Administration (including the "isolationist" ones of the twenties).[21]

Neither culturally nor geopolitically, *Grécistes* contend, do Europeans share common bonds with the US. They reject notions of an Atlantic community and point to those innumerable instances when America has thwarted the most vital European interests.[22] Such especially was the case during the Cold War. Not only did the US collude with Soviet Russia, it refused to contest the postwar division of Europe, it passed up those few opportunities that would have reunified Germany or aided anti-Soviet rebellions, and, in the Helsinki Accords of 1975, it legally sanctioned Europe's divided status. At the same time, it actively promoted the dissolution of Europe's colonial empires, morally supported the Turks in their invasion of Greek Cypress, eased the Europeans out of the Middle East and the Persian Gulf, abetted Islamic incursions on Europe's periphery, and stymied virtually every European effort to act autonomously. Its two-decade long alliance with radical Islam (hardly mitigated by the recent Likudization of the Bush Administration) was also at the expense of its European "alliance," especially in restoring the "Muslim bolt" blocking Europe's Eurasian land routes and in supporting Turkish efforts to "Lebanonize" the Continent.[23]

Since Hitler's defeat, the US has indeed shown its European "allies" little but contempt, acting as if they were vassals with no choice but to passively submit to its hegemonic interest. François Mitterrand (1916–96), whose Socialist government was the most pro-American in French history, admitted as much in his posthumous testament, where he noted that the US has been in "a permanent state of war" with Europe, unwilling to cede any part of its world power to its allies or make any concession to their national interests.[24] Recent military forays in Southeastern Europe constitute simply the latest in its ongoing effort to maintain a Continental presence that keeps Europeans from settling their own affairs—all the while giving the US Army new lands to occupy, Wall Street financiers new countries to rebuild, and Big Oil new sources to exploit.[25]

The North Atlantic Treaty Organization was (and remains) the principal institutional framework of the US-European "alliance." Ostensibly a military coalition of states to resist the threat of Soviet invasion (although its real purpose, as numerous mainstream commentators noted at its founding, was to prevent the resurgence of an independent Germany and to ensure America's postwar hegemony over Europe), NATO was not actually an alliance, but, according to De Gaulle, the auspices under which "America's European protectorate" was to be organized.[26] NATO's rationale was thus less a matter of European security than of extending the Monroe Doctrine to Western and Central Europe. From the beginning, there was not the slightest pretext of parity. The US took command of the alliance's forces and the Europeans were relegated to subordinate positions.[27] American troops, moreover, were allowed to occupy strategic areas of Europe, especially in Germany, and to develop a vast infrastructure to support them.[28] Europeans were also expected to support US defense initiatives, while the US commitment to Europe remained qualified.[29] Once the Soviets developed intercontinental ballistic missiles capable of reaching the American mainland, many European leaders feared the US would simply retreat to its North American redoubt if ever it came to a nuclear exchange with the Soviets.[30]

To justify Europe's submission to American power, a new ideology, "Atlanticism," was developed to foster the illusion that America was not only Europe's loyal defender, but heir to its civilization.[31] For *Grécistes* and other New Rightists, this liberal ideology sought nothing so much as to prevent "the unification of the Old World centers of power in a coalition hostile to [US] interests" (Nicholas Spykman). As such, those conservative intellectuals embracing Atlanticism were seen as little better than the *clercs de gauche*, who put Soviet interests above those of Europe.[32] Decades before Communism's fall, the GRECE began advocating a general withdrawal from NATO.[33] Against the superpowers, it upheld a "third way"—*ni Washington, ni Moscow!*—that put European interests foremost. Anything weakening the *condominium américo-soviétique*, it maintained, would be good for the Continent. That NATO continues to exist, "defending" Europe from a "now non-existent threat from a nonexistent country [i.e., the Soviet Union]," and continues to extend its American protectorate eastward, in parody of Hitler's *Drang nach Osten*, simply testifies to the servility of Europe's collaborationist elites.[34]

As long as it was subject to Yalta, the Continent remained dependent on the superpowers. The Soviet collapse (and hence the collapse of Yalta's principal pillar) was consequently an event of world-historical significance. Although initially disconcerted by the loss of a convenient adversary, the US quickly turned the demise of Russian communism into a vindication of its liberal market democracy. The most self-congratulatory expression of this triumphalist response came from the State Department's Francis Fukuyama and his *End of History*, which pronounced the cessation of ideological conflict and the worldwide triumph of American-style liberalism.[35]

*Grécistes*, conversely, interpreted the Cold War's conclusion as marking not the end but the return of history. One filiation of the Enlightenment's Great Narrative may have ended in 1989, but to think that history as a whole had ended or that reason had finally won out over the irrational forces of darkness would be to think in the same illusory way as those who thought the Bolshevik Revolution of 1917 represented the next higher stage of civilization.[36] *Grécistes* have also not forgotten that the spiritual degradations and injustices of nineteenth-century liberal society were responsible for the birth of Communism.[37] However monolithic its present global hegemony, they predict that America's liberal order is likely to give rise to even more challenging forms of anti-liberalism. This especially seems likely since "after a long parenthesis, liberal capitalism appears to have regained the arrogance and elan of its origins."[38]

The demise of the Soviet empire also brought old identities and long repressed ethnic grievances to the surface, altering "the patterns of cohesion, disintegration, and conflict in the post-Cold War world."[39] Samuel Huntington's contention that the end of the US-SU condominium would lead to a "clash of civilizations" was a prescient anticipation of what the new era would presage—just as the 9/11 terrorist attack on the symbols of America's global domination dramatically illustrated the potentially violent and destabilizing nature of these clashes.[40] In reopening conflicts between enrootment and cosmopolitanism that the Cold War had closed off, the events of 1989 also re-posed the question of European identity.[41] In the last decade, *Grécistes* and other identitarians have been repeatedly frustrated by the Continent's failure to reassert its civilizational project and resist US unilateralism (though with the advent of the US's "war on terrorism" in 2001, which "institutionalized a permanent state of planetary conflict" [Emmanuel Todd], this changed for a time, as France and Germany hesitated in following the US in its quixotic crusade).[42]

Despite her present doldrums, Europe's prospects are far from spent. By virtually every significant index, the EU stands higher than the US, except in the most decisive category of all: leadership, particularly at the head of a great military power. Europeans are better educated and more skilled than Americans, their cultural resources more prodigious, their economy more productive, their population and markets larger, their creativity higher, their scientific and technological capacity of greater potential. As a union, Europe possesses all the means of supplanting US hegemony.[43] If ever her political and military confidence should catch up with her economic and intellectual powers (and the arrogant tendency of recent US Administrations to use aggression and violence to augment its waning powers may perhaps accelerate this prospect), her geopolitical ambitions are eventually bound to clash with those of the US Europe's present subordination to the transatlantic colossus is thus not "objective," but reflects the inferiority complex of the collaborationist elites making up *le parti américain*—elites who have dissipated or neutralized virtually every expression of Europe's will to power over the last half century.[44] For this reason, *Grécistes* claim "Americans are only as strong as we are weak."[45] If resolute leaders should ever emerge, the Continent possesses both the means and the ability to accomplish great things. The first step toward Europe's ascension may, indeed, have already begun, as the identitarian current represented by the GRECE and other New Right tendencies poses an increasingly lucid alternative to the once dominant Atlanticist ideology.

## Third World Alliance

The Third Way *Grécistes* advocated during the Cold War took its most notable expression in 1986 with the publication of Benoist's *Europe, Tiers monde, même combat*. In this work, Benoist called for an alliance between Europe and the Third World, particularly the Arab Middle East, in order to undermine the *blocs* and weaken their hold on Europe.[46] In a period when Jean-Marie Le Pen's National Front was beginning to attract the Right electorate with anti-immigrant appeals, the GRECE's "Third Worldism" signaled a major departure for the anti-liberal forces. It also signaled an opening to the Left, whose infatuation with the Third World had begun to unravel. Given the Left's unitary model of humanity, it has always been uncomfortable with national and cultural specificities, which were massively reasserted once the imperial powers retreated. That behind the facade of their progressive anti-colonial struggle, Third World peoples, like the European "proletariat," had failed to uphold the liberal democratic values the Left thought universal was cause for many former Sixty-Eighters to take their distance from them—that they proved to be anti-secular, anti-human rights, anti-rationalist, and, in some cases, anti-Semitic, led to outright disaffection.

Against both ends of the political spectrum, then, the GRECE of the eighties rallied to the Third World, affiliating with national-populist forces in Africa, Asia, and Latin America, as they resisted the US-SU condominium. Its Third Worldism, however, had little to do with the liberals' love of the "noble savage" or with white racial guilt, but followed from its geopolitical hostility to the *bloc* system and, philosophically, from its "differentialist" anthropology. Like postmodernists, *Grécistes* rejected both the colonial and the postcolonial variants of the Great Narrative. In their view, the Third World was no Rousseauian paradise, but a complex of diverse peoples, whose different cultures and histories ill-fit the liberal narrative. Only in assuming a universalist perspective, they believed, was it possible to interpret the Third World as somehow "undeveloped," destined to follow in the West's footsteps.[47]

Whether propounded by international financiers or well-meaning Leftists, notions of development, they claimed, rest on a linear concept of history, with the world's peoples situated at different stages in an evolutionary process whose culmination is to resemble the American system. Every modernizing society, in this view, is expected to converge on a single set of axial principles, as economic development pushes it along a common "developmental path." Walt Rostow's *The Stages of Economic Growth*, which challenged socialist schemes for postcolonial development by arguing that Third World countries would eventually "catch up" with the industrial West provided they emulate the Western capitalist model, was the most notable expression of this developmentalist view that measured all the world by its own standard.[48] Even Marxist Third Worldists, like Andre Gunder Frank, who criticized Rostow's capitalist argument and claimed Third World underdevelopment stemmed from its dependency on the West, not its lack of capitalization, accepted a purely economist model of development.[49] Both liberal developmentalist ideology and its Marxist dependency critique assumed, then, that Third World modernization would continue along Western lines and ought to be understood in economic and perhaps political terms, but not biocultural or civilizational ones.[50]

In opposing the prevailing notions of economic modernization, *Grécistes* in the eighties argued for culturally specific forms of economic growth. Just as late nineteenth-century Japan industrialized without abandoning its Japanese identity, *Grécistes* called on non-Western peoples to "develop" their societies on the basis of their own experiences and values.[51] What purpose, they asked, was there to development if it led to self-destruction? In fact, it was on just this point that *Grécistes* criticized the liberal model as it applied to Europe. Economic development, they stressed, ought not to be an end in itself. Under the laws of global capitalism, however, this is inevitably the case. Thus it is that the developmental policies propounded by international bankers in their computer-lined offices in New York dictate that Europe, like the Third World, sacrifice the logic of her own destiny for the sake of their financial markets.

Since the fall of the Soviet Union, the need for a Third Way between the *blocs* has lost much of its former relevance. The main international tensions now run between the liberal capitalist forces associated with America's New World Order and those identitarian forces—in Europe and elsewhere—that oppose them. The GRECE's Third Worldism has thus lost much of its original significance, even if the present alignment still dictates an identitarian orientation to the "periphery," as it resists the homogenizing forces of the "center."[52]

## The System That Destroys Nations

The GRECE's Third Worldism was part of its Third Way alternative to the US-SU condominium. But it also expressed its refusal to identify Europe with the "West." This constituted a particularly important facet of the GRECE's contribution to the Right in these years, when America stood as Europe's alleged defender. As a notion, the "West" for New Rightists no longer denoted Europe, the Atlantic alliance, or even what Americans call "Western civilization." As Guillaume Faye defined it in *Le système à tuer les peuples* (1981), the West had ceased to represent a geographic or civilizational entity and had become an ideological concept linked to the transnational system of US-style liberal capitalism.[53]

As the first country whose economy absorbed its society, the US is the pre-eminent incarnation of the West. But the West—*l'américanosphère*—is not, Faye insists, the US *per se*. Rather, it is the world system which strives to subject all planetary activities to its usurious logic.[54] This makes the West a technoeconomic system, not a civilization. A civilization serves human needs, while the West is a "megamachine" (Serge Latouche), whose production of prosperity, progress, and individual "liberation" creates a highly materialist form of social reality geared to market principles, but ultimately indifferent to those who have to live within its mechanical world.[55] The West's banks, multinationals, and various transnational institutions, for instance, operate in the interests of its system, but not for the sake of ethnicity, history, or destiny. A Singapore banker, as such, may be more "Western" than a Breton peasant, who still tills the soil and lives in the spirit of his ancestors.[56]

The West, moreover, is not led, only managed. Indeed, it is not men, but the system's regulatory logic that directs it. As such, this logic compels it to extend itself to every facet of existence and to every corner of the globe, as everything is integrated to accord with its systemic imperatives. Life is thereby disembedded from its given context, contractual relations are substituted for organic ones, history and memory are supplanted by electronic sources of "news and information," and the "present" is transformed into an "eternal now." As a totalitarian aggregate that denatures man, eliminates non-functional identities, and converts the most personal dimensions of everyday life into economic transactions, the West knows only the inorganic imperatives of its technoeconomic logic. This gigantic anti-culture thus changes all it touches. It feels no compulsion, for example, to pose the question "why?" or to address the strivings of the human spirit. Its system is its own justification. Similarly, it converts the most rudimentary cultural expressions—dress, food, leisure—into purchasing decisions, creating in the process a sociality devoid of life, warmth, and meaning. The "West" thus "kills" the peoples it dominates through a numbing economic deculturation that devitalizes everything it touches.[57] "Far from being an expression of Europe, it is the enemy of Europe" (Zinoviev).[58]

To the degree Europe still possesses a culture, a history, and a destiny, it does not belong to the West.[59] By contrast, the Europe affiliated with the West is simply a zone—more or less identical to the system's other zones.⁶⁰ The languages spoken there might differ from those of the North American or East Asian zones, red wine might be preferred to Coca-Cola or tea, and people might read more books than elsewhere, but these differences are mainly atmospheric, reflecting the ambiance of earlier ages. The same technoeconomic logic governs the European zone as the others. Slight differences in lifestyle and consumption patterns alone distinguish them. Like Christianity and its various secular offshoots, the West does not recognize frontiers, nations, and peoples, all of which it subjects to the same universal standards. As Benoist wrote in 1986, "Europe no longer exists as a strategic concept, economic entity, political power, or distinct cultural reality."⁶¹

Following the fall of the Berlin Wall, the Italian Catholic philosopher Augusto Del Noce argued that "Marxism died in the East because it triumphed in the West." Like New Rightists, Del Noce believed Marxism was never a radical alternative to, only a variant of, liberal capitalism. In his view, the global system represented by the West had come to resemble this variant, incorporating all the basic Marxist principles: atheism and materialism, cosmopolitanism and universalism, the primacy of practice over philosophy, economism, technological Prometheanism, and egalitarian homogenization. The single aspect of the Marxist project the system failed to realize was the one thing in it that was great: its denunciation and hope of transcending the alienation born of capitalist social relations. By contrast, Kant's vision of the Enlightenment, in which reason treats man purely as an end, has been completely inverted.⁶² Closer in spirit to the Marxian than the Kantian concept of the Enlightenment, the West now threatens Europe's very existence.

To survive, it is imperative, New Rightists contend, that Europeans oppose the West with a Ghibelline vision of a Continental imperium stretching from Galway to Vladivostok.

## Notes to Chapter VII

1. Cf. Lloyd C. Gardner, *Spheres of Influence: The Great Powers Partition Europe, from Munich to Yalta* (Chicago: Ivan R. Dee, 1993).
2. Hans-Dietrich Sander, "Stalins grösster Fehler oder die Arcilleferse der Grossmächte," *Staatsbriefe* (May 2000); Frank Kofsky, *Harry S. Truman and the War Scare of 1948: A Successful Campaign to Scare the Nation* (New York: St. Martin's Press, 1995).
3. Alain de Benoist, "L'ennemi principal" (Part II), *Éléments* 41 (March–April 1982); Alain de Benoist, *Orientations pour des années décisives* (Paris: Le Labyrinthe, 1982), 29. Cf. Dirk Bavendamm, *Roosevelts Krieg: Amerikanische*

*Politik und Strategie, 1937–1945* (Munich: Herbig, 1993); Arthur Conte, *Yalta ou le partage du monde* (Paris: Robert Laffont, 1964); Jean-Gilles Malliarakis, *Yalta et la naissance des blocs* (Paris: Éds. Albatros, 1982).
4. Jean-Louis Cartry, "Pour une défense non-alignée," *Éléments* 41 (March–April 1982); Guillaume Faye, *Nouvelle discours à la nation européenne* (Paris: Éds. Albatros, 1985), 37; Pierre-Marie Gallois, *La France sort-elle de l'histoire? Superpuissances et declin national* (Lausanne: L'Âge d'Homme, 1998), 19.
5. Gallois, *La France sort-elle de l'histoire?*, 89ff.
6. Benoist, *Orientations pour des années décisives*, 31–32; Guillaume Faye, "L'audace de la puissance," *Éléments* 41 (March–April 1982). Cf. Régis Debray, *Les empires contre l'Europe* (Paris: Gallimard, 1985).
7. Martin Heidegger, *Introduction to Metaphysics*, trans. Ralph Manheim (New Haven, CT: Yale University Press, 1952), 37. Cf. Pierre Drieu la Rochelle, *Genève ou Moscou* (Paris: Gallimard, 1928); Serge-Christophe Kolm, *Le libéralisme modern* (Paris: PUF, 1984). Georges Duhamel, who was similarly appalled by America's technoeconomic civilization, characterized it as "a sort of bourgeois communism." See his *America the Menace: Scenes from the Life of the Future*, trans. Charles Miner Thompson (London: George Allen and Unwin, 1931), 116.
8. Maiastra, *Renaissance de l'Occident?* (Paris: Plon, 1979), 33–34; Pierre Krebs, *Das Thule-Seminar: Geistesgegenwart du Zukunft in der Morgenröte des Ethnos* (Horn: Burkhart Weecke Verlag, 1994), 33–38. As Keyserling describes it: "Both countries are fundamentally socialist. But America expresses its socialism in the form of a general prosperity, and Russia in that of a general poverty." Quoted in Alain de Benoist, *Vu de Droite: Anthologie critique des idées contemporaines*, 5th ed. (Paris: Copernic, 1979), 400.
9. Robert de Herte, "Pourquoi nous sommes anticommuniste," *Éléments* 57–58 (Spring 1986); Guillaume Faye, "Pour en finir avec la civilisation occidentale," *Éléments* 34 (April–May 1980); Oswald Spengler, *The Hour of Decision*, trans. Charles Francis Atkinson (New York: Knopf, 1934), 67–68.
10. Alain de Benoist, *Les idées à l'endroit* (Paris: Hallier, 1979), 273; "Entretien avec Alain de Benoist," *Jeune nation solidariste: Organe de Troisième Voie* 196–197 (March–April 1985). Cf. Henry Steele Commager, *The Empire of Reason: How Europe Imagined and America Realized the Enlightenment* (New York: Phoenix, 2000).
11. Faye, *Nouvelle discours à la nation européenne*, 73.
12. Yockey: "Bolshevism means . . . the destruction of the West and of its culture. The *Communist Manifesto* sets forth a program to accomplish this on the economic-social side. In the ten demands that it makes, only nine are possible, and all these have been realized in the United States, but not one of them in Russia." See "The World in Flames" (1961), in *The Thoughts of Francis Parker Yockey* (London: The Rising Press, 2001). In this spirit, one German identitarian argues that America, not Soviet Russia, ought to be viewed as the true homeland of Karl Marx. See Krebs, *Das Thule-Seminar*, 39.
13. Robert de Herte, "Ni des esclaves, ni de robots," *Éléments* 34 (April–May 1980); Benoist, "L'ennemi principal" (Part II). The Canadian geopoliticist Donald William notes that anti-Soviet revolts occurred in East Germany (1953), Hungary (1956), Czechoslovakia (1968), and Poland (1980–85), but also

argues that the following should be viewed as revolts against the American empire: Guatemala (1951), the Dominican Republic (1965), Nicaragua (1972), Vietnam (1965–75), Chile (1973), Grenada (1983), and Panama (1989). See *Le choc des temps: Géopolitiques* (Montreal: Éds. Sciences et Culture, 2000), 53–55. According to Chalmers Johnson, during the Cold War the US killed many millions more than the Soviets in order to maintain its Latin American and East Asian empires. See his *Blowback: The Costs and Consequences of American Empire* (New York: Henry Holt, 2000), 22–28.

14. Benoist, *Orientations pour des années décisives*, 76; Alain de Benoist, "Pour une déclaration du droit des peuples," in *La cause des peuples: Actes du XVe colloque national du GRECE* (Paris: Le Labyrinthe, 1982).
15. Michael Lind, *Up from Conservatism: Why the Right is Wrong for America* (New York: The Free Press, 1996), 45; Murray N. Rothbard, "Life in the Old Right" (1994), in *The Paleoconservatives: New Voices from the Old Right*, ed. Joseph Scotchie (New Brunswick, NJ: Transaction Publishers, 1999).
16. Quoted in Alain de Benoist, *Europe, Tiers monde, même combat* (Paris: Robert Laffont, 1986), 16.
17. Cf. Alexandre Zinoviev, *Homo Sovieticus*, trans. Jacques Michaut (Paris: Julliard/L'Âge d'Homme, 1982).
18. Bertrand Laget, "La guerre civile européenne," *Éléments* 98 (May 2000); Ernst Nolte, *Der europäische Bürgerkrieg, 1917–1945: Nationalsozialismus und Bolshewismus* (Berlin: Propyläen, 1987).
19. Cf. Geir Lundestad, ed., *No End to Alliance: The United States and Western Europe, Past, Present and Future* (New York: St. Martin's Press, 1998), 171.
20. Hermann Keyserling, *America Set Free* (New York: Harper and Brothers, 1929), 84; Leon Degrelle, *Hitler: Born at Versailles* (Newport Beach, CA: IHR, 1987).
21. Walter A. McDougall, *Promised Land, Crusader State: The American Encounter with the World since 1776* (Boston: Houghton Mifflin, 1997), 145; Jean-Jacques Mourreau, "L'Europe malade de Versailles," *Éléments* 69 (Fall 1990); Nikolaj von Kreitor, "NATO and the Architects of the American *Lebensraum*," at Eurocombate (http://www.geocities.ws/eurocombate). Cf. Werner Links, "The United States and Western Europe: Dimensions of Cooperation and Competition," in *No End to Alliance: The United States and Western Europe, Past, Present and Future*, ed. Geir Lundestad (New York: St. Martin's Press, 1998); François-Georges Dreyfus, *1919–1939: L'engrenage* (Paris: Fallois, 2002).
22. Faye, "Pour en finir avec la civilisation occidentale"; Frédéric Julien, *Les États-Unis contre l'Europe: L'impossible alliance* (Paris: Le Labyrinthe, 1987).
23. Alexandre Del Valle, *Islamisme et États-Unis: Une alliance contre l'Europe*, 2nd ed. (Lausanne: L'Âge d'Homme, 1999), 286–88. Also Richard Labévière, *Les dollars de la terreur: Les États-Unis et les islamistes* (Paris: Grasset, 1999); Gilberto Oneto, "Sarrasins et cow-boys unis contre l'Europe" (2000), at *Synergon* (http://www.geocities.com/spartacorps/synergon). Skeptics might be reminded that Osama bin Laden, the Taliban regime of Afghanistan, and Saddam Hussein were all, at times, in the pay of the CIA. Cf. John K. Cooley, *Unholy Wars: Afghanistan, America, and International Terrorism*, 2nd ed. (Herndon, VA: Pluto Press, 2000).

24. From Georges-Marc Benamou, *Le dernier Mitterrand*, quoted in Alain de Benoist, *Dernière année: Notes pour conclure le siècle* (Lausanne: L'Âge d'Homme, 2001), 187.
25. Charles Champetier, "La Yougoslavie en ruine: Une guerre contre l'Europe," *Éléments* 95 (June 1999). The Balkans are not a source of oil, but if the vast Central Asian reserves are to be marketed, a pipeline from the Black Sea to the Adriatic is needed. Hence the strategic importance of the region.
26. Jacques Thibau, *La France colonisée* (Paris: Flammarion, 1980), 277; Robert Steuckers, "Sécurité et défense en Europe," in *Le défi de Disneyland: Actes du XXe colloque national de la revue "Éléments"* (Paris: Le Labyrinthe, 1987). Cf. Bob Djurdjevic, "A Bear in Sheep's Clothing," *Chronicles* (December 1998).
27. Since the end of the Cold War, US unilateralism has increased to the point where even Zbigniew Brzezinski acknowledges that it now treats its allies "as if they were [members] of the [former] Warsaw Pact. The US issues orders and they have to follow." See the transcript of CNN's *Late Night with Wolf Blitzer* (March 2, 2003). Also Konrad Pingel, "Der amerikanische Globalismus und die geostrategischen Imperative," *Staatsbriefe* (May–June 2001). It should be noted, though, that the increasingly unilateralist character of US policy, inspired by the Bush Administration's Likudization, is now threatening to disrupt NATO. Bush and his Jewish advisers have indeed done more to promote the cause of European independence than any previous Administration.
28. As Frank Costigliola documents, the US military occupation after 1945 led not only to US economic domination of Europe, it dominated all facets of French life. For example, beginning in the late 1940s, the US surreptitiously took control of several mainstream newspapers, infiltrated the major trade unions, broke strikes, manipulated public opinion, and "purchased" a number of key politicians and cabinet ministers. Its control of Germany, Italy, and Britain was even more extensive, for their governments were already subservient to the US. See *France and the United States: The Cold Alliance since World War II* (New York: Twayne, 1992), 64–88.
29. Fabrice Laroche, "Une nouvelle résistance," *Éléments* 16 (June 1976); Jean-Baptiste Duroselle, *France and the United States: From the Beginnings to the Present*, trans. Derek Coltman (Chicago: University of Chicago Press, 1978), 184.
30. "Entretien avec le General Gallois," *Éléments* 41 (March–April 1982).
31. Cf. Lundestad, *No End of Alliance*, 21.
32. Henri Gerfaut, "Une certaine idée de l'Europe," *Éléments* 53 (Spring 1985).
33. Marco Tarchi, "Prolégomènes à l'unification de l'Europe," in *Crépuscule des blocs, aurore des peuples: Actes du XXIIIe colloque national du GRECE* (Paris: GRECE, 1990).
34. Louis Sorel, "Le nouvel atlantisme contre l'Europe," *Éléments* 94 (February 1999); Zbigniew Brzezinski, *The Grand Chessboard: American Primacy and Its Geostrategic Imperatives* (New York: Basic Books, 1997), 59.
35. Francis Fukuyama, *The End of History and the Last Man* (New York: Avon, 1993).
36. Alain de Benoist, "Le retour de l'histoire," in *Crépuscule des blocs, aurore des peuples: Actes du XXIIIe colloque national du GRECE* (Paris: GRECE, 1990);

Alain de Benoist, "Les retrouvailles de l'Europe," *Éléments* 67 (Winter 1989). Emmanuel Todd, who was one of the first to predict the imminent fall of the USSR—*La chute finale: Essai sur la décomposition de la sphère soviétique* (Paris: Robert Laffont, 1976)—now predicts the imminent collapse of the other Enlightenment project: see *Après l'empire: Essai sur la décomposition du système américain* (Paris: Gallimard, 2002). Also see Immanuel Wallerstein, "The Eagle Has Crash Landed," *Foreign Policy* (July–August 2002). The second American war on Iraq, which is beginning as I finish these lines, appears to confirm the virtuality of American power and its impending demise—even though there is little doubt that the Washingtonian Goliath will crush the Mesopotamian David.

37. Pierre Vial, ed., *Pour une renaissance culturelle: Le GRECE prend la parole* (Paris: Copernic, 1979), 32.
38. Alain de Benoist, "Introduction," in *L'écume et les galets, 1991-1999: Dix ans d'actualité vue d'ailleurs* (Paris: Le Labyrinthe, 2000).
39. Pierre Vial, "Union soviétique: La revanche des peuples," *Éléments* 67 (Winter 1989–90); Samuel P. Huntington, *The Clash of Civilizations and the Remaking of World Order* (New York: Simon and Schuster, 1996), 36. Cf. Roland Breton, *L'ethnopolitique* (Paris: PUF, 1995).
40. Samuel P. Huntington, "The Clash of Civilizations?," *Foreign Affairs* 72:3 (Summer 1993). Though accepting the general contours of Huntington's thesis, *Grécistes* refuse to follow him in identifying "Western Civilization" with the heritage of liberalism, in conflating US civilization with European civilization, in believing that global harmony depends on the political culture of liberal democracy, in separating the Orthodox Slavic realm from Catholic Europe, in confusing religion with civilization, and in all those numerous instances where he distorts his argument to fit American policy objectives. See François Labeaume, "Vers un choc des civilisations," *Cartouches: L'actualité des idées* 2 (Spring 1997). Since 9/11, *Grécistes* also resist the use of Huntington's thesis to justify America's empire-building "war on terrorism." See Alain de Benoist, "The 20th Century Ended September 11," *Telos* 121 (Fall 2001).
41. Benoist, "Les retrouvailles de l'Europe."
42. Cercle Héraclite, "La France de Mickey," *Éléments* 57-58 (Spring 1986); Louis Sorel, "L'Hamlet européenne," *Res Publica Europaea* 14 (January 2000). Pierre Krebs writes: *"Die Berliner Mauer ist zwar gefallen, doch es haben sich in den Köpfern Hunderte von Mauern wiederaufgabaut."* See "Das Deutschtum am Scheideweg," *Elemente der Metapolitik zur europäischen Neugeburt* 6 (1998).
43. Charles Champetier, "Vive l'Europe libre!," *Éléments* 96 (November 1999); Patrick Nesles, "La mondialisation, c'est la guerre," *Éléments* 98 (May 2000). Cf. Charles A. Kupchan, *The End of the American Era: U.S. Foreign Policy and the Geopolitics of the Twenty-first Century* (New York: Knopf, 2002), 119–59.
44. Faye, *Nouveau discours à la nation européenne*, 53–57, 61.
45. Guillaume Faye, *L'Archéofuturisme* (Paris: L'Æncre, 1998), 102.
46. The GRECE's Third World turn was suggested even earlier. See Benoist, "L'ennemi principal" (Part II).
47. Robert de Herte, "Le développement en question," *Éléments* 48-49 (Winter 1983-84).

48. W. W. Rostow, *The Stages of Economic Growth* (Cambridge: Cambridge University Press, 1960).
49. Andre Gunder Frank, *World Accumulation, 1492–1789* (New York: Monthly Review Press, 1978).
50. Benoist, *Europe, Tiers monde, même combat,* 184–85.
51. Alain de Benoist, "Pour le Tiers monde, quelle solution?," *Éléments* 48–49 (Winter 1983–84).
52. Georges Feltin-Tracol, "L'Europe entre Djihad et McWorld," *Cartouches: L'actualité des idées* 5 (August 1998); Alain de Benoist, "Huit réflexions sur la mort du communisme," *Éléments* 71 (Fall 1991); François Labeaume, "La guerre des intellectuels," *Éléments* 95 (June 1999).
53. Guillaume Faye, *Le système à tuer les peuples* (Paris: Copernic, 1981). Also Benoist, *Orientations pour des années décisives,* 30–31; Benoist, *Europe, Tiers monde, même combat,* 14. Faye's notion of the "West" anticipates Robertson's notion of "globality" and later theories of globalization—although Faye is more partisan (realistic?) in emphasizing its negative American impetus. Cf. Roland Robertson, "Interpreting Globality," in *World Realities and International Studies Today,* ed. Roland Robertson (Glenside: Pennsylvania Council on International Education, 1983).
54. Cf. Serge Latouche, *The Westernization of the World: The Significance, Scope, and Limits of the Drive towards Global Uniformity,* trans. Rosemary Morris (Cambridge: Polity, 1996).
55. Faye, *Le système à tuer les peuples,* 22–23.
56. Faye, *Le système à tuer les peuples,* 29–30.
57. Faye, *Le système à tuer les peuples,* 63–80, 139, 166; Alain de Benoist, "Recensions," *Nouvelle École* 37 (Spring 1982).
58. Guillaume Faye, "Panem et Circenses: A Critique of 'The West,'" *The Scorpion* 9 (Spring 1986).
59. Marco Tarchi, "Droite et gauche: Deux essences introuvables," in *Gauche-Droite: La fin d'un système: Actes du XXVIIIe colloque national du GRECE* (Paris: Le Labyrinthe, 1995). Cf. Immanuel Wallerstein, "Does the Western World Still Exist?," *Binghamton University Commentary* 112 (May 1, 2003).
60. Pierre Krebs, *Im Kampf um das Wesen* (Horn: Burkhart Weecke Verlag, 1997), 65.
61. Alain de Benoist, "L'Europe sous tutelle," *Éléments* 59 (Summer 1986). A work that extends and updates Faye's argument is Alexandre Zinoviev, *La grande rupture: Sociologie d'un monde bouleversé,* trans. Slobodan Despot (Lausanne: L'Âge d'Homme, 1999).
62. Augusto Del Noce, "Le marxisme meurt à l'Est parce qu'il s'est réalisé à l'Ouest," *Krisis* 6 (October 1990). Also Augusto Del Noce, "Contestation et valeurs," in *L'époque de la sécularisation,* trans. Philippe Baillet (Paris: Éds. des Syrtes, 2001). Cf. Flora Montcorbier, *Le Communisme du marché* (Lausanne: L'Âge d'Homme, 1999).

## Chapter VIII

# Imperium

Unlike globalists and Atlanticists, who tout its wealth and economic prominence, New Rightists believe Europe is in decline.[1] The Continent, they observe, no longer lives according to European criteria. Self-serving technocracies, pillars of *le parti américain*, manage its lands with the multinationals' generic conception of man, disparaging its particularistic cultures and historic legacies.[2] In the collaborationist spirit of 1945, these technocracies act more American than European, promote their people's deculturation, and passively accept their subordination to global market forces. Many Europeans have even been made to feel that "the past is an embarrassment and the future is named America."[3] In this vein, one minister (Françoise Giroud) floated the idea of adopting English as France's national language and reserving French as its classical language—its Latin.[4]

This weakening of cultural identity has been compounded by a stunted system of socialization, educational policies denigrating traditional standards, a proliferation of social pathologies, and a vast influx of inassimilable Afro-Asian immigrants, totally alien, if not hostile to the France's European civilization.[5] Buttressed by the liberal "Right" and the social democratic Left, as they converge in extolling market values, the "cabal of materialist gangsters" (Yockey) managing the Continent focuses almost exclusively on "the battle for exports," indifferent to the dissolution of social solidarities and a common cultural vision.[6] Indeed, their loss is routinely extolled in the name of global economic modernization and the glories of diversity. But more consequential than even these assaults on European identity has been the loss of national sovereignty that came in the wake of the "Thirty Years' War between the United States and Germany" (Immanuel Wallerstein), when Europe was occupied by the two extra-European powers. The subsequent fall of the Berlin Wall and the end of the Cold War seem only to have altered the character of this heteronomy. Europe in the New Right's view has never been as prostrate as it is today.[7]

## The Decline of the Nation-State

In the current European debate over national sovereignty, New Rightists distinguish themselves from all the major parties. In opposition to Gaullists and *Lépenistes* on the Right and Jacobin nationalists on the Left, both of whom think the nation-state is the one indispensable source of sovereignty, they do not take their stand in its defense. Power, they claim, no longer resides at the apex of the national political system. Like postmodernists, they see the nation-state as a vestige of modernity and globalization as testament to the fact that society has become less controllable, the state less central, and the distinction between domestic and foreign affairs less clear-cut. As the global forces of pluralism and discontinuity blur traditional boundaries and give rise to various transnational and non-statist political movements challenging conventional political functions, notions of territoriality, sovereignty, and authority have been progressively emptied of their former significance.[8] Though accepting the nation-state's obsolescence and favoring a unified Europe as the critical threshold below which survival is no longer possible, New Rightists nevertheless oppose the prevalent model of European unity, as well as postmodernist proposals to do away with the state altogether.

Historically, the principle of sovereignty, upon which the nation-state was legitimated as a specific political form, received its key formulation in Jean Bodin's *Six livres de la république* (1576). Like later liberal theorists, Bodin believed sovereign power (the supreme political authority) was compromised by those traditional intermediary bodies standing between the governed and the government. Against the prevailing Roman and feudal concepts, he conceived of the state as resting not on the *polis* or the estates, but on reason's opposition to particularistic customs and institutions. He thus advocated a form of sovereignty that would be "one and indivisible," with the state's subjects uniformly subordinate to the king. This centralizing concept of sovereignty would later be taken up by Hobbes and Rousseau and came to dominate Enlightenment thought. By the time it reached the National Assembly in 1789, the liberal revolutionaries had ceased identifying sovereignty with the monarchy and instead vested it in the "people"—or the "nation." The revolutionaries also went a step beyond Bodin, conflating notions of state and nation, which up to then had been separate. The citizen, as a consequence, was henceforth transformed into a rights-bearing abstraction, the nation into a homogeneous territory shorn of its various particularisms, and the nation-state into a contractual association of uniform citizens subject to a single law, a single market, and a single form of national identity.[9]

Bodin's Jacobin descendants would thus proscribe everything obstructing the citizens' identification with the state. (In Saint-Just's incomparable expression: "*Ce qui constitue la République, c'est la destruction totale de ce qui lui est opposé.*") Indeed, an inorganic or ahistorical concept of the nation, analogous to the liberal idea of the individual and associated with the centralized institutions of the nation-state, was imposed at the expense of all historical identities. Those intermediary bodies (corporations, guilds, orders, communes) that had previously mediated the individual's relationship to the state were likewise abolished, as were the political significance of blood-ties and local particularisms. At the same time, nationalism's liberal impulse lent the nation a rationalist, expansionist, and messianic character, attuned to the modernist project. Following the Revolution of 1789, the liberal state would foster a national identity whose abstract legal character negated every particularistic expression of identity. Similarly, the Jacobin concept of national sovereignty restricted citizenship to voting and oriented the individual to the private sphere, reducing him, in effect, to "a consumer of government" (Quentin Skinner).[10]

The Bodinian concept also contained the seed of egalitarianism, for it presupposed a homogenized political society whose subjects were "equally" subordinate to their sovereign.[11] According to Benoist, the late eighteenth-century revolutionaries simply took this concept to its logical conclusion. The Jacobin Republic (like the American Republic) would serve, then, less as a cultural or historical than as a political identity, for the individual it embraced was stripped of his qualifying particularisms and united with others on the sole basis of his political affiliations: that is, he and other nationals were united as a undifferentiated mass. This would transform the nation (traditionally an *ethnos*) into an atomized body of equal individuals (a *demos*). In this spirit the Republic compelled Bretons, Alsatians, and others to give up their languages for French, abandon their regional institutions, and refashion themselves according to the Parisian model of the central state.[12] That the liberal state born in 1789 was an abstraction—a stepping stone to a more encompassing form of universal government—should come, thus, as no surprise.

For the Counter-Enlightenment, liberal nationalism represented another variant of modern rationalism, justifying the destruction of historical institutions and transcendent values for the sake of bourgeois social relations. When, late in the nineteenth century, a large part of the Right, in reaction to Marxist internationalism, rallied to the nationalist cause, it was careful to distance itself from the liberal concept of the nation, appealing not to abstract man or universal rights, but to the nation's specific linguistic, territorial, ethnic, and historical identities.[13] Yet even though the Right's notion of the nation rejected universalist postulates and a materialist interpretation of history, the identity it extolled, like its Left variant, tended to oppose those local particularisms that differed from its own unitary notion of the nation. More seriously, its nationalism rejected the civilizational unity of the West, pitting its petty-statism against "the large-space thinking of the European imperium" (Yockey). Right-wing nationalists, as a consequence, often ended up affecting on the national level what globalists presently attempt at the planetary level: that is, they too endeavored to establish a uniform model of identity.[14] *Grécistes* stress thus that both the Left and Right variants of the nation-state merged with the leveling impetus of liberal modernization and did so at Europe's expense.[15]

But more than criticizing national sovereigntists for recycling a variant of the Jacobin ideal, New Rightists claim they conceive of the nation-state in nineteenth-century rather than twentieth-century terms.[16] For with the advent of globalization, the nation-state ceases, in effect, to be an autonomous body. Half of all French legislation today originates with the European Union (EU), the euro has supplanted the franc, the European Court of Justice has become the highest court of appeal, the Paris bourse has fallen into alien hands, and most sources of news, information, and entertainment are provided by multinational or American firms. Even war-making powers and military defense (which Max Weber defined as the very basis of the state) have been taken over by NATO and other supranational institutions. Above all, not a single European state today has the capacity to resist the powers of international finance.[17]

With the advent of globalization, the nation-state has ceased to be the master of its own house. As Daniel Bell puts it, it has become too small to treat the big problems and too big to treat the small ones. Many postmodernists even see it as giving way to a "global community based on principles of cyberspace and multilayered, overlapping identities" (Peter van Ham) linked to the deterritorialization of political power. Indeed, the personnel that today makes up the state—the faceless, narrowly educated, and deracinated bureaucrats comprising the New Class—is loyal not to the nation, but to those transnational, global, and abstract entities associated with America's New World Order. As such, their principal commitment is to certain globalist abstractions rather than to the people they rule. Although national sovereignty remains a concern of identitarians, they claim sovereigntists overestimate the nation-state's capacity to defend national identities within an international context premised on the diminishment of state power. Moreover, the Jacobin principle of sovereignty that once crushed local and regional particularisms and the New Class forces charged with its present exercise seem an unlikely alternative to the global forces warring on national identity. A more effective and sympathetic system, they argue, is required, for the future—if it is to be European—obviously belongs to neither the nation-state nor the New Class' global village, but rather to those civilizational entities capable of defending culturally-defined territories from the hostile forces arrayed against them.[18]

Against the Bodinian concept of sovereignty, which lent itself to modernity's anti-traditionalist impetus and to several historical variants of political absolutism (monarchical, republican, managerial, and totalitarian), *Grécistes* contrapose the theoretical legacy of Johannes Althusius, an early federalist championing the communal character of political man and the divided nature of sovereign power. In his *Politica* (1603), Althusius envisaged the state as a federation in which diverse communities were to be integrated into a larger political entity on the basis of their distinctions. Ranging from guilds and corporations to towns and provinces, these communities were to retain their sovereignty when federating, delegating to the federation only those powers that could not be effectively exercised within their own realm.[19] As an aggregate of such communities, Althusius' federation was organized from the simple to the complex, with "each successive level [drawing] its legitimacy and its capacity to act from the autonomy of the lower level."[20]

Within this ascending system of federated communities, sovereignty was never totally alienated, only delegated. The Prince derived his sovereignty from all the various bodies comprising the federation, which authorized its use at the highest level of the state—but there alone. This made the Prince not the exclusive proprietor of sovereignty, only its occasional trustee. Thus, while his power was the highest in the federation, it was nevertheless limited. Each level—from the local to the federal—was to exercise the sovereignty necessary for carrying out its designated functions. Power was delegated to the next higher body only when it could not be properly exercised at its own level. The legitimacy of the superior body was thereby vested in its specific tasks and in the consent of the lower bodies. This principle that decisions were to be reached at the lowest relevant level—*"subsidiarity"*—also made sovereignty a distribution of competence, a notion antithetical to Bodin's, which concentrated all competence at the state's pinnacle.[21] Similarly, subsidiarity returned authority to the family, the community, and the region, restoring those autonomous intermediary bodies (Burke's "little platoons") that once constituted the principal sources of European freedom.

For New Rightists, who believe Europe's spiritual and cultural identity comes from the plurality of its varied nations and peoples, federation avoids many of the anti-identitarian ramifications of the nation-state, as well as the EU's homogenizing economic logic. For within Althusius' encompassing vision, people and community were sustained in both their sovereignty and particularity, just as laws, languages, and institutions were allowed to differ from one community, region, or nation to another, whenever they comply with the *politica*'s more embracing forms of unity. In contrast to the centralized nation-state, with its uniform mass of rights-bearing individuals, and the EU, with its centripetal market, Althusius' polity organized the state as a community of different communities, with multi-level networks of power, authority, and cooperation. Through federation, the organic sense of community formerly animating European peoples was to be revived and the leveling homogenization that comes with modern forms of nationalism avoided.

Following the Treaty of Westphalia (1648), the Bodinian model came to dominate the European state system. Until quite recently, it concentrated power better than earlier state forms and functioned relatively effectively. Beginning, though, with the Second European Civil War (1939–45), when the era of continental powers commenced, the nation-state began losing control of its economy and institutions, just as the Renaissance city-states had at the dawn of the modern age. With the advent of globalization, the nation-state has faltered entirely. A defense of sovereignty, New Rightists contend, is now no longer possible at its level: only a Europe-wide response holds out the prospect of shielding the Continent's autonomy from America's global order. Such a response, they emphasize, need not eliminate the nation or even the nation-state, merely subsume it to a more suitable federal framework. The key here is subsidiarity, in which Europe—its different, but closely related peoples, languages, and communities—functions as a continuum stretching from the neighborhood to the continental, without any level appropriating the prerogatives and identities of the others.

## The Imperial Idea

Since the advent of the Cold War, when the nation-state was integrated into the East-West system of *blocs*, the "family of peoples"—the "ethnosphere" (Faye)—constituting Europe has been groping its way toward unification. From the Coal and Steel Community of the early 1950s to the present European Union, this process has occurred mainly at the economic level. The development, though, of a European Common

Market, Monetary System, and Central Bank, however necessary to economic unity, is not, New Rightists argue, a meaningful way of constructing "Europe."[22] Against the economist view of the "Eurocrats"—whose bureaucratic imperatives ignore culture, forsake a political project, and promote a centralizing economic homogenization indifferent or hostile to national particularisms—they warn that once the market becomes the one true God, everything and everyone will be sacrificed to its interests. Money will then become the sole European standard and the usurious principles corrosive of identity will move to the center of Continental life. As Maurice Bardèche noted at the beginning of the Cold War, "the reign of money is that of the foreigner."[23]

In this context, it is worth noting that the Common Market has long been a creature of US interests.[24] Economic integration was initially promoted under the auspices of the Marshall Plan, encouraged by organizations such as the General Agreement on Tariffs and Trade and those institutions based on the Bretton Woods Agreement of 1944 (specifically the International Monetary Fund and the World Bank), and designed to undergird America's postwar market empire. Integration has since remained subservient to US policy concerns, facilitating America's penetration of European economies, complementing NATO, promoting the wholesale adoption of American techniques, products, and institutions, and, finally, serving as part of an incipient world federation based on the US system. Just as the "Pentagon's Foreign Legion" (NATO) lacks parity with the US, the Common Market has usually refrained from demanding reciprocity with US markets. Numerous economic sectors have consequently suffered for the sake of American interests, with the *Grande Marché* doing little to extricate Europeans from their heteronomous relationship with the US. In Benoist's characterization, "the United States of Europe risks becoming the Europe of the United States."[25] (Relatedly, the chief historian of US-EU relations, Geir Lundestad, describes the EU as America's "empire by integration.")[26]

Economic unity and the development of supranational agencies to facilitate trade do not, then, denote European sovereignty, but rather the potential dissolution of all sovereignty, as the political sinks entirely into the economic.[27] If not constructed in tandem with European political independence, New Rightists fear an economically unified Europe will lead to a further loss of sovereignty—and, worse, to an abandonment of what makes Europe European. To achieve a meaningful union—*une véritable Europe européenne* with a destining project—a political force, rooted in the Continent's civilizational traditions, is needed. Unity, in a word, is not realizable solely at the economic level, but demands a cultural project to revive the civilizational heritage that Europeans as a whole share. For only at this level can they be made to understand the need to act as a concerted political force on the world stage. New Rightists do not, of course, oppose economic unity—they, in fact, call for a Continental trade *bloc*, a *Großraumautarkie*, to serve as a geo-economic alternative to the monetarist, free trade dogmas of the globalists. But however crucial, they believe economic unity ought to be subordinate to the civilizational, political, and ethnocultural requirements of unification.[28]

Against Atlanticists, philo-Americans, and ultraliberals, all of whom advocate a cosmopolitan Europe centered on a market, New Rightists take their stand as patriots of the European idea. Like sovereigntists opposed to Americanization and globalization, they criticize the EU for its economism and "bureaucratic vampirism." In their view, the Eurocrats want only a "phantom Europe"—"a free trade zone governed on the theoretical level by ultraliberal monetary principles and, on the practical level, by administrators and bankers who lack both a political project and democratic legitimacy."[29] Such policies, they contend, are no antidote to a Europe deprived of ideals, values, and myths. They are not even economically convincing, for the Eurocrats' ultraliberalism, geared to the interests of bankers and international financiers, abrogates the possibility of a Continental industrial policy, "nationalized" enterprises, and a meaningful political economy.

Worse, the market forces propelling the unification process have the potential to subject Europe to globalism's most Darwinian effects, threatening as they do to obliterate her historical institutions and regional identities for the sake of powerful international speculators.[30] Instead of entrusting Europe's future to New Class operatives opposed to all that is native to her peoples, New Rightists insist that Europeans need "saints, thinkers, heroes, and prophets" to realize a civilizational project of Continental scope.[31] Without such men to lead them, Europeans will almost certainly "succumb to the totalitarianism of consumption, the homogenization of culture, and the corporate organization of decadence."[32] But however critical of the EU's failings, New Rightists nevertheless remain committed to unification. The big question in their view is what form unity will take—a question, they contend, which boils down to two fundamental options: the cosmopolitan and the imperial.

From the age of Frederick II (the late twelfth and early thirteenth centuries), the proponents of the European idea have divided into two major camps: the Guelphs (the cosmopolitan partisans of the Pope) and the Ghibellines (the champions of the Holy Roman Emperor).[33] After 1945, the liberals revived the Guelphs' cause, promoting a weak political structure for an economically united Europe (just as their thirteenth-century counterparts sought to strengthen the Pope, and his powerful financial supporters, at the emperor's expense). New Right Ghibellines, by contrast, advocate a strong state with a semi-autarkic market. Countering the Guelphs' economist vision of unity, they evoke the *Reichsidee*.[34] Since the fall of Rome, this idea, with its virile concept of aristocracy and its sacerdotal sense of power, has continued to influence the European state system, especially after its reincarnation in the Holy Roman Empire of the Hohenstaufens.[35] One might even argue that all considerations of European unity, even those infected with the Guelphs' mercantile virus, as the Treaty of Rome suggests, reflect the powerful nostalgia associated with it.[36]

In contrast to a nation-state, which organizes an ethnocultural identity associated with a specific territory, an imperial order refers to a sovereign ideal linking a space with a spiritual authority—an ideal such as the medieval principle of *ordo ducit ad Deum* (an order leading to God).[37] Since its ideal is "spiritual and supranational," an empire "belongs to a higher order than the parts comprising it." This enables it to accommodate differences, which it seeks to integrate rather than abolish, and to remain open to evolving economic and social forms, as they unfold within the spirit of its ideal.[38] The Flemish New Rightist Luc Pauwells thus writes that the Europe of the imperial idea "will never be 'completed': it is an unfinished symphony, always in the process of becoming, never perfected, an enterprise and a heritage for generations to come."[39] Unlike the Eurocrats' "superstate," which conceives of Continental unity in terms of market exchanges and a ubiquitous administrative apparatus, the imperial idea derived from the aristocratic animus of the Roman imperium envisages Europe as a complex "mosaic" of different Indo-European peoples, whose regional languages, schools, and institutions are to be preserved—and revitalized—in the interests of their larger civilizational project.[40]

From this Ghibelline perspective, the British Empire, Napoleon's Continental empire, the Soviet Empire, Hitler's New Order, and America's New World Order were (or are) imperialist, but not imperiums.[41] That is, they were (or are) empires not in the classical Roman sense of having derived their authority from a spiritual principle whose elaboration resembles an organic growth. Instead, they arose as aggressive extensions of the nation-state. As Arnaud Guyot-Jeannin formulates it: "*L'impérialisme impose. L'empire compose.*"[42] The American empire, for example, projects its "homogeneous system of consumption and technoeconomic practices" on the whole world, but, like the former Soviet empire, it addresses only the lowest realm of human existence—and then only with the intent to "enslave and unify" according to its assimilationist model.[43] The only historical cases conforming to the New Right's imperial idea have been those of Rome, Byzantium, the Hohenstaufens, and the Hapsburgs. In these traditionalist empires, cultural, linguistic, national, and social boundaries did not coincide (as in a nation) nor were they subordinate to a single model of life (as the *pax americana* dictates). Rather, their unity rested on an affiliation to a common ideal, upon whose basis their differences were integrated.[44]

Without a great political project envisaging a European imperium, New Rightists fear EU-style unification will end up turning the Continent into a gigantic, soulless Switzerland, enhancing, perhaps, its economic prowess, but leaving it powerless in the field of international relations.[45] Such a Europe would, in fact, do nothing to alter its status as an "American valet" and a *Lebensraum* for the non-white Muslim peoples of the South. Against the tepid unitary ideas of the Brussels shopkeepers, who weigh Europe's future in metric tons of steel and units of exports, not history and culture, the imperial idea appeals to what is most exalted in, and hence innermost to, the heritage identitarians champion.[46]

For too long, Europe's New Class has been obsessed with GNPs and growth rates. But if Europe is to become great again, it needs to rediscover politics, tap its peoples' will to power, and give Europeans a government, not merely a system of management, that looks beyond quotidian, market-based concerns to the primordial in their ancestral heritage.[47] Clausewitz says, "A people has nothing higher to respect than the dignity and liberty of its own existence."[48] Just as human existence entails more than animal survival, dignity and liberty are more than the right to make purchasing decisions or pursue individual pleasures. If they are to take European form, dignity and liberty can only be exercised on the basis of those heroic possibilities posed by the myths, tradition, blood, and history of her peoples. If ever, though, Europeans should awake to the dictates of their destiny and heed the patriots among them, *la Grande Nation* of Mozart and De Gaulle, of Jan Sobieski and William Shakespeare, which means nothing to the Eurocrats, might again become meaningful.

## The Geopolitics of Eurosiberia

While Europe has yet to achieve political unification, it is still more than a geographic concept. For millennia, it constituted a civilizational realm, made up of kindred peoples and language groups stemming from the Indo-Europeans, Greek thought, and Latin institutions. Product of this historical matrix, Europeans have acquired a distinct mental constitution, just as surely as they have always had a racial one.[49] Throughout the ancient and medieval eras, this common heritage took civilizational form, first under the Roman Empire, later under the Roman Church. Then, with the advent of modernity, the rise of monarchical states, the Reformation, and a century of fratricidal religious war, Europe's principal political expression became the nation-state. Notwithstanding the divisive nationalist rivalries it fostered, the nation-state tended to intensify "interculturality and competition around common identities."[50]

The European civil wars of the twentieth century and the Cold War that followed, in reversing this process of interstate competition, further enhanced the trend toward interculturality. Combined with the fall of the Berlin Wall and the dissolution of the ideological *blocs*, economic integration continues to nurture at least the economic and institutional basis of a civilizational identity. As an earlier patriot of the European idea notes: "A bit of history divides Europeans, but much unites them."[51] Ill-conceived and haphazard as the process of reconciling national differences may be, Europe is nevertheless groping its way toward unity. The exact form it will take remains, of course, an open question and, if the reigning New Class elites prevail, it may ultimately serve as but a prelude to some sort of American-dominated one-world formation. But as this process proceeds in a world in which ideological alignments are increasingly giving way to ones based on culture and race, Europeans come face to face with the *geopolitical* challenges of what Samuel P. Huntington calls "the clash of civilizations."[52]

Geopolitics—the study of environmental influences, particularly the strategic actions of states, on the evolution of peoples and their territories—evokes a good deal of suspicion in the English-speaking world.[53] Since 1945, it has been associated with Hitler's war-making quest for *Lebensraum*.[54] Geopolitics is also suspect because it differs from the politically correct disciplines of "political science" and "international relations" in representing a form of thought that studies continental conflicts irrespective of established ideological or moral references. For more than two centuries, however, longer than the term has existed, all the great powers have practiced geopolitics and many of its major theorists have been English and American. Typically, Zbigniew Brzezinski, in a significant recent work in the field, refers to it as "geostrategy," while US academics favor the term "political geography."[55] With considerably less circumlocution, European identitarians engage in similar geopolitical theorizing, for thinking in terms of space and power, territory and politics, has become an inescapable facet of their project.[56]

Carl Schmitt writes: "World history is the history of the struggle between the maritime powers and the continental powers."[57] The idea that land and sea are in perpetual conflict is central to almost all schools of geopolitical thought. The Punic Wars, which pitted maritime Carthage against overland Rome, represent the purest expression of this geopolitical paradigm. In the modern era, the "Anglo-Saxons" (the British, followed by the Americans) have taken over the Carthaginians' part, while Germany, Austria, and Russia assumed the Roman part. Given this clash between sea and land, the key to maritime (or thalassocratic) supremacy—which civilizationally represents a sea-going nomadism hostile to rooted cultures and settled inland peoples—is containment of the Eurasian landmass, the world's "heartland," which is invulnerable to sea power. Only a strong anchorage in its rimlands (or coastlands), Western Europe being the foremost, makes it possible for a thalassocracy to restrain the continental land potential of a Germany or a Russia. Those controlling these rimlands are thus able to control the heartland and hence the world.[58]

Nineteenth-century Britain occupied India and parts of the Middle East and kept Europe divided through a balance-of-power policy. Since supplanting Britain as the world's chief maritime power, US policy pursues a similar geopolitical logic. For even more than Britain, America's mercantile thalassocracy acts as a force for cosmopolitanism, atomization, and the destruction of the European *ethnos*. Adapted from a strategy first worked out by Halford Mackinder, its continental island endeavors to maintain its hegemony over Eurasia through its occupation of Western and Central Europe, its alliance with Islam (though Washington's recent Likudization may make this increasingly difficult), and the strategic use of its cultural and economic powers.[59] US geopolicy has, in fact, changed little since the Cold War's end, for it still aims at containing Russia, dominating the rimlands surrounding it, and universalizing its deculturated way of life. If ever the US should lose control of Europe—or what Brzezinski calls "America's essential geopolitical bridgehead on the Eurasian continent"—it will lose its ability to contain the heartland, and hence the world.[60]

In endeavoring to maintain its increasingly fragile world hegemony, nineteenth- and early twentieth-century Britain had an extremely destructive impact on Europe: the two European civil wars, among others, were motivated in large part by misguided British efforts to prevent a German continental challenge to its thalassocracy.[61] Britain's heir (and since 1939, lord), the US, plays a similarly destructive role.[62] As secret Pentagon documents, as well as numerous public policy statements, demonstrate, US strategy pivots on suppressing every potential challenge to its global hegemony, especially those that might come from Russia or a unified Europe.[63] The most explicit of the Pentagon documents, the Wolfowitz memo ("Defense Policy Guidance"), leaked to the *New York Times* in early 1992, played a major role in the Clinton Administration's effort to enlarge its interventionist capacities for the sake of its unipolar order.[64] The present [i.e., 2003] Bush Administration (comprised of Big Oil magnates, the satraps of the Military-Industrial Complex, and Zionism's imperialist vanguard) has not only signed on to these policies, its "jackbooted Wilsonism" (Pierre Hassner), unilateralist doctrine of "preventative war," and empire-building "war on terrorism" are proving to be even more adventurist than the unipolar doctrines of the Clinton Administration.[65] Significantly, US policy continues to be animated by the simplistic one-world ideologies of the Rooseveltian New Class and the Manichean dichotomies of the Cold Warriors, both of which have imparted a megalomaniacal slant to America's relationship to the Rest of the World. If its reaction to 9/11 is any gauge, US schemes for world supremacy are likely to provoke not only continued international, but increasingly domestic resistance—as the international havoc wrought by its military and corporate forces "blow back" to haunt the American mainland.[66] Indeed, the arrogance, mendacity, and witlessness of the highest governmental echelons in suppressing every challenge to their rule seem bent on putting the US on a collision course with its friends and allies—and especially with reality.

Against the US's thalassocratic tradition, New Rightists ally with "continentalists" represented by that lineage of geopolitical thinkers stretching from Friedrich Ratzel and Karl Haushofer to Jean Thiriart and Heinrich Jordis von Lohausen, all of whom emphasize the spiritual bonds linking organically formed peoples to their native lands and national traditions. Like these thinkers, they identify with the most ancient of Europe's geopolitical principles: *Delenda est Carthago!* (Carthage must be destroyed!). They therefore advocate a rimland-heartland—a Euro-Russian—alliance to serve as the basis of a continental *bloc* to counter the deracinating forces of the *pax americana*. Animated by its "hierarchical, communitarian, and heroic world view" (Alexander Dugin), such a *bloc* has the potential, they believe, to restore Russia and Europe to great power status and curb the anti-identitarian impetus of America's New World Order.

The possibility of such an East-West alliance acquired special pertinence in the wake of the Cold War, for with the demise of Soviet Communism, Europe's "blind solidarity" with the US lost its former *raison d'être*. This, combined with the fact that the EU's economic might, product of a continental world, is hampered by its tutelage to the US and that the European New Class, however subaltern, finds its subservience a burden, further enhances the possibility of such a continentalism. The severe rifts in the Atlantic alliance in the period leading up to the second American war on Iraq—"the first great 'crime against humanity' of the twenty-first century" (Benoist)—are (as I write) already revealing the potential divisiveness of these geopolitical contradictions, as American schemes for world conquest become increasingly insupportable to its "allies."[67] An East-West realignment, in which the tellurocratic forces of hierarchy, order, and rootedness unite against the thalassocratic principles of nihilism, rootlessness, and effeminate egalitarianism, is, however, contingent on the cooperation of the two principal European peoples.

At the time of the Franco-Prussian War (1870), Ernest Renan wrote that the great tragedy of European history was that the Germans did not understand the French and the French did not understand the Germans.[68] While this situation lingers in parts, *Grécistes* and other identitarian bearers of the European idea strive to overcome it.[69] It was De Gaulle who led the way in rejecting a technoeconomic concept of Europe and affirming the primacy of her political identity. By the late 1940s, he had come to realize that Franco-German amity was key to overturning the anti-European Yalta system.[70] Throughout his career, as an opponent of the thalassocratic powers, he continued to promote Franco-German cooperation, though Germany's US-controlled leadership repeatedly stymied him.[71] Unlike many subsequent Gaullists, the General did not fear a unified Germany, for he believed it was essential to European unity and that unity around a "Carolingian pole" was crucial to any reassertion of French grandeur in the world.[72] But what De Gaulle did not fully appreciate and what separates him (and many old-style nationalists) from GRECE-style identitarians is the incompatibility of the French national tradition with that of the German imperial tradition.

In favoring European unity, French New Rightists do so in opposition to their own national tradition, which has long opposed a consolidation of the European powers at the expense of the French state. France, though, has not always been anti-imperial, even if it was the first to betray the imperial tradition.[73] They point out that Clovis, the reputed founder of the nation, was actually the ruler of a Franco-Germanic empire that lasted until the late tenth century, when Hugh Capet abandoned the Roman idea of empire and embarked on a process of monarchical centralization—a process that laid the foundations for the modern nation-state. In consolidating their dynastic ambitions, subsequent Capetians were obliged to amalgamate the various peoples comprising the "hexagon," creating, in effect, the French nation out of a disparate assortment of Bretons, Alsatians, Flamands, Gascons, Occitans, Basques, Normans, and others. As such, the languages, institutions, and identities of these peoples were supplanted by those of Paris and the Île-de-France. As an "anti-empire," then, the French state arose on the ruins of her ancient provincial institutions and communities. In this sense, France is an "artificial" nation, created by the state. After 1789, revolutionary liberals continued the Capetian project, completing the nation-making process of centralization, homogenization, and assimilation.[74] The republican tradition spawned by the Revolution would thus adhere to a highly standardized definition of national identity—for this alone conformed with its uniform model of citizenship.[75]

Germans, by contrast, have rarely confused nationality and citizenship. The Holy Roman Empire (founded by Otto I in 962) politically united them with other central European peoples in a federated imperium, whose political divisions were dynastic rather than national. As a consequence, it was not through the state that medieval Germans came to identify themselves as a people, for the "nation" was always divided by political borders. This sometimes left them apolitical, but it also enabled them to define themselves in broader terms. Before nineteenth-century liberals took up the national idea, the *Vaterland* was mainly a cultural, linguistic concept. Germans thus rarely felt the urge to express themselves politically and instead treated their national identity as a "world-open" cultural construct. In contrast to the French national tradition (which transmitted a canonized culture as part of the process of political socialization), the German cultural tradition was always in the process of elaboration, as the Germans themselves grew and expanded as a people.[76] It was only late in the nineteenth century that they achieved any political unity and then only partially. In truth, there has never been a German nation-state (not even at the height of the Hitler regime—for Swiss, Austro-Hungarian, Baltic, and various Eastern European Germans remained outside it). Historically, *Deutschland* was simply all the lands settled by people of German speech and blood. Even today, the imperial idea, with its federal political forms, remains strong in German politics. The *Bundesrepublik*, in this respect, contrasts sharply with De Gaulle's highly centralized Fifth Republic.

Because the nation-state no longer works and federation seems the sole feasible basis of European unity, New Rightists tend not to fear Germany in the way many French sovereigntists do. In their view, the nation is closed, the empire open. In advocating European unity, they consequently favor a concept modeled on the German imperial idea—only the culture and people they appeal to are not German, but European.[77] This by no means implies that France does not have much to contribute to European unity. In many ways, France mirrors Europe and remains pivotal to the unification process. The nation forged by the Capetians arose from an amalgam of different, though closely related peoples and languages. Ethnically, this made the French the most representative of Europe's peoples, combining a blend of Celtic, Germanic, and Greco-Roman strains—the Continent's chief ethnic components—along with later Slavic admixtures from Poland and Russia and even Armenians from Europe's lost Eastern marches.[78]

In addition, France's extraordinary cultural legacy has brought to Europe a spirit of analytical detachment, a sense of refinement, form, and style, and a linguistic gift for eloquence, clarity, and sophistication that is unique among the world's peoples. Above all, France is the sole European nation to have asserted itself as a power in the post-1945 world, arming itself with nuclear weapons, attempting to act as an autonomous diplomatic force, and, under De Gaulle, refusing its client status.[79] Of the various European nations, only the French are militarily comparable—not in size, of course, but in their technological and offensive potential—to the US. Finally, France's destiny, as De Gaulle affirmed, is to make history. France, in truth, cannot be France without grandeur. The "legacy of forty kings" has imbued the country with a pre-eminently political and martial idea of its essence.[80] As Brzezinski writes, France is the single European country with "the will and ambition for a Grand Europe."[81] Although the German experience embodies a sounder political basis for unification, all historical reflections on Europe's future are likely to focus on France. The French, however, will play this world-historical role only if they discard their specific national pretensions. In a world where their cultural and political identity is threatened by Americanization and their biological existence by Third World colonization, their national destiny now depends on their commitment to the European project.[82] For this reason, most identitarians believe their national and regional identities are now irreparably linked to their European identity.[83]

While the Soviet collapse in 1991 seemed to diminish the imperative of European unity, at the same time, it made the prospect potentially more fateful, as the peoples of Russia, Ukraine, the Baltic states, and Eastern Europe rejoined *le grand espace eurasiatique*. De Gaulle considered the Russians a European people and at the height of the Cold War talked of a "Europe from the Atlantic to the Urals." Free now of the Soviet yoke, the prospect of such a Europe, this time stretching from Galway to Vladivostok, from Iceland to Armenia, seems even more of a possibility. Indeed, Russia for identitarians has become key to the international situation, for it remains the single European power capable of challenging the cosmopolitan dictatorship represented by the "Yankee thalassocracy." Moreover, as Slavs, they belong to the one European family to have resisted the effeminizing forces of liberal modernity and retained something of the old warrior ethos. Not a few Europeanists believe Europe's future is now tied to this potential "Piedmont." The sun, they say, rises in the East.[84]

Given the nature of the existing geopolitical realities, the GRECE has long sympathized with Russia, even during the Cold War. This was especially evident in its positive assessment of National Bolshevism.[85] Informed by the interwar activities of Ernst Niekisch, this revolutionary nationalist offshoot of the Conservative Revolution advocated an *Ostorientierung* to break with the Western liberal powers (principally Britain and the US) and facilitate a *rapprochement* between German nationalism and Russian socialism. Niekisch's legacy—especially in posing the Prussian/Spartan virtues of honor, service, and order as an antidote to liberalism's individualistic, hedonistic, and predatory spirit—still influences much of the anti-liberal Right. At the same time, it is seen as a credible alternative not only to the most important anti-liberal regimes of the twentieth century (principally Communism and fascism), but one that incorporates all that was great in these regimes while transcending their evident failings.[86]

Like National Bolsheviks, *Grécistes* believe Communism never affected the Russian spirit to the degree liberalism influenced the American.[87] More importantly, Russia for them represents a less globalized and commercialized version of Europe, lacking its "extreme individualism, militant soullessness, religious indifference ... [and] mass culture" (Gennady Zyuganov). Although the former empire of the tsars has had an ambiguous historical relation to the West and retains certain Asiatic characteristics alien to Europe, the Russians are a Christian Indo-European people, rooted in racial, linguistic, cultural, and historical structures akin to Europeans.[88]

As a Continental power "naturally" opposed to the thalassocratic forces, Russia has an inherent geopolitical affinity with Europe.[89] As Vladimir Putin said in flawless German before a standing ovation of the Bundestag (September 25, 2001): "Between Russia and America, there is an ocean. Between Russia and Germany, there is a great history."[90] If European capital and know-how continues to penetrate eastward, contributing to Russia's recovery, the former Soviet Union holds out the prospect of becoming a vast continental power, with an abundance of natural resources (especially oil), an immense reservoir of human talent, and a will to power. A Eurasian *rapprochement* (which is already occurring in certain areas of trade, research, and development) would portend an empire of unparalleled immensity and a possible "staging area of a new anti-bourgeois, anti-American revolution" (Dugin). It would not be at all "unnatural," then, if European and Russian destinies should merge and an "Empire of the Sun," spanning 14 time zones, arise.[91]

As the GRECE predicted in 1991, once free of its Communist masters Russia would be plundered by the West and reduced to neo-colonial status.[92] "Communism," Benoist writes, "impoverished Russia, capitalism [has] wrecked it."[93] The former superpower (which passed into American receivership under the terms of the "Second Treaty of Versailles" [Nikolai von Kreitor]) approached Third World status during the 1990s. As its social and economic infrastructure crumbled, NATO intruded ever further into its former spheres of influence and US policy (animated by the Russophobic ranks of the Pentagon and State Department) promoted (and continues to promote) various "de-Russification" campaigns in Ukraine and Central Asia. Relatedly, the murderous NATO air war against Serbia, as Alexandre Del Valle and others have demonstrated, aimed not merely at securing US control of the strategically situated Balkans, but at preventing a possible *rapprochement* between Europe and the Orthodox Slavic world.[94] As Brzezinski in *The Grand Chessboard* and Wolfowitz in the Pentagon documents argue, US interests demand Russia's dismemberment and its marginalization in world affairs.

The US, though, is not alone in hoping to plunder and fragment it. While NATO encroaches on its western spheres of influence, Russia is simultaneously threatened from the south and east by potentially aggressive Third World peoples, mainly Muslims and Chinese, who covet its land and resources. Throughout the 1990s, when its indigenous liberals served as "the errand boys of the West" (Iver Neumann), the Russian Federation remained relatively helpless in face of these threats—to such an extent that the country's very existence hung in the balance. With Putin's ascent, it seems to have recovered from the alcoholic torpor of the Yeltsin years, as it resumes the "power politics" befitting a great nation. Its bloody war with Islam in Chechnya (whose Muslim insurgents were supported by the petrol monarchies and, via Pakistan's security apparatus, the US) marks the sole European effort to date to defend the Continent's biocultural integrity from the anti-European south.[95]

As suggested above, a great many New Rightists now look to Russia as a potential liberator. Several times in its history, when its people seemed on the verge of extinction, they have staged extraordinary resurgences. If this should ever reoccur, Europe is likely to be swept up in Russia's elan. But perhaps the most significant variable in the Russian situation is its openness. There is not a single European country today that is free of or directly aligned against America's cosmopolitan order. While Russia is neither free of nor explicitly opposed to the US, it is nevertheless in transition; and this transition, especially if it continues its current national-patriotic course, has the potential of altering the present world alignment. The geopolitical affinity of Russian and European interests—their joint subjugation to international capital, as well as the dangers posed by American military might and the Third World's demographic assault—could conceivably lead to a situation in which their fates merge. Many European, as well as Russian, nationalists now, in fact, advocate just such an alliance.[96] If ever, then, a Eurasian imperium stretching from the Atlantic to the Pacific—Eurosiberia—should arise, it would constitute a powerful counterweight to US hegemony and a definite spur to Europe's ascension.[97] This is only an idea, of course. But ideas, especially ones pregnant with possibility, have a way sometimes of changing the world.[98]

## Organic Democracy

As an imperium embracing the Indo-European biocultural zone, Eurosiberia suggests the possible geographical framework of unity. The *Reichsidee*, however, is politically neutral. It could conceivably take monarchical, republican, managerial, totalitarian, or some other form.[99] For the GRECE, it is envisaged as a federal democracy, for no other governmental form seems feasible, except the liberal one of total administrative control. This, though, raises the question: what is democracy? As the "moral Esperanto of the present nation-state" (R. B. J. Walker), the term has come to bear numerous inflated significations, even the most Orwellian ones.[100] The liberal plutocracies, with the US at their head, never, for example, tire of extolling their democratic virtues—even as they subject their populations to increasingly undemocratic control and their public business to an ever more nihilistic spoils system. Communists in their day were no less blatant in making "democracy" an empty verbalism. While labeling their Eastern European satellites "people's democracies," they carried out the most heinous crimes and exercised the most ruthless despotism. To say, then, that one is a democrat today has about as much significance as when Kim Il Sung of North Korea, Pol Pot of the Khmer Rouge, or the intellectually challenged members of the House of Bush claim to be democrats.[101]

In advocating democracy, New Rightists refer not to its liberal simulacrum, with its emphasis on elections and the "rule of law," nor do they refer to the so-called "popular democracies," which tyrannized their populations in the name of social equality. Their reference, instead, is to those early European forms of self-governance which gave rise to the term. But even in the etymological sense of "the rule of the people," "democracy" has been interpreted in various contradictory ways. For example, in the modern period, it is usually taken to mean electoral politics, parliamentarism, and legal proceduralism, all of whose "representational" forms tend to culminate in opportunism, careerism, corruption, and an asocial individualism; or else the term is associated with a certain licentious way of life based on individual autonomy. Postmodernists even advance a notion of "cosmopolitan democracy" that, for the sake of unlimited self-constructions, dispenses with any idea of people or nation.

When New Rightists speak of "the rule of the people," their reference, then, is not to these modern or postmodern associations, but rather to the ancient Greek notion that only an assembled people has the right to decide its "common good." Democracy, in this sense, is based on access to the public square (*agora*), where the key political decisions are made in direct consultation with the citizenry.[102] Benoist points out that even before the reforms of Clisthenes, Athenians were entitled to gather and speak in the *agora*, which belonged to "everyone" and constituted the axis around which the *polis* revolved. Unlike the modern liberal concept, classical citizenship was based not on abstract "inalienable rights," but on membership (derived from kinship) in the city.[103]

The *polis*, as such, was not any politically united body of people, but a citizenry reflecting an ethnically homogeneous and culturally cohesive community sharing the same underlying sentiments and values. This organic notion of citizenship made ancient democracy relatively harmonious, for it functioned not as a market in which rival interests competed, but as an extended family in which concern for the common good, even when interpreted differently, was uppermost.[104] In many respects, ancient democracy was entirely superfluous, for the people *qua* a people implicitly agreed on fundamentals. The minor matters over which citizens (*polites*) differed and submitted to public debate rarely affected their common attachments. Benoist notes that the Latin root of "liberty," *liberi*, means "children"—that is, "derived from the same stock." In this sense, democratic "freedoms" did not imply liberation from communal restraints, but belonging to—and hence involved in the life of—one's own "people."[105] This made freedom "organic" and even pre-political, entailing a community of kindred beings bound by "blood and soil." Accordingly, Greek democracy excluded slaves and metics, who were not—and never could be—of the community. For those, however, whose fathers' land it was and who were willing to defend it, citizenship was automatic.

This made the *demos* of Greek democracy indistinguishable from its *ethnos*. One was born rather than became an Athenian, since the condition of being an Athenian implied history and kinship.[106] The fundamental unanimity of the people was consequently never at issue. Collective and individual interests, like public and private, closely overlapped. It is relevant to note in this context that Greek democracy collapsed in the age of Alexander, when his Near Eastern conquests destroyed the *polis*' ethnic foundations. Classical writers (Aristotle especially) were thus wont to view the mixing of divergent peoples and cultures as an inevitable source of political disorder, for such mixtures failed to generate a shared sense of the public good.[107]

Unlike the virtualist character of modern liberal democracy, with its judicial concept resting on representational forms of an increasingly abstract and simulated kind and unlike the postmodern condition, where there is no people and no determinate expressions of authority, ancient democracy was pre-eminently communal.[108] In Schmitt's formulation, "essential to the concept of democracy is the people, not humanity."[109] Democratic rights went with being a member of a specific community, not with being human. Political equality was accordingly a "gift" of the local pagan deities, who resembled the people worshipping them. (Pagan temples, not coincidentally, surrounded the *agora*.)[110] In distinction to liberalism's abstract, procedural concept of rights—which allows the individual to detach himself from communal ties and do whatever he pleases—ancient and medieval notions of freedom held that one was free to the degree one was able to participate in the community.[111] Indeed, the ancients believed freedom was possible only through public participation, not refuge in private life. With the loss of this notion, an organic concept of the people was also lost. Since the French and American Revolutions universalized "the rights of man," "the people" everywhere has been reconceptualized to mean a simple plurality of individuals, whose "equal" and "inalienable" rights transcend communal, national, or ethnoracial attachments. Yet, in elevating the individual above the people (the private sphere above the public), the liberals' rights-based order abolishes even the possibility of popular sovereignty, which becomes the province of "a rather dubious class of persons" (Schmitt)—professional politicians—who alone are responsible for shepherding the so-called "citizenry."

Like Schmitt, New Rightists believe that in genuinely democratic states group identity, group rights, and group projects, anchored in culturally informed concepts of the good, take precedent over individualist or abstract humanitarian ideals. Such a group-oriented state necessarily stands above the "interests," representing the collective aspirations of those who feel themselves to be part of an extended family. As Napoleon put it, *la politique, c'est le destin*. If individuals rooted in specific cultures and communities possess a state expressing their will to exist as a people, then this state cannot but assume the force of a destiny—for destiny is nothing other than the logic inherent in a people's project. For this reason, New Rightists envisage their Eurosiberian imperium as a sovereign democratic federation made up of various self-governing communities, representing both the *ethos* and the *ethnos* of the different European families. This makes it identifiable not with the modern *demos*, understood in the liberal sense as congeries of faceless unrelated individuals, but rather with those transcendent affiliations implicit in the existence of *un peuple* or *ein Volk*.[112]

Rather than an unfortunate side-effect of modern society, New Rightists believe that the professionalization of contemporary politics—based on a party system, which, by definition, subordinates the people's general welfare to a "part" of the people—is an unavoidable offshoot not simply of liberalism's evasion of the political, but of its inherent antipathy to any concept of popular sovereignty—for a people represents a place, a history, and a destiny, which invariably contradicts liberalism's atemporal, abstract, and universalist principles.[113] Despite the ceaseless slogans and simulations to the contrary, the atomized masses of modern democracies are thus routinely excluded from any meaningful exercise of power, unless one considers the ballot—"the sum of private opinions" (Schmitt), which reduces everyone and everything to the lowest common denominator—such an exercise. (As Baudrillard notes: "The whole art of politics today is to whip up popular indifference.")[114]

Contrary to the claims of its apologists, the present lack of democratic participation has little to do with society's size and complexity. At a time when power is variously diffused and the state has abandoned many of its traditional functions, the multitude of existing associations and communities could easily serve as democratic arenas. Yet, instead of multiplying "public spaces within which an active citizenry could be reborn," liberal power is exercised from the top down, with local associations and communities deprived of significant decision-making powers, or else power is exerted through market and techno-administrative networks immune to popular consultation, as policy supplants politics. Decentralization, delegation of responsibility, and plebiscitary referendums are similarly avoided. Even when referendums are "staged," they tend to address only secondary issues. (And if such referendums should happen to produce results unfavorable to New Class elites, constitutional principles are invariably invoked to nullify them.)

In this spirit, the entire governmental apparatus of the so-called democracies today is geared to lobbying by big business and powerful minority interests, not citizen participation. The only public debates are accordingly those of the governing elites, which frame the issues, control the discussion, and interpret the results for a largely muzzled public. There are, in fact, no longer citizens in these polities who participate in political life or control their destiny, only TV viewers who vote and consume as programmed.[115] One might argue that liberal democracies know no popular will because they rest not on a people, but on aggregates of special interests, on money, and on those who know "how to pull the wires controlling the public mind."[116]

Against such fraudulent forms of governance, the New Right appeals to Europe's longest memory, envisaging a democratic imperium of organic communities that, in subsuming all the various anti-liberal principles surveyed in the chapters above, anticipates a radical identitarian order faithful to its people's biocultural heritage.

## Notes to Chapter VIII

1. Julien Freund, *La Décadence* (Paris: Sirey, 1984); Karlheinz Weissmann, "Was Ist Dekadence?," *Junge Freiheit* (November 2, 2001); Dominique Venner, *Histoire et tradition des européens: 30,000 ans d'identité* (Paris: Rocher, 2002), 11.
2. Guillaume Faye, *Le système à tuer les peuples* (Paris: Copernic, 1981), 144. Cf. Pierre-Patrice Belesta, "L'Europe contre les peuples: La leçon par l'Irlande," *Écrits de Paris* 634 (July 2001).
3. Thomas Molnar, *The Emerging Atlantic Culture* (New Brunswick, NJ: Transaction Publishers, 1994).
4. Alain de Benoist, "Vers l'indépendance! Pour une Europe souveraine" (1986), in *La ligne de mire I: Discours aux citoyens européens, 1972-1987* (Paris: Le Labyrinthe, 1995).
5. Alain de Benoist, "L'Europe sous tutelle," *Éléments* 59 (Summer 1986). Cf. Philippe Malaud, *La révolution libérale* (Paris: Masson, 1976).
6. Alain de Benoist, "Idéologies: c'est la lutte finale" (1984), in *La ligne de mire I*; Alain de Benoist, "Die Religion der Menschenrechte," in *Mut zur Identität: Alternative zum Prinzip der Gleichheit*, ed. Pierre Krebs (Struckum: Verlag für Ganzheitliche Forschung und Kultur, 1988). See also Pierre Thuillier, *La grande implosion: Rapport sur l'effondrement de l'Occident, 1999-2002* (Paris: Fayard, 1995); Benjamin R. Barber, *Jihad vs. McWorld: How Globalism and Tribalism Are Reshaping the World* (New York: Ballantine Books, 1996).
7. Robert de Herte, "L'escroquerie libérale," *Éléments* 68 (Summer 1990); Benoist, "Vers l'indépendance!"
8. Alain de Benoist, "Face à la mondialisation," in *Les grandes peurs de l'an 2000: Actes du XXXe colloque national du GRECE* (Paris: GRECE, 1997). Cf. Barber, *Jihad vs. McWorld*, 39; James Good and Irving Velody, "Postmodernity and the Political," in *The Politics of Postmodernity*, ed. James Good and Irving Velody

(Cambridge: Cambridge University Press, 1998); Peter van Ham, *European Integration and the Postmodern Condition: Governance, Democracy, Identity* (London: Routledge, 2001). Perhaps the most influential view of postmodern politics has been that of "Tony Blair's foreign policy guru," Robert Cooper. See his "The Post-Modern State," in *Re-ordering the World: The Long-Term Implications of September 11*, ed. Mark Leonard (London: Foreign Policy Center, 2002); also Robert Cooper, "The New Liberal Imperialism," *The Observer* (April 7, 2002).

9. Alain de Benoist, "Qu'est-ce que la souveraineté?," *Éléments* 96 (November 1999).
10. Alain de Benoist, *Critique du nationalisme et crise de la représentation* (Paris: GRECE pamphlet, n.d.), 7–15.
11. Benoist, "Qu'est-ce que la souveraineté?"
12. Pierre Maugué, "La France n'a pas commencé en 1789," *Éléments* 64 (December 1988).
13. In this context, Charles Maurras provides an important reference: "*Une patrie,*" he writes, "*est un syndicat de famille, composé par l'histoire et la géographie; son organisation exclut le principe de la liberté des individus, et leur égalité, mais elle implique, en revanche, une fraternité réelle, profonde, organique, reconnue par les lois, vérifiée par les mœurs et dont la circonscription des frontières n'est rien que le signe naturel.*" See Xavier Cheneseau, ed., *Maurras l'indomptable* (Paris: Éds. de l'Homme Libre, 2000), 38.
14. Benoist, "Qu'est-ce que la souveraineté?"
15. Arnaud Guyot-Jeannin, "La Droite et la nation," in *Aux sources de la Droite: Pour en finir avec les clichés*, ed. Arnaud Guyot-Jeannin (Lausanne: L'Âge d'Homme, 2000); Maugué, "La France n'a pas commencé en 1789." Cf. Bernard Chantebout, "La Nation," *Krisis* 5 (April 1990). The Right is not necessarily nationalist. This holds not only for the GRECE, but for several significant historical cases. For example, see Arnaud Imatz, *José Antonio: La Phalange espagnole et le national-syndicalisme*, 2nd ed. (Paris: Godefroy de Bouillon, 2000), 250–55; Julius Evola, "Metternich," in *Explorations: Hommes et problèmes*, trans. Philippe Baillet (Puiseaux: Pardès, 1989). The GRECE's position should also not be confused with recent Left/liberal attempts to characterize the nation as a modernist "invention"—a "purely historical moment"—without significant roots in real peoples and histories, such as Ernest Gellner, *Thought and Change* (London: Weidenfeld and Nicolson, 1964); Benedict Anderson, *Imagined Communities: Reflections on the Origins and Spread of Nationalism*, 2nd ed. (London: Verso, 1991); and E. J. Hobsbawm, *Nations and Nationalism since 1780: Programme, Myth, Reality* (Cambridge: Cambridge University Press, 1990).
16. Letter of Jacques Marlaud to Régis Debray, December 13, 2000, *Le Lien express* 4 (February 2001); Charles Champetier, "Réflexions sur la question corse," *Éléments* 99 (November 2000).
17. Zygmunt Bauman, *Globalization: The Human Consequences* (New York: Columbia University Press, 1998), 65–69.
18. Alain de Benoist, "Les limites du souverainisme," *Éléments* 96 (November 1999). Cf. Susan Strange, *The Retreat of the State: The Diffusion of Power in the World Economy* (Cambridge: Cambridge University Press, 1996).

19. Johannes Althusius, *Politica: Politics Methodically Set Forth and Illustrated with Sacred and Profane Examples*, trans. Frederick S. Carney (Indianapolis: Liberty Fund, 1995); Alain de Benoist, "Johannes Althusius," *Krisis* 22 (March 1999).
20. Benoist, "Qu'est-ce que la souveraineté?"
21. "Les équivoques du principe de subsidiarité: Entretien avec Jean-Louis Clergerie," *Krisis* 22 (March 1999).
22. Alain de Benoist, "Maastricht et la mémoire de l'avenir" (1992), in *La ligne de mire II: Discours aux citoyen européens, 1988-1995* (Paris: Le Labyrinthe, 1996); Robert de Herte, "L'Europe de 1992: Un mauvais conte de fées," *Éléments* 65 (Spring 1989).
23. Maurice Bardèche, *L'œuf de Christophe Colomb* (Paris: Éds. Déterna, 2002), 149.
24. Philippe de Saint-Robert, "La reine morte: Considérations sur la souveraineté française," in *Europe: Le nouveau monde. Actes du XXVIe colloque national du GRECE* (Paris: GRECE, 1993); Jean-Baptiste Duroselle, *France and the United States: From the Beginnings to the Present*, trans. Derek Coltman (Chicago: University of Chicago Press, 1978), 190.
25. Robert de Herte, "L'Europe réunifiée," *Éléments* 30 (June 1979).
26. Geir Lundestad, *"Empire" by Integration: The United States and European Integration, 1945-1997* (Oxford: Oxford University Press, 1998).
27. Charles Champetier, "Pour en finir avec Bruxelles," *Éléments* 69 (Fall 1990); Molnar, *The Emerging Atlantic Culture*, 43; "L'Europe et l'Amérique au miroir de Maastricht: Face à face avec Jean-Luc Mélenchon et Gilbert Pérol," *Krisis* 13-14 (April 1993).
28. Charles Champetier, "Maastricht: Non," *Éléments* 75 (September 1992); Alain de Benoist, "Citoyen de quelle Europe?" (1991), in *L'écume et les galets, 1991-1999: Dix ans d'actualité vue d'ailleurs* (Paris: Le Labyrinthe, 2000).
29. "Three Interviews with Alain de Benoist," *Telos* 98-99 (Winter 1993-Spring 1994).
30. Alain de Benoist, "La mémoire de l'avenir," in *Europe: Le nouveau monde. Actes du XXVIe colloque national du GRECE* (Paris: GRECE, 1993). Postmodern advocates of European unity reject not only the Continent's cultural heritage, they call for an "active forgetfulness," oriented to a future construction based on "multifarious senses of we"—i.e., based on an identification not with Europe, but with the world at large. Similarly, their notion of European identity is not cultural or civilizational, but materialist, conceived in terms of "lifestyles." See Ham, *European Integration and the Postmodern Condition*, 70-73.
31. As L. L. Matthias notes: *"Certains hommes d'État ont pu faire de grandes affaires, mais rarement un homme d'affaires a su agir en homme d'État."* See *Autopsie des États-Unis* (Paris: Seuil, 1955), 139.
32. Guillaume Faye, *Nouvelle discours à la nation européenne* (Paris: Éds. Albatros, 1985), 57.
33. The significance of these terms, as well as their ongoing resonance within the European Right, owes much to the influence of Julius Evola. See Philippe Baillet, "Evola, le dernier gibelin," *Éléments* 38 (Spring 1981); Julius Evola, *The Mystery of the Grail: Initiation and Magic in the Quest for the Spirit*, trans. Guido Stucco (Rochester, VT: Inner Traditions, 1997). Also Jean-Gilles Malliarakis, "L'héritage gibelin," *Jeune nation solidariste: Organe de Troisième*

## IMPERIUM       251

Voie 3 (May–June 1985); Hans-Dietrich Sander, "Der ghibellinische und der guelfische in der deutschen Geschichte," *Staatsbriefe* (April 2002).

34. Marco Tarchi, "Prolégomènes à l'unification de l'Europe," in *Crépuscule des blocs, aurore des peuples: Actes du XXIIIe colloque national du GRECE* (Paris: GRECE, 1990); Jean-Claude Valla, "De Charlemagne à Napoléon," *Éléments* 38 (Spring 1981). Cf. Ulick Varange (Francis Parker Yockey), *Imperium: The Philosophy of History and Politics* (Costa Mesa, CA: Noontide Press, 1962 [1948]); Jean Thiriart, *Un empire de 400 millions d'hommes, Europe* (Brussels, 1964). Since the end of the Cold War, the imperial idea has moved to the center of GRECE concerns. Its first formulation, though, reaches back to its formative period. See Giorgio Locchi, "Le règne, l'empire, l'imperium," *Nouvelle École* 20 (September 1972).

35. Cf. Francis Rapp, *Le Saint-Empire romain germanique: D'Otton le Grand à Charles Quint* (Paris: Tallandier, 1999).

36. Alain de Benoist, *L'empire intérieur* (Paris: Fata Morgana, 1995), 107. On the controversies surrounding the imperial idea, see the introductory essay in Maurice Duverger, ed., *Le concept d'empire* (Paris: PUF, 1980). The New Right's understanding of the *Reichsidee* is based on the Roman experience, especially as interpreted by Julius Evola. See his *Revolt Against the Modern World*, trans. Guido Stucco (Rochester, VT: Inner Traditions, 1995), 287–311.

37. Benoist, *L'empire intérieur*, 117; Julius Evola, "Sur les prémisses spirituelles de l'empire" (1937), in *Essais politiques*, trans. Gérard Boulanger and François Maistre (Puiseaux: Pardès, 1988).

38. Benoist, *L'empire intérieur*, 117–19; Julius Evola, "L'Europe ou la conjugaison du déclin" (1951), in *L'Europe ou le déclin de l'Occident*, trans. Rémi Perrin (Paris: Perrin et Perrin, 1997).

39. Luc Pauwells, *L'Europe impérieuse: Du long chemin de la CEE libérale à l'empire européenne* (Paris: GRECE, n.d.), 22.

40. Alain de Benoist, "L'idée d'empire" (1990), in *La ligne de mire II*; Robert de Herte, "La France: Le détonation de l'Europe," *Éléments* 38 (Spring 1981); Julius Evola, "United Europe: The Spiritual Pre-Requisite," *The Scorpion* 9 (Spring 1986). If the imperial idea is able to reconcile the one and the many, one might wonder why biocultural homogeneity is of such importance to the identitarian project? Besides the fact that all identity is ultimately biocultural, there are two answers to this. First, the imperial idea is a Roman one, rooted in a cultural experience distinct to Europe; it is not readily exportable and lacks resonance with non-Europeans. Secondly (and more importantly), within the various communities making up an imperium, democracy, education, and institutional life require a common body of beliefs and values (a shared bioculture), without which such a body would be impossible to sustain.

41. According to Joseph A. Schumpeter: "Imperialism is the objectless disposition on the part of the state to unlimited forcible expansion." See *Imperialism and Social Classes*, trans. Heinz Norden (New York: Augustus M. Kelley, 1952), 7.

42. Arnaud Guyot-Jeannin, *Révolution spirituelle contre le monde moderne* (Neuilly-sur-Seine: Cercle Sol Invictus, 2000), 53.

43. Cf. Roger Garaudy, *Les États-Unis, avant-garde de la décadence: La nouveau désordre international* (Beirut: Al Fihrist, 1998), 19.

44. Benoist, *L'empire intérieur*, 131.
45. Robert de Herte, "Entre jacobinisme et séparatisme," *Éléments* 12 (September 1975).
46. Tarchi, "Prolégomènes à l'unification de l'Europe."
47. Pierre Joannon, "Pavane pour une Europe défunte," *Éléments* 19 (January 1977).
48. Jean-Jacques Mourreau, "Adresse aux princes," in *Crépuscule des blocs, aurore des peuples: Actes du XXIIIe colloque national du GRECE* (Paris: GRECE, 1990); Alain de Benoist, *Les idées à l'endroit* (Paris: Hallier, 1979), 49–54.
49. Maiastra, *Renaissance de l'Occident?* (Paris: Plon, 1979), 299.
50. Claude Karnoouh, "Logos without Ethos: On Interculturality and Multiculturalism," *Telos* 110 (Winter 1998).
51. Quoted in Christian Bouchet, *Les nouveaux nationalistes* (Paris: Éds. Déterna, 2001), 217.
52. Samuel P. Huntington, *The Clash of Civilizations and the Remaking of World Order* (New York: Simon and Schuster, 1996).
53. Pierre M. Gallois, *Réquisitoire: Entretiens avec Lydwine Helly* (Lausanne: L'Âge d'Homme, 2001), 133.
54. Cf. Michel Korinman, *Quand l'Allemagne pensait le monde: Grandeur et décadence d'une géopolitique* (Paris: Fayard, 1990).
55. Zbigniew Brzezinski, *The Grand Chessboard: American Primacy and Its Geostrategic Imperatives* (New York: Basic Books, 1997). In this context, it is revealing to note that the US Army, while plundering German science and technology in 1945, confiscated the entire personal library of General Haushofer. For a survey of geopolitics' current status in the US academy, see John Agnew, *Making Political Geography* (London: Arnold, 2002).
56. Alain de Benoist, *Vu de Droite: Anthologie critique des idées contemporaines*, 5th ed. (Paris: Copernic, 1979), 237–54; Heinrich Jordis von Lohausen, *Les empires et la puissance: La géopolitique aujourd'hui*, trans. Elfriede Popelier and Jean-Louis Pesteil, 2nd ed. (Paris: Le Labyrinthe, 1996); Pierre M. Gallois, *Géopolitique: Les voies de la puissance*, 2nd ed. (Lausanne: L'Âge d'Homme, 2000).
57. Carl Schmitt, *Terre et mer: Un point de vue sur l'histoire mondiale*, trans. Jean-Louis Pesteil (Paris: Le Labyrinthe, 1985), 23.
58. Halford Mackinder, "The Geographical Pivot of History," in *Democratic Ideals and Realities* (New York: Norton, 1962).
59. Jean-François Tacheau, *Stratégies d'expansion du nouvel empire global* (Lausanne: L'Âge d'Homme, 2001).
60. Charles Champetier, "Vers l'Europe libre," *Éléments* 96 (November 1999); Brzezinksi, *The Grand Chessboard*, 59; Friedrich S. Felde, "Washingtons Weltherrschaft," *Staatsbriefe* (April 1998). The US aggression on Iraq in 2003, which is beginning as I finish these lines, appears to have inaugurated a watershed in world affairs—alienating the Europeans, discrediting the UN and other US-controlled bodies comprising the institutional basis of its global order, and discarding the "new liberal imperialism" for a Zionist-inspired policy of old-fashioned *Machtpolitik*. This, however, does little to diminish the accuracy of the New Right's previous characterization of US policy.

61. Brian W. Blouet, *Geopolitics and Globalization in the Twentieth Century* (London: Reaktion Books, 2001), 35–45; Niall Ferguson, *The Pity of War* (New York: Basic Books, 1999). A war that leaves the victor qualitatively worse off—and the two European civil wars of the twentieth century not only finished off the already bankrupt British Empire, it reduced the mother country to a third-rate power—can be nothing other than "misguided." Joseph Chamberlain's idea of an Anglo-German partnership represented one lost alternative to Britain's—and Europe's—tragedy in this century.

62. Donald William, *Le choc des temps: Géopolitiques* (Montreal: Éds. Sciences et Culture, 2000), 25–26.

63. As one international policy expert writes: "The American aspiration to freeze historical development by working to keep the world unipolar is doomed. In the not very long run, the task will exceed America's economic, military, and political resources; and the very effect to maintain a hegemonic position is the surest way to undermine it." See Kenneth N. Waltz, "Intimations of Multipolarity," in *The New World Order: Contrasting Theories*, ed. Birthe Hansen and Bertel Heurlin (New York: St. Martin's Press, 2000). Also Chalmers Johnson, *Blowback: The Costs and Consequences of American Empire* (New York: Henry Holt, 2000), 220–29; Hans-Dietrich Sander, "Das erste Kriegsziel der amerikanische Politik," *Staatsbriefe* (December 1999).

64. *New York Times* (March 8, 1992). Also Patrick J. Buchanan, *A Republic, Not an Empire: Reclaiming America's Destiny* (Washington, DC: Regnery, 1999), 7–22; Alain de Benoist, "Les gendarmes du monde" (1992), in *L'écume et les galets*.

65. Alain de Benoist, "George W. Bush: l'ennemi américain," *Le Lien express* 8 (June 2001). Cf. Susan Bryce, "Who Is George W. Bush?," *New Dawn* 65 (March–April 2001).

66. Noam Chomsky, *9-11* (New York: Seven Stories Press, 2001).

67. Philippe Grasset, "Europe in the Making?" (2002), at *De Defensa* (http://www.dedefensa.org); Emmanuel Todd, *Après empire: Essai sur la décomposition du système américain* (Paris: Gallimard, 2002). (Actually, the very opposite of what I expected in 2003 has since occurred, with Europeans [pre-eminently France and the UK] subsequently integrating themselves even more intimately into the Americanosphere.)

68. *Journal des débats* (September 18, 1870); cited in Alain de Benoist, "Une certaine idée de l'Allemagne," *Éléments* 30 (June 1979).

69. Benoist, "Une certaine idée de l'Allemagne."

70. Jean-Jacques Mourreau, "De Gaulle, visionnaire de l'Europe," *Éléments* 68 (Summer 1990). While supporting De Gaulle's opposition to the superpowers, *Grécistes* nonetheless consider him a nationalist rather than a Europeanist. See Pauwells, *L'empire impérieuse*, 17–18.

71. Pierre-Marie Gallois, *La France sort-elle de l'histoire? Superpuissances et déclin national* (Lausanne: L'Âge d'Homme, 1998), 117–18. Not coincidentally, it was one of the pioneers of the German New Right and a major influence on Benoist who was responsible for making Gaullist policy objectives familiar to his countrymen. See Armin Mohler, *Die Fünfte Republik: Was Steht hinter de Gaulle* (Munich: Piper, 1963) and *Was die Deutschen Fürchten* (Stuttgart: Seewald,

1965). On Mohler, see Marc Ludder and Robert Steuckers, "Armin Mohler et la Nouvelle Droite," *Vouloir* 11 (1999).
72. Mourreau, "De Gaulle, visionnaire de l'Europe." De Gaulle's legacy remains much in dispute. At various times, nationalists have criticized him for being a Jacobin, an enemy of the nation, a lackey of the Anglo-Saxons, the Communists, the Rothschilds, or the Masons. See, for example, Philippe Ploncard d'Assac, *Le nationalisme français: Origines, doctrine et solutions* (Paris: Duquesne Diffusion, 2000), 29–31; Pierre Monnier, *Quand grossissent les têtes molles: Essai sur la têtemollité* (Paris: Éds. Déterna, 2000), 25–26, 100–1; Henri-Christian Giraud, *De Gaulle et les communistes*, 2 vols. (Paris: Albin Michel, 1988–89); Alain Pascal, *La trahison des initiés: La Franc-Maçonnerie du combat politique à la guerre de religion* (Paris: L'Æncre, 1998), 120–22.
73. Venner, *Histoire et tradition des européens*, 157; Pierre Vial, "Où va la France?," *Terre et peuple: La revue* 11 (Spring 2002).
74. Benoist, *L'empire intérieur*, 142–46; Carl Schmitt, "La formation de l'esprit français par les légistes" (1942), in *Du politique*, ed. Alain de Benoist (Puiseaux: Pardès, 1990). Cf. Karlheinz Weissmann, *Nation?* (Bad Vilbel: Ed. Antaios, 2001); Brian Jenkins and Nigel Copsey, "Nation, Nationalism and National Identity in France," in *Nations and Identity in Contemporary Europe*, ed. Brian Jenkins and Spyros A. Sofos (London: Routledge, 1996).
75. This process was still underway as late as the Third Republic. See Eugen Weber, *Peasants into Frenchmen: The Modernization of Rural France, 1870–1914* (Stanford, CA: Stanford University Press, 1976).
76. Benoist, "Une certaine idée de l'Allemagne"; Benoist, *Les idées à l'endroit*, 226. Cf. Louis Dumont, *German Ideology: From France to Germany and Back* (Chicago: University of Chicago Press, 1994).
77. Pauwells, *L'empire impérieuse*, 20. Not a few French sovereignists see German federalism as a plot to weaken France and foster Germany's domination of Europe. For example, see Pierre Hillard, *Minorités et régionalismes dans l'Europe fédérale des régions: Enquête sur le plan allemand qui va bouleverser l'Europe* (Paris: François-Xavier de Guibert, 2000).
78. Pierre Vial, "A la croisée des destins," *Éléments* 38 (Spring 1981); Jean Haudry, "Les racines du peuple français," in *Les origines de la France*, ed. Jacques Robichez (Saint-Cloud: Éds. Nationales, n.d.).
79. Frank Costigliola, *France and the United States: The Cold Alliance since World War II* (New York: Twayne, 1992), 24.
80. Michel Marmin and Jean-Claude Valla, "Pourquoi la France?," *Éléments* 38 (Spring 1981).
81. Brzezinski, *The Grand Chessboard*, 63.
82. Guillaume Faye, "La France en Europe," in *Une certaine idée de la France: Actes du XIXe colloque national du GRECE* (Paris: Le Labyrinthe, 1985).
83. Jean-Gilles Malliarakis, "Contre Moscou sans Washington," *Jeune nation solidariste: Organe de Troisième Voie* 9 (May–June 1986).
84. Alain de Benoist, "Le retour de l'histoire," in *Crépuscule des blocs, aurore des peuples: Actes du XXIIIe colloque national du GRECE* (Paris: GRECE, 1990).
85. Alain de Benoist, "L'ennemi principal" (Part II), *Éléments* 41 (March–April 1982); Guillaume Faye, "L'audace de la puissance," *Éléments* 56 (Winter 1985);

IMPERIUM                                                                        255

Pierre Krebs, *Die europäische Wiedergeburt* (Tübingen: Grabert, 1982), 74–77; Alain de Benoist, "Préface," in Ernst Niekisch, *Hitler: Une fatalité allemande et autres écrits nationaux-bolcheviks*, trans. Imke Mieulet (Puiseaux: Pardès, 1991). For a succinct formulation of National Bolshevik principles by one of its foremost living proponents, see Alexandre Dougine (Dugin), "La métaphysique du National-Bolchevisme," at *Archivio Eurasia* (http://utenti.tripod.it/archivEurasia). On Niekisch, see Friedrich Kabermann, *Widerstand und Entscheidung eines deutschen Revolutionärs: Leben und Denken von Ernst Niekisch* (Koblenz: Verlag S. Bublies, 1993); Birgit Rätsch-Langejürgen, *Das Prinzip Widerstand: Leben und Wirken von Ernst Niekisch* (Bonn: Bouvier, 1997).

86. Benoist, "Préface," in Niekisch, *Hitler*; F. Lapeyre, "Ernst Niekisch, un destin allemand," *Éléments* 73 (Spring 1992). Cf. Karl Otto Paetel, *Nationalbolschewismus und nationalrevolutionäre Bewegungen in Deutschland* (Schnellbach: Bublies, 1999); Karlheinz Weissmann, *Die preussische Dimension: Ein Essay* (Munich: Herbig, 2001). Niekisch's National Bolshevism ought not to be confused with went by the same term in the Soviet Union. On the latter, see Mikhail Agursky, *The Third Rome: National Bolshevism in the USSR* (Boulder, CO: Westview Press, 1987). There are several other tendencies associated with the term; see Louis Dupeux, *National Bolchevisme: Stratégie communiste et dynamique conservatrice*, 2 vols. (Paris: H. Champion, 1979).

87. Benoist, "L'ennemi principal" (Part II).

88. Georges Nivat, *Vers la fin du mythe russe: Essais sur la culture russe* (Lausanne: L'Âge d'Homme, 1982).

89. Alexandre Dougine, "La Russie, l'Europe, le Monde," *Éléments* 73 (Spring 1992); Alain de Benoist, *Orientations pour des années décisives* (Paris: Le Labyrinthe, 1982), 72–73.

90. "Die Rede der Präsidenten des Russichen Föderation," at *Paris-Berlin-Moscou* (http://www.paris-berlin-moscou.org). Also Wolfgang Strauss, "Deutschrussische Affinitäten," *Staatsbriefe* (January–February 1998).

91. Pierre Vial, "La troisième Rome," *Éléments* 57–58 (Spring 1986). Cf. Gerhoch Reiseggen, *Wir Werden Schamlos Irregeführt: Vom 11. September zum Irak-Krieg* (Tübingen: Hohenrain, 2003).

92. Alain de Benoist, "Huit réflexions sur la mort du communisme," *Éléments* 71 (Fall 1991). On the collusion between the West and the former Soviet ruling class, as they jointly plundered the country, see Alexandre Zinoviev, *La suprasociété globale et la Russie*, trans. Gérard Conio (Lausanne: L'Âge d'Homme, 2000).

93. Alain de Benoist, *Dernière année: Notes pour conclure le siècle* (Lausanne: L'Âge d'Homme, 2001), 95. This is also the opinion of one World Bank insider: see Joseph E. Stiglitz, *Globalization and Its Discontents* (New York: Norton, 2002), 133–34.

94. Alexandre Del Valle, *Guerres contre l'Europe: Bosnie-Kosovo-Tchétchénie* (Paris: Éds. des Syrtes, 2000). The anti-Russian impetus of US foreign policy is especially clear to Russian geopoliticists. See Natalija Narocnickaja, "Russland und Europa in 20. Jahrhundert" (2000), at *Synergon* (http://www.geocities.com/spartacorps/synergon).

95. Michel Chossudovsky, *War and Globalization: The Truth Behind September 11* (Shanty Bay, Canada: Global Outlook, 2002), 27–28, 74, 113. The Russia of Vladimir Putin, who is obviously no creature of Washington, has already distinguished itself from the Russia of the corrupt "Yeltsin family." Since his election, the country's elites have become more conscious of the international threats they face and, despite several pro-Americans still in Putin's government, begun to counter the aggressive anti-Russian thrust of US policy. Putin also seems to realize that Europe represents a potential counterweight to American hegemony and needs to be cultivated as such. Finally, the post-Yeltsin system has a decidedly national-patriotic character, unlike the "family's" liberal orientation. See Victor Loupan, *Le défi russe* (Paris: Éds. des Syrtes, 2000); Wolfgang Seiffert, *Wladimar W. Putin: Wiedergeburt einer Weltmacht?* (Munich: Langen Müller, 2001).

96. For example, Walter Laqueur, *Black Hundred: The Rise of the Extreme Right in Russia* (New York: Harper Perennial, 1993), 162, 266; Guillaume Faye, "La guerre nécessaire," *Terre et peuple: La revue* 10 (Winter 2001); Gennady N. Seleznew, "International Aspects of Eurasism," at *Archivio Eurasia* (http://utenti.tripod.it/ArchivEurasia); but, most importantly, the following speech delivered to the Russian Duma by one of its deputies: Alexey Mitrofanov, "Anti-NATO: Ein neues Gedanke für russische Geopolitik, Taktik und Strategie für die heutige Zeit," at *Reich Europa* (http://www.esclarmonde.de.vu). Cf. Marlène Laruelle, *L'idéologie eurasiste russe ou comment penser l'empire* (Paris: L'Harmattan, 2001). That this Eurasian strategy has begun to worry the liberal plutocracies is evident in several recent criticisms of Alexander Dugin, Russia's foremost geopoliticist. See *Financial Times* (December 2, 2000); *Le Monde* (January 18, 2001, and June 8, 2001).

97. Louis Sorel, "Le Grand Triangle," *Res Publica Europaea: Information et analyses géopolitique* 17 (May 2001). Cf. Franck de La Rivière, *L'Europe de Gibraltar à Vladivostok* (Lausanne: L'Âge d'Homme, 2001); Henri de Grossouvre, *Paris-Berlin-Moscou: La voie de l'indépendance et de la paix* (Lausanne: L'Âge d'Homme, 2000).

98. It should be noted that the GRECE's National Bolshevism has been marred by inconsistency and hesitancy. For example, it formally rejects association with Alexander Dugin's Eurasianist movement, it failed to support Russia's war in Chechnya, and it has been critical of Russian efforts to re-establish its dominance in the former Soviet lands. The identitarian tendency that has been most Eurasianist (and the most geopolitically sophisticated) is the Synergon/Europa movement of Robert Steuckers. See the journal *Vouloir* and the website at http://www.geocities.com/spartacorps/synergon. It might also be added that Steuckers, a former *Gréciste*, has consistently taken the logic of GRECE-style identitarianism in directions that the now aging GRECE hesitates to follow. See Robert Steuckers, "La redécouverte des facteurs 'Russe,' 'Sibérie,' et 'Eurasie' dans la Nouvelle Droite en France," at *Archivio Eurasia* (http://utenti.tipod.it/ArchivEurasia).

99. Benoist, "L'idée d'empire."

# IMPERIUM

100. Robert de Herte, "Réinventer la démocratie," *Éléments* 52 (Winter 1985). Cf. George Orwell, *Selected Essays* (London: Penguin, 1957), 149; Vladimir Volkoff, *Pourquoi je suis moyennement démocrate* (Paris: Rocher, 2002).
101. Alain de Benoist, *Démocratie: Le problème* (Paris: Le Labyrinthe, 1985), 7.
102. Alain de Benoist, "Plädoyer für eine organische Demokratie," *Elemente für die europäische Wiedergeburt* 1 (July 1986).
103. Benoist, *Démocratie*, 13.
104. Alain de Benoist, "Peut-on encore être démocrate?," *Éléments* 52 (Winter 1985). Cf. Aristotle, *The Politics*, trans. T. A. Sinclair (London: Penguin, 1981), 167–71.
105. Benoist, *Démocratie*, 14.
106. Bernard Marillier, *Indo-Européens* (Puiseaux: Pardès, 1998), 62–64.
107. Cf. Irenäus Eibl-Eibesfeldt, *Der Mensch—Das riskierte Wesen. Zur Naturgeschichte menschlischer Unvernunft* (Munich: Piper, 1988).
108. Guillaume Faye, "Peut-on encore être démocrate?," *Éléments* 52 (Winter 1985).
109. Quoted in Alain de Benoist, "De quelques évolutions idéologiques à gauche," *Éléments* 99 (November 2000).
110. According to Joseph de Maistre: "*La politique et la religion se fondent ensemble.*" See his *Considérations sur la France* (Lyons: E. Vitte, 1924), 71.
111. On the liberal definition of freedom as "freedom from coercion," see J. G. Merquior, *Liberalism, Old and New* (Boston: Twayne, 1991), 5–9.
112. Alain de Benoist and Guillaume Faye, "Pour un État souverain," *Éléments* 44 (January 1983).
113. Benoist, *Démocratie*, 31; Armin Mohler, *Von rechts gesehen* (Stuttgart: Seewald, 1974), 108–11.
114. Jean Baudrillard, *Cool Memories II*, trans. Chris Turner (Durham, NC: Duke University Press, 1996), 16.
115. Alain de Benoist, "Vers une démocratie organique," *Éléments* 52 (Winter 1985). Karlheinz Weissmann makes an analogous observation about the ancient Germanic concept of liberty (*Freiheit*), which was etymologically related to notions of friend (*Freund*) and peace (*Friede*). See *Alles was recht(s) ist: Ideen, Köpfe und Perspektiven der politischen Rechten* (Graz: Stocker, 2000), 253.
116. Alain de Benoist, "Huit thèses sur la démocratie," *Éléments* 52 (Winter 1985).

# Conclusion

The New Right's metapolitical project hinges on the question of identity. What, though, is "identity"? Etymologically, the word derives from the late Latin *identitas*, meaning "singularly or peculiarly formed." *Identitas*, in turn, derives from the early Latin *idem*, suggesting "sameness and continuity." Today, in most Indo-European languages, "identity" has come to denote "the quality or condition of being the same," even when this "sameness" is subject to growth and development. In this sense, identity is at issue whenever there arises a question of distinguishing one form of being from another or one form of being in its different stages of becoming. In reference to a people (to its nature, spirit, or cosmos), identity signifies that which renders it "incomparable and irreplaceable" vis-à-vis another.[1] For the individual, identity affects the way he conceives of himself, relates to others, and situates himself in the larger world.

Despite being fundamental to the human condition, the modern age—especially the late modern age with its diverse, immanent, and nihilistic references makes an authentic realization of identity less and less possible. "Inauthenticity" (the condition of not being "real"—not an expression of *Dasein*—not a "being-at-home-with-itself"—and hence something deformed or pathological) comes then whenever Europeans are swept along by fashion or force, fail to recognize the distinct ground of their existence, and/or sacrifice their future possibility to some present distraction.

Once such a false identity takes hold, life is subject to determinations that are no longer its own. The ensuing pseudomorphosis culminates in the loss of *Dasein*—the loss of the very condition for being a being situated in a specific time and space. The loss of Europe's distinct ethnocultural identity implies, as such, the loss of Europe itself.

## Liberalism's War on Identity

If identity is primary in a world where nothing is primary any longer, then man's being can be fully realized only in reference to those significations that authentically ground him—that is, in reference to that which anchors him in a specific culture, in a specific period of history, in a specific people. With the multiple roles and relativist value systems fostered by late modern (or postmodern) society, these significations have been progressively drained of meaning, causing *Dasein* to "fall away from itself."[2] The resulting loss of identity, as identitarians from one end of the Continent to the other contend, has been an annihilating chaos, threatening the European's very existence.[3] For once man's being is distorted or obliterated, so too is his world.

As argued in all the above chapters, the single most consequential force assailing these identitarian significations, and hence compromising the integrity of European being, is liberalism (classical, progressivist, or neoconservative), which conceives of man in the way modern science conceives of inert matter. On the basis of its simplistic reductions, the European is rendered into a quantitative abstraction, undifferentiated from the rest of humanity. So reduced, he is subjected to laws that isolate and decontextualize him, limit his motivation to material self-interest, relate him to other individuals through faceless contractual arrangements, and, most damagingly, lock him into a mono-directional temporality at odds with his world-open nature. Then, as the instrumentalist dictates of this condition override deeply rooted meanings, life is made barren and new anxieties arise to haunt it.[4] With postmodernity, the process assumes nihilistic proportion, as historically formed peoples are transformed into consumerist tribes and identity is reduced to an array of vacuous lifestyle choices threatening the last vestiges of their ancient heritage. By severing Europeans from all that makes them a distinct people, liberalism is creating the worst possible world for them. As José Ortega y Gasset warns: "Europeans do not know how to live unless they are engaged in some great enterprise. When this is lacking, they grow petty and feeble and their souls disintegrate."[5]

No people today is more afflicted by liberalism's petty, enfeebling, and disintegrating effects than Europeans.[6] If present conditions persists, everything that has distinguished them over the ages and inspired their great enterprises will be sacrificed on the altar of the present chaos. The Continent will then cease to be European, as it is altered by the introduction of alien gene pools; as Arabic, Turkish and other non-European languages achieve parity with its own languages; as Islam takes its place along side of, and then crowds out, Christianity; as social practices, mores, behaviors, and institutions are reshaped by outsiders, and as the regnant elites, driven by the quantitative logic of their economic appetites, do everything in their power to turn the Continent into a "multiracial ensemble" alien to the last 30,000 years of history. Faced with the prospect of extinction, New Rightists claim Europeans have but a single alternative: to abandon the liberal practices that have stupefied them over the last half century and carry out a conservative revolution to recapture the truth of their originary being. For only when their longest memories are again reflected in the principles guiding them into the future will they regain the living unity of their culture.[7] In Heidegger's formulation: "Identity is the actualization of a heritage."[8] Without it, Europeans cease to be who they are.

Given the opposition to whomever resists the "narcotizing pluralism" of the present world system, the future is heralding a showdown between those intent on defending the integrity of their identity and those committed to dissolving it in the universalist solvent of America's global market. Since the ascent of the New World Order more than a decade ago, identitarian movements and, in some cases, a violent "process of ethnification" (Wallerstein), have moved closer to the center of the world stage, as the market fundamentalism of the "Washington Consensus" extends the tentacular grasp of its homogenizing order to all the world's peoples.[9]

In this struggle between the liberal Moloch and those opposing its "warm death" (Lorenz), Benoist observes that one combatant arms itself in the name of humanity, the other mobilizes for the sake of a specific people; one pursues liberation, the other liberty; one upholds the virtualist forms of representative democracy, the other the communal practices of a self-determining people; one resists difference, the other uniformity; one seeks to integrate Europe into a homogenizing global system, the other supports a world in which Europeans and others are free to pursue their own destiny, as they, and not financial interests headquartered in New York, see fit.[10] Such struggles—rather than the exhausted Left-Right antagonisms of modernity—are, indeed, the ones which New Right identitarians now prepare Europeans to fight. They ought to be seen, then, as part of that larger movement resisting the liberalization (or Americanization) of the world, as they mobilize around the idea, formulated long ago by Charles Maurras, that blood alone is able to prevail against the rapacious forces of money.[11]

## The New Right Project

Every social order engenders conflicts specific to it. In the heyday of liberal modernity, the national market, the nation-state, and philosophies allied to the natural sciences formed the principal sites of modernist contention. Today, with the looming of postmodernity, global markets, transnational bodies, and new *épistémès* are beginning to supplant these sites. The discursive impact of this transformation and the political alignments they suggest have had an especially disconcerting effect on the politics of both Left and Right.

A good deal of ideological, not to mention existential uncertainty, accompanies the waning of the modern age. Acculturated by the Marxist sensibility of the state university (rather than the organic ontology of the Irish hedge school), most postmodernists have sought to reformulate the liberal project in ways favoring New Class designs (by advancing multiculturalism, individual license, minority interests, and the elimination of established barriers and borders). Those, on the other hand, who might benefit from the anti-liberal implications of the postmodern *épistémè* (that is, conservatives, traditionalists, ethnonationalists, Right-wing anti-globalists, and other contemporary anti-liberals resisting the usurious forces assaulting the integrity of their culture and community) have often been the most reluctant to accept its illuminations—or even to admit that it sheds light of any sort—given postmodernity's frequently perverse effects on contemporary life and thought.[12]

Foremost among New Rightists, *Grécistes* see postmodernism as bearing more than a tangential relationship to the anti-liberal tradition and its opposition to "the new liberal imperialism."[13] Postmodernism's exposure of rationalism's often fictitious postulates, the primacy it accords to culture and community, the wealth of possibility it sees shut out by the liberal *status quo*, the straightjacket of managerial discourse it opposes—these have long informed the different schools of Counter-Enlightenment thought. In contrast to many conservatives and traditionalists, who view postmodernism as simply another unpalatable expression of liberalism's "constructionist idealism," *Grécistes* are qualitatively more receptive to its critique. Thus, whenever postmodernists tear the veil from modernity's unstated assumptions, equate reason with symbolization and power, posit the primacy of context, and affirm freedom and identity, they find not another fashionably perverse assault on "the order of things," but a validation of certain key aspects of the heritage they defend. They do not, of course, follow postmodernists in making the metanarrative collapse an excuse for anti-identitarian practices. Nor do they find inspiration in its orientation to the Left, which has not only abandoned the "people" for the sake of feminists, homosexuals, and non-white "minorities," but does so in ways fostering the most radical quantitative impulses of the New World Order.

New Rightists approach postmodernism in ways that make it compatible with the traditional—and revolutionary—possibilities still latent in the European idea. Accepting the world's intrinsic lack of coherence and the relativity of its different orders of value need not, then, trivialize or discredit the European heritage. From the identitarian's perspective, postmodernism's anti-foundationalist broadsides constitute an emphatic justification of tradition's particularity and the fact that we are who we are only because we make certain decisions to identify with and defend *our* particular system of truth. The constructed (that is, the human or cultural) character of the historical narrative, the multiplicity of these narratives, and their absence of closure are cause for affirmation and commitment, not despair, for culturally relative "truths" born of one's own identity are necessarily more meaningful than those that are not.

Organic forms of identity may lack the sort of philosophical foundations modernity claimed for itself, but New Rightists believe they are irreplaceable in enabling a people to grow and evolve in the inmost spirit of its being. Without these forms, a people (as all the above has sought to prove) cannot sustain itself in the fullness of its being. The art of historical survival—what Raymond Ruyer calls *chronopolitique*—consequently dictates that a people jealously, intolerantly if need be, defend its myths, beliefs, lifestyles, language, institutions, and, above all, its specific genetic heritage, for these alone enable it to be what it is and what it might be. There is, in truth, no other *raison d'être* for it. As Benoist argues, a people is heir to a unique fraction of history; it is not an arbitrary territorial grouping, an abstract social construct, or a momentary collection of individuals whose ultimate identity is with humanity. Embodied in an identity forged in the inextricable symbiosis of race, culture, and time, a people's history instills in it a common feeling of belonging together, of having a common destiny, but especially of knowing where it came from and where it is going.[14] Apart from such feelings, there is no people. Liberalism, for this reason, wants people to forget the heritage that makes them a people; it thus treats the past as a burden and encourages individuals to travel light.

Refusing all truck with liberalism's "now time," New Rightists believe that only in appropriating a past alive in the present is a meaningful future possible. Paraphrasing Heidegger, we might say that in apprehending "what will be" in terms of "what has been," identitarians formed in the GRECE's New School of European Culture represent both the most radical and futural of contemporary schools of thought.[15] They accordingly take their stand with Ernst Jünger in predicting either a return of the ancient gods or an annihilating chaos.

Without the promptings of their originary spirit, nothing, they believe, is likely to save them from the imposition of liberalism's inherently self-destructive *cosmopolis*.[16] If Europeans are to have a future, they will have to return to the font of their being—to the lands their ancestors settled, to the traditions and myths that have sustained them over the ages, to the Faustian impulses that have provoked all that is great in their heritage—and to do so in the willful spirit of world-open man.

Europe's rebirth (and this is the New Right's ultimate goal) looms over the Continent. Heirs to *la civilisation indo-européenne* (Dumézil), its peoples possess all the elements necessary for a thriving imperium. They need simply look beyond their petty differences to consolidate the ties that bind them to the same biocivilization. The New Right's project aims in this way at making Europeans aware of the immense possibilities inherent in their heritage.

## Critique of the GRECE

Because New Rightists affirm their European identity and resist liberal subversions, they are routinely labeled "fascists" or "racists." Such characterizations naturally tell us more about liberalism's inability to tolerate opposed views than they do about the New Right itself, for in attaching an accusatory label like "fascist" or "racist" to whatever displeases or challenges it, liberalism simply dismisses the need to explain itself or rebuff its critics. That proponents of the so-called "open society" should smear or muzzle their critics is more than another abnormality of late modernity, for it attests to an inability to legitimate a discredited (and increasingly dysfunctional) project.[17] There are, however, serious criticisms to be made of the New Right, but these, to be sure, derive from identitarian, not liberal, criteria.

Since its founding, the GRECE, the original and most enduring of the tendencies gathered under the New Right's banner, has designated liberal modernity as Europe's chief "enemy." Because the United States is the world's foremost liberal power, the GRECE's anti-liberalism has been closely associated with its anti-Americanism.[18] One might wonder (at least Guillaume Faye does) if the GRECE has accurately identified Europe's enemy.[19] This Schmittian notion presumes that politics divides the world into friends and foes, designating the latter as those threatening the survival of the body politic.

From an identitarian perspective, there seems little doubt that America endangers Europe. But it is less certain that it constitutes its principal enemy. As indicated in an earlier chapter, a massive influx of Third World peoples is presently convulsing European life. Unlike rival New Rightists, especially those emphasizing the biocultural component of identity, *Grécistes* view their intrusion into the European *Lebensraum* as symptomatic of capitalism's insatiable quest for cheap labor and its willingness to elevate economic interests above every other consideration.[20] They consequently direct their fire not against immigration *per se*, but against the liberal market system fostering it. At the same time, however, they champion *la cause des peuples* and *le droit à la différence*, defending particularistic identities from the homogenizing forces of the global market. And this, as we have seen, has led to a qualified multiculturalism.

For their identitarian critics, *Grécistes* have failed to distinguish between Europe's enemy and its provisional adversary (between what Schmitt distinguishes as the difference between *Feind* and *Gegner*).[21] For although the American order in Europe deculturates, deracinates, and alienates Europeans, the GRECE's critics claim that it does not threaten them with immediate physical annihilation, which is not the case with immigration. The disintegration of a culture, they contend, can be stopped at any time, once a people finds its way back to its originary sources. The mixing of races and diverse cultures, however, is irrevocable. For this reason, these identitarians believe the growth of alien immigrant populations, in threatening Europe's biological stock, constitutes the single greatest danger to its survival. The American system may therefore mean a slow death through deculturation and even be ultimately responsible for the Third World invasion, but if present trends continue, within a generation Europeans will be a hounded minority in their own lands. This will create a non-white Europe opposed to everything that defines Europe.[22]

Along with underestimating the dangers of immigration, *Grécistes* harbor an implicit admiration for Islam's anti-modernism. This leads them to look on the Muslim world—in Europe and elsewhere—as a potential ally in the struggle against American deculturation.[23] The GRECE's identitarian critics again disagree. Americanism and Islamization, they observe, are not incompatible, but closely related phenomena.[24] For example, France's new Islamic culture—*la culture black-beur*, with its Negro hoodlum attire, the cacophony of its rap music, its narcissistic character structure, and its contempt for Europe's high culture—is largely a product of American cultural influence. Likewise, the ethnic chaos—the ongoing *intifada*—that comes with Third World colonization strengthens the US's hold over Europe, for it weakens social stability and fosters a cosmopolitanism advantageous to American practices.

Between the threat posed by the "mental colonization" of the US Culture Industry and its consumer society and the actual colonization that comes with Islamization, the GRECE's identitarian critics tend to identify the latter as the more pressing danger—even if they recognize that immigration is ultimately a product of the deculturating imperatives of America's economic civilization.[25] For however detestable

Americanism may be, it is, Guillaume Faye observes, easier to get rid of a McDonald's than a mosque.[26] The great hegemon of the West may represent a dangerous adversary, and one which must be opposed if Europeans are to reclaim their identity, but the immediate threat to European existence—in the most elemental biocultural sense—comes from the Muslim lands to the south, whose immigrants are presently renting Europe's social fabric, erasing her culture and memory, and transforming her demography beyond recognition.[27]

As the Algerian revolutionary Houari Boumediène boasts, the Islamic world today carries in the wombs of its women the weapons that one day will conquer Europe. In colonizing the Continent, Muslims, in effect, prepare the basis for its outright conquest.[28] For this reason, the more advanced identitarians call not simply for an end to immigration, but for a military reconquest of their homeland. The Christian-Muslim struggle for Kosovo (in which the United States allied with Islam against Christian Serbia), they believe, was merely the opening salvo in a more cataclysmic struggle for the Continent's future.[29] The GRECE, on the other hand, has accommodated itself to what some identitarians perceive as the principal enemy.[30]

The GRECE's questionable designation of Europe's enemy is linked to another problematical feature of its project. As already noted, its analytically detached metapolitics has culminated in a qualified form of multiculturalism. An analogous failing inheres in its identitarianism, which is more intellectual than biocultural. For in championing *la cause des peuples* and *le droite à la différence*, the GRECE has ended up recuperating many of the egalitarian principles it formally rejects.[31] It does this by making ethnopluralism a universal (or Kantian) right, detached from any specific context: yet, only the self-hating white multiculturalist, steeped in the rationalist myths of liberal modernity, believes in the equal worth of all peoples and their right to transform Europe in their own image. Every healthy people—and thus every genuine identitarian—holds to the superiority of their own ways. Long-existing nations, the Chinese and Jews pre-eminently, owe their historical endurance precisely to their ethnocentrism. Even Americans would be without their world-conquering confidence if they did not believe in the superiority of their way of life (however evil it may actually be).

If one's own civilization is not felt to be superior to others, there hardly seems reason to defend it.[32] In this vein, Christopher Dawson, one of the greatest twentieth-century historians, attributed the end of the European age less to the decline of Europe's economic and political powers after

1945 than to the "loss of faith in the uniqueness of [her] culture."[33] After two horrific world wars, Europeans had lost faith in themselves.

But Europeans do not need to justify who they are. Giorgio Locchi warned early on that ethnopluralism contradicts the very principle of an identitarian politics, for a civilization and a people exist only *vis-à-vis* other peoples and civilizations. In refusing to accept the primacy of their own people and in refusing to put their interests ahead of others, *le droit à la différence* became simply another form of liberal pluralism, in which the struggle is not for *our* culture and *our* people, but for that of all the others. As Julien Freund says, pluralism is the night in which all cats are gray.[34]

Europe, moreover, is hardly one among many equally worthy civilizations. By all accounts, it is in a league of its own.[35] The Belgian National Bolshevik Jean Thiriart claims that European culture "is the culture of civilized people everywhere, whether it be Tokyo, Moscow, Singapore, or Pasadena."[36] Its achievement and creative vitality are similarly ranked as the highest of any civilization. Its superiority, in fact, has never been in question, only its present lack of self-confidence. This, however, is key. A civilization is sustainable only as long as its members believe in themselves.[37] For reasons touched on in the above pages, Europeans no longer believe in themselves. Having abandoned the identity of their blood and spirit and hence their will to power, their extraordinary civilization now faces the prospect of extinction, as it mixes with alien peoples, abandons its ancient traditions, and ignores its incomparable heritage. The GRECE's ethnopluralism, in its lack of self-assertion, simply enhances the prospect of decline.

The failings that follow from the GRECE's decontextualization of identity are no less evident in its anti-Americanism and anti-Christianism. The few American thinkers to have examined its ideas with detachment characterize its anti-Americanism as a caricature, based on a Hollywood depiction of American life.[38] Caricature, however, is not the real problem with its anti-Americanism, which, in truth, highlights a great many American foibles and affirms many traditional European assessments.

From an identitarian perspective, the GRECE's anti-Americanism fails less because of its exaggerated character, than because of the subservient or "colonial" mentality it reflects. Its fixation on America causes it not only to mischaracterize the chief enemy, but to vent a *ressentiment* that is entirely inappropriate to Nietzsche's "good European." America is admittedly Europe's adversary (and in itself *the* great force for evil in the world). But as *Grécistes* themselves acknowledge, America is strong only to the degree Europe is weak. It is not America that keeps Europe servile, but the complicity of her vassalized elites.³⁹ The Continent's subaltern status in an American-dominated world is thus ultimately a European problem. The GRECE's heaviest fire ought, as such, to be directed against those European collaborators who make this subjugation possible. But such has not been the case. A metapolitics motivated by the real-world political concerns of European identity would undoubtedly be less concerned with America's sins (which are innumerable) and more with discrediting the *collabos*, whose treason has left the Continent prey to America's predatory world market system.

There is another telling problem with its anti-Americanism. As Europeans succumb to the deculturating influences of America's liberal empire, they betray themselves. This goes without saying. But what passes for Americanism today has become no less a threat to European Americans—and not solely to those of us "who look to the sacred soil of Europe for their origin, their inspiration, and their spiritual home" (Yockey). There are two key issues here: America's European essence and the possible biological demise of Euro-America. *Grécistes* have consistently underestimated the degree to which America is (or, at least, was) a European country. Despite the anti-European animus of its Puritan founders and the Hebraizing character of its liberal modernist values, its lands were settled by peoples of European stock, developed in accordance with European principles (however much these were modified or revised), and retained an ethnoracial identity with Europe (without which its settlement of North America would have resembled the anti-identitarian process characteristic of Mexico and many parts of Latin America). As one of America's greatest Europeanist writes, "America belongs spiritually, and will always belong, to the Western Civilization of which it is a colonial transplantation, and no part of the *true* America belongs to [those] . . . outside of this civilization."⁴⁰ Given its European origins, identitarians cannot completely dismiss this "European nation on a foreign shore" (H. Millard).

Such especially seems the case for those "segments" of the American population whose primary identity is European.⁴¹ With only a cursory familiarity with the country's historical complexities and an inability to "follow an American dynamic in American rather than European terms" (Robert Wiebe), *Grécistes* underestimate the degree to which white Southerners and European immigrants (especially the "Catholic, Irish-led working class") developed a parallel society contesting the nihilistic atomization of Anglo-Protestant market society, actively rebuffing the Yankee (anti-European) model of Americanism and, at times, asserting an anti-US expression of Americanism (in identifying with the religious and cultural heritage of the "old country" rather than the Low Church anti-culture of the capitalist Northeast). Indeed, it was the decimation of urban Catholic America and the American South by New Class elites in the post-Rooseveltian age, especially in their racial, housing, and immigration policies, that prepared the system whose globalist principles are presently colonizing the Rest of the World. An identitarian opposition to "Americanism" ought, therefore, to distinguish between European Americans, threatened by the anti-identitarian forces of US-style liberalism, and those New Class descendants of the Puritan Elect (a great many of whom it turns out are Jewish, given that "Calvin was a Judaizer") who constitute the brunt of this threat.

Like Europeans, these European Americans are under assault by multiculturalism and Third World immigration, which promises their extinction as a "people" (however weakly they understand their "peoplehood"); by managerialism, which renders them into passive consumers; by globalization, which rents the fabric of their communities and undermines their economic viability; by a Culture Industry whose sewage contaminates their heritage; and by school systems, universities, government bureaucracies, and remote planners who reject their moral order and their right to be who they are. European-style identitarianism speaks almost as directly to the concerns of these Americans experiencing America's transformation into "an unstable and fragmented multicultural collective," as it does to Europeans witnessing the de-Europeanization of their own lands.

An identitarian anti-Americanism offers America's European stock a platform on which it might resume the ethnogenesis sidetracked a century and a half ago—by forging (in the struggle for their own republic in North America) an American nation explicitly based on Europe's racial and cultural heritage and on the European heritage that is native to the US. The fate of Europeans on both sides of the Atlantic seems, in fact, to hinge now on their common struggle against the same liberal Moloch, whether it is called "Americanism," "modernity," "liberalism," or "globalization."

A similar failing affects the GRECE's anti-Christianism. It is philosophically possible, of course, to emphasize the non-European origins of early Christian belief and its distorting effect on European life. But after 1,500 years, it seems reasonable to assume that Christianity has come to express something enduring—and not all of it negative—in the European spirit. Indeed, if world history teaches anything, it is that civilization—its cultures, traditions, and peoples—tend to reshape foreign religions rather than succumb to them outright. This introduces several factors ignored or minimized by *Grécistes*.

The first involves the evident difference between ecclesiastical and popular Christianity. As pagan Europe was Christianized by the Roman Church after the Empire's collapse, the ecclesiastical establishment was forced to accommodate itself to popular belief. To this degree, popular Christianity continued to serve as a vehicle of the European spirit, incorporating significant facets of the not so repressed pagan sensibility. The glory of medieval Christendom—its universities, Gothic cathedrals, epic poems, chivalric knights, fair ladies, and Grail Quests—was, on this account, no less a testament to the glory of Celtic-Germanic paganism, as Europe's root peoples transformed this so-called "Semitic" religion into a vehicle of their own spirit.

A second factor relates to the chasm separating historical Christianity from modern Christianity. In both its neo-Catholic and Protestant distillations, modern Christianity assimilates much of the Left's egalitarian and universalist blather, which *Grécistes* take as proof of its inherent anti-identitarianism. In this spirit, the modern Church orients to the whole world, neglecting the people and culture that made it what it is. Yet, historical Christianity, in either its medieval or early modern forms, recognized ethnocultural differences, affirmed the existence of nations, prohibited or frowned on mixed marriages, accepted racial differences, and recognized hierarchic inequalities. In view of what James C. Russell calls the "Germanization of medieval Christianity," it is deceptive to treat the Christian heritage as if it constituted a faithful distillation of its "primitive" Near Eastern origins and did not become a "European folk religion." Indeed, any monolithic interpretation of Christianity that fails to recognize its complex and multifarious historical expressions does an injustice to it.

A third problem with the GRECE's anti-Christianism relates to the fact that de-Christianization is irreparably linked to Europe's "despiritualization." As the Traditionalist René Guénon observes, despiritualization is a form of "de-traditionalization." Whatever was of "value in the modern world," Guénon understood, "came to it from Christianity, or at any rate through Christianity, for Christianity [brought] with it the whole heritage of former traditions"—that is, of the pagan past, of the Germanic-Celtic "barbarians," the Hellenic philosophical tradition that undergirds the European idea, and the Roman imperium, which was the idea's first incarnation.[42] The influence of these former traditions embodied in Christian culture is especially acute in all that separates it from the materialistic and anti-metaphysical disposition of the other Abrahamic religions. Christianity was also instrumental in serving as the medium through which the common people participated in European high culture, transcending the rudimentary anthropological limits of everyday life and connecting with their aristocracy.[43]

To categorically reject Christianity, as *Grécistes* do, not only dismisses much of what remains vital in both the pagan spirit and the Continent's high culture, it simply hastens the present nihilistic despiritualization (and hence destruction) of Europe. Modernization and the Left project after all were born in opposition to the Catholic Church and its transcendent order. Finally, as Julius Evola argues, paganism will never be revived as a religion. Its principles and values live on solely within the Christian, specifically the pre-Tridentine Catholic or Gothic tradition, for it remains the tradition that best preserves all that is enduring in paganism. Because there is no religious option outside Christianity that is meaningfully available to Europeans, only a misleading emphasis on the Near Eastern intellectual origins of early Christianity can justify its categorical dismissal.[44]

For better or worse, Christianity is Europe's religion. Instead of frontally opposing it, *Grécistes* might emphasize its assimilation of European values, including those of the Indo-European past and the Roman imperial tradition; recognize how the particularistic application of these beliefs historically served the needs of group survival (in favoring neighborly love), not those of non-European outgroups; and focus their criticisms on those prelates (Marxists, Masons, homosexuals, etc.) who have abandoned these inspirations for the woolly-minded humanitarianism and "politically correct ecumenicalism" that presently passes for Christianity. As not a few identitarians note, the categorical nature of the GRECE's anti-Christianism plays into the hands of the Left, which seeks a complete desacralization to speed its Utopian constructions.[45]

## Achievement

These are serious criticisms of and, from an identitarian perspective, major flaws in the GRECE's project.[46] Yet, however compromising, such flaws, I believe, are compensated by the various contributions it has made to the forces of anti-liberalism over the last three decades—especially in launching the careers of such New Right tribunes—in addition to the Pope Himself, Alain de Benoist—as Guillaume Faye, Robert Steuckers, Pierre Vial, Pierre Krebs, Tomislav Sunic, and Jean-Claude Valla, all of whom presently stand in the vanguard of Europe's future. While the GRECE's abandonment of metapolitics, its hyper-intellectualism, and its concessions to the reigning liberal ideas, especially multiculturalism, renders it increasingly tangential to the rising forces of European identitarianism, these forces are likely to succeed only to the degree they take up where it left off.

Any concluding assessment of the GRECE's achievement ought probably to begin by acknowledging that its metapolitics has had almost no impact on the political class (with a few individual exceptions), the professorate, or the reigning New Class elites. Yet, beyond the Establishment, among various anti-system forces, such as the National Front, the Mouvement National Républicain, the Vlaams Blok, the Alleanza Nazionale, and a host of new national-populist formations challenging the liberal oligarchs, it has led the way in subverting the dominant discourse and posing a viable alternative to it. In the ranks of the young and the undoctrinaire, among a growing number of identitarian, radical Right, and revolutionary nationalist organizations, and in that nebulous underground made up of Dark Wave bands and esoteric traditionalists, its ideas have found a similarly receptive audience. The growing indifference to Left-Right managerial discourse also augments its audience.[47] Nearly every distillations of anti-liberalism in France, a great many in Germany, Italy, and Belgium, but more and more throughout Europe, now reflect the ideas broached in the above chapters. The GRECE's metapolitical emphasis on culture, its philosophical critique of liberal rationalism, its preference for tragic-heroic rather than economic values, its paganism, archeofuturism, anti-Americanism, European nationalism, and tellurocratic geopolitics have indeed become central to the concerns of nearly all who presently fight in Europe's name.[48]

What long-range effect the GRECE's identitarianism will have on the rising generation remains, of course, still to be seen, but certain of its engagements, especially in the realm of ideas, can already be positively assessed. It has, for example, been instrumental in popularizing such neglected French thinkers as Georges Dumézil and in introducing Right-wing audiences to many foreign, especially German, thinkers, such as Carl Schmitt, Arnold Gehlen, Ernst Niekisch, Armin Mohler, Ernst Jünger, and others. A growing interest in the Indo-Europeans, the life sciences, paganism, myth, postmodernism, as well as numerous histories and personalities ignored by the academic *nomenklatura*, have also sprung from GRECE publications. Less directly (for it comes from identitarians influenced by it), it has generated renewed interest in the ancient, medieval, and epic traditions of European thought, convincing many of the ways in which they are superior, especially in their reasonability, to modern liberal beliefs.

The GRECE has also been far ahead of other political tendencies in anticipating the principal fault lines of the late modern (or postmodern) age. Early in its history, it identified the American threat to Europe, rejected the belief that commerce establishes a reign of universal harmony and that markets are the panacea they are made out to be, predicted the disruptive return of identitarian questions and Samuel Huntington's "clash of civilizations," called for and expected the reunification of Germany, claimed European unity would be achieved despite the resistance of the nation-state and the *blocs*, anticipated the collapse of Soviet Communism and the impending demise of American imperial power, dissected the spiritual void programmed by consumer society, revived an interest in the rich and varied literature critical of liberalism, exposed the inquisitional nature of political correctness, and foresaw the anti-identitarian implications of globalization, mass immigration, and multiculturalism.[49] The list could be extended.

Above all, the GRECE has been instrumental in rearming Right-wing thought, after postwar liberalism quarantined virtually every tendency refusing to pay homage to it. In its allegiance to the present liberal order, the mainstream Right has, of course, been hostile to it, especially to its anti-liberalism and anti-Americanism. Yet, this false Right can no longer pose as the sole viable alternative to the Left. Its uncritical support of the world market and globalism's anti-identitarian implications has, indeed, made it an unapologetic convert to liberal modernity. As to the Left, the GRECE has absorbed its most perspicacious insights and supported it whenever it has resisted the technoeconomic onslaught of global capital and its managerial state. Some of the most brilliant Left intellectuals—Jean Baudrillard, Régis Debray, Louis Dumont, Michel Maffesoli, *et cetera*—have also gotten their most sympathetic hearing from *Grécistes*, who have engaged their ideas in ways that the Left, in the spirit of bourgeois complacency, refuses. This, of course, has not prevented the GRECE from attacking the Left's hegemony and turning its key ideas against it. The Left, as a consequence, can no longer expect its principles to be quite so readily taken for granted, now that the GRECE and similar tendencies have exposed the anti-European racism implicit in its multiculturalism, the anti-democratic character of its rationalist politics, the inquisitional intent of its political correctness, the collaborationist character of its Americanism, its obscurantist rejection of the life sciences, the anti-communal implications of its economism, and the indefensibility of its defining philosophical premises.

More generally, the GRECE's rejection of Right-Left politics anticipates the postmodern divide between "the periphery and the center." In an age when Europe's survival is at stake, modernist political contentions have lost much of their former relevance. Once symbolizing the polarizing forces of progress and tradition, Right and Left have ceased to address the burning questions facing most Europeans in the twenty-first century—and, indeed, these two wings no longer represent clearly distinct alternatives. If they are

# CONCLUSION

to survive as political categories, they will certainly need to be redefined, for Europeans today stand at the dawn of an entirely new era of struggle.

Paul Piccone, the former editor of *Telos*, suggests that the identitarian New Right may, in fact, represent "a major paradigm shift threatening the displacement of traditional Left-Right divisions."[50] Evident in the escalating worldwide conflict between identitarians and globalists, patriots and cosmopolitans, such a reorientation has long been latent in liberal modernist societies; since the Soviet collapse, it has moved closer to the center of political life. In this sense, the French presidential election of 2002—called by some "the first real election since 1945"—was especially noteworthy in inaugurating a new era in European politics. Jean-Marie Le Pen's defeat, in face of every dirty trick and slander of the unified oligarchy (a defeat whose final vote count resembled that of a banana republic), nevertheless represented a moral victory for identitarians and a damning condemnation of the Left, which went on record favoring a crook to a nationalist (*plutôt un escroc qu'un facho!*).

Contrary to the reports of the controlled media, Le Pen's small but impressive showing was not simply a protest vote, but a rebellion against the present liberal system. This was especially evident in the climate of civil war and the totalitarian mobilization of state and society that occurred between the two rounds of balloting.[51] As one identitarian characterizes it, the election of 2002 effectively terminated the Left-Right system of politics, for all future struggles will increasingly pit Europeans mobilizing for the *Reconquista* against the corrupt Left-leaning oligarchy and its nebulous Islamic and Islamophile constituency.[52] In this mutation of the political system, it is difficult, then, not to see the beginning of Piccone's "paradigm shift."

The former *Gréciste* Guillaume Faye has compared the New Right to a spermatozoon: though powerless to change the world, it has the capacity to fertilize situations, disseminating ideas that may affect the future.[53] These ideas will need to be powerful. For as we enter the twenty-first century, Faye predicts a future of fire and storm—in which the one-worlders' "global village" gives way to clashing civilizations and rival biocultural *blocs*.[54]

In this scenario anticipating modernity's interregnum, Faye allots no part to the liberal elites who make up *le parti américain*. Recruited from the ranks of corporate management, a corrupt political class, and a university system committed to the banalities of New Class ideology, this "bloodless, sexless, raceless, classless" crew at the helm of *le Titanic Europa* (G.-A. Amaudruz) has been responsible for a disaster unprecedented in European history—more catastrophic, arguably, than anything perpetuated by the Huns or the Turks.[55] Unconscious that a society can appear to function normally, even after having lost its soul, these elites defend "the worst kind of society to have ever existed . . . because [it is] the most subservient to the tyranny of the economic and the reification of social relations." It now even threatens Europe's ethnocultural existence.[56]

Less cretinized generations would almost certainly have considered the misdeeds of Europe's Americanized *nomenklatura* cause for revolt.[57] Its days, though, are already numbered. Like the modernist enterprise, the legitimacy of its foul "reign of quantity" has begun to slip. Once the stormy weather arrives, as it inevitably will, its unmoored ideals and designer social forms are likely to be swept away, as were those of the other Enlightenment project. At that point, it may be clearer that the New School of European Culture has stood for what is most enduring in the Continent's inimitable heritage—and for what is likely to be most enduring in the heritage to come.

## Notes to Conclusion

1. Gordon Marshall, ed., *The Concise Oxford Dictionary of Sociology* (Oxford: Oxford University Press, 1994), 232; *The Oxford Universal Dictionary*, 3rd ed. (Oxford: Clarendon Press, 1955), 951; Guillaume Faye, *Pourquoi nous combattons: Manifeste de la Résistance européenne* (Paris: L'Æncre, 2001), 146–49.
2. Martin Heidegger, *Being and Time*, trans. John Macquarrie and Edward Robinson (New York: Harper and Row, 1962), § 38 (tense changed).
3. Karlheinz Weissmann, "Arnold Gehlen: Von der Aktualität eines zu Unrecht Vergessenen," *Criticón* 153 (January 1997); Leslie Holmes and Philomena Murray, eds., *Citizenship and Identity in Europe* (Aldershot, UK: Ashgate, 1999), 1–24. Cf. Charles Taylor, *Sources of the Self: The Making of Modern Identity* (Cambridge: Cambridge University Press, 1989). Even academics are beginning to realize that "the central issue informing contemporary debates in social and cultural theory" increasingly derives from the conflict between identity and cosmopolitanism. See Craig Calhoun, *Critical Social Theory: Culture, History, and the Challenge of Difference* (Oxford: Blackwell, 1995), xii.
4. Cf. Pierre Chaunu, *Histoire et décadence* (Paris: Perrin, 1981).
5. Quoted in Michael Walker, "We, the Other Europeans," *The Scorpion* 9 (Spring 1986). In the same spirit, Guillaume Faye writes: "*Pour ne pas mourir, nous sommes condamnés à l'angoisse et à la grandeur. Nous ne sommes pas une civilisation faite pour le bonheur.*" See *Nouveau discours à la nation européenne*, 2nd ed. (Paris: L'Æncre, 1999), 130.
6. On the sociohistorical backdrop to the current identitarian crisis, see Richard Kuisel, "Modernization and Identity," *French Politics and Society* 14:1 (Winter 1996); Dave Russell and Mark Mitchell, "Fortress Europe, National Identity, and Citizenship," in *Europe: The Cold Divide*, ed. Fergus Carr (London: Macmillan, 1998).

7. Jacques Marlaud, "Notre conception de l'identité," in *Crépuscule des blocs, aurore des peuples: Actes du XXIIIe colloque national du GRECE* (Paris: GRECE, 1990); Pierre Krebs, *Das Thule-Seminar: Geistesgegenwart der Zukunft in der Morgenröte des Ethnos* (Horn: Burkhart Weecke Verlag, 1994), 14.
8. Quoted in Yvan Blot, "L'identité française et son héritage antique," in *Les origines de la France*, ed. Jacques Robichez (Saint-Cloud: Éds. Nationales, n.d.).
9. Ronald Gläser, "Kulturelle Konflikte Verstakte Spürbar," *Junge Freiheit* (October 26, 2001). Cf. Benjamin R. Barber, *Jihad vs. McWorld: How Globalism and Tribalism Are Reshaping the World* (New York: Ballantine Books, 1996), 205-32; Neva Welton and Linda Wolf, eds., *Global Uprisings: Confronting the Tyrannies of the 21st Century* (Gabriola Island, Canada: New Society Publishers, 2001); John Gray, *False Dawn: The Delusions of Global Capital* (New York: The New Press, 1998), 209-11.
10. Guillaume Faye, "Le système contre les peuples," in *La cause des peuples: Actes du XVe colloque national du GRECE* (Paris: Le Labyrinthe, 1982); Alain de Benoist, *L'écume et les galets, 1991-1999: Dix ans d'actualité vue d'ailleurs* (Paris: Le Labyrinthe, 2000), 22. Even the oily apologist of the Washington Consensus, Thomas Friedman, acknowledges the prospect of such a scenario. See *The Lexus and the Olive Tree* (New York: Farrar, Straus and Giroux, 1999), 212.
11. Alain de Benoist, "Identité et mondialisation," *Le Lien express* 9 (October 2001); "Interview de Guillaume Faye," at *Vlaamse Jongeren Mechelen* (http://www.vjm.cc/vjm). In the second volume of *The Decline of the West*, trans. Charles Francis Atkinson (New York: Knopf, 1928 [1922]), 507, Oswald Spengler makes a similar argument: "Money is overthrown and abolished only by blood."
12. This reluctance has much to do with the Right's "realism." Unlike the Left (whose idealism disposes it to seeing the world as a mere construction to be reshaped in terms of its imagined Utopia), the Right roots itself in foundational beliefs—including those, alas, of the modern order.
13. John Schwarzmantel, *The Age of Ideology: Political Ideologies from the American Revolution to Postmodern Times* (New York: New York University Press, 1998), 118-30.
14. Alain de Benoist, "Pour une déclaration du droit des peuples," in *La cause des peuples: Actes du XVe colloque national du GRECE* (Paris: Le Labyrinthe, 1982).
15. Heidegger: "Whoever wants to go very far back... into the first beginning—must think ahead to and carry out a great future." See *Contributions to Philosophy (From Enowning)*, trans. Parvis Emad and Kenneth Maly (Bloomington: Indiana University Press, 1994), § 23.
16. Robert de Herte, "Œcuménopolis," *Éléments* 24-25 (Winter 1977-78).
17. As one Left/liberal historian admits: "We are rapidly approaching the point at which scholarship becomes propaganda, ceases to liberate the spirit of the human individual, and simply replaces the old dogmas with new ones." See Glen Jeansonne, *Women of the Far Right: The Mothers' Movement and World War II* (Chicago: University of Chicago Press, 1996), 186.
18. Alain de Benoist, "L'ennemi principal," *Éléments* 41 (March-April 1982); Alain de Benoist, "Qu'est-ce que l'identité? Réflexions sur un concept-clef," *Éléments* 77 (n.d. [c. Spring 1993]).
19. Faye, *Nouveau discours à la nation européenne*, 147-49.

20. Alain de Benoist, "Immigration et logique du capital," *Le Lien express* 9 (October 2001); Robert de Herte, "Avec les immigrées contre le nouvel esclavage," *Éléments* 45 (Spring 1983).
21. Guillaume Faye, "L'impérialisme américain: Menace majeure ou tigre du papier?," *Terre et peuple: La revue* 12 (Summer 2002).
22. Pierre Vial, *Une terre, un peuple* (Villeurbanne: Terre et Peuple, 2000), 66; Jean-Raphaël de Sourel, *La fin de l'Europe et de sa civilisation humaniste* (Paris: Éds. des Écrivains, 1999).
23. Robert de Herte, "Le réveil de l'Islam," *Éléments* 53 (Spring 1985).
24. Alexandre Del Valle, *Islamisme et États-Unis: Une alliance contre l'Europe*, 2nd ed. (Lausanne: L'Âge d'Homme, 1999). This anti-Islamic identitarianism has been sharply criticized by *Grécistes*. See Arnaud Guyot-Jeannin, "Europe-Islam: Même combat contre l'Occident!," *Cartouches: L'actualité des idées* 5 (August 1998); M. Thibault, "Alexandre Del Valle, un homme sous influence," *Le Lien express* 9 (October 2001).
25. Pierre Vial, "Où va la France?," *Terre et peuple: La revue* 11 (Spring 2002).
26. Faye, *Nouveau discours à la nation européenne*, 210.
27. Guillaume Faye, *La colonisation de l'Europe: Discours vrai sur l'immigration et l'Islam* (Paris: L'Æncre, 2000).
28. Del Valle, *Islamisme et États-Unis*, 199–247.
29. *Inter alia*, see Pierre-Marie Gallois, *Le soleil d'Allah aveugle l'Occident* (Lausanne: L'Âge d'Homme, 1995); David Pujadas and Ahmed Salam, *La tentation du Jihad: L'Islam radical en France* (Paris: J. C. Lattès, 1995); Christian Bouchet, *Les nouveaux nationalistes* (Paris: Éds. Déterna, 2001).
30. Arnaud Guyot-Jeannin, "La Droite et l'identité," in *Aux sources de la Droite: Pour en finir avec les clichés*, ed. Arnaud Guyot-Jeannin (Lausanne: L'Âge d'Homme, 2000).
31. As the French nationalist Philippe Ploncard d'Assac warns: "*Les mots étant les drapeaux des idées et leurs véhicules, il est évident que le changement de vocabulaire entraîne fatalement, insensiblement, le changement des idées. On fini par penser comme l'on parle et agir comme l'on pense.*" See *Le nationalisme français: Origines, doctrine et solutions* (Paris: Duquesne Diffusion, 2000), 40.
32. Henry de Montherlant in *Le maître de Santiago*: "*Si nous ne somme pas les meilleurs, nous n'avons pas de raison d'être.*" Quoted in "Entretien avec Jean Mabire," *Réfléchir et agir* 9 (Summer 2001).
33. Christopher Dawson, *Dynamics of World History*, ed. John J. Mulloy (Wilmington, DE: ISI Books, 2002), 421.
34. Julien Freund, "Le pluralisme des valeurs," in *La fin d'un monde—Crise ou déclin? Actes du XVIIIe colloque national du GRECE* (Paris: Le Labyrinthe, 1985).
35. Faye, *Pourquoi nous combattons*, 72–73; Claude Lévi-Strauss, *Race et histoire* (Paris: Denoël, 1987), 51–52.
36. Jean Thiriart, "Responses to 14 Questions," at *Archivio Eurasia* (http://utenti.tripod.it/ArchivEurasia).
37. Guillaume Faye, "Dans les replis du déclin: La métamorphose," in *La fin d'un monde—Crise ou déclin? Actes du XVIIIe colloque national du GRECE* (Paris: Le Labyrinthe, 1985); Jean-Pierre Blanchard, *Mythes et races: Précis de sociologie identitaire* (Paris: Éds. Déterna, 2000).

38. Paul Gottfried, "Alain de Benoist's Anti-Americanism," *Telos* 98-99 (Winter 1993-Spring 1994); Paul Piccone and Gary Ulmen, "Introduction," *Telos* 117 (Fall 1999). There are those, however, who claim "the caricatures of American life found in comics and Hollywood are not caricature." See Marcus Cunliffe, "The Anatomy of Anti-Americanism," in *Anti-Americanism in Europe*, ed. Rob Kroes (Amsterdam: Free University Press, 1986).
39. Faye, *Nouveau discours à la nation européenne*, 135. Cf. Pierre M. Gallois, *Réquisitoire: Entretiens avec Lydwine Helly* (Lausanne: L'Âge d'Homme, 2001), 7.
40. Francis Parker Yockey, "The Destiny of America" (1955), in *The Thoughts of Francis Parker Yockey* (London: The Rising Press, 2001). (My emphasis.)
41. Robert H. Wiebe, *The Segmented Society: An Introduction to the Meaning of America* (New York: Oxford University Press, 1975).
42. René Guénon, *The Crisis of the Modern World*, trans. Arthur Osborne (Ghent, NY: Sophia Perennis, 1996 [1927]), 139.
43. Nicolas Berdyaev, *The Fate of Man in the Modern World*, trans. Donald A. Lowrie (Ann Arbor: University of Michigan Press, 1935), 114.
44. Cf. Christopher Dawson, "Sociology as a Science," in *Science for a New World*, ed. J. Arthur Thomson and J. G. Crowther (New York: Harper and Brothers, 1934).
45. For example, Robert Barrot, *Il est trop tard* (Paris: Godefroy de Bouillon, 2001), 8; Kevin MacDonald, "What Makes Western Culture Unique?," *The Occidental Quarterly: A Journal of Western Thought and Opinion* 2:2 (Summer 2002).
46. For the GRECE's response to some of these criticisms, see "Entretien avec Alain de Benoist," *Réfléchir et agir* 11 (Spring 2002).
47. Gregory Flynn, ed., *Remaking the Hexagon: The New France in the New Europe* (Boulder, CO: Westview Press, 1995), 191, 204.
48. For example, every nationalist interviewed in Bouchet's *Les nouveaux nationalistes* identified with those specifically GRECE ideas that would have been heretical for an earlier generation of nationalists.
49. *Manifeste pour une renaissance européenne: À la découverte du GRECE, son histoire, ses idées, son organisation* (Paris: GRECE, 2000), 11-12.
50. Paul Piccone, "Confronting the French New Right: Old Prejudices or a New Political Paradigm?," *Telos* 98-99 (Winter 1993-Spring 1994). Piccone's positive assessment of the New Right derives from the Frankfurt School's opposition to the "dialectic of Enlightenment"—i.e., to the social rationalization and the highly managed social systems that come with modernization. He and other *Telos* editors who have begun translating Benoist into English are, however, supportive of his identitarianism only at the economic and social levels, for their critique of "instrumental reason" and the homogenizing mechanization of life it creates dismisses not only the New Right's concept of a strong state, but, more importantly, its affirmation of the biocultural specificity of European life. Hence, Piccone's bizarre contention that Americans should see the Mexican colonization of the Southwest as an "enrichment." On the Left-Right breakup in the US, see Samuel Francis, "Paleo-Malthusians," *Chronicles* (December 1998); Patrick J. Buchanan, *The Great Betrayal: How American Sovereignty and Social Justice Are Being Sacrificed to the Gods of the Global Economy* (Boston: Little, Brown, 1998), 108.

51. Yves Daoudal, *Le tour infernal, 21 Avril–5 Mai: Analyse d'une fantasmagorie électorale* (Paris: Godefroy de Bouillon, 2003).
52. Guillaume Faye, "Analyse de la présidentielle," *J'ai tout compris!*, supplement to no. 21 (May 2002). While Le Pen's National Front rhetorically threatens the liberal oligarchy and rallies many anti-liberals, it is hardly the ideal party for identitarians. For example, it is nationalist rather than Europeanist; assimilationist rather than separatist; "liberal" rather than anti-capitalist. The more advanced identitarians now argue that it has ceased to represent them and that the way forward will occur only after it vacates the scene. See Norbert de la Aixe, "'Remettez-nous ça, garçon!,'" *Réfléchir et agir* 12 (Summer 2002).
53. "Entretien avec Guillaume Faye," *Éléments* 92 (July 1998). On Faye's contribution to what remains most vital in New Right thought, see Robert Steuckers, "L'apport de Guillaume Faye à la Nouvelle Droite et petite histoire de son éviction," at *Vlaamse Jongeren Mechelen* (http://www.vjm.cc/vjm/index3.htm).
54. Guillaume Faye, "XXIe siècle Europe: Un arbre dans la tempête," *Terre et peuple: La revue* 2 (Winter 1999); Raymond Ruyer, *Les cent prochains siècles: Le destin historique de l'homme selon la Nouvelle Gnose américaine* (Paris: Fayard, 1977), 199–207; Paul-Marie Coûteaux, *L'Europe vers la guerre* (Paris: Éds. Michalon, 2000); Jean Parvulesco, "Vladimir Poutine et l'Europe eurasiatique de la Fin" (2000), at *Synergon* (http://www.geocities.com/spartacorps/synergon). Cf. Robert D. Kaplan, *The Coming Anarchy: Shattering the Dreams of the Post Cold War* (New York: Random House, 2000); Samuel P. Huntington, *The Clash of Civilizations and the Remaking of World Order* (New York: Simon and Schuster, 1996); Thomas W. Chittum, *Civil War II: The Coming Breakup of America* (Show Low, AZ: American Eagle Publications, 1996); Alain Minc, *Le nouveau Moyen Âge* (Paris: Gallimard, 1993); Richard C. Longworth, *Global Squeeze: The Coming Crisis for First-World Nations* (Chicago: Contemporary Books, 1998).
55. Cf. Giorgio Freda, *La désintégration du système*, trans. Éric Houllefort (Paris: Totalité, 1980).
56. "Vers des nouvelles convergences: Entretien avec Alain de Benoist," *Éléments* 56 (Winter 1985).
57. Pierre Thuillier, *La grande implosion: Rapport sur l'effondrement de l'Occident, 1999–2002* (Paris: Fayard, 1999), 14–21; Pierre-Marie Gallois, *La France sort-elle de l'histoire? Superpuissances et déclin national* (Lausanne: L'Âge d'Homme, 1998), 149; Guillaume Faye, *L'Archéofuturisme* (Paris: L'Æncre, 1998), 57; Emmanuel Lévy, "L'avant-guerre civile," *Éléments* 96 (November 1999); Alain de Benoist, "*Secessio plebis*: Une situation pré-révolutionnaire" (1996), in *L'écume et les galets*. Also Peter Glotz, Rita Süssmuth, and Konrad Seitz, *Die planlosen Eliten: Versaümen Wir Deutsche die Zukunft* (Munich: Ferenczy bei Bruckmann, 1992); Alfred Mechtersheimer, "Weshalb das 'System' nicht länger funktioniert," *Nation und Europa: Deutsche Monatshefte* (March 2003); Christopher Lasch, *The Revolt of the Elites and the Betrayal of Democracy* (New York: Norton, 1995). Patrick Buchanan makes a similarly negative characterization of American elites, claiming they are "today reenacting every folly that brought previous empires to ruin." See *The Great Betrayal*, 4.

# Index

## A

Abellio, Raymond, 44
Alexander the Great, 246
*Algérie française*, 29, 30, 52n12, 101
Alleanza Nazionale, 271
Althusius, Johannes, 230–31
    *Politica*, 230
Amaudruz, Gaston Armand, 273
Ambrose, Stephen, 188
Americanization, 18, 30, 35, 182, 212, 233, 241, 260
Anti-Communism, 29, 62, 117n77, 176, 212
Archeofuturism, 146, 164–65, 175nn118, 126, 126, 271
Ardrey, Robert, 44
Arendt, Hannah, 108
Aristotle, 77, 86, 166n5, 246
Aron, Raymond, 108
Aron, Robert, 193
Atlanticism, 215, 216, 233

## B

Badinter, Robert, 106
Bardèche, Maurice, 176, 202n7, 232
Barrès, Maurice, 48
Barsamian, David, 111
Baudelaire, Charles, 178
Baudrillard, Jean, 37, 39, 48, 109, 194, 203n39, 207n88, 247, 272
Beauvoir, Simone de, 98
Beethoven, Ludwig van, 194

Bell, Daniel, 229
Benoist, Alain de, 26, 30, 44, 45, 46, 47, 92, 95, 99, 100, 107, 108, 110, 127, 128, 133, 135, 137, 138, 150, 157, 161, 162, 165, 176, 182, 186, 195, 196, 209n105, 220, 228, 232, 239, 245, 260, 262, 271
    and America, 175n120
    and history/memory, 172n78
    relationship to GREGE, 59n81
    *Europe, Tiers Monde, même combat*, 217
    *Vu de Droite*, 26
Bentham, Jeremy, 41
Berger, Peter, 32
Berlin, Isaiah, 14
Berkeley, 33
Bernstein, Eduard, 16
Bible, 12, 148
Bioculture, 67, 101
Bloch, Ernst, 125
Boas, Franz, 75n28
Bodin, Jean, 227, 230, 231
    *Six livres de la république*, 227
Bonald, Louis de, 48
Boumediène, Houari, 265
Bourgeoisie, 9, 12, 14, 15, 16, 18, 24n34, 31, 49, 64, 77, 81, 100, 112n14, 176
    and Cartesianism, 80, 81
    and Enlightenment, 14
    and liberalism, 77
    and Protestantism, 12

Bowie, Jim, 188
Brasillach, Robert, 176
Brogan, Denis William, 188
Brzezinski, Zbigniew, 108, 223n27, 236, 237, 241, 343
Bücher, Karl, 93
Burke, Edmund, 15, 23n31, 24n34, 48, 230
Burnham, James, 117n77, 180, 182
Bush, George H. W., 197
Bush, George W., 106, 184, 196, 197, 206n58, 214

## C

Calvin, John, 12, 178, 268
Calvinism, Calvinists, 126, 177, 179, 181, 183, 189, 197, 198. 206n63, 268
Capet, Hugh, 239
Capitalism, 92
Carrrel, Alexis, 99
Carter Administration, 106
Cartesianism, 78–81, 83
Catholicism, Roman, 43, 47, 78, 126, 166n4, 178
  Irish, 181
  and Benoist, 45
  and Judaism, 140n10
  and history/time, concept of, 146–48
Cau, Jean, 212
*Cause du peoples, la*, 45, 264, 265
Celts, 130
Celtic Twilight, 175n123
Champetier, Charles, 96
Chernobyl, 16
Chesterton, G.K., 185
Christianity, 16, 32, 45, 125–28, 131, 166n5, 220
  and dualism, 127
  and paganism, 139n8

*Chronicles*, 181
CIA, 32, 199, 222n23
Civil Rights Revolution, 199
Clausewitz, Carl von, 235
Clinton, Bill, Clinton Administration, 184, 194, 238
Clisthenes, 245
Clovis, 239
Cold War, 28, 45, 108, 109, 196, 210–16, 222n13, 226, 231, 232, 236, 237, 238, 242
Collaborationism, 27, 28
Collingwood, R. G., 160, 173n90
Communism, Communists, 27, 45, 46, 108, 215, 242, 243, 244
Communist Party, French (PCF), 27, 176
Comte, Auguste, 153
Connolly, William, 36, 39, 55n61
Conservative Revolution, 46–50, 60n92
Constable, John, 93
Consumerism, 30, 32, 109
Counter-Enlightenment, 14, 15, 48, 62, 211–12, 228, 261
Crockett, Davy, 188
Culture, Gehlen's definition of, 66–69
  Locchi's functional model of, 69–71
  Locchi's organic model of, 69–71
*Culture, black-beur, la*, 264
Culture Industry, 32, 53n26, 62, 198, 264, 268

## D

Dahmer, Jeffery, 89
Dar-al-Harb, 102, 103
Dawson, Christopher, 13, 147, 265
Debord, Guy, 36, 48
Debray, Régis, 34, 48, 272

De Gaulle, Charles, 28, 29, 32, 33, 53n24, 61, 214, 235, 239, 241, 254n72
Deleuze, Gilles, 37
Del Noce, Augusto, 32, 220
Del Valle, Alexandre, 243
Democracy, organic, 244–48
Derrida, Jacques, 37
Descartes, René, 77–83, 130, 160, 193
Dewey, John, 88
*Dirty Dozen*, 188
Diwald, Hellmut, 174n104
Doolittle, Eliza, 88
Dostoevsky, Fyodor, 49
*Droit à la différence, le*, 45, 104–5, 264, 265, 266
Dryden, John, 13
Dugin, Alexandre, 238, 243, 256nn96–98
Dumézil, Georges, 149–51, 168nn23–25, 169n31, 179, 263, 271
Dun, Robert, 74n17, 124n158
Dumont, Louis, 48, 272

## E

East India Empire, Portuguese, 11
*Edda*, 128, 148
Eibl-Eibesfeldt, Irenäus, 44
*Éléments*, 58n70, 96
Eliade, Mircea, 134, 153, 154
Eliot, T. S., 180
Empiricism, 81–83
Enlightenment, 13–14, 15, 16, 17, 23n30, 41, 55n61, 83, 108, 184, 186, 196, 211, 220, 227, 274
  of Kant, 84–85
Eternal Return, 151–56
Europe-Action, 30
Europe, idea of, 43, 58n69, 233
European Union (EU), 217, 229, 231–35, 238

Eurosiberia, 235–44, 247
Evola, Julius, 18, 19, 22n22, 32, 44, 47, 49, 74n17, 132, 161, 170n33, 176, 195, 250n33 270
*Ex oriente lux* thesis, 148, 149, 167nn16, 167n19, 19

## F

Fascism, 18, 19, 27, 35, 47, 51n6, 56n68, 242
Faye, Guillaume, 54n42, 72, 92, 105, 164, 168n22, 175n118, 219, 225n53, 231, 263, 265, 270, 273
  *Système à tuer les peoples, Le*, 219
Feminism, 34, 98–100, 107, 125
  differentialist feminism, 99
*Figaro Magazine, Le*, 26
Finkelstein, Norman, 199
First European Civil War (1914–18), 49, 62
Fischer, David Hackett, 182
Flynt, Larry, 196
Fontenelle, Bernard le Bovier de, 13
Ford, John, 191
Fortuyn, Pim, 19
Foucault, Michel, 9, 37, 41, 48, 156
Franco-Prussian War (1870), 239
Frank, Andre Gunder, 218
Frankfurt School of Social Research, 30, 48, 277n50
Frazer, James G., 149
Frederick II, 233
Freedom, liberal notion of, 109, 111, 257n111
Freund, Julien, 44, 266
Freyer, Hans, 49
Friedrich, Carl J., 108
Frontier, 191
Fukuyama, Francis, 215
  *End of History*, 215

## G

Gandillon, André, 102
Gehlen, Arnold, 44, 45, 65, 66–69, 103, 136, 271
   and Lorenz, 74n25, 75n28
   and fundament of culture, 65–66
Genghis Khan, 189
Geopolitics, 236–37
Ghibellines, 220, 233–34
Giroud, Françoise, 226
Giscard d'Estaing, Valéry, 61
Globalization, 35, 76n47, 103, 198, 225n53, 227, 229, 231, 233, 268, 272
Gobineau, Arthur de, 89
Godard, Jean-Luc, 34
Goethe, 89, 179
Gramsci, Antonio, 62, 63, 64, 65, 73n13, 74n17, 104
   *Prison Notebooks*, 62
Gray, John, 17
Great Depression, 183
Great Narrative *(grand récit)*, 36–39, 41, 215, 217
*Großraumautarkie*, 233
Groupement de Recherche et d'Études pour la Civilisation Européenne (GRECE), 31, 42, 46
   Commission des Traditions, 138
   media discovery of, 26
   and multiculturalism, 175n126
   and identity, 42
   and paganism, 45
   and Right, 46–47
   and Islam, 264
   founding of, 27, 30–31
   tendencies within, 46–47, 59n82, 140n12
   critique of, 263–70, 276n31
Guelphs, 233–34
Guénon, René, 47, 79, 84, 112n5, 197, 269
Guevara, Che, 33
Guizot, François, 85
Guyot-Jeannin, Arnaud, 234

## H

Habermas, Jürgen, 84
Haider, Jörg, 19
Hain, Peter, 201
Ham, Peter van, 229
Hassan, Ihab, 39
Hassner, Pierre, 238
Haushofer, Karl, 238, 252n55
Hawthorne, Nathaniel, 182
Hazard, Paul, 147
Heidegger, Martin, 21n20, 40, 44, 79, 125, 156–64, 211, 260, 262
   and memory, history, and truth, 172n78
   and myth, 135
   and tradition, 161
   and 'what is', 173n94
Helsinki Accords, 214
Heraclitus, 66, 130
Hesiod, 130
History, linear concept of, 146–47, 161
Hitler, Adolf, 108, 198, 213, 214, 215, 234, 236, 240
Hobbes, Thomas, 227
Holy Roman Empire, 234, 240
Homer, 130, 131, 151
*Homo oeconomicus* (Economic Man), myth of, 85
Human rights, 101, 106–7, 121nn123,139, 246
Hume, David, 80
Huntington, Samuel P., 22n22, 119n194, 216, 224n40, 236, 272
Hussein, Saddam, 176
Husserl, Edmund, 65
Huxley, Aldous, 110

# INDEX

## I

Identity, 40, 41, 42, 43, 51n6, 76n44, 83, 98, 99, 164–65, 216, 258–60, 262
  definition of, 258, 260
Ideology, definition of, 73n5
*Iliad*, 128, 148
Immigrants, immigration, 19, 35, 101–4, 119n94, 181, 187, 200, 226, 264–65
Imperial idea (*Reichsidee*), 231–35, 244, 251nn34–36, 251n40
  definition of, 234
Imperium, 45, 115n59, 226, 234, 244
Individualism, individuality, 35, 84–88
  and egalitarianism, 88–89
  New Right critique of, 86–87
Indo-Europeans, 43, 137, 139, 149–51, 165, 166n5, 168n22, 169n33, 234, 235, 242, 271
Inquisition, liberal, 46, 56n68, 59n79, 110, 123n156, 124n158, 263, 275n17
Iraq, First US War on (1991), 176, 199
Iraq, Second US War on (2003), 252n60
Irish America, 201n4, 267–68
Irving, David, 196
Islam, 102–3, 119nn97, 119n106, 214, 237, 243
  and GRECE, 264

## J

James, Henry, 180
Jefferson, Thomas, 185, 198, 204n42
Jews, Judaism, 11, 48, 102, 125, 140n10, 177–78, 179, 197, 199, 206n58, 265, 268

Jordis von Lohausen, Heinrich, 238
Jünger, Ernst, 44, 129, 193, 262, 271

## K

Kant, Immanuel, 39, 82–85, 113n17, 220
Kennedy, Robert, 197
Keyserling, Hermann, 176, 190, 192, 221n8
Kim Il Sung, 244
Kirk, Russell, 20n10, 24n32, 137, 204n41
Krebs, Pierre, 97, 105, 140n12, 270
Kreitor, Nikolai von, 243

## L

Labor movement, 23n26, 104
La Rocque, François de, 29
Latouche, Serge, 16, 219
Le Bon, Gustave, 48, 53n22, 137, 141n23
Left, definition of, 9–10, 20n6
  and modernity, 16
  and ideas, 48
  anti-liberal, 22n24
  as establishment, 19
  as salvation religion, 21n13
  obsolescence of, 260, 272
  New Left, 27, 42, 62
  *gauche caviar*, 35
Lenin, V.I., 30, 63, 64
  *What Is To be Done?*, 63
Le Pen, Jean-Marie, 19, 217, 273
Lévi-Strauss, Claude, 67, 149, 165, 196
Liberalism, definition of, 77
  and 'classical liberalism', 116n67
Lincoln, Abraham, 189
Lind, Michael, 203n38
List, Friedrich, 93, 115n56

Livingston, Donald W., 204n40
Locchi, Giorgio, 44, 45, 69, 70, 134, 151, 154, 266
Locke, John, 81–82, 94, 95
*Logos*, 133
London, Jack, 180
Longest memory, 148–52, 164–65, 248, 260
Lorenz, Konrad, 44, 45, 189, 260
Lorrain, Claude, 93
Lundestad, Geir, 232
Lyotard, Jean-François, 36, 37, 143n53
*Le Condition postmoderne*, 42

# M

Mabire, Jean, 29
Mackinder, Halford, 237
Maffesoli, Michel, 38, 272
Maistre, Joseph de, 22n22, 48, 188, 206n59, 257n110
Malia, Martin, 212
Manifest Destiny, 181
Marcuse, Herbert, 33
Markale, Jean, 130
Market, New Right view of, 92–93
Marshall Plan, 232
Marx, Karl, 15, 30, 33, 63, 106, 112n12, 121n126, 221n12
Marxism, 16, 30, 33, 34, 40, 63, 87, 112n12, 166n10, 218, 220, 228
Maulnier, Thierry, 44
Maurras, Charles, 29, 48–49, 94, 249n13, 260
May Events of 1968, 31–36
Mencken, H. L., 194
Metapolitics, definition of, 65
critique of, 74n17
GRECE abandonment of, 104–5, 120n119
Millard, H., 267

Miller, Henry, 194
*Air-Conditioned Nightmare*, 194
*Millet* system, 103, 120n109
Milton, John, 147
Mitterand, François, 35, 61, 214
Mnemosyne, 153
Modernity, 9, 11–19, 21n11, 38–43, 49, 50, 55n61, 71, 72, 76n44, 96, 97, 106, 136, 138, 147, 152, 160,162, 236, 262, 268
  totalitarian, 18
  and postmodernity, 36–37, 261
  and René Guénon, 112n5
  and Jean-François Lyotard, 143n53
  and Friedrich Nietzsche, 159
  and objective truth, 173n78
  and Left/Right, 260, 272
  and America, 175, 178, 184–90, 203n39
  and Europe, 203n38
  and tradition, 230
  and deviralization, 242
  as enemy, 263, 265
Moeller van den Bruck, Arthur, 10, 49
Mohler, Armin, 24n34, 44, 253n71, 271
Molnar, Thomas, 16, 28, 52n10, 179
Monroe Doctrine, 180, 198, 214
Mother Theresa, 89
Mouvement National Républicain, 271
Mozart, Wolfgang Amadeus, 235
Müller, Adam, 94
Multiculturalism, 34, 35, 101, 103, 104, 105, 106, 107, 120n119, 261, 268, 270, 272
  GRECE accommodation to, 104–5, 120n115, 175n126, 264
Mussolini, Benito, 62
Myth, 133–36, 142n48, 146

and modernity, 133, 144n69
and science, 143n50

# N

Napoleon, 234, 246
Nation, nation-state, 35-36, 93, 96, 97, 227-31, 234, 236, 240, 249n15
and modernity, 227
National Front, 19, 104-5, 115n53, 217, 227, 271, 278n52
National Socialism, 27, 30, 149
NATO, 214-15, 223n27, 229, 232, 243
Neumann, Iver, 243
New Class, 17, 23n30, 28, 89, 95, 99, 100, 205n48, 229, 230, 233, 235, 236, 238, 239, 247, 261, 268, 271
and monoclass, 28, 52n10
New Deal, 182
New Science of the 17th century, 13, 21n18, 43, 77
*New York Times*, 238
New World Order, 106, 175, 201, 229, 230, 234, 238, 260
Niekisch, Ernst, 22n24, 49, 242, 255n86, 271
Nietzsche, Friedrich, 40, 44, 48, 69, 81, 88, 126, 128, 147, 148, 151-56, 159, 161, 162, 163, 164, 178, 266
and Last Man, 34, 54n35, 195
and myth, 144n67
'9/11', 103, 199, 216, 224n40, 238
Nock, Albert Jay, 185
Nolte, Ernst, 213
*Nouvelle École*, 31, 58n70
*Nouvelle Observateur, La*, 26

# O

Oakeshott, Michael, 112n12
Oberlercher, Reinhold, 22n24, 178
*Origin of Species, The*, 135
Ortega y Gasset, José, 259
O'Sullivan, John, 181
Otto I, 240
Outlaw, 192

# P

Paganism, 45, 128-33, 246, 271, 269-70
Paine, Thomas, 180
Pareto, Vilfredo, 48
Parkinson, C. Northcote, 177
*Parti américain, le*, 30, 35, 104, 211, 216, 226, 273
Pascal, Alain, 30
Pauwels, Louis, 128
Pauwels, Luc, 234
People, English concept of, 86
Percy, Walker, 183
Pétain, Marshal, 27, 31
Philosophical Anthropology, 44
Piccone, Paul, 89, 205n48, 273, 277n50
Pilgrim Fathers, 176
Pingel, Konrad, 107
Plessner, Helmuth, 65
Poe, Edgar Allen, 180
Pol Pot, 244
*Polis*, 245, 246
Popular Front, French (1936-38), 27
Postmodernism, 36-42, 261
and identity, 259
and myth, 143n53
and Marxism, 40
and paganism, 143n53
Poujade, Pierre, 28
Pound, Ezra, 180

*Pravda*, 111
*Principia Mathematica*, 135
Private sphere, 89, 94, 96, 182, 228, 246
Protagoras, 68
Protestantism, Protestants, 12, 16, 126, 177–84
Public sphere, 96, 247
Puritans, 12, 177–85, 188, 189, 191, 192, 197, 268
Putin, Vladimir, 242, 243, 253n95

## Q

Quantification, 78–79, 91

## R

Racism, 19, 56n68, 76n44, 102, 104, 105, 168n22, 272
  Differentialist racism, 76n44
Ranke, Leopold von, 158
Rassemblement du Peuple Français (RPF), 28
Ratzel, Friedrich, 238
Reagan, Ronald, 18, 26, 27, 34, 50n5
Reformation, Protestant, 11–12, 13, 97, 236
Renan, Ernest, 239
Renfrew, Colin, 148
Revolution, Civil Rights, 199
Revolution, Dual, 18, 25n38
Revolution of 1688, Whig, 14, 21n11, 23n31
Revolution of 1789, French, 14, 17, 48, 97, 227, 228, 240, 246
Revolution of 1917, Bolshevik, 63, 215
Right, definition of, 9–11, 14, 15, 20n2, 20n10
  American Right, 17
  False Right, 17, 18, 19, 20n10, 24n34, 50m5, 272
  True Right, 10, 15, 17, 18, 19, 20n10, 22n22, 48
  New Right, 27, 30
  obsolescence of, 261, 272
  realism of, 275n12
  and ideas, 48
*Rig Veda*, 128, 149
Robespierre, 46
Robichez, Jacques, 101
Roosevelt, Franklin D., 189, 210
Rorty, Richard, 38, 55n61, 79, 96, 190
Rostov, Walt, 217
  *Stages of Economic Growth*, 217
Roszak, Theodore, 82
Rougier, Louis, 44, 45
Rousseau, Jean-Jacques, 46, 227
Rufer, Hermann, 211
Ruggiero, Guido de, 80
Russell, James C., 126, 269
Ruyer, Raymond, 44, 162, 262

## S

Sade, Marquis de, 33
Saint-Just, 46, 228
Salomon, Ernst von, 191
Sandel, Michael, 186
Santayana, George, 185, 193
Sartre, Jean-Paul, 34
*Saving Private Ryan*, 188
Scheler, Max, 65, 107
Schmitt, Carl, 49, 94, 117n75, 205n46, 237, 246, 247, 263, 264, 271
Scruton, Roger, 204n40
Second European Civil War (1939–45), 27, 109, 231
Second nature (*zweite nature*), 66, 155

## INDEX

Secularization, 12–13
Self-made man, 195, 208n92
Serrano, Andres, 194
Sex and gender, concept of, 98, 117n79
Shakespeare, William, 235
*Sharia*, 102
Skinner, Quentin, 228
Smith, Adam, 17, 23n31
Socialism, 15–16, 19, 23n26, 54n42, 61, 106
Solzhenitsyn, Alexandr, 111
Sombart, Werner, 49, 193
Sorel, Georges, 22n24, 48
Soviet Union (USSR), 16, 28, 111, 185, 196, 210–16, 218, 234, 241
Spann, Othmar, 93, 115n56
SPD, 35
Spengler, Oswald, 16, 49, 146, 176
Spykman, Nicholas, 215
Staël, Madame de, 65
Stalin, Joseph, 108, 210
State, 14, 63, 64, 65, 93–97, 186, 187, 188, 240, 247
Stendhal, 180
Sternhell, Zeev, 48
Steuckers, Robert, 53n24, 58n77, 103, 105, 256n98, 270
Stoddard, Lothrop, 180
Subject-object relations, 78
Subsidarity, 230–31
*Sunday Times* of London, 101
Sunic, Tomislav, 60n94, 270

### T

*Táin Bó Cuailnge*, 135
Talmon, Jacob, 108
Taylor, Charles, 93
*Terre et people*, 190
Thalassocracy, 237
Thatcher, Margaret, 18, 26, 27, 50n5

Third Worldism, 34, 45, 217–18
Thiriart, Jean, 238, 266
Thompson, Jim, 191
Thompson, William I., 196
Thucydides, 146
Time, Christian/Modernist concept of, 146–48
Tocqueville, Alexis de, 192
Todd, Emmanuel, 187, 216, 223n36
Tönnies, Ferdinand, 48
Totalitarianism, 46, 91, 108–11, 122n143, 123n156, 219, 233
Tradition, 10–17, 19, 22, 33, 38, 48, 62, 69, 72, 76n45, 79, 81, 83, 85, 98, 125, 127, 133, 134, 135, 136–39, 144n69, 159, 160, 161, 163, 164, 178, 184, 185, 187, 192, 203n39, 206n58, 210, 232, 240, 262, 263, 266, 269, 270, 272
*Traditions d'Europe*, 138
Travis, William, 188
Tripartite ideology, 150–51, 169n28, 169n33
Twain, Mark, 179

### U

Universalism, 35, 39, 57n68, 67, 71, 89–91
New Right critique of, 90–91
US-SU condominium, 210–16, 218

### V

Valla, Jean-Claude, 270
Vattimo, Gianni, 9, 37, 39, 152, 163
Veblen, Thorstein, 180
Venner, Dominique, 29, 100, 137, 138, 188
Veyne, Paul, 133
Vial, Pierre, 58n77, 105, 138, 270
Vichy (regime), 27, 49

Vico, Giambattista, 146
Vidal, Gore, 195
Vietnam, 106, 176, 189
Vlaams Blok, 271
Voltaire, 46
*Voluspá*, 135

# W

Walker, R. B. J., 244
Wallerstein, Immanuel, 226, 260
War Between the States (1861–65), 183, 202n7
War of Position, definition of, 64
Washington, George, 180, 186, 191
Weaver, Richard, 194
Weber, Max, 183, 229
West, the, 218–20
Westphalia, Treaty of, 231
Wiebe, Robert, 52n10, 204n44, 267
Wilson, Woodrow, 196, 213
Winthrop, John, 177
Wittgenstein, Ludwig, 37, 86
Wolfowitz, Paul, 238, 243
Wood, Gordon S., 180, 185
World-openness, definition of, 66

# Y

Yalta, 210, 215, 239
Yockey, Francis Parker, 28, 81, 117n77, 176, 180, 206n60, 221n12, 226, 229, 267

# Z

Zedong, Mao, 33
Zinoview, Alexandre, 46, 108, 219
Zyuganov, Gennady, 242

# Other titles published by Arktos:

*Beyond Human Rights*
by Alain de Benoist

*Manifesto for a European Renaissance*
by Alain de Benoist & Charles Champetier

*The Problem of Democracy*
by Alain de Benoist

*Revolution from Above*
by Kerry Bolton

*The Fourth Political Theory*
by Alexander Dugin

*Fascism Viewed from the Right*
by Julius Evola

*Notes on the Third Reich*
by Julius Evola

*Metaphysics of War*
by Julius Evola

*The Path of Cinnabar*
by Julius Evola

*Archeofuturism*
by Guillaume Faye

*Convergence of Catastrophes*
by Guillaume Faye

*Why We Fight*
by Guillaume Faye

*The WASP Question*
by Andrew Fraser

*War and Democracy*
by Paul Gottfried

*The Saga of the Aryan Race*
by Porus Homi Havewala

*Homo Maximus*
by Lars Holger Holm

*The Owls of Afrasiab*
by Lars Holger Holm

*De Naturae Natura*
by Alexander Jacob

*The Biocentric Worldview*
by Ludwig Klages

*Fighting for the Essence*
by Pierre Krebs

*Can Life Prevail?*
by Pentti Linkola

*Germany's Third Empire*
by Arthur Moeller van den Bruck

*Guillaume Faye and the Battle of Europe*
by Michael O'Meara

*The Ten Commandments of Propaganda*
by Brian Anse Patrick

*A Handbook of Traditional Living*
by Raido

*The Agni and the Ecstasy*
by Steven J. Rosen

*The Jedi in the Lotus*
by Steven J. Rosen

*It Cannot Be Stormed*
by Ernst von Salomon

*Tradition & Revolution*
by Troy Southgate

*Against Democracy and Equality*
by Tomislav Sunic

*The Arctic Home in the Vedas*
by Bal Gangadhar Tilak

*The Initiate: Journal of Traditional Studies*
by David J. Wingfield (ed.)